# ADVOCATE

# OF

# DIALOGE

_____ COMPILED BY _____

ALİ ÜNAL & ALPHONSE WILLIAMS

Copyright © 2000 by The Fountain

Published by The Fountain

9900 Main St. #504

Fairfax, Virginia 22031 USA

www.fountainlink.com

Library of Congress Cataloging-in-Publication Data

Ünal, Ali
Williams, Alphonse

Advocate of dialogue : Fethullah Gülen / compiled by Ali Ünal
(translator) and Alphonse Williams.

p. cm.

Includes bibliographical references and index.

ISBN  0-9704370-1-3

1. Gülen, Fethullah. 2. Scholars, Muslim--Turkey--Biography.
3. Islam and politics. 4. Islam--Essence, genius, nature.
I. Ünal, Ali; Williams, Alphonse

BP80.G8 V65 2000

297'.092--dc21

00-011608

*Printed and bound in Turkey*

# Table of Contents

# Foreword

At a time when fame makes many people perplexed, we wonder, "Can there be a person who despises fame?" Anyone who knows Fethullah Gülen (Hodjaefendi) even a little will respond in the affirmative. This man has always been guided by the golden principle: "By itself, fame is hypocrisy, an attractive honey that poisons hearts. It makes people slaves of others."

Then why are we publicizing him in *The Voice of Tolerance: Fethullah Gülen*? Does this contradict the above principle? No, it does not. It is not Gülen himself who wants us to publicize him, but we think that as an intellectual and scholar of the highest caliber, his ideas, mission, and offers to humanity for a better world should be known.

Gülen himself says:

> While striving in the way of God and for the benefit of people, we try to do good deeds everywhere. These are stages on the way, but never the goals. Like this world. Our Prophet, upon him be peace and blessings, guides us with the following: "What is my relation with this world? In this world, I am like a traveler who sits under the shade of a tree and then gets up and leaves." Sincere people necessarily pass and leave through these stages.

> On this journey, hearts are fixed on God's approval. Nothing should be expected from this world or even the next in return. We lower ourselves if we incline toward the world for any reason other than seeing that the people's faith and well-being are secured.

Even though this fact is exhibited in his life, we thought that it was necessary to prepare this book. Through it, we hope to make Fethullah Gülen better known by the public and to set the historical record straight.

In preparing this book, we collected Gülen's biography and interviews with various journalists and columnists in order to present a clear picture of his intellectual world through his writings, speeches, and poems. We then divided it into nine chapters, each of which deals with one or more specific areas. We have included articles on his activities, his efforts for dialogue and tolerance, accounts of talks he has given on these topics, and how they are viewed by the media. In addition, we present published material concerning his views on education and service to humanity via the schools attributed to him by the media, as well as his views and what has motivated him to pursue such a noble mission for over 40 years.

Chapter One, "Who Is Fethullah Gülen?," deals with his upbringing, the early spiritual influences that shaped his life, and how he saw his life. Born in 1938 in the small 50-60-house village of Korucuk, Erzurum province, Gülen entered a world that was undergoing rapid change. The Ottoman State, having collapsed during World War I, was being transformed by Mustafa Kemal Atatürk into a modern European republic known as Turkey. To speed up this process, Atatürk made several revolutions: he abolished the sultanate (1922); proclaimed the Turkish Republic (1923); abolished the caliphate, Ministry of Religious Affairs, and religious schools and courts (1924); suppressed Sufi brotherhoods and closed sacred tombs as places of worship; adopted a new Civil Code in place of the Shari'a (the religious law of Islam) (1926); and introduced the Latin alphabet in place of the Ottoman Arabic-based script (1928).

Coming from a family steeped in religious devotion, Gülen does not reject modern knowledge. He is well read in European philosophy and literature, and has a commanding knowledge of modern science. When his views are sought on how to best serve others, his advice is always: "A mosque would be nice; a school would be better; the combination of the two would be the best."

He has spoken and written a great deal on the reconciliation of religion and science. A retired religious official who spent his professional life in the Ministry of Religious Affairs as a preacher, he has neither displayed opposition to the Turkish Republic's government nor engaged in political activity. He has devoted himself to intellectual and spiritual enlightenment, the well-being of people, and the realization of social peace. In addition, he has worked for the realization of effective dialogue, as well as an atmosphere of tolerance, respect, and understanding, especially among the followers of different religions. He is widely known for his ideas to promote education both in Turkey and abroad.

Chapter Two, "Religion, Islam, and Tolerance," deals with Gülen's views of Islam, Prophet Muhammad, the Qur'an, and how Islam has shaped the Turkish people. He confronts head-on problems that are plaguing Turkey: the attempted politicization of religion by people with agendas; Sunni–Alawi tension and how others are exploiting it to keep Turkey off-balance; as well as such undesirable activities as fundamentalism, dogmatism, and coercion.

Perhaps one of his most interesting assertions is that Islam reached Turkey from Central Asia. This region produced some of the most important figures in the history of Islam, and it was from such people that Turkey received Islam. The Central Asians transferred their deep spirituality and tolerance to the Seljuks, who passed it on to the Ottomans. These were the people who would set up the Ottoman State, whose tolerance for religious and ethnic minorities amazed visiting Europeans.

His essay "Lesser and Greater Jihad" (p. 70) sheds light on a concept that gets a lot of play in the Western media. Gülen reminds us of its true meaning: the very personal spiritual struggle to determine whether good or evil will predominate in a person's life. And it is this understanding of jihad, the "greater jihad," that continues to occupy his life. The "lesser jihad" (its military aspect) is conducted mainly for self-defense and to present Islam's message to humanity. Gülen contends that this concept has been distorted by Orientalists and many of their adherents, especially those who have apostatized from Islam.

Chapter Three, "Religion and Society," analyzes several important subjects: the essential lack of conflict between religion and science and modern knowledge, his vision of what Turkey can become, and how true Muslims can be recognized.

His view of the role of modern science differs markedly from that of other Muslim leaders, and has been a constant thread running through all of his other activities. After reminding us that the Muslims led the world in science for 500 years, he asks: "What is there for us to fear from science?"

The Muslim intelligentsia, seeking to maintain the purity of Islam after the Mongol and Crusader invasions, froze Islamic thought to some extent. In addition, due to a misunderstanding of Imam al-Ghazali's writings, religion and science gradually became separate spheres of activity, with the end result that science was expelled from the religious universities and schools. Disregarding the Qur'an's command to pursue knowledge and science, and unable to meet Europe on equal terms, the Islamic world's long decline began. If this process is ever to be stopped, science must regain its central place in the education systems of Islamic countries.

The second part of this chapter presents Gülen's view of what society would be like if Muslims really applied the Qur'anic teaching to their lives. While many might consider this section highly idealized, it must be remembered that such a society did exist under Prophet Muhammad and the four Rightly Guided Caliphs. And for the last 14 centuries, it has existed in the lives of countless individual Muslims scattered over the world. Listening to him speak of friendship, "righteous servants," ideal men and women, and so many other facets of daily social life build within us the desire to work for his vision so that it may come true.

Chapter Four, "The Individual and Human Rights," deals with several contentious issues: human rights in Islam, how Islam views the individual, and the role of women and polygamy. Gülen's view on these issues is not often heard in the Western media. Instead of imposing the headscarf on women, he says:

> The headscarf isn't one of Islam's main principles or condi-
> tions. It's against the spirit of Islam to regard uncovered
> women as outside of religion. We have so many things in
> common. First, we must try to come together on the pillars of
> faith and principles or main commandments of worship.
> Then we can discuss other matters. Where the main pillars of
> Islam are attacked by its enemies and not observed by its fol-
> lowers as they must be, we cannot divide on matters of sec-
> ondary importance.

Instead of another Muslim man of religion telling women how
they should dress and behave, and what is their "proper" role in
society, he reminds us how the Prophet and early Muslims honored
women, and how each gender complements the other and is entitled
to the respect necessary to make a perfect whole.

Chapter Five, "Religion and Politics," deals with the very sensitive issue of Islam's role in a modern, secular society. This issue
is of vital importance for the contemporary Muslim world, as various governments base their claim to legitimacy upon it. As Islam
played a fundamental role in the Muslims' struggle for independence from their colonial masters, it gradually became highly politi-
cized and often a justification for violence.

Gülen maintains that Muslims must follow the way shown by
the Qur'an and exemplified by the Prophet and Companions. Islam
never pursues a political goal; rather, it seeks to obtain God's
approval and good pleasure in all moments of life. Thus Islam must
be dealt with as a religion based primarily on belief, worship and
good conduct, not as a purely social, economic, and political ideology or system. This is why he does not oppose the Turkish government, regularly meets with high state officials and politicians, and
conducts his activities within the framework of Turkish law.

Chapter Six, "Dialogue," and Chapter Seven, "Interfaith
Meetings and Activities," explores one of the several issues for
which Gülen is known: his ceaseless quest for interfaith dialogue
between Muslims, Jews, and Christians. But Gülen does far more
than just utter pleasant words about the need for dialogue in a theoretical context—he lives it.

In his capacity as a Muslim citizen of Turkey, he has met such non-Muslim luminaries as Pope John Paul II, Greek Orthodox Patriarch Bartolomeos I, and Israel's Sephardic Head Rabbi Eliyahu Bakshi Doron. He speaks to all of them with one voice:

> All of us believe in the same God. We might understand certain things differently, but why should that keep us from working together to uplift humanity and turn it toward God? Why should we let our differences divide us against the onslaught of atheism and unbelief sweeping the modern world?

He continually meets with people from all social segments of Turkey: artists, entertainers, journalists, scholars, and politicians. And to all of them, he gives the same message: "Show tolerance to those with different ideas and beliefs, love each other, work for unity, and serve others by educating them." No one is turned away, even those who oppose what he is doing. In his early 60s and suffering from diabetes and other physical problems, he remains an active author and speaker, a person wholly committed to the uplifting of humanity through education and moral regeneration.

Chapter Eight, "Educational Activities," and Chapter Nine, "A Teacher of Minds and Hearts," deals with Gülen's other well-known activity: his serving as the inspiration for a drive for scientific and modern education on a scale that is perhaps unique. As of this writing, more than 700 schools and universities have been opened mainly in Turkey and Central Asia, but also in such far-flung countries as Cambodia, Vietnam, Mongolia, Brazil, Russia, the United States, Romania, Albania, and others. The purpose of these schools is to provide young men and women with the modern skills and good morality that will make them valuable assets to their societies, and to give them the skills necessary to raise their standard of living. The emphasis is science (e.g., chemistry, mathematics, engineering, physics, computer science), for this is the knowledge suitable to our age.

While many people from all walks of life and different worldviews are realizing this portion of his vision, Gülen's very life represents the other: how a true Muslim should be. Those who have had any degree of contact with him cannot help but notice how he moves in a circle of love for God, the Prophet, and humanity; of humility and compassion; and a desire to usher in another "Age of Bliss." One cannot read such selections as "The Leading, Exalted Spirits" (p. 101), "Love, Compassion, Tolerance, and Forgiving: The Pillars of Dialogue" (p. 253), and "The Journey beyond Being" (p. 360) without being affected.

This book represents our desire to make Gülen's ideas better known to a larger audience. On behalf of *The Fountain*, I would like to express my sincere thanks and respects to everyone, from media personnel and politicians to scholars and businessmen, whose writing and views compose this book's main material.

In addition, I would like to take the opportunity to recognize the work of all those who have helped prepare and publish this work. Great care has been taken in assembling its contents. It is my sincere wish that it will bring good to those who read it, and that it will encourage all of us to strive for realizing the world envisioned by the author.

Editor

**Note:** All footnotes, unless otherwise indicated, are from *Merriam-Webster's Collegiate Dictionary*, 10th ed. (Merriam-Webster: 1999) or from *Encyclopedia Britannica*, 1999-2000 at www.britannica.com.

CHAPTER 1

# Who Is
# Fethullah Gülen?

## Introduction

Known by his plain and austere lifestyle, Fethullah Gülen, affectionately called Hodjaefendi, is a scholar of extraordinary proportions. This man for all seasons was born in Erzurum in 1938.[1] Upon graduation from a Divinity school (*madrasa*) in Erzurum in 1958, he obtained his license and began to preach and teach about the importance of mutual understanding and tolerance. His services and activities, which began during the 1960s, have made him one of Turkey's most well-known and respected public figures.

Though simple in outward appearance, he is original in thought and action. He embraces all humanity, and is deeply averse to unbelief, injustice, and deviation. His belief and feelings are profound, and his ideas and approach to problems are both wise and rational. A living model of love, zeal, and emotion, he is exceptionally balanced in his thought, behavior, and treatment of issues.

Turkish intellectuals and scholars acknowledge, either tacitly or explicitly, that he is one of the most serious and significant thinkers and writers, and among the wisest activists, of twentieth-century Turkey or even of the Muslim world. But such accolades of his leadership of a new Islamic intellectual, social, and spiritu-

---

[1] Erzurum is a city in eastern Turkey. Located on a caravan route from Anatolia to Iran, it has been a major commercial and military center since antiquity. It is now a major rail station on the Ankara–Iran route.

al revival—a revival with the potential to embrace great areas of the world—do not deter him from striving to be no more than a humble servant of God and a friend to all. Desire for fame is the same as show-off and pretentiousness, a "poisonous honey" that extinguishes the heart's spiritual vigor, is one of the golden rules he follows.

Gülen has spent his adult life voicing the cries and laments, as well as the beliefs and aspirations, of Muslims in particular and of humanity in general. He bears his own sorrows, but those of others crush him. He feels that each blow delivered at humanity is delivered first at his own heart. He feels so deeply and inwardly connected to creation that he said:

> "Whenever I see a leaf falling
> from its branch in autumn,
> I feel as much pain as if
> my arms had been amputated."

## The Historical and Social Background

Certain times, conditions, and even places are like wombs that, when impregnated by certain events, give birth to certain personalities.

When the twentieth century arrived, one important thinker commented, the world witnessed the collapse of "a great, unlucky continent; a glorious, unfortunate state; and a valuable, unprotected nation." With the words "a very noble nation, alas, was disgraced," M. Akif Ersoy lamented the decay of the Turkish people and the Ottoman State.[2]

Centuries earlier, Turkish tribes had suddenly gushed forward like a spring from Central Asia's high mountains and plateaus and, wave upon wave, flowed to the West. First settling in Anatolia, they

---

[2] Mehmed Akif Ersoy (1873-1936): Turkey's national poet and composer of the national anthem. Ersoy was an educator who used his masterly narrative poems to give a vivid critical picture of pre-World War I conditions in Turkey. His powerful and dramatic style, though expressed in traditional meters, testifies to his deep concern for the people's sorrows.

gradually became heirs to a magnificent civilization under the calm, serene shadow of which a considerably chaotic part of the world had lived for five centuries. As the bearers of this civilization, they advanced far into Europe's heart, embroidering the lands they conquered with wonderful works of art and civilization. However, in common with human beings, civilizations and states undergo birth, youth, maturity, old age, and death, as they were determined in the eternal past.

Any judgment made in past eternity occurs within the framework of specific causes and humanity's partial free will. If this were not so, we would justifiably be fatalistic, for fatalism contradicts the mind and logic, as well as historical, sociological, and even psychological truths.

Our bodies age and draw closer to the grave. Like a new day appearing on the horizon with a baby's innocence, we experience the morning of youth, the noon of maturity, the afternoon of old age, and then we experience the sunset and are gone. The same thing is repeated in the seasons, which occur within a predestined framework. Civilizations and states follow the same procedure, but are apparently dependent on their representatives' choices and conduct.

All historical events occur in a similar way and framework, and thus teach us something. Seeing the similarities between these events, between the development of one state and civilization and decay of the other, we can derive accurate conclusions and valuable lessons.

In establishing this universal truth, we must never forget that human beings are not, as materialists claim, "organic" machines. Rather, we have a physical and a spiritual aspect, many mixed and perplexing feelings, and a curious and questioning mind or reason that makes us sorry for the past and worry about the future. In addition, we have other special faculties, among them a heart that is contented only with special "food."

To perform our particular duty, responsibility, and function, and so become truly human and attain real happiness, we must be nurtured emotionally and spiritually, mentally and physically. Thus, although we cannot control our birth and death or meet many of our needs, and live within a certain social framework, each of us has a free will to direct his or her life. Therefore, we seem to be individuals who make human history. We are accountable for our acts and receive what we have earned. This is the difference between human history and the life of "nature."

### Our Old Cities

With their external appearance, inner depth, good proportions, surrounding vineyards and orchards, cascading streams and breezy atmosphere, our old cities softened all hearts. They enchanted all dreams, and intoxicated those who stopped for a while in them.

Colorful lights from beyond rained on the cities; familiarity, love, and affection gushed out of the ground; and city inhabitants breathed a unique communion each moment in the city's bosom. These galleries of beauty-the cities-were a corner of Paradise that everyone strongly desired and to which they ran.

In the people's inspired faces and the buildings' enchanting proportions, we felt that everything bowed to divinity and was progressing in a profound atmosphere within boundaries drawn by celestial inspiration, as if swimming meaningfully and symmetrically, harmoniously, and brightly.

Especially during the latter years and despite various faults due to aged institutions, this atmosphere with all its beauty developed by sighs and laments of love, by ardor constantly being carried away to ecstasy, and by spiritual pleasures that could make the pleasures of Paradise be forgotten, was like the final destination that we could reach...[3]

The Islamic civilization inherited by the Ottomans viewed humanity and life as a whole. On the one hand, it valued science as the "mind's light," understanding that as God's vicegerent on Earth, humanity has the authority to improve the world with knowledge. On the other hand, it based its spiritual foundation on the dynamics

---

[3] Fethullah Gülen, *Zamanin Altin Dilimi* (The Golden Slice of Time) (Izmir: 1994), 43-48.

and values of Islam, and thereby showed itself as a civilization of the mind, heart, and spirit.

This civilization saw nature, the subject matter of sciences, as a place of manifestations of the natural laws derived from the Creator's Attributes of Will and Power. It never perceived scientific "laws" as incompatible with Islam, which is a complete and harmonious system of the laws coming from the Creator's Attribute of Speech (*Kalam*). In the West, science was separated from religion and brought more harm than good. This mistaken approach also enslaved humanity to the very objects that men and women produced and used, thereby depriving them of all sublime values. It gives no significance to human life, but can kill hundreds of thousands in an instant.

Islamic civilization accepted science as an expression of religion on a different level. By wedding the heart and mind on the individual level, and religion and scientific knowledge on the social level, it presented true bliss to a significant part of humanity for centuries. In his monumental *Introduction to the History of Sciences*, Sarton divided history into chronological period and named each one after its most influential scientist.[4]

The 350-year period from the eighth century to the latter half of the eleventh century carries only the names of Muslim scientists: the Harizmî and the Bîrûnî periods, for example.[5] Sarton also identifies hundreds of Muslim scientists who had an impact on their era.

---

[4] George Alfred Leon Sarton (1884-1956): Belgian-born U.S. scholar and writer whose research and publications on the history of science did much to make the subject an independent discipline.

[5] Muhammad Ibn Musa al-Khorezmi (c.780-850) (also al-Khorezmi or al-Khawarazmi): Chief mathematician in the "House of Wisdom," an academy of sciences established in Baghdad by Caliph al-Ma'mun. He wrote *Kitab al-Muhtasar fi Hisab al-Gabr wa al-Muqubala*, from which *algebra* is derived. Abu Rayhan al-Biruni (973-1048): Well-known figure associated with the court of Sultan Mahmud Ghaznawi, a famous 11th-century Muslim sultan. Al-Biruni was a versatile scholar and scientist who was active in physics, metaphysics, mathematics, geography, and history.

These scientists were not experts only in their particular fields or imprisoned in materialist aspects, as is the usual case today, but were experts in many fields. Most were also people of the spirit, mind, and heart. Similarly, many great Sufis were simultaneously mathematicians, astronomers, doctors, historians, and chemists.

In the mid-thirteenth century, Islamic civilization suffered a great shock in the form of the Mongol invasion. But despite its 500-year existence, it was full of life in spirit, nature, and essential dynamics due to the vital energy flowing from its main resources. It recovered quickly. This time, Islamic civilization developed a new branch spreading from Anatolia to Europe, and gained greater splendor with the Ottoman State. However, about the beginning of the nineteenth century, its "wing" of science was broken, and it suffered a decline in its spiritual power. By this time, the West had transformed its scientific knowledge into a source of great strength and launched its colonial expansion.

This development was largely based on some socio-psychological factors created by the European Renaissance or even before. Europe's intoxication with materialism and its hunger for material wealth led its people to search for the world's riches. The power gained through geographical and scientific discoveries and technological inventions eventually led them to world domination. Already collapsing, the Ottoman State could not withstand it. After the Turkish-Russian war of 1877–78,[6] the First and Second Balkan Wars, and the First World War were deeply felt in every Turkish family. Finally, the invasion and division of Anatolia by the Allied forces were added to these.

Together with all these defeats, Europe's apparent dazzling power and material superiority dulled the ever-bright principles of belief, beginning with belief in God, the purpose of creation and life for Muslims. Islam was the victim of Muslims' degradation. The

---

[6] Russia imposed the Treaty of San Stefano on Turkey, and seized Tulcea province; the Chilia, Sulina, Mahmudia, Isaccea, Macin, Babadag, Hârsova, Kunstendje, and Medgidia districts; the islands in the Danube Delta; and the Serpents' Island.

Qur'an was pushed aside, and the Muslims' minds and hearts, hope and love, enthusiasm and feelings were paralyzed. Geographically and socially, the Muslim world came to resemble ruins where owls nested. Over this grievous situation, Ersoy would wail:

> I became like an owl lamenting over the ruins,
> Having seen this heavenly land in its fall.
> If I had lived in the "Time of Rose,"[7]
> I would become a nightingale;
> O Lord, if only You had brought me earlier![7]

### *Our Homes from Past to Future*

Our old, well-proportioned houses once gushed forth happiness and serenity, and spirituality and peace flowed from them. The light that enveloped their surroundings reminded us more of moon and stars. Now we are trying to catch them in our dreams. We are consoled with dreams of them, and we live with the desire to realize those sweet dreams once more.

With their interiors and exteriors and their residents, our houses were the most humane, spacious, sacred places, and the most exposed to the other world. When looked carefully, they seemed as if heavenly kiosks with the *houris* of Paradise in them,"[8] and eternity was felt in the light-diffusing atmosphere surrounding them. The halls (*selamlik*[9]) where guests were received were open to the outer world and connoted places of worship and education, and places where earthly pleasures were tasted. The harem sections reminded one of heavenly kiosks and dervish lodges. The synchronization and fusion of these warm homes with the human spirit was so perfect and meaningful that their inhabitants listened to the poetry of the past and the future together, and felt the idea of immortality permeate their hearts…[10]

---

[7] The period of Prophet Muhammad and the rightly guided caliphs. This period is affectionately called the "Time of the Rose," especially in Sufi and Ottoman–Turkish literature.

[8] Houri: A beautiful maiden who will live with the blessed in Paradise.

[9] Selamlik: A palace's public court or a part of a house where visitors were received. It was normally reserved for formal use and access.

[10] Gülen, *Zamanin Altin Dilimi*, 31-36.

## A Different Home

According to Fethullah Gülen: "Poems, like entreaties, express the ups and downs and enthusiastic and sorrowful moods in one's inner world. To the extent that individuals are concentrated on exalted truths, they become like divine breaths." Gülen, a scholar, philosopher, and poet faced such a world when he was born in November 1938.

One important operative rule in God's universe is that the biggest things grow in the bosom of the smallest things. For example, the seeds of the approximately 30-ton sequoia trees in Ecuador weigh only 0.7 mg. Hiding an ocean in a drop, God uses an invisible sperm as the basic material of the human organism. In the same way, to the extent that people understand their feebleness, poverty, and nothingness before God, they will be powerful with His strength, rich with His wealth, and exist with His eternal existence.

People who have had an impact on history appear in the most unexpected places. According to legend, Rome is said to have been founded by two brothers, Romulus and Remus, who sucked milk from a wolf. Considering the criteria of human superiority, as the French historian Lamartine[11] said and as modern computers confirm, Prophet Muhammad,[12] the greatest person of all time, was raised in an arid valley in the middle of a desert. The Ottoman State rose on the shoulders of a small, insignificant Seljuqid prin-

---

[11] Alphonse-Marie-Louis de Prat de Lamartine (1790-1869): French poet best known for his Méditations poetiques, which strongly influenced the Romantic movement in French literature.

[12] In any publication dealing with the Prophet Muhammad, his name or title is followed by the phrase "upon him be peace and blessings," to show our respect for him and because it is a religious requirement to do so. A similar phrase is used for his Companions and other illustrious Muslims: "May God be pleased with him (or her)." However, as this practice might be distracting to non-Muslim readers, these phrases do not appear in this book, on the understanding that they are assumed and that no disrespect is intended.

cipality.[13] Even though Gülen attributes no greatness to himself, he is a very important person.

He was born in Korucuk, a small village of 50-60 houses, in the Hasankale district of Erzurum province. His ancestors came from Ahlat, a small town in Bitlis province located among the mountains near Lake Van in eastern Turkey. Escaping from Umayyad and Abbasid oppression, the Prophet's descendants had settled in those mountainous regions, where they "blossomed like snow flowers" and established spiritual paths to reach God. Bitlis and its surroundings thus attained the distinction of being the region where the Turkish tribes and Islamic spirit first mingled and fused.

Gülen awoke to life in a hearth permeated with the spirit of Islam. He describes his impressions about family and childhood:

> The first person from my ancestors to settle in Korucuk was my great-grandfather Molla Ahmed, son of Hursid Aga, son of Halil Efendi. Molla Ahmed was an extraordinary person distinguished by his knowledge and piety. During the last thirty years of his life, he never stretched out his legs to lie on a bed and sleep due to his respect to God. It was said that when he became sleepy, he would sit down, rest his forehead on his right hand, and nap a little.
>
> My grandfather Samil Aga resembled his father in some ways, for he was also like a man of the next world. His seriousness and dignity inspired awe in the village people. In addition to his influence, my grandmother Mûnise Hanim had perhaps an even greater influence upon me. She was a unique woman who spoke very little and tried to fully reflect Islam with her state of being. My father also had a great influence on me. He lived carefully to follow Islam, had eyes full of tears, and did not waste his time. Although raised in a small

---

[13] Any of several Turkish dynasties ruling over a great part of western Asia in the 11th–13th centuries. A group of Central Asian nomadic Turkish warriors, they established themselves in the Middle East during the 11th century as guardians of the declining 'Abbasid caliphate. After 1055, they founded the Great Seljuk sultanate (Iran, Iraq, and Syria). They helped prevent the Fatimids of Egypt from making Shi'a Islam dominant throughout the Middle East and, in the 12th century, blocked the Crusader states' inland expansion. Their defeat of the Byzantines at the Battle of Manzikert (1071) opened the way for the Turkish occupation of Anatolia.

village amidst material poverty, scarcity, and drought, according to one who knew him closely, he seemed to have received a "royal upbringing." This generous, noble lover of knowledge had an agile mind that revealed itself in subtleties and was tied to Islam with all his heart. My maternal grandmother, Hatice Hanim, was a monument of purity in every respect. Her daughter Refia Hanim, my mother, was a symbol of compassion and profundity. She taught the Qur'an to all the village women and me at a time when even reciting Qur'an was prosecuted.

Guests, especially scholars, were frequent in our house. We paid great attention to host them. During my childhood and youth, I never sat with my peers or age group; instead, I was always with elder people and listened to them talk about things of mind and heart.

My father constantly adorned his comments with witty remarks he had heard or made up. This shows that he had a fine mind. I was impressed that he would never step over the line of what was proper in our relationship. In both his love and his anger, he protected that boundary. He was bound to the Prophet's Companions to the extreme, and instilled in my siblings and me his love of them.

Outside of my family, Muhammed Lütfi Efendi had a very great influence on me.[14] Every word out of his appeared as an inspiration flowing from another realm. We listened attentively whenever he talked, for it was as if we were hearing celestial things that had previously come down to Earth.

I cannot say that I fully understood him, because he passed away when I was not even 16 years old. Despite this, because he was the one who first awakened my consciousness and perception, I tried to grasp his points with my mind and natural talents, since my age prevented me from comprehending him. My intuition, sensitivity, and feelings of today are due to my sensations in his presence.[15]

---

[14] Muhammed Lütfi Efendi (d. 1954): Born in Alvar (Hasankale district, Erzurum). Later known as Efe Hazretleri or Alvarli Efe, he was an influential Sufi master and poet who had a *divan* of his own. Gülen received spiritual lessons from him when he was 10-15 years old.

[15] Fethullah Gülen, *Küçük Dünyam* (My Small World). Interviewed by Latif Erdogan, *Zaman*.

As Gülen points out, this unique home was like a guesthouse for all knowledgeable and spiritually evolved people in the region. Due to this early contact, young Gülen found himself in a circle of knowledge and spirituality almost from birth.

Gülen received his first Arabic and Persian training from his father, who enjoyed reading books and constantly read the Qur'an or murmured poems. Ramiz Efendi was obsessed with Prophet Muhammad and the Companions, and his books on them were either worn or torn from being read so often. He instilled this love of the Companions in his son, which was to be one of the most important aspects of Gülen. This explains his great love of the Prophet and his Companions, which rose like the smoke from an incense burner in his father's house.

### Our Old Villages

The deep serenity, contemplative calmness, and magical nature that surround our imagination when thinking about our old villages no longer exist.

The slice of silence that we sense and become exhilarated by today in a cove or a grove was always the natural and permanent atmosphere of our old villages. There was such a warm bond and sweet balance between former villages and cities that villagers did not envy the city and city life, and city dwellers did not look down upon villagers. In fact, city dwellers sometimes actually came to live in the villages. The village, considered a small city at that time, was a place of divine beauty where city dwellers went for amusement and relaxation, and to be close to nature. A pleasant silence and calm always dominated the old villages. The morning sunlight, the mewing of sheep and lambs, and the cries of insects and birds would strike our hearts in sweet waves of pleasure and add their voices to the nature's deep, inner chorus. In the evening, existence would shroud itself in the covers of dusk, a mysterious condition that would cast a spell on people and produce dreams. The nights always resonated with a song of silence and calm.

In this world-the next-door neighbor to the next world-the call to prayer and the prayer litanies, the language of the beyond would call us to a different concert and take us around in a deeper and more spiritual atmosphere. As long as

we feel thoughts and ideas belonging to that sacred period,
we cannot break with our past and remain detached from our
future…[16]

## First Training and Psychological Background

Humanity has a distinctive place among creation. In the universe comprised of different realms and worlds, God's Names,
which give existence and meaning to every thing, event, and phenomenon, manifest differently in each realm. Thus the same Name
manifests one way in the social field, another way in the sciences,
and still another in religion. In other words, the same truth appears
in different colors, tones, and shapes in different receptacles.

In each realm, however, humanity's place is unique: People
serve as mirrors to God's Names, see with His vision, and hear with
His hearing. They also have strength from His Power, knowledge
from His Knowledge, and will from His Will. Yet there are manifestations that appear to be opposite at first glance. For example,
how are eternal Mercy and Compassion compatible with eternal
punishment in Hell? Every Name has its own particular place and
field of manifestation. As these Names are reflected in the same
manner, they cause conflicting feelings to arise in each individual.
Anger and mercy, compassion and the desire to punish the exist side
by side, and it is each individual's duty to transform these conflicting feelings into a lace of harmony.

Similarly, just as each of our five external senses has its unique
function and wants to be fulfilled with its own "nourishment," each
of our internal senses and faculties has its own function and wants
its special fulfillment. The mind, thought, memory, reasoning, and
the ability to learn are "mental faculties." Each one has a special
meaning and function for the individual in which they are found, a
special area in which to operate, and an environment in which to
obtain "nutrition." Similarly, each inner faculty (e.g., feelings, the
heart, and the spirit) performs unique functions. To the extent that

---

[16] Gülen, *Zamanin Altin Dilimi*, 37-42.

one's internal and external faculties are nurtured with their special "nourishment" and are satisfied, people establish harmony and attain peace in their inner and outer worlds.

When the necessary relation and harmony is established between mind and heart, reason and spirit, material and spiritual, people can perform their actions within a framework of "wisdom," use such externally oriented capacities as strength and passion within certain limits, and keep them in balance. In short, establishing internal "justice"—balance and the middle, moderate way—leads to just and balanced external relations. If the mind is sacrificed for the spirit or vice versa, or the mind and the spirit for strength, passion, or the body, only a "half" or a "quarter" person will appear. Such a condition will be reflected in society. Raising a complete person of both internal and external balance, justice, and peace means considering all human emotions, feelings, and faculties and then training them to achieve the desired result.

## Years of Education

Destiny directed Gülen to put into effect all the aptitudes and characteristics brought by creation in a just and balanced manner. In his own words:

> My first teacher was my mother. At that time, our village had no elementary school. Later one opened.
>
> I began praying when I was 4 years old, and have never missed a prayer since. One of my teachers was extremely hostile to religion and could not accept this activity. Another teacher, Belma, liked me very much and would say: "One day a young lieutenant will pass over Galata Bridge.[17] It is as if I am watching him now."
>
> I ran all of the errands for my family, helped my mother with the housework, and herded our cattle and sheep. In my spare

---

[17] The bridge at a port and commercial section of Istanbul. It was a symbolic link between the traditional city of Istanbul proper (site of the empire's imperial palace and principal religious and secular institutions) and Galata, Beyoglu, Sisli and Harbiye districts (home to many non-Muslims, foreign merchants, and diplomats).

time, I read books or memorized the Qur'an. When my father was an imam at Alvar village, I learned to read the Qur'an with the correct pronunciation and rhythm from Haci Sidki Efendi of Hasankale, our district. I had no place to stay in Hasankale, so I walked back and forth on the 7 to 8 km. road.

My first Arabic teacher was my father. Later I was taught by Muhammed Lütfi Efendi's grandson, Sadi Efendi. I was studying at Erzurum when I learned that my grandfather and grandmother had died. I was extremely shaken. Day and night I prayed: "Lord, take my soul too so that I can reunite with them." Such depth of feeling was common in my family.

One of my siblings died during my childhood. For years I visited her grave and cried. One of the most shocking events of my life was Muhammed Lütfi Efendi's death. With his death, the world saw another void that could not be filled, and this "old mother of humanity" would groan once again.

My father had to leave Alvar. After a period of time in Artuzu, he settled in Erzurum. While studying there, I could fit all my belongings in a hand-carried box. I continued my education under very difficult conditions. We prepared our food in the same place where we slept. Most of the time we had to bathe in ice-cold water.

Once, the place we stayed in was so narrow that I would have to stretch my foot toward my friend while sleeping. Considering this disrespectful, I did not lie down. Our books were on the room's other side. How could I extend my legs toward them? Also, this side faced Makka. The only other wall faced Korucuk. Thinking that my father might be there and that this would be disrespect to him, I could not extend my legs in that direction either. I sat like this for several nights without sleeping. Not once in my life did I extend my feet toward Korucuk, where my father was born and buried. This is how much respect I have for my parents.

While studying the religious sciences, I read other books and studied the Sufi practices. For me, impacts of the religious sciences and Sufism always produced the same rhythm.

Being very energetic and active, I did not neglect physical exercise. I also was very determined, maybe even courageous. I would quickly climb the high cypress tree in front of the Kursunlu Mosque, and then enjoy the surrounding view. I really liked walking on the top of the minaret's pinnacles.

I was very careful about how I dressed. My clothes were very clean and a little expensive for that time. Sometimes I would be hungry for days, but I never wore pants that were not pressed or shoes that were not polished. When I could not find an iron, I would put my pants under the bed so that they would look pressed.[18]

Gülen is naturally energetic and active, honorable, extremely brave and bold, and a supporter of order and orderliness. In addition, he has a serious historical consciousness and is full of heroic feelings. If his natural abilities had not been disciplined and balanced, he easily could have been a ruthless ruler. He is extremely devoted to his friends and relatives, sensitive, compassionate, and kind. However, he and his family have suffered great deprivation and sorrow, such as the simultaneous deaths of a brother, his grandfather, and paternal grandmother. If he had not been brought up in a circle where the religious sciences and spirituality were studied together, he could have retreated into a life of mystical seclusion.

Gülen also studied positive sciences, literature, history, and philosophy. His education that began in his father's home continued in Erzurum with Muhammed Lütfi Efendi. In fact, his spiritual and religious training have never ended. While in school, he met students of Bediüzzaman Said Nursî and was introduced to the *Risale-i Nur*, in one respect a complete and contemporary Islamic school of thought that contributed a great deal to his intellectual and spiritual formation.[19]

---

[18] Gülen, *Küçük Dünyam*. Interviewed by Latif Erdogan, *Zaman*.

[19] Bediüzzaman Said Nursî (1876-1960): An Islamic scholar of the highest standing with a wide knowledge of modern science and the contemporary world. He believed that humanity could be saved from is crises and achieve true progress and happiness only by knowing its true nature, and by recognizing and submitting to God. His *Risale-i Nur* (Treatise of Light) deals with the Qur'anic descriptions of Divine activity in the universe. Containing logical proofs and explanations of all Qur'anic truths (e.g., Divine Existence and Unity, the Prophets and revealed Scriptures, angels, resurrection, the Hereafter, and destiny [predestination]), it is his reply to those who deny them in the name of science. In it, he shows their many discrepancies and illogical statements.

A person is truly human if he or she learns,
and teaches, and inspires others. It is difficult to regard
as truly human someone who is ignorant and has
no desire to learn. It is also questionable
whether a learned person who does not renew
and reform himself or herself to set an example
for others is truly human.

Meanwhile, he continued his modern education in science and philosophy, literature and history. While gaining a deep comprehension of the main principles of modern sciences (e.g., physics, chemistry, biology, and astronomy), he read such Existentialist philosophers as Camus, Sartre, and Marcuse in French.[20] He was introduced to other Eastern (Islamic and non-Islamic) and Western philosophies through their main sources.

This produced a man of enthusiastic love and deep spirituality and, simultaneously, of broad knowledge, comprehensive logic, discernment, and wisdom. The public knows Gülen as a man of insight and sagacity, clearness, softness and generosity, pain and pleading, dignity and piety, compassion, mercy and tolerance. On the other hand, he is known for his "heroic life," unending hope, idealism, and measured discipline. Finally, he is a symbol of patience. Those close to him know him as a man of education and deep spirituality.

---

[20] Albert Camus (1913-60): French novelist, essayist, and playwright, best known for *L'Étranger* (The Stranger), *La Peste* (The Plague), and *La Chute* (The Fall) and his work for leftist causes. He received the 1957 Nobel Prize for Literature. Jean-Paul Sartre (1905-80): French philosopher, dramatist, and novelist. A major exponent of Existentialism, his best known works include *Nausea, Being and Nothingness*, and *No Exit*. He was awarded, and declined, the 1964 Nobel Prize for Literature. Herbert Marcuse (1898-1979): German-born U.S. political philosopher. His Marxist critical philosophy and Freudian psychological analyses of 20th-century Western society were popular among student leftist radicals, especially after the 1968 student rebellions in West Berlin, New York's Columbia University, and the Sorbonne in Paris.

## Fethullah Hodja or Hodjaefendi[21]

When he was about 20 years old, Gülen left Erzurum for Edirne, Turkey's most western province. Years of deprivation, solitude, and surveillance followed a period of military service that was particularly fertile in Mamak and Iskenderun.[22] During his military service, one of his commanders encouraged him to read the Western classics. After returning to Edirne and therefrom to Kirklareli, Gülen unexpectedly found himself in Izmir in 1966.[23] While in Edirne he was known as the Hodja from Erzurum; when he went to Erzurum he was called the Hodja from Edirne. In Izmir he was known as Fethullah Hodja or Hodjaefendi.

Fethullah Gülen relates his days in Edirne, military service and appointment to Izmir as follows:

### Edirne

My father wanted me to leave Erzurum. With my mother's consent, I was sent to Edirne, where our relative Hüseyin Top Hodja would look out for me.[24]

I was eating and sleeping very little. I became so ascetic that I had to be hospitalized for 15 days. Despite my solitary lifestyle, I had good relations with prominent people in Edirne. In fact, the Head of the Military Branch, a colonel from the Black Sea, once told me: "We're fellow townsmen. You can't be from Erzurum." I had a close friendship with Resûl Bey, the Chief of Police.[25] I also struck up friendship with patrons of the city's coffeehouses.

---

[21] *Hodja* (in Turkish Hoca) is a title for imams, religious scholars, or religiously knowledgeable people. *Hodjaefendi* (in Turkish *Hocaefendi*) a combination of titles *hoca* and *efendi* (a title of respect for men of knowledge or position).

[22] Cities in Ankara and Hatay provinces, respectively.

[23] Kirklareli is a province in the Thrace region. Izmir is Turkey's third largest city and one of its largest ports.

[24] Hüseyin Top Hoca: A relative of Gülen who settled in Edirne after being assigned as an imam there. He worked for the Religious Affairs Department.

[25] *Bey*: A title given to men to show respect or reverence. It is still used in Turkey and Egypt as a courtesy.

I developed my habits here. I liked this region so much that sometimes I would get upset with the Bosphorus (Istanbul Strait) for separating Thrace, especially Edirne, from Anatolia.

I invested my money in books that I considered beneficial, and would give books and magazines to others as gifts. For this reason, I often had financial problems.

I do not give the appearance of being a person who likes to talk and meet with others. However, I have always been very open, and wherever I go I have made and kept good relations with my friends. Also, sitting a lot in the presence of older people and gaining the right to talk with them helped me feel comfortable while talking with others. However, I was always careful not to overstep the boundaries of good manners.

### *Military Service*

I reported to my unit on November 11, 1960 at Mamak. It was a period of coup. I was in Talât Aydemir's unit.[26]

One day while training, the squadron commander called me and asked: "Are you the hodja?" He added: "My wife is ill. I'll bring her and you can 'recite' (prayers) to her." I replied: "I don't know how to 'recite' like that (for curing people). If you believe reading will be effective, you can do it." Later I came to understand that he had been testing me. In later days, he protected me a lot. They gave me an easy job: radio operator.

As I was not entirely fulfilling my military service, I thought that the military's food would not be *halal* (religiously permissible) for me. I even bought my uniform from a military student.

I had reported for service in November. In December, the Talât Aydemir event exploded. And Mamak, with its 15,000 personnel supported it.

---

[26] Talât Aydemir: A colonel who commanded the Mamak Armored Division, he was notorious for his unsuccessful coup d'état attempt of May 21 1963. Together with Fethi Gurcan, he was executed for his second attempt, after which martial law was declared.

Although Aydemir had been a part of the May 27th coup, he later revolted against his comrades.[27] If he had been successful, he would have been another Mussolini. He and his supporters were all potential dictators, and they mocked spirituality.

Eight months after I had reported to service, lots were drawn and I was sent to Iskenderun. There, I spent my spare time reading the Qur'an and other books. A very good commander there insisted that I read the Western classics. As a result, I read both Western and Eastern religious and non-religious classics.

Once I was so malnourished that I had to be hospitalized for exhaustion and jaundice. After I was released, they gave me a 3-month leave for a climate change. I returned to Erzurum, which I had left 4 years earlier. While I was in Erzurum, I went back and forth to the *Halk Evi* (the local town hall). Once I even gave a seminar there on Mawlana Rumi.[28]

Three months later I returned to my unit. I eventually completed my military service and was discharged. I returned to Erzurum and then again went to Edirne.

### Edirne, Kirklareli, and Finally Izmir

In that second term of my residence in Edirne, I stayed with my superior Suat Yildirim, who was the mufti there. When I met with some pressure during my duty, I asked to be transferred to Kirklareli. I did not stay there long. During my yearly leave, I was transferred to Izmir. I went to Kestanepazari Qur'anic school in Izmir. At Kestanepazari, I was busy with students. My official duty was not limited to Izmir, for I was expected to travel in Turkey's Aegean Zone.[29] From time to

---

[27] The May 27 coup d'état was organized by left-wing generals and colonels in cooperation with the leftist media and intellectuals in 1960. It toppled Adnan Menderes, prime minister and leader of the right-wing Democrat Party.

[28] Jalal ad-Din al-Rumi (1207-73, also called Mawlana): The greatest Sufi mystic and poet, famous for his lyrics and didactic epic *Masnavi-ye Ma'navi* (Spiritual Couplets), which widely influenced Muslim mystical thought and literature. After his death, his disciples were organized as the Mawlawiyah order (the Whirling Dervishes).

[29] Turkey has 7 geographical zones: the Marmara, Black Sea, Aegean, Central Anatolian, Mediterranean, Eastern Anatolian, and South-eastern Anatolian zones.

time I would go to coffeehouses to explain things to the men
who were wasting time there.

Most students at Kestanepazari were talented. I was not being
paid there, because I did not want any payment for what I was
doing (not to spoil my sincerity). At night I would visit the
dormitory and put the blankets back to those who had taken
theirs aside. After 5 years, I had to leave Kestanepazari for
various reasons.[30]

His service in the field of education, beginning in the
Kestanepazari Qur'anic School and continuing while a travelling
preacher throughout western Anatolia, gained popularity in the
1970s. These were the days when his idea to serve Islam, Turkey,
and humanity in the name of servanthood to God by raising "perfect" human beings—people who combine spirituality with intellectual training, religious and natural sciences; who wed mind and
heart; who find true happiness in helping others—began to sprout.

In Gülen's dreams and imagination, even in his writings and
poems, was a legendary purebred "horse" that only understood
how tired it was when, stopping for a moment on the slope of a
hill, its heart stopped beating and it died. A true human being had
to be like that horse: his or her life was to be so dedicated to serving others that tiredness would be felt only when his or her heart
stopped beating. With sad and deep looks, a heart burning with
lofty ideals, a spirit intoxicated with breezes coming from the
worlds beyond, with a heart crushed by troubles coming upon
humanity, and with profound feelings, he or she had to be
equipped with the diamond truths of faith, ruby knowledge,
chrysolite love, emerald enthusiasm, pearl-coral contemplation,
and the consciousness of infinite servanthood, helplessness, and
poverty before God.

Be so tolerant that your chest becomes as wide as oceans.
Get inspired with faith and love of human beings. Let there
be no troubled souls to whom you do not offer a hand and
about whom you remain unconcerned.

---

[30] Gülen, *Küçük Dünyam*. Interviewed by Latif Erdogan, Zaman.

After the military coup of March 12, 1971, Hodjaefendi was arrested under suspicion of "changing the social, political, and economic bases of the regime in Turkey; establishing an association and secret organization for this purpose and thereby abusing the people's religious feelings." Released 6 months later after his acquittal by the court, he returned to his previous official position.

After this, he was sent to Edremit, then to Manisa, and finally to Bornova/Izmir, where he worked until September 12, 1980.[31] During this time, he influenced people throughout the country with his sermons, private talks, and conferences on religious knowledge as well as social, economic, and philosophical topics. Especially impressive were his answers to university students who felt their faith questioned by modern philosophy and science. His words influenced many social sectors: from students to teachers, public officials to workers, shopkeepers to traders and business people.

Gülen pointed out that service to one's country should be made in the framework of following basic principles:

- Constant positive action that leaves no room for confusion, fighting, and anarchy
- Absence of worldly, material, and other-worldly expectations in return for service
- Actions, adorned with moral virtues, that build trust and confidence
- Activities that bring people and society together
- Patience and compassion
- Positive and action-oriented people, instead of creating opposition or being reactionary.

In this way, a volunteer service "bazaar" was opened for God's approval. The small group that started to form around his opinions served people in the light of his advice. Now, many people from all walks of life and different opinions participate in this service.

---

[31] Edremit is a town in Balikesir province. Manisa is a city in western Turkey, 20 miles northeast of Izmir.

They continue to serve without thought of material gain. They preach, teach, and establish private educational institutions all over the world. They also publish books and magazines, as well as dailies and weeklies, participate in television and radio broadcasts, and fund need-based scholarships for students. The companies and foundations set up by his followers, all of whom agree on the need to serve humanity especially in the field of education, have founded and are operating about 300 high schools and universities from England to Australia, the United States and Russia, and in South Africa.

Gülen's understanding of service permits no expectation of material or political gain. Sincerity and purity of intention should never be harmed or contaminated. Tolerance, love, and patience have top priority, and avoiding reactionary activities and engaging in positive action are emphasized. The generation kneaded with this understanding of service has attracted broad attention in a short period of time.

## Further Remarks

Known for his ardent endeavor to strengthen bonds among people, Gülen maintains that there are more bonds bringing people together than separating them. And so he works tirelessly for a sincere, profound dialogue and tolerance. He was a founder of the Foundation of Writers and Journalists, a group that promotes dialogue and tolerance among all social strata and has received a warm welcome from almost all walks of life. He regularly visits and receives leading Turkish and international figures: the Vatican Ambassador to Turkey; the Patriarchs of Turkey's Orthodox, Greek Orthodox, and Armenian communities; the Chief Rabbi of Turkey's Jewish community; and leading journalists, columnists, television and movie stars, and intellectuals.

He firmly believes that if you wish to control masses in an unquestioned manner, simply starve them for knowledge. As people can escape tyranny only through education, he asserts that the road to social justice is paved with adequate and universal education, for only this will give people the sufficient understanding and tolerance to respect the rights of others. To this end, he encourages society's elite, community and business leaders, as well as industrialists, to support quality education for the needy.

> Applaud the good for their goodness; appreciate those who have believing hearts; be kind to the believers. Approach unbelievers so gently that their envy and hatred would melt away. Like a Messiah, revive people with your breath.

His tireless efforts have begun to bear fruit. For example, graduates from private schools in Turkey and Central Asia, established by private donations and run as trusts, have taken top honors in university placement tests and consistently finish at the top in International Science Olympiads. They have produced several world champions, especially in mathematics, physics, chemistry, and biology. In July 1997, a chemistry team from Izmir Yamanlar High School took the top honors in the Chemistry Olympiad held in Calgary, Canada.

Gülen maintains: "If a nation expects to be ignorant and free, in a state of civilization, it expects what never was and will never be." He has inspired the use of mass media, notably television, to inform those without any formal education about pressing social issues.

"As a political and governing system, democracy is the only alternative left in the world," he maintains. In spite of its many shortcomings, he states that no one has yet designed a better governing system. We must make it work. People shall always demand freedom of choice in their affairs, especially in their expression of spiritual and religious views.

> There is a mutually supportive and perfective relation between an individual's actions and inner life. We may call it a "virtuous circle." Attitudes like determination, perseverance, and resoluteness illuminate such a person's inner conscience; the brightness of one's inner conscience strengthens one's willpower, and one's resolve stimulates one to higher horizons.

"Do not despair in the face of adversity, and do not yield to those without direction," he emphasizes, lest we give up hope. He views desperation as a quicksand that buries human progress and kills the will to succeed, a noose that chokes and drowns people.

With his acute perception, Gülen perceives that the world's spiritual climate is undergoing a positive change. He envisions a twenty-first century in which we shall witness the sprouting of a spiritual dynamic that will revive the now-dormant moral values. He envisions an age of tolerance and understanding that will lead to cooperation among civilizations and their ultimate fusion into one body. The human spirit shall triumph in the form of an intercivilizational dialogue and a sharing of values.

Gülen successfully bridges the past with the future. His deep desire to find solutions for contemporary social problems has resulted in gem-like sentences set one after another in his writings and speeches, like priceless pearls on a string. In his inimitable style and choice of vocabulary, he offers a way out of the "material quicksand" in which humanity finds itself today:

> Souls without love cannot be elevated to the horizon of human perfection. Even if such people lived hundreds of years, the could make no advances on the path of perfection. Those who are deprived of love entangled in the nets of selfishness, are unable to love anybody else, and die unaware of the love deeply implanted in the very being of existence.

"Today's men and women are searching for their Creator and the purpose of their creation," Gülen contends. He gives practical, convincing answers to such questions as: Why was I born? What is the purpose of my life? What is the meaning of death, and what does it demand from me? In his speeches and writings, one encounters statements like: "Humanity has come to a crossroads: one leads to despair, the other to salvation. May God give us the wisdom to make the right choice." His works represent a search for the truth.

He believes that there should be no material shortages in the world, and sees no justification for people dying of starvation. Basing himself on his firm belief that inequitably distributed wealth should be channeled through private charities to the needy, he has spearheaded the establishment of many charitable organizations to pursue this noble goal.

A unique social activist, Gülen has synthesized the positive sciences with divinity, reconciling all "apparent" conflicts between the two. In his writings and oral presentations, he brings the ideologies and philosophies of East (in particular of Islam) and those of the West closer together.

> Compassion is the beginning of being; without it everything is chaos. Everything has come into existence through compassion, and by compassion it continues to exist in harmony. The Earth was put in order by messages coming from the other side of the heavens. Everything from the macrocosm to the microcosm has achieved an extraordinary harmony thanks to compassion.

"As for getting others to accept your ways," Gülen tells us, "the days of getting things done by brute force are over. In today's enlightened world, the only way to get others to accept your ideas is by persuasion and convincing argument. Those who use brute force to reach their goals are intellectually bankrupt."

In their daily lives, people must maintain the delicate balance between material and spiritual values if they are to enjoy serenity and true happiness. Unbridled greed must be guarded against.

A true leader who leads by example, he lives as he preaches and thus presents a living, ideal model to emulate. As a student of the Hadith,[32] Qur'anic commentary (*tafsir*), and Islamic jurisprudence (*fiqh*), as well as philosophy and Sufism,[33] Gülen occupies his rightful place among his contemporaries in the Islamic sciences.

---

[32] Hadith (or Hadit) is Arabic for *news* or *story*. In religious terms, it is used for the spoken traditions attributed to Prophet Muhammad. They are revered and received as a major source of religious law and moral guidance. The development of Hadith was a vital element during the first three centuries of Islamic history, and its study provides a broad index to the mind and ethos of Islam.

[33] Sufism: A spiritual Islamic belief and practice through which Muslims seek to find Divine love and knowledge through a direct personal experience of God.

> Love is the most crucial element in every being, a most radiant light and a great power that can resist and overcome every force. Love elevates every soul that absorbs it, and prepares it for the journey to eternity. Souls that have made contact with eternity through love exert themselves to implant in all other souls what they receive from eternity. They dedicate their lives to this sacred duty, for the sake of which they endure every kind of hardship to the end. Just as they pronounce "love" with their last breath, they also breathe love while being raised on the Day of Judgment.

Throughout his life, Gülen has tasted almost nothing of worldly pleasure. He has spent his bachelor life studying, teaching, traveling, writing, and speaking. Always he feels the sufferings of people coming from the spiritual wasteland of the twentieth century.

> Only those who overflow with love will build the happy and enlightened world of the future. Their lips smiling with love, their hearts brimming with love, their eyes radiating love and the most tender human feelings—such are the heroes of love who always receive messages of love from the rising and setting of the sun and from the flickering light of the stars.

## Interview Excerpts

[The following are excerpts from the interviews made by various journalists with Gülen.]

### *His Compassion*

Q: You have suffered a lot in your life. How did you overcome events that could have smothered your enthusiasm and smashed you?

A: I was once pursued for 6 years as if I were a traitor. It bothered me, but I forgot and forgave it. I don't feel hostility toward anyone now. Even then I approached the matter logically, not emotionally. I've forgiven the people who did this. If one day I see the faith of people secured and a peaceful atmosphere surrounding the world, then everything will have been worthwhile.[34]

---

[34] Nevval Sevindi, "Fethullah Gülen Ile New York Sohbeti" (An Interview with Fethullah Gülen in New York), *Yeni Yüzyil*, August 1997.

Q: Why did they pursue you for years after the September 12th coup?

A: A newspaper columnist instigated action against me. In one of my last sermons in Bornova, I talked about *al-Shari'a al-Fitriya*. God has two collections of laws: one, issuing from His Attribute of Speech, consists of the principles of religion, also called the Shari'a. However, in the narrow sense they mean the political laws of Islam. The other, issuing from His Attributes of Will and Power, consists of the principles to govern the universe and life, "the laws of nature" that are the subject matter of science. In Islamic terminology, this is called *al-Shari'a al-Fitriya*. Respecting these two collections of laws will make us prosperous in this world and the next, while opposing them will lead us to ruin. The Muslim world remained behind the West because it neglected *al-Shari'a al-Fitriya*.

I explained this matter to the congregation. I encouraged them to undertake scientific research and advancement. However, the next day a columnist wrote about this and claimed I had made propaganda for the Shari'a, meaning the political laws of Islam.

The public prosecutor's office investigated this matter officially. Later, this office understood its mistake and referred the case to the head office of the religious affairs department. This office declared that no action was needed. But I guess that, just as today some people are allergic to the word *Shari'a*, the martial law commander in Izmir was bothered by that word. He put me under surveillance. That situation was very difficult. Of course some people supported me, but it was very hard to make the military regime understand.[35]

Q: In your videotaped sermons, which I watched to get to know you, I notice you weep frequently. What makes you so softhearted?

A: I guess the biggest factor is that this is how God created me. On the other hand, I grew up in a place that resembled "ruined

---

[35] Nuriye Akman, "Fethullah Hoca Anlatiyor" (Fethullah Hodja Is Explaining), *Sabah*, 23–30 January 1995.

towns, ruined homes." In Akif's words, "homeless deserts, headless communities, days without work, evenings with no thought for tomorrow, being dominated, oppression ..." Seeing those, I can't help but feel sad when I wistfully remember the past. It's made me softhearted like a child.[36]

### His Literary Formation

Q: Do you read any books on topics other than religion?

A: I try to read as much as I can. Regardless of the subject, I try to read at least 200 pages a day.[37]

Q: Where does your love of reading come from?

A: In my childhood, usually accounts of the Companions' heroic deeds were read at home. I read many books like the one about Abu Muslim al-Khorasani, which can be considered as legends from Islam's early period.[38] Around the age of 18 to 20, I was drawn to books on jurisprudence and philosophy. I also read about Darwinism and relevant topics. Some books led me to other books, and so it continued. During my military service, a very wise commander who had a deep knowledge of Sufism and loved the Eastern (Islamic) and Western classics advised me to read Western classics. I read many famous Western writers, among them Rousseau, Balzac, Dostoyevski, Pushkin, Tolstoy, and the Existentialists.[39]

Q: Which Western writers influenced you?

---

[36] Ibid.

[37] Ertugrul Özkök, "Hoca Efendi Anlatiyor" (Hodjaefendi Is Explaining), *Hürriyet*, 23–30 January 1995.

[38] Abu Muslim al-Khorasani (d. 755): Leader of a movement in Khorasan. As an agent for the 'Abbasid family, he was instrumental in the downfall of the Umayyad caliphate and in placing the 'Abbasids on the throne.

[39] Eyüp Can, "Fethullah Gülen Ile Ufuk Turu" (A Tour of Horizon with Fethullah Gülen), *Zaman*, August 1995.

A: One must admire Kant.[40] Although Bertrand Russell criticized him bitterly and described him as one who overturned the history of philosophy, Kant was an important philosopher. He was well-known in Turkish theology schools. If you like, I'll relate to you an interesting anecdote related to Kant. In the proficiency test for preachers and muftis, they asked: "In his book, *A Critique of Pure Reason*, the German philosopher Kant separated intelligence into two types: practical and theoretical. He said that theoretical intelligence could not know God and that practical intelligence could. What do you understand from this view, and how do you evaluate it?" Those who had not studied philosophy couldn't answer that question. In fact, one of my friends taking the test apparently didn't understand the question. He asked me jokingly: "What might this Kant thing be?" I told him in jest: "Put some sugar in hot water, stir it well, squeeze a little lemon in it, and you'll have a *kant*." (In Turkey, a beverage called *kant* is prepared this way.)

Descartes caught my interest due to his theological perspective. Many more recent people have attracted my attention. For example, although he is a pantheist, I admire Sir James Jeans very much.[41] Before 1960, I carefully read his *Unknown Universe*. As his view of the universe slightly resembles that of Muhyiddin Ibn al-Arabi, I liked him very much.[42] Another significant figure is Eddington, an astrophysicist who is Jeans' contemporary.[43]

---

[40] Immanuel Kant (1724-1804): German philosopher whose comprehensive and systematic work in the theory of knowledge, ethics, and aesthetics greatly influenced all subsequent European philosophy, especially Kantianism and Idealism.

[41] Sir James Jeans (1877-1946): English physicist and mathematician who was the first to propose that matter is continuously created throughout the universe.

[42] Muhyiddin Ibn al-'Arabi (1165-1240): Muslim mystic, philosopher, poet, and sage. He is considered one of the world's great spiritual teachers. He also was known as Muhyiddin (the Revivifier of Religion) and Shaykh al-Akbar (the Greatest Master).

[43] Sir Arthur Stanley Eddington (1882-1944): English astronomer, physicist, and mathematician. He did his greatest work in astrophysics, investigating the motion, internal structure, and evolution of stars. He was the first expositor of the theory of relativity in the English language.

Q: The writers you mentioned are related to either philosophy or physics. How about literary writers?

A: For a long time I've nurtured a great admiration for Shakespeare. Besides him, one of the writers I greatly appreciate is Victor Hugo, who was exploited by the communists. I read his novels when I was still a child. I also read Tolstoy at a very early age, and admired both Dostoyevski and Pushkin.[44]

### Poetry

Q: We know you write poems. Let's talk a little about literature. Which writers and poets you like?

A: There are definitely people I prefer due to their influence in the intellectual arena. In general, I like the works of all talented people and artists. Just as I've been amazed at someone's movie, I feel wonder at Picasso's pictures. In literature, such people as Shakespeare, Dostoyevski, and Pushkin amaze me.

In Turkey, there are several literary men whose poetry and prose I appreciate. However, I admire the poets Yahya Kemal,[45] Mehmed Akif, and Necip Fazil.[46] In both prose and poetry, I also should mention Sezai Karakoç.[47] Among the Tanzimat[48] and the suc-

---

[44] Eyüp Can, "Fethullah Gülen Ile Ufuk Turu," *Zaman*, August 1995.

[45] Yahya Kemal Beyatli (1884-1958): A Turkish poet initially followed independent courses and later joined the National Literature movement. He made his debut in 1912 and won fame during the War of Independence.

[46] Necip Fazil Kisakurek (1905-83): Educated at the Naval School and Istanbul University Literature Faculty. He expressed spiritual–Sufi tendencies in his poems and plays, skillfully using the Turkish language in an original and modern style to reflect his colorful character.

[47] Sezai Karakoç (1933- ): A Turkish poet combining Islamic thought with the surrealism in modern poetry. He uses spirituality and life-stories of prophets and saints. His similes and synthesis opened an untried page in Turkish poetry.

[48] Tanzimat (Reorganization): A series of Ottoman reforms undertaken between 1839-76 by sultans Abdülmecid I and Abdülaziz. Heavily influenced by European ideas, these reforms were intended to effectuate a fundamental change from a Shari'a-based empire to a more secular state.

ceeding generations, Namik Kemal,[49] Sinasi,[50] Recaizade,[51] and Refik Halid[52] are very admirable and talented. Tevfik Fikret wasn't difficult to read.[53] Among Western writers I also like Balzac. Although he's considered a realist, his Lily of the Valley shows his romanticism. There might be parallels between Iranian poetry and French literature. I can mention Sa'di,[54] Hafez,[55] Nizami,[56] and Anvari[57] are among the Persian writers that I have read.[58]

---

[49] (Mehmed) Namik Kemal (1840-88): A Turkish prose writer and poet who greatly influenced the Young Turk and Turkish nationalist movements. He is best-known for *vatan* (fatherland) and *hürriyet* (freedom), ideas modeled after European concepts that he virtually introduced into Turkish poetry.

[50] Ibrahim Sinasi (Efendi) (1826-71): Founded and led a Western movement in 19th-century Turkish literature. He is considered the founder of modern Ottoman literature, and was probably the first to direct literary expression to the masses.

[51] Recaizade Mahmud Ekrem (1847-1914): An outstanding figure of 19th-century Turkish literature who came under Namik Kemal's influence. He had considerable influence on literary taste, ideas, and work of later Turkish poets.

[52] Refik Halid Karay attained his literary identity later in the National Literature Movement. He was a pioneer of the "domestic literature/domestic story."

[53] Tevfik Fikret (Mehmed Tevfik) (1867-1915): A prominent Turkish poet who tried to define a new literature by writing in an obscure style and using many rare Arabic and Persian words. Greatly influenced by the French Symbolist poets, he sought to adapt Turkish poetry to Western themes and verse forms.

[54] Sa'di (1213-91): One of the greatest poets in classical Persian literature. Author of Bustan and Gulistan, he is remembered as a great panegyrist and lyricist, author of several masterly general odes on human experience, and for his lament of Baghdad's fall to the Mongols in 1258.

[55] Hafez (1325/26-89/90): One of the finest lyric poets of Persia. He received a classical religious education, lectured on Qur'anic and other theological subjects, and wrote commentaries on religious classics.

[56] Nizami (1141-1209): The greatest romantic epic poet in Persian literature. He brought a colloquial and realistic style to the Persian epic.

[57] Anvari (1126-89): Considered one of the greatest panegyrists of Persian literature. He wrote with great technical skill, erudition, and a strong satirical wit.

[58] Nevval Sevindi, "Fethullah Gülen Ile New York Sohbeti," *Yeni Yüzyil*, August 1997.

## Music

Q: Do you listen to music?

A: Until I was 16 years old, I was in contact with some players of Sufi music while I lived in Erzurum. As is known, Sufi or our classical music was born in the dervish lodges and hostels. Hymns and similar poetry attracted me to our classical music. For example, I listened to Itrî[59] and Dede Efendi.[60] I also admired Haci Arif Bey as if he were a saint.[61]

Q: Were you interested in Western classical music?

A: In fact, I admire some of Western musicians also. Others have asked this very question. They asked me: "Can you criticize Mozart?" Even if I say certain things about him, it wouldn't be a critique. We can say that Beethoven complemented Mozart's unfinished work. Western classical music's concertos and symphonies are really serious, dignified, and rich. But saying this, of course, is not a critique. However, just as I greatly admire every genius—God created them with certain talents—I greatly appreciate them as well.[62]

---

[59] Buhurizade Mustafa Itri (1640-1712): A Turkish composer considered one of the founders of the Ottoman music tradition. He composed many light tunes in the form of *turku* (folk song), none of which have survived.

[60] Hamamizade Ismail Dede Efendi (1778-1845): One of the greatest Turkish composers. He created masterpieces in all forms and modes of Turkish music, and developed various composite musical modes: *sultan yegah, neveser, saba buselik, hicaz buselik,* and *Araban kürdi.* His greatest works are the seven Mevlevi pieces for Samah. More than 200 of his compositions are available today.

[61] Haci Arif Bey (1831-85): The composer who started the classical era of Turkish music. He composed more than 1,000 songs and numerous religious pieces, and published a 600-page journal of lyrics called *mecmuai Arif* (1873). More than 200 of his songs (composed in 22 modes), 7 religious works, and a composition in the nehavent form have survived.

[62] Ertugrul Özkök, "Hoca Efendi Anlatiyor," *Hürriyet,* 23–30 January 1995.

### *Properties and Possessions*

Q: You don't have a house. How about your belongings?

A: I have a quilt, bed sheets, and books. I have a long-standing will that all my books go to a foundation. As long as it exists, that property belongs to the foundation. I own no property. I eat wherever is convenient. Sometimes my friends prepare food; sometimes I make it myself. I have diabetes and high blood pressure. I eat low-calorie food, between 1,200-1,800 calories a day. Sometimes I make due with cheese and olives.[63]

### *Daily Tasks*

Q: Who takes care of the daily tasks of a sensitive and shy person like yourself?

A: Because I have been alone all my life, I've always tried to be self-sufficient. I've washed my own clothes for 40 years. There was no machine; I washed them by hand. I cooked my own food. In fact, because of my mother's illnesses, I would help her prepare food during my childhood. I lived alone here and there; I lived alone for years in Edirne. In Izmir I stayed alone in a small cottage. I rented a new house 5 or 6 years later, and I was alone there, too. Guests would come and I would prepare food and tea for them. This continued until the September 12th military coup.[64]

### *Temper*

Q: You appear to be good-natured. Don't you ever get angry?

A: I'm usually so calm and easygoing that everyone might think: "If I tie a rope to him, I could lead him to water (anywhere)." But due to my sensitivity, I may sometimes get angry. However, I'm careful to keep my anger limited to those closest to me. In order not to hurt anyone, I exhaust my anger privately.[65]

---

[63] Nuriye Akman, "Fethullah Hoca Anlatiyor," *Sabah*, 23–30 January 1995.

[64] Ibid.

[65] Ibid.

### Leadership

Q: You always emphasize that you're not a sheikh (or the leader of a dervish order), nor do you show any tendency to accept that you are a leader of a religious community. However, I would like to discuss your leadership.

A: I've never called myself a leader. I'm an ordinary man. A leader is someone with capabilities, genius, charisma, and high performance. I don't have any of those.

Q: Can humility change the reality? Since a group has gathered around your name, don't you automatically become a leader?

A: I insist on saying "I am not a leader" because I expressed my thoughts for 30 years on pulpits (of mosques), and people sharing the same feelings and thoughts responded. For example, I said to them: "Establish university preparatory courses. Establish schools." As an expression of their respect for me, they listened to what I said. This might be a mistake, but they listened and we met at this point. I saw that just as I was saying "schools," I found a lot of people were saying "schools." They come to ask about other, especially religious, issues as well. Sometimes they even ask about economic matters. I tell them that "such issues require subject-specific expertise," and send them to experts.

Q: In your writings and sermons, you recommend suffering hardship to develop spiritually. You have suffered, but now people bow before you to kiss your hand. What do you feel?

A: Extremely uncomfortable. I don't approve such a principle.[66]

### Perception of His "Self"

Q: Looking at the mirror of fate, how do you see yourself?

A: There is an attraction toward me here, and there's my own view. In my own view I am an ordinary man trying to be a true human. During my youth, there was an Imam of Alvar whom I

---

[66] Ibid.

admired very much. He frequently said with an Azeri accent: *Herkes yakhshi men yaman; herkes bugday, men saman* (Everyone is good, I am not; everyone is wheat, I'm the straw). I always repeat the same thing.[67]

### Fethullahçi (Follower of Fethullah)

Q: You never liked the term *Fethullahçi*. But whether you like it or not, those close to you are called *Fethullahçi*. Why?

A: Those using this term may perceive us as a dervish order. In fact, they also call me a "leader of a religious brotherhood." I'm just as uncomfortable with that as I am with *Fethullahçi*. Actually I'm bothered by such suffixes as *-ci* or *cu* (*-ean, -an* or *-ist* in English), because this means division. In Islam, there is and can be no room for such definitions, for *Tawhid* is the essence and foundation of Islam.[68] Muslims cannot be called even *Muhammedci* (Muhammadan), as some Orientalists do either intentionally or mistakenly.[69]

### The Hodja Spoke

By N. Kemal Zeybek

On Wednesday evening I watched Fethullah Gülen Hodja on Kanal D (a private TV channel). If only his views would be broadcast frequently and then spread all over our country. This is the religious knowledge we need. Knowledgeable ... Sincere ... Profound faith ... Determined ... Successful in service to others ... Not using religion, business, and politics as a tool ... Tied to his religion, but respectful of other religions and belief ... In other words, a real Muslim ...

---

[67] Ibid.

[68] Ibid.

[69] *Tawhid*: The belief in One Almighty God, Creator of all universe and life. God is the ultimate Master and Power, who must be served, obeyed, and worshipped at all times during an individual's life.

### A Means for a Relationship with the Creator

The Hodja says: "Religion is the relationship between people and their Creator. The feeling of religion lives in the heart's depths and on the inner world's emerald green hills. If you turn it into a display of forms, you'll kill it. Politicizing religion will harm religion before it harms a government's life." In other words, making religion a political instrument opens the way to its destruction.[70]

## Twenty-first Century Utopia and the Dervish Tradition

By Nevval Sevindi (anthropologist, researcher and writer)

One feels Gülen's asceticism, an extension of the dervish tradition, and the depth of his inner world and love, which give meaning to life and contain the roots of a strong endurance. This endurance, nurtured by an ideal, carries this country's spirit in such a way that it cannot be kept in a certain mold.

He sets targets, recommends plans and projects, and seeks to raise a generation that believes in itself. He writes and speaks about a restructuring woven with virtues that will regain for twenty-first-century Turkey its lost values. He believes in the individual and that without going deep inside and interrogating oneself, a heart–mind integration cannot be forged.

Saying: "Don't forget Pascal in Ghazali's bright horizon; don't fail to salute Pasteur in the laboratory when performing the dance of the whirling dervishes with Mawlana," Gülen signals that Turkey is pregnant with a cultural synthesis that is elevated in both worlds.

### Turning the Other Cheek

At first Gülen displays a refined and modest reserve before others. It is obvious that he does not enjoy leaving the richness of his inner world to face routine questions. He is accustomed to winding around the curves and on the edge of his inner world's boundaries. He does not talk loudly or in anger or command. He does not know how to say "No," and suffers the results. He accepts the axiom of

---

[70] *Son Havadis*, 21 April 1997.

"turning the other cheek." I understand that ugly politics and politicians play a big role in his high blood pressure and diabetes.

### He Appreciates Modern Science
### and Free Enterprise

Gülen has faith in the victory of hope and will. Trusting in the individual and newness, he explains the importance of integrating the mind and heart through love: "Until ignorance dries up, the masses can't attain enlightenment." He sees self-renewal as the only condition of continued existence. He sleeps two or three hours a day, eats little, and reads a lot.

He genuinely believes in and encourages free enterprise. According to him, believers both in Turkey and abroad must be wealthy. He emphasizes education arm-in-arm with development, and economic and cultural togetherness for the future... He recommends the dynamic of knowledge against ignorance, work against poverty, and solidarity and wealth.

### A Tripod Encompassing Life's Economic,
### Cultural, and Spiritual Aspects

Gülen's understanding, which rests on a tripod, encompasses life's "economic, cultural, and spiritual" dimensions. The tripod of economics, education, and religion is the main dynamic of his view's vitality. As long as knowledge is not operative in life, it has no value for him. As long as the ways of earning money are not learned and money is not spent to benefit the country, it is greed itself. Unless methodology and system replace memorization, he believes that education cannot be beneficial.

Gülen activates people to solve their problems, produce plans and programs, earn money, and make their knowledge operative in their lives. He recommends that education result not only in learning, but also produce people as social creatures with spiritual and all other values.

### Turkish Renaissance

Gülen is nurturing and enlarging the 1,000-year-old Anatolian Turkish–Islamic traditions under today's conditions. At the same time, he's using his religious knowledge and depth for today. He believes in a Turkish renaissance.

If only people could come out of their small cages and move to not only a broad horizon of the heart, but also to a wide mental horizon as well. If only the foundation of this polarized society—where everyone sits in his or her own cell and believes all other ideas to be hostile—were to become green and we were to take our rightful place in the world. If only we could open the closed doors of a world that produces no ideas, and if people could understand that they have nothing to fear except themselves. If only we could build bridges to each other and understand each other by talking and debating. As the Hodja said: "If keeping your eyes closed to the future is blindness, then disinterest in the past is misfortune."

### The Cultural Islamic Synthesis in Modern Turkey

Intellectuals who do not produce a national cultural synthesis and who deny the Seljuqid-Ottoman synthesis have not reached the people. Their baseless, imitative view blew them about like the wind. Since they could not throw off their exploited coercive mentality, they could not produce an ideology for the rising Turkish middle class. Intellectuals and bureaucracies that could not produce a synthesis from this country's history, conditions, and culture have always imposed their own view, belittling everything except themselves.

Gülen is a child of the Republic of Turkey, and approximately the same age. He is not an imitator, for he knows how to produce new value from the materials at hand. He does not see knowledge as a heap of rocks, but as a mental activity or process that will create a pyramid or a building. For this reason he is alone. Struggling with fixed ambitions, arguments, and habits, he is having a difficult journey.

He is the "Muslim European Turk" that the Republican ideology wanted to create: a new synthesis of full religion and Western formation. A synthesis that could surpass the Ottoman would be determined by the new Republic of Turkey. An understanding of Islam that looks with Anatolia's eye of the heart, shows affection, and loves with heartfelt Muslimness. It is the Islamic understanding that found spiritual expression in Yunus, Hadji Bektash, and Mawlana, and that encompasses the whole world.

This cultural richness made people inside the Ottoman borders identify with Muslimness, like the Bosnians. In one of the twentieth century's last bloody wars, this *Muslimness* could not be torn out. Today Turkey still controls the geography of Ottoman culture. The breadth of these borders is an expression of our cultural richness. Central Asia is the place from whence we came, and Europe is the place to which we went. Turkey must forego sleeping on this treasure. At the end of 70 years, the Turkish middle class and rising Anatolian bourgeoisie want their need for an ideology fulfilled.

### Humanity's Scientific and Spiritual Knowledge
Returning to and leaning on the original source of religion, the Hodja brings a new perspective and horizon. It is new because instead of hearsay, superstition, and traditional customs, there is an effort to base belief on knowledge. The mind and spirit are found together in the human being. People with internal gaps to be filled should not spend their lives with only money and commands. These internal gaps can be filled, and thus closed, with scientific and spiritual knowledge. This is why the Hodja emphasizes individual freedom, education, and free enterprise.

### Educational Missionaries Opening
### Horizons in Central Asia
Young people from Central Asia's Turkish republics are pouring into Turkish universities via the TCS and YÖS (college level replacement tests for foreign students) examinations. They have been specially trained, passed the necessary exams, and earned first-place honors in different branches. In Tajikistan, the most hesitant republic, supporters of Iran and the Isma'ili sect could not realize their goals, for the people chose Turkish education.[71] While last year

---

[71] Isma'ili: A Shi'a sect most active as a religio-political movement during the 9th–13th century through its subsects, the Fatimids, Qarmatians, and Assassins. They stress the dual nature of Qur'anic interpretation (exoteric and esoteric) and distinguish between the ordinary Muslim and the initiated Isma'ili.

23 students came to Turkey from Tajikistan, this year 99 people passed the exam and came.[72]

### *The Hodja Is a Very Respected Person*
### *Who Pays Respect to Everyone*

By Nuriye Akman

I first asked for an appointment with Fethullah Hodja about 2 years ago. Later, his talk with Çiller renewed my desire to see him.... Of course, not only myself, but also all reporters wanted to see him.

Q: Before your meeting, were you told by others such things as "Ask the Hodja this" or "Don't say that"?

A: They had prepared a headscarf for me, for they thought it would be more appropriate. When they asked the Hodja about it, he said: "You've made a mistake; let her come as she is."

Q: What are your impressions of Hodja Efendi?

A: Generally he's a person who speaks little and doesn't talk unless asked a question. He's very shy. I knew he was shy, and it was the first time he was speaking with a woman reporter. The Hodja is a very respected person who pays respect to everyone. He's like a now-forgotten, refined gentleman that we've read about or seen in old films. He frequently says *Estagfirullah* (I ask God's forgiveness. I'm not one of the kind you describe), especially when you praise him. He speaks in a refined way. While sitting, he keeps his legs closely together and sits in a straight position without moving. He's extremely modest. Before doing something, he always asks permission, even before drinking a glass of water. The Hodja speaks distinctly and fluently in a low voice. He knows what he's going to say, and he speaks clearly.

Q: Were you able to publish the full interview?

---

[72] Nevval Sevindi, *Fethullah Gülen'le New York Sohbeti* (The New York Interview with Fethullah Gülen) (Istanbul: Sabah Kitaplari, 1997).

A: We filmed parts of his talk. This was a big sacrifice for him, because he sweats due to shyness. He doesn't feel comfortable being in the limelight. While posing for photographs, he asked: "Haven't you tortured me enough?" But he says these pleasantly. Actually he did feel under a lot of pressure.

Q: After the interview was published, what kind of favorable or unfavorable reaction did you get?

A: Some top-ranking government officials called. "We thought Hodja Efendi was a man wearing a turban and baggy trousers with clogs on his feet whose head should be broken and who was anti-secular. You confused us," they said.[73]

## His Works

In addition to his books, Gülen contributes to several journals and magazines. He writes the editorial page for *Sizinti, Yeni Ümit* (New Hope), *Yagmur* (Rain), and *The Fountain* magazines. His sermons and discourses have been recorded on thousands of tapes and videocassettes. In addition, many books have been compiled from his articles, sermons, and answers to questions he has been asked over the years. Some of his books are as follows:

- *Asrın Getirdiği Tereddütler* (4 vols.; vol. 1 has appeared as Questions and Answers about Faith)
- *Kalbin Zümrüt Tepeleri* (translated as :Key Concepts in the Practice of Sufism)
- *Çağ ve Nesil* (This Era and the Young Generation)
- *Ölçü veya Yoldaki Işıklar* (4 vols.; vol. 1 has appeared as Pearls of Wisdom)
- *Zamanın Altın Dilimi* (The Golden Part of Time)
- *Renkler Kuşağında Hakikat Tomurcukları* (2 vols.; vol. 1 has appeared as Truth through Colors)
- *Kırık Mızrap* (Broken Plectrum), a collection of verse

---

[73] Interviewed by the weekly *Nokta*.

- *Fatiha Üzerine Mülahazalar* (Reflections on *Surat al-Fatiha*)
- *Sonsuz Nur* (2 vols., Prophet Muhammad: Aspects of His Life)
- *Yitirilmiş Cennet'e Doğru* (Towards the Lost Paradise)
- *İnancın Gölgesinde* (The Essentials of Islamic Faith).

Some of his books, such as *Asrın Getirdiği Tereddütler*, *İnancın Gölgesinde*, *Sonsuz Nur*, *Kırık Mızrap*, have been translated into German, Russian, Albanian, and Bulgarian.

## CHAPTER 2

# Religion, Islam, and Tolerance

> Fethullah Gülen is a religious scholar and very careful in living Islam in his daily life. However, there are different understandings of Islam. Thus some people, especially those describing ideas, movements, persons, and organizations by making generalizations and naming, mention different "versions" of Islam: Militant Islam, Political Islam, Cultural Islam, and so on. To understand Fethullah Gülen's view and practice of Islam, the following excerpts from his writings and interviews are of considerable significance.

## The Irrepressible Power of Religion

Regardless of changes, advancements in science and technology, and new ways of thinking, the feeling of attachment to a religion always has been the primary factor in forming humanity's scientific and intellectual life, developing human virtues, and establishing new civilizations. With its charm and power, religion is still and will be the most influential element and power in people's lives. This reality will continue to exist. The existence of two great civilizations in recent history, one based mainly on Islam and the other owing a good deal to Christianity, proves this argument.

In contrast to some of the Muslim world's so-called Westernized intellectuals, who seem to be ashamed of their religion and history, Western people appreciate the roots of their culture and civilization. While paying tribute to that important cultural root through Christian political parties, Western people continue to present global messages of hope and salvation in the name of Jesus. This also supports the argument that religion gradually will grow more influential and play a unique role in the future, just as it did in the past.

Following the near-global collapse of communism, the Orthodox Church is restoring its influence in the former communist bloc. Christian parties have come to power in some European countries, and people take oaths on the Bible in official or nonofficial environs. Religious education is taken seriously at schools and colleges, and is propagated through the mass media... All this indicates that, even after distortion and corruption, religion cannot be defeated.

Until recently, only theologians were defending religion. But now many scientists, among them biologists, anthropologists, zoologists, physicians, physicists, psychologists, and sociologists, are working to show the eternity of its truth.

It is a pity that, contrary to the trends in the West, some Muslim intellectual circles remain stuck in a materialist philosophy and have set their hearts upon a Marxist utopia. Fortunately, their lack of sound reasoning and insight, as well as intellectual separation from the majority, means that few people pay attention to them.

People who can draw the right conclusions from what they read and observe know that positivism was dethroned long ago in scientific and intellectual studies. They also know that the physical sciences, spirituality, morality, and other forms of knowledge based on intuition and inspiration are irreplaceable in human life. Furthermore, right now it is hard to claim that positivistic and materialistic scientists can apply a moral perspective to their work. In irresponsible hands, science and its products become deadly weapons. Unless combined with moral reflection, science is apt to bring about new kinds and degrees of disasters, like Hiroshima and Nagasaki.

Many products of science and technology, like nuclear power, are neutral, for the end result depends upon how they are used. In the hands of virtuous people who have deep, heartfelt, and strong relations with the Creator, they are like tame animals ready to serve humanity. They are a cause of fear for the unjust and oppressors, and a promise of support and hope of security for the innocent and oppressed.

Great thinkers opine that science and knowledge can have positive value if used to benefit humanity by virtuous people with high moral standards. Einstein said that science teaches us the relations between phenomena and how phenomena exist together under their specific conditions. He added that science, which consists of the knowledge of what already is, does not teach us what should be; only religion teaches us how things should be and to which goals we should aspire. Einstein also believed that religion points out our goals, and that science can be very helpful in showing us how to reach those goals. Religion should define the limits of science by directing science to its objective and then teaching it how to pursue that objective. Science without religion is crippled, while religion without science is blind.

If we restrict our thinking to scientific confines, the world will appear as a dull, one-dimensional mechanism. However, in regard to its miraculous birth and inevitable death and its amazing operation, science has nothing to say about the universe and existence. Such areas belong to religion. Scientists such as Sir J. Jean and Eddington have suggested new and primarily God-based ways for science to follow, in opposition to materialistic trends and attitudes. They also have tried to remove the obstacles in front of science.

We hope and believe that science will draw closer to religion, and that scientists will realize the absolute necessity of belief in God.[74]

## The Qur'an

- The Qur'an descended from the Highest of the High, in accordance with humanity's merit and value, and considering the human heart, spirit, mind, and physical being. Containing the most perfect messages, it is a collection of Divine Laws.

- Followed today by more than a billion people, the Qur'an is a unique book that, with its eternal and unvarying divine principles, guides everyone to the shortest and most illuminated road to bliss.

---

[74] Fethullah Gülen, *Günler Bahari Soluklarken* (As Days Approach Spring) (Izmir: T.Ö.V. Yayinevi, 1997), 88-92.

- The Qur'an has been a light source for the most magnificent and enlightened communities that have ruled the world, that produced thousands of scholars, philosophers, and thinkers. In this sense, no other rule is equal to its rule.

- Since the day it was revealed, the Qur'an has encountered many objections and criticisms. However, the Qur'an has always emerged unscathed and so continues to manifest its victory.

- The Qur'an crystallizes in the heart, illumines the spirit, and exhibits truths from cover to cover. Only believers who can sense all the beauty of the universe in a single flower and see rainstorms in a drop of water can perceive and understand its real countenance.

- The Qur'an has such a style that Arab and foreign linguists and literary people who heard its verses bowed before it. Those who recognized its truth and understood its contents bowed before this masterpiece of eloquence.

- Muslims can reach unity only by affirming and believing the Qur'an. Those who cannot do so cannot be Muslims or establish any lasting unity.

- Saying that "faith is a matter of conscience" means "I affirm God, His Prophet, and the Qur'an" with my tongue and my conscience. Every act of worship connected to this understanding manifests this affirmation.

- When humanity was floundering in the brutality of ignorance and unbelief, the Qur'an burst forth in a flood of enlightenment that drowned the world in its light. The Qur'an engendered an unparalleled revolution with no equal. History is witness enough!

- The Qur'an teaches in a most balanced way the meaning and nature of humanity; truth and wisdom; as well as God's Essence, Attributes, and Names. No other book can equal it in this field. Look at the wisdom of scholarly saints and the ideas of true philosophers, and then you will understand.

- The Qur'an is the unique book ordering true justice, real freedom, balanced equality, goodness, honor, virtue, and compassion for all creation. It is also the unique book forbidding polytheism, oppression, injustice, ignorance, bribery, interest, lying, and bearing false witness.

- The Qur'an is the only book that, while protecting orphans, the poor and the innocent, puts the king and the slave, the commander and the private, the plaintiff and the defendant at the same table and then judges them.

- Claiming that the Qur'an is a source of superstition is nothing more than repeating the words uttered by ignorant Arabs 14 centuries ago. Such a view ridicules wisdom and true philosophy.

- If only those who criticize the Qur'an and its contents could produce something to guarantee the order, harmony, peace, and safety of human life even in a short, temporary period.... Actually, it is very difficult to understand this perversity and obstinacy when faced with the miserable and unbalanced civilizations based on principles contrary to the Qur'an, and the troubled, depressed, and moaning hearts of those deprived of its light.

- The most orderly life for humanity is that instructed by the Qur'an. In fact, some of the good things that are today universally commended and applauded are the exact things encouraged by the Qur'an centuries ago. So, whose fault it is if Muslims are in a miserable situation today?

- Those who criticize the Qur'an, as if it were their profession, generally have only a vague and superficial knowledge of its contents. It is ironic that such people feel free to vent their opinions without researching or even reading it. Actually, there is no difference between their attitude and the obstinacy that some ignorant people show in the face of (physical) sciences. It seems that we will continue to wait for people to awaken to truth.

- Those who have faith in Prophet Muhammad and the Qur'an have faith in God. Those who do not believe in the Qur'an do not believe in Prophet Muhammad, and those who do not believe in Prophet Muhammad do not believe in God. These are the true dimensions of being a Muslim.

- The Qur'an enables people to rise to the highest level, namely the station of being addressed by God. Those who are conscious of being in this position hear their Lord speak to them through the Qur'an. If they take an oath that they speak with their Lord, they will not be among liars.

- Even though we are still in this world, when we enter the Qur'an's enlightened climate we feel that we are passing through the grave and the intermediate world, experiencing the Day of Judgment and the Sirat,[75] shuddering at the horror of Hell, and walking on Heaven's tranquil slopes.

- Those who have avoided Muslims from understanding the Qur'an and perceiving it in depth have removed Islam's spirit and essence from them.

- Soon, and under humanity's gazes of commendation and amazement, the streams of knowledge, technique, and art flowing toward the Qur'anic ocean will fall into their essential source and unite with it. At that time, scholars, researchers, and artists will find themselves in that same ocean.

- It should not be too hard to see the future as the Age of the Qur'an, for it is the word of One Who sees the past, present, and future simultaneously.[76]

---

[75] Sirat: The bridge leading over the deep gulf of Hell to Paradise.

[76] Fethullah Gülen, *Ölçü veya Yoldaki Isiklar* (Criteria or Lights of the Way) (Izmir: T.Ö.V. Yayinevi, 1990), 3:78-87.

## Prophet Muhammad

*   Humanity came to know and favor the true civilization through Prophet Muhammad. All efforts exerted after him for the sake of true civilization have been no more than following or mimicking the principles he brought and adjusting them to new conditions. For this reason, he rightfully deserves the title "the founder of true civilization."

*   Prophet Muhammad rejected indolence and laziness, esteemed labor as a mode of worship, and applauded those who work hard. He directed his followers to horizons beyond the age in which they lived, and taught them how they could be the means of balance in the world.

*   Prophet Muhammad is unequalled: He appeared as a sword of valor and eloquence against unbelief and savagery, proclaimed the truth with the clearest voice, and showed humanity the ways leading to the existence.

*   If ever someone hated ignorance, unbelief, and brutality, that person is Prophet Muhammad. Those who search for truth and thirst for true knowledge eventually will discover him and embrace his path.

*   Prophet Muhammad proclaimed true freedom to humanity, and ingrained in human consciousness that all human beings are equal before the law. He established that superiority lies in virtue, piety, and morality. He regarded proclaiming the truth against all oppressors and oppressive thoughts as a kind of worship.

*   Prophet Muhammad called upon us to protect religion, life, reason, property; the integrity of family and lineage; and to strive for this purpose. In a remarkably balanced way, he proclaimed that no other duty could equal this struggle.

*   Prophet Muhammad unveiled the transitory nature of this world and death, and showed the grave to be a waiting room opening to the realm of eternal bliss. He led every heart seeking happiness, regardless of place or time, to the fountain of Khadr, and enabled them to drink the elixir of immortality.[77]

## Religion

*   Since its appearance on Earth, humanity has found true peace and happiness in religion. As it is impossible to talk of morality and virtue where people do not practice the true religion, it also is difficult to imagine real happiness, for morality and virtue originate in a good, clear conscience. Religion is what makes one's conscience good and clear, for it is a connection between humanity and God.

---

[77] Ibid., 3:28-31.

- Religion is the best school, the most blessed institution founded to inculcate good moral qualities in people. It is open to everyone, from the youngest to the oldest, and only those who attend it attain peace, satisfaction, and freedom. Those without religion, by contrast, cannot save themselves from losing everything, including their true identity.

- Religion is the collection of Divine principles that guide people to what is good, not by force but by appealing to their free will. All principles that secure our spiritual and material progress, and thereby our happiness in both worlds, are found in religion.

- Religion means recognition of God in His absolute and transcendental Unity, acquiring spiritual purity by acting in His way, arranging relationships in His name and according to His commandments, and feeling a profound interest in and love for all creation on His account.

- Sooner or later, those who do not recognize religion will come to hate such high values as chastity, patriotism, and love of humanity.

- Immorality is a disease caused by the lack of religion, and anarchy is a product of this same lack.

- Do atheists, who devote their lives to attacking religion, not have some obligation to demonstrate atheism's benefits and good consequences, if any?

- Religion and science are two faces of the same truth. Religion guides us to the true path that leads to happiness. Science, when understood and used properly, is like a torch that provides us with a light to follow the same path.

- All the beautiful "roses" of laudable virtues are grown in the "gardens" of religion, as are the most illustrious "fruits" of the tree of creation, such as prophets, saints, and scholars of high achievement. Although atheists deliberately ignore them, they will never be able to remove them from the hearts and pages regardless of how hard they try.

- Nothing in true religion is contrary to sound thinking, common sense, and knowledge. Therefore true religion cannot be criticized from any rational point of view. Those who do not accept religion either are devoid of sound thinking and reasoning or have a wrong conception of knowledge and science.

- Religion is an inexhaustible and blessed source that lays the foundation of true civilization. Religion elevates us so high in spirit and feelings that we make contact with ethereal worlds, where we are "fed" to full satiation with all kinds of beauty, virtues, and goodness.

- Virtues should be sought in the practice of religion. It rarely happens that an atheist has laudable virtues or that a religious person has none.

- Men and women attain true humanity by means of religion, which distinguishes them from animals. For atheists, there is no difference between human beings and animals.

- Religion is the path established by God, while atheism is Satan's path. This is why the struggle between religion and atheism has existed since the time of Adam and will continue till the Last Day.[78]

## Worship

- Worship means sincere acknowledgement of oneself as a servant and of God as the sole and true Object of Worship. It consists in a servant designing his or her life in accordance with the relations between a true servant and the True Object of Worship, in light of the fact that the created is the former and the Creator is the latter.

- Worship means one's thankfulness for the bounties bestowed, such as life, consciousness, power of perception, and faith. Neglecting the duty of worship is crude ingratitude.

- Worship is a road to travel, opened by the Being who commands us to belief. It is a set of good manners that He ordered us to observe, so that we could reach Him and finally obtain happiness in both this and next life. Those who cannot find this way and acquire these manners cannot reach God, the Truth.

- Worship is the safest way to reach the most unshakable certainty in one's conscience about the greatest truth, which is known only theoretically at the outset. In each station on this way, along which consciousness seeks certainty on the wings of reverence and respect, a person experiences a different taste of glimpsing the Beloved.

- Some souls, shut off to the truth, spend their lives studying only certain theoretical issues. Even if they live in the enchanting company of the most eloquent, articulate tongues and the most fascinating expressions of the truth, they cannot advance even an inch toward it.

- Worship is a blessed, growing resource that feeds a person's thoughts and will of being good, righteous, and virtuous. It is a mysterious elixir that tames and reforms the self's innate tendencies toward evil. One who engages in worship a few times a day by reflecting on Divine truths and remembrance of God, enters the way of perfection and also protection against the temptations of the carnal self.

- Worship is developing our potential, which can make us like angels, so that we can be fitted for Paradise and control our bestial inclinations and poten-

---

[78] Ibid., 2:76-81.

tialities. So far in human history, many people have surpassed angels by means of their worship, while many others have refused to worship and thus have sunk to the lowest of the low.

- The most meritorious act or benefit of worship is recognition and love of God Almighty and serving humanity. If there is something more meritorious and commendable, it is seeking God's approval and pleasure in whatever one does and, to "stand firm uprightly on the straight path as you have been commanded (12:112)" by always pursuing the truest and highest ideal in life.

## Morals

- Morals are a set of noble principles that originate from exalted spirituality and govern human conduct. For this reason, people who neglect spirituality, and are therefore lacking in spiritual values, cannot sustain conduct in accordance with these principles.

- Preferring the interests of others to one's own is exalted spirituality and liberality. One day, those who always do good without expecting any return will bow before God in wonder and admiration when, unexpectedly, they meet the accumulated results of their considerate nature and all the good deeds they have done.

- Just because you are learned does not mean you are truly human. Learned people are freed from carrying the burden of superfluous information and attain eminence to the extent that they serve humanity and set a good example for others through their high morals and virtues. Otherwise, they are no more those who have wasted their lives. Those with high morals and virtues, even if they lack education and are as dense as iron, sometimes may prove to be useful and valuable, and even as precious as gold.

- Never deceive anyone, even if they deceive you. Fidelity and uprightness are two of the highest virtues. Even if following this advice brings you loss, which it usually does, always be faithful and upright.

- Morals were once thought of as virtues. Today they are regarded as a collection of rules for social behavior. I wish people would behave in accordance with these rules, even though they are not virtuous!

- In the past people would say: "The principles of good conduct are no longer practiced; we only see them recorded in books." Today they say: "The principles of good conduct are outdated; whatever remains of them is recorded in old books." Whatever they say, those principles are worth sacrifice of many new things, even though people try to present them as outdated.[79]

---

[79] Ibid., 2:59-61.

## The Universality of Islam

The issues brought forth by time and changing circumstances are referred to as secondary methods (*furuat*) of jurisprudence. For example, when sea trade was not so complex, Islam, Christianity, and Judaism had no specific rules for it. Such matters are to be referred to *ijtihad* in the light of basic principles of Islamic belief, morality, and lifestyle.[80]

Time and conditions are important means to interpret the Qur'an. The Qur'an is like a rose that develops a new petal every passing day and continues to blossom. In order to discover its depth and obtain its jewels in its deeper layers, a new interpretation should be made at least every 25 years.

The Hanafi understanding and Turkish interpretation dominates more than three-fourths of the Islamic world.[81] This understanding is very dear to me. If you like, you can call this Turkish Islam. Just as I see no serious canonical obstacle to this, I don't think it should upset anyone. Actually, I think the world needs an interpretation of the Qur'an and Sunna that explains, addresses and belongs to everyone.

Societies that have never founded states, never known the spirit of Sufism, never experienced the events that the Turkish nation

[80] *Ijtihad* (Arabic: effort): In Islamic law, this is the independent or original interpretation of problems not precisely covered by the Qur'an, Hadith, and *ijma'* (scholarly consensus). In the early Muslim community, every adequately qualified jurist could exercise such original thinking, mainly *ra'y* (personal judgment) and *qiyas* (analogical reasoning).

[81] Hanafi (also Hanafiyah, Madhhab Hanifah, and Hanafites): A Sunni schools of religious law incorporating the legal opinions of the ancient Iraqi schools of Kufa and Basra. It was developed from the teachings of Imam Abu Hanifah (c. 700-67) by such disciples as Abu Yusuf (d. 798) and Muhammad al-Shaybani (749/750-805), and eventually became the official Islamic legal interpretation for the 'Abbasids, Seljuqs, and Ottomans. Hanafis acknowledge the Qur'an and Hadith as primary sources of law, but accept *ra'y* (personal judgment) in the absence of precedent. The school currently predominates in Central Asia, India, Pakistan, Turkey, and the countries of the former Ottoman State.

has faced because of the great states it has founded, and have never gained the centuries of experience it gained cannot really say anything in the name of universality. Therefore when evaluating the Turkish version and experience of Islam, and why it accepted the Hanafi school of law as its formal code of law, the history of Islam in general and Turkish history in particular should be kept in mind.

Turkish Islam is composed of the main, unchanging principles of Islam found in the Qur'an and Sunna, as well as in the forms that its aspects open to interpretation assumed during Turkish history, together with Sufism. More than any other Muslim country, Sufism has spread among the Turks in both Central Asia and Turkey. This is why Turkish Islam always has been broader, deeper, more tolerant and inclusive, and based on love. If we can breathe this spirit into the modern world's carcass, I hope it will revive.

## Islam Is Misunderstood

We must review our understanding of Islam. Islam is not a religion for a particular time. Bediüzzaman asks: "Why, in this world, do others advance and we go backward?" Since Islam is misunderstood, implemented incorrectly, and perceived as a simple religion belonging to the past, today the Islamic world is in a pitiful state.

As Muslims, we must ask ourselves why. Taking the Qur'an and Sunna as our main sources and respecting the great people of the past, in the consciousness that we are all children of time, we must question the past and present. I am looking for laborers of thought and researchers to establish the necessary balance between the constant and changing aspects of Islam and, considering such juridical rules as abrogation, particularization, generalization, and restriction, who can present Islam to the modern understanding. During Islam's first 5 centuries of Islam were the period when there were, a time when the freedom of thought was very broad, many researchers and scholars were involved in such an undertaking. Only in such an atmosphere can great scholars and thinkers be raised.[82]

---

[82] Hulusi Turgut, "Nurculuk," *Sabah*, 23–31 January 1997.

## *Neo-Salafiyah and Islam's Universality*[83]

Q: Some people think that taking the tenets of the Qur'an and Sunna just as they are and applying them to our lives will solve all problems. Can this understanding be reconciled with Islam's universality?

A: Some people believe that doing so represents an important step in the name of universality. But of course this is not possible. If you don't use the logic by which the doctrines of the Qur'an and Sunna can be interpreted, and if you fail to see that their aspects change over time and according to conditions, you can't attain universality.

Each doctrine is a nucleus, a seed of life that can fulfil its purpose only when it finds the soil, air, and water necessary for its germination and growth. If people who can apply the logic and approach of the great Hanafi jurists to the present time and conditions do not appear, and if society avoids this option (unlike the Ottomans), then we cannot go anywhere.[84]

### *"Turkish Islam"*

Q: How do you evaluate the expression "Turkish Muslimness"?

A: This expression might appear to conflict with Islam's universality. Islam is the religion of humanity. If that was not the case, even though they protected their own customs and traditions, Turks and other nations would not have entered Islam so eagerly. Ismail Hami Danismend notes that in the tenth and eleventh cen-

---

[83] In traditional Islamic scholarship, *Salafi* (early Muslim) means someone who died within the first 400 years after the Prophet, such as Abu Hanifa, Malik, Shafi'i, and Ahmad ibn Hanbal. Those who died after this time are *Khalaf* (latter-day Muslims). *Salafi* was revived as a slogan and movement by followers of Muhammad 'Abduh (a student of Jamal al-Din al-Afghani) approximately 100 years ago. Like similar movements, its basic claim was that Islam had not been properly understood by anyone since the Prophet and the early Muslims, and themselves.

[84] Eyüp Can, "Fethullah Gülen Ile Ufuk Turu."

turies, thousands of tents of Turkish people became Muslim all at once.[85]

I would like to mention something here: Muslims entered Samarkand, Tashkent, and Bukhara in 80 AH. Otherwise, scholars like Bukhari,[86] Muslim,[87] and Tirmidhi[88] couldn't have appeared in the third Islamic century. In 50 AH they entered Sind (now in Pakistan). This is a very early period. After 50 years, all of Central Asia embraced Islam. That wave spread from there to Asia Minor.

Q: Where did those who were raised in Central Asia carry Islam?

A: Islam appeared in Makka and Madina, then followed a road toward Asia. Although it entered eastern Anatolia while advancing toward Asia, it was spread and established in Anatolia by Central Asian Turks. The whole world of Islam is indebted to Makka and Madina. Our second indebtedness is to Central Asia.

We owe many things to Central Asia, be it in the fields of Hadith, *tafsir* (Qur'anic commentary), and jurisprudence, or because of the renaissance that took place there in the fourth and fifth Islamic centuries. In that early period, Islam was protected and

[85] Ismail Hami Danismend (d. 1967): A Turkish historian whose expertise was mainly the Ottoman and Seljuqid periods.

[86] Al-Bukhari (810-70): One of the greatest Hadith compilers and scholars. His chief work is accepted by Sunni Muslims as a major source of religion. From the approximately 600,000 traditions he gathered, he selected only about 7,275 as completely reliable for inclusion in his *Al-Jami' al-Sahih* (The Authentic Collection).

[87] Muslim ibn al-Hajjaj (817-75): One of the chief Hadith authorities. He traveled widely. His great work, the *Sahih* (The Genuine), is compiled from the approximately 300,000 traditions he collected in Arabia, Egypt, Syria, and Iraq.

[88] Al-Tirmidhi (d. c.892): Arab scholar and author of one of the six canonical Hadith collections. His canonical collection *Al-Jami' al-Sahih* (The Sound Collections) includes every spoken tradition used to support a legal decision, as well as material on theological questions, religious practice, and popular belief and custom.

developed in a way compatible with the Qur'an, Sunna, *ijma'* (scholarly consensus), and *qiyas* (analogical reasoning). The influence of qiyas in a society's morality, psychological make-up, and socioeconomic conditions can't be denied. The social structure's influence also cannot be denied.

The Turkish nation interpreted Islam in the areas open to interpretation. From this viewpoint, it attained a very broad spectrum and became the religion of great states. For this reason, I think the term *Turkish Muslimness* is appropriate. Another aspect of this is that in addition to profound devotion to the Qur'an and Sunna, the Turks always have been open to Sufism, Islam's spiritual aspect. Sufism has spread among Turks more than others.

Q: Can you be called a Muslim Turkist?

A: For me, being Muslim is an essential, for it encompasses my bliss in this world and the next. But among my general thoughts and perceptions I believe, as expressed by one of our famous poets, that the Turkish nation put its true values on a solid foundation after becoming Muslim. Turks reached their zenith as a nation only after becoming Muslim. I look at myself as a Muslim Turk from this perspective. I have never thought of separating the two. Being Muslim is my only guarantee for happiness in this world and the afterlife. But I didn't think of my being Turkish as separate from my being Muslim. At the same time, I am very far from racism.

Q: Islam is a universal religion. Are there also Turkish traces in it?

A: Islam is universal with respect to its principles. Details can be interpreted differently. It's my humble opinion that the Turkish nation has interpreted those interpretable matters quite well. If Ottoman tolerance existed today in the world, I believe there would be a very good basis for dialogue not only among Muslims but also humanity. In a world that is becoming more and more globalized, being open to dialogue is very important.[89]

---

[89] Özkök, "Hoca Efendi Anlatiyor."

## Islam and Turks

Fethullah Gülen said that the contact between Central Asian Turks and Islam began in 50 AH, and that their conversion took place usually in large groups. Islam was carried to Anatolia from there. This is his explanation:

Muslims residing within modern Turkey's borders did not receive Islam directly from Makka and Madina. This might make some people uncomfortable. In 50 AH, Central Asia began to embrace Islam. In the first Islamic century, some prominent people came to Makka and Madina from the region between modern Turkmenistan and Afghanistan.

The late Ismail Hami Danismend claimed that Turkish tribes became Muslim in large groups. According to some, the founders of the Hanafi school either were Turkish or had a connection with Turks.[90] The greatest Hadith scholars also emerged and grew up in places where Turks were densely concentrated.[91] Jurisprudence, Hadith, and Qur'anic commentary developed in Central Asia. In the fifth and sixth Islamic centuries, Islam was entrusted to the Seljuqid states, and then passed to their heirs: the Ottomans.

Islam, with all its light and dimensions, went to Central Asia. Its interpretable aspects were interpreted there. The foundation for *ijtihad* (independent judgement reached through reasoning based on the Qur'an and Sunna) was evaluated there. It is no coincidence that the Hanafi school of jurisprudence found its most prominent representatives in that region,[92] or that Islamic jurisprudence gained universality via such newly developed methods such as *istihsan* (preferring closed to open analogy, or preferring an exceptional law to the general one), *istishab* (preserving the existing legal situation and accepting it as the norm), and *sedd-i zerayi* (prohibiting that which leads to what is forbidden.)

---

[90] Abu Hanifa, Abu Yusuf, and Imam Muhammad.

[91] Such as Imam Bukhari, Imam Muslim, Tirmidhi, and Nasa'i.

[92] Such as Marginani, Hulvani, and Sarakhsi.

In addition to Islamic jurisprudence, Sufism and the Maturidi branch of the Ahl al-Sunna were widely spread in these Turkish areas.[93] It is undeniable that the seed of Islam sown and germinated in Makka and Madina grew and became a universal tree in these regions. This is why I use the term "Turkish Islam" or "Turkish Muslimness" to express this fact.[94]

Q: What should the Turkish identity be like in the twenty-first century?

A: The factor of Islam definitely should be included. But it should not be a world that is fighting with America and Europe. In line with contemporary realities, it should take Western thought, evaluate it, and respect that which complies with its own spirit and spiritual roots. The Turkish world should be very different, broader, and able to help maintain world peace.

Q: Does the *European Muslim* identity indicated in the Tanzimat edict describe us? Can we say that the Turkish-Muslim identity will be European in the future?

A: If both Europe and Turkey could come to a mutually acceptable agreement, the future could be promising. But this demands intelligent people with one eye on the larger world and one eye on their own world. It demands evolved people who can observe both worlds, architects who can build a brand new world.

More specifically, in my opinion, the West and the East each represent an aspect of humanity. The West represents the mind and activism, while the East represents the heart and spirit. So, giving up their centuries-old clashes, these two worlds should come together for a happier, more peaceful world.[95]

---

[93] Abu Mansur Muhammad al-Maturidi al-Samarqandi (d. 944). Titular head of the Maturidiyah school of theology, which came to be one of the most important foundations of Islamic doctrine.

[94] Turgut, "Nurculuk."

[95] Sevindi, "Fethullah Gülen Ile New York Sohbeti."

## Islam and Dogmatism

Q: What's Islam's attitude toward dogmatism?

A: If dogmatism means to accept or copy something blindly without leaving any room for free thought and the use of mental faculties, then there is no dogmatism in Islam. Especially under the conception of religion that has developed in the West, knowing and believing are considered as different things. However, in Islam they complement each other. The Qur'an insists that everyone should use his or her mental faculties (e.g., thinking, reasoning, reflecting, pondering, criticizing, evaluating, etc.).

Q: And Qur'anic verses that are decisive in canonical law...?

A: There are fixed, unchanging aspects of creation and life. As the laws of nature and the essential aspects of humanity (e.g., its nature, basic needs, feelings) never change, a religion addressing humanity must have constant principles and perpetual values.

Such moral standards as truthfulness, chastity, honesty, respect for elders (especially parents), compassion, love, and helpfulness are always universally accepted values. Also, it is universally accepted that people should refrain from adultery and fornication, robbery, deception, alcohol, gambling, and indecent ways of making a living. Accepting and considering such standards and values while making laws is not dogmatism.

However, as in all other religions, Islam has experienced some dogmatist attitudes. For example, the Zahiriyah began during 'Ali's reign as a consequence of Kharijite extremism.[96] They accepted

---

[96] Zahiriyah (Arabic: Literalists): Followers of an Islamic legal school that insisted on strict adherence to the literal text (*zahir*) of the Qur'an and Hadith as the only source of Muslim law. Founded in Iraq by Dawud Khalaf in the 9th century, it spread to Iran, North Africa, and Muslim Spain. Although strongly attacked by orthodox theologians, it survived for about 500 years and seems finally to have merged with the Hanbali school. The Kharijites (or Khawarij) emerged after Mu'awiya wrested the caliphate from 'Ali. Those who opposed 'Ali's acceptance of the arbitration, which they regarded as a ruse, left and rejected both parties' claims. They were known for their puritanism and fanaticism.

verses with their external meaning only, and refused to consider such basic rules as abrogation, particularization, and generalization. In the beginning, it did not become a school of thought. However, people like Dawud al-Zahiri[97] and Ibn al-Hazm[98] established it as a system in Andalusia[99] and published books on it. Later on this school passed into the hands of some influential persons like Ibn Taymiyah,[100] and influenced such scholars as Ibn al-Qayyim al-Jawziya,[101] Imam Dhahabi,[102] and Ibn Kathir.[103] It subsequently gave

---

[97] Dawud ibn 'Ali ibn Khalaf Dhahiri of Isfahan (d. 883): Founder of the Zahiriyah school of thought.

[98] Ibn Hazm (994-1064): A Muslim litterateur, historian, jurist, and theologian of Islamic Spain famed for his literary productivity, breadth of learning, and mastery of the Arabic language. A leading exponent of the Zahiri (literalist) school of jurisprudence, he produced some 400 works on jurisprudence, logic, history, ethics, comparative religion, and theology.

[99] Al-Andalus originally meant the entire Iberian peninsula. After the Muslim conquest, it became part of the independent Ummayad caliphate of Córdoba, founded by 'Abd al-Rahman III in 929. After its breakup in the early 11th century, Andalusia was divided into several small kingdoms, the largest of which were Málaga, Seville, and Córdoba.

[100] Ibn Taymiya (1263-1328): One of Islam's most forceful theologians who, as a member of the Pietist school founded by Ibn Hanbal in the beginning, supposedly sought the return of Islam to the Qur'an and the Sunna. He is also the source of the Wahhabiyah, a mid-18th-century traditionalist movement of Islam.

[101] Ibn al-Qayyim al-Jawziyya (1292-1350): Studied under his father, the local attendant (*qayyim*) of al-Jawziyya school, concentrating on Islamic jurisprudence, theology, and Hadith. He finally joined the study circle of Imam Ibn Taymiya, and became his closest student and disciple, and eventual successor.

[102] Al-Dhahabi (673-748): Considered the head of masters, perspicuous *hadith* critic and expert examiner, encyclopedic historian and biographer, and foremost authority in the canonical readings of the Qur'an.

[103] Ibn Kathir (1300-73): Muslim theologian and historian who became a leading intellectual figure of 14th-century Syria. He is best remembered for his 14-volume history of Islam, *Al-Bidaya wa al-Nihaya* (The Beginning and the End), a work that utilized nearly all available sources and formed the basis of several writings by later historians.

rise to Wahhabiyah.[104] However, such people have always represented only a small minority.[105]

## Sunni Islam and Free Thought

Q: You indicated that during one period, the Ottoman
madrasas froze artistic, aesthetic, and intellectual movements
because of the *madrasas*' extremist position (being closed to
physical sciences and Sufism). Some claim that Sunni Islam
(beginning with Imam Ghazali) obstructed philosophy, art, and
free thought. As one who emphasizes Sunni Islam in this century, how do you evaluate this criticism?

A: Sunni Islam cannot be opposed to aesthetics, art, beauty,
and the expressions of beauty. If it could be so, the magnificent
Islamic civilization that flourished in the first 5 centuries of Islam
would never have occurred. During this period, in addition to
Hadith, Qur'anic commentary, and jurisprudence being at their
zenith, the positive sciences, philosophy, Sufism, literature, and
architecture realized considerably high degrees of development.
Although a pause was observed after this, the Ottoman period saw
the further and unprecedented advancement of such fine arts as
architecture, music, literature, and calligraphy.

If anything could constrain art and free thought, it would be
jurisprudence. But history shows that when jurisprudence's codifi-
cation was the most advanced, art and free thought were also at their
most advanced level. Andalusia is a wonderful example of this.
Authors of Islamic science and history, such as Seyyed Hossein

---

[104] Wahhabi: A member of the Muslim puritan movement founded by Muhammad
ibn 'Abd al-Wahhab in 18th-century Najd (Arabia), and adopted in 1744 by the
Saudi family. They stress God's absolute oneness (tawhid), deny all acts implying polytheism (e.g., visiting tombs and venerating saints), advocate a return to
the original teachings of Islam, and condemn all innovations. Their theology and
jurisprudence are based, respectively, on the teachings of Ibn Taymiyah and on
Hanbali legal school. The stress literal belief in the Qur'an and Hadith and the
establishment of a Muslim state based only on Islamic law.

[105] Can, "Fethullah Gülen Ile Ufuk Turu."

Nasr[106] and Roger Garoudy,[107] don't hesitate to express their amazement and awe. Islamic civilization is represented by tolerance, peace, and love kneaded in the midst of free thought and belief.[108]

## Islam and Art

Q: What is Islam's view on art?

A: As shown by the Qur'an, it is to see creation as it is and then to represent it abstractly. Abstraction is one of the most pronounced characteristics of Islamic art.

Q: As you emphasized, there are written criticisms on Islamic art. But when it comes to the relationship between theory and practice, not very concrete things are said.

A: When explaining this, because we can't express some things according to our own way of thinking, we might fall into dualism. We can get into a dilemma. For this reason, I've left expressing my opinion on art to later. If God gives me the opportunity, I am thinking of writing on this subject sometime in the future.[109]

## Beards and Turbans

A: I see the robe, turban, beard, and loose trousers as details. Muslims shouldn't be drowning in detail. Today many Muslims may be doing this. Choosing not to wear a turban, robe, or loose trousers shouldn't be construed as weakening the Muslim Turkish identity. From imams to members of Parliament, from governors

---

[106] Professor Seyyed Hossein Nasr (1933- ): A leading expert on Islamic science and spirituality and University Professor of Islamic Studies at George Washington University. He has written numerous books, including *Man and Nature: The Spiritual Crisis of Modern Man* (1998), *Religion and the Order of Nature* (1996) and *Knowledge and the Sacred* (1989).

[107] Roger Garoudy (1914- ): French intellectual, head of Islam and the West Association.

[108] Can, "Fethullah Gülen Ile Ufuk Turu."

[109] Ibid.

to district officials, no one should be categorized as a sinner because of such things.[110]

## Headscarves

Q: How important is it for a Muslim woman to cover her head?

A: This issue is not as important as the essentials of faith and the pillars of Islam. It's a matter of secondary importance in *fiqh*. Faith in God was revealed to our Prophet in Makka. Then came the daily prescribed prayers. Such commands as giving alms, fasting, and pilgrimage came in Madina. In the sixteenth or seventeenth year of Muhammad's prophethood, Muslim women's heads were still uncovered. It was not included in the pillars of Islam or the essentials of faith. Those issues to which Islam gives priority should, out of our own devotion, be given priority while becoming a Muslim and communicating Islam to others.

Q: If I remember correctly, you gave the same message in the 1990s when this issue created a lot of social tension.

A: Maybe I said the same thing. Let's not drown in detail. Let's not sacrifice the important for the trivial.[111]

## Religion Allows No Coercion in Its Name

Q: You say that religion does not allow any coercion in its name. But isn't there contrary behavior in Turkey?

A: If this religion is from God, if it has fused with human nature. If it is a message from God's Attribute of Speech, like a book or humanity created by His Power and Will, it does not create any contradiction between human life and the universe He created. Religion, humanity, and the universe are three different versions and expressions of the same truth. From this perspective, I don't believe or see any probability that the spirit of religion will conflict with human nature.

---

[110] Akman, "Fethullah Hoca Anlatiyor."

[111] Özkök, "Hoca Efendi Anlatiyor."

Q: What should be said about those who, in the name of religion, say, "wear this or that"?

A: One day a "natural" selection will occur and everything will return to its essence. In other words, religion will reveal its true reality. Thoughts that were added to religion later on will be removed. Those who appear strict and bigoted, who give room only to themselves in religious matters, may one day be crushed by their way of thinking. Religion will remain in its original form then, and its universality will reappear. As a result, everyone will find his or her place.[112]

## Will Islam Be Implemented by Force?

Q: Some are worried that all of this is pretension (*taqiya*) and that tomorrow, when an administration based on Islamic principles comes to power, these fourth- or fifth-degree matters will be imposed, and it will be mandatory to, say, cover the head.

A: This is perhaps due to a lack of knowledge regarding Islamic principles. If such a mistake were to be made, it would be contrary to what Islam teaches, something done without knowing Islam. In other words, those who accept Islam follow its commandments naturally. As for those who don't believe in Islam, leave them to their own understanding and lifestyle, for Islam's commands are obligatory only for Muslims. If there is anxiety that people will be forced to do this when Islamic principles are carried over into public life, it should be understood that such a forceful act is not Islamic.[113]

## Islam, Theocracy, and Tyranny

Q: In Islam, is there despotism or theocracy as the media assert?

A: Some people, just as they can use everything for evil, can exploit Islam and abuse religion for despotic rule. But this doesn't mean that Islam has a despotic side. I think such a claim is

---

[112] Ibid.

[113] Ibid.

due to a non-comprehension of this issue. Islam has nothing to do with theocracy, which is, in one respect, a system of government put forth by the Church's interpretation. In Islam there is no church and no clergy. In the meaning as Westerners understand it, the Office of Religious Affairs has no authority to determine laws for the community.

Q: At this point, fundamentalism always appears...

A: In the words of Ziya Pasa: "There was no such thing before, this is a new rumor."[114] Fundamentalism means fanatical and dogmatic adherence to a belief. As a movement, it appeared in America in the first quarter of the twentieth century. It cannot be denied that it has influenced several American presidents. It has nothing to do with Islam, even though some people ascribe Iranian and Saudi movements to fundamentalism and try to blacken Islam's name. It is a mistake to consider Islam as fundamentalism or Muslims as fundamentalists. The matter is locked up in conceptual confusion. First this has to be clarified.[115]

## "Political Islam" and Religious-oriented Parties

Q: I'm very curious about several things. Europe has Christian Democrat political parties, which are legal and don't cause conflict like ours (religious parties) do. Why is there conflict in Turkey over religious-oriented parties? Is there a mistake in their positions, or is political organization in Islam different from that of the West?

---

[114] Ziya Pasha (d. 1880): Translator of Rousseau's *Émile* (a popular textbook for 19th-century Muslim intellectuals). He was among the first to write in a less traditional idiom and to complain in his poetry about the pitiable conditions of Muslims under the victorious Christians. Together with Sinasi (d. 1871) and Namik Kemal (d. 1888), he founded an influential Turkish journal, *Tasvir-i Efkâr* (Picture of Ideas). The essential themes of their articles, novels, poems, and dramas are fatherland (*vatan*), freedom of thought, democracy, and constitutionalism. He also was a member and advocate of the Young Ottomans, a secret nationalist organization formed in Istanbul in June 1865.

[115] Can, "Fethullah Gülen Ile Ufuk Turu."

A: First of all, I think that as Muslims we don't know Islam with all its aspects. When we adopt it as an ideology rather than as a religion, we are eager to quarrel about how Islam should be understood and lived. And so we are not open to dialogue. Second, Turkey has some people who are extremely apprehensive of even the least manifestation of Islam. It seems to me that in this new era of Turkish history, some of us have not yet learned how to live together in a society. Actually there's nothing to fight about. As was mentioned a little earlier, the basis of being a Muslim, as Prophet Muhammad demonstrated, is love, forgiveness, and generosity to others.

On the other hand, some tend to show Islam as something frightful. Regardless of whether they do so for their own security or to protect their position in the world balance, some powers present Islam as a religion and a governmental system that usurps, occupies, and operates by force. Unfortunately, some so-called Muslims engage in movements that support this image. Actually, these movements are derived from the understanding and interpretation of certain people, who cloak them in the name of Islam.[116]

## Partisanship

Q: Necmettin Erbakan is active in politics as a representative of Islam in Turkey. You're following a different path. Isn't Erbakan's attempt to establish a political framework for living Islam a good thing? He's pursuing this struggle.

A: It may be good according to him.

Q: But, practically speaking, you're not doing what he's doing.

A: I think I've found a better work. I pursue the way to "faith in God, knowledge of God, love of God, and spiritual pleasure." If I had accepted and approved of everything he did, I would do the same thing.

---

[116] Özkök, "Hoca Efendi Anlatiyor."

Q: Which things in him don't you approve of?

A: I never investigated or inquired into that. I'm just following my way. I have no time or intention to show enmity to others. The Qur'an teaches us: "You must be busy with yourselves; don't allow others' following different ways to keep you busy." I have only two hands. Sometimes they are enough to do what I have to do and sometimes not. If I had four hands, I would use them for my work.[117]

## The Alawis in Turkey and Sunni–Alawi Unity[118]

Q: You attribute a great deal of importance to Sufism, which also seems to have an important place in the Alawis' life and worldview. As you know, they form a significant section of Turkish society. What is your idea on this subject?

A: Perhaps society as a whole needs to make some adjustments. This is what Sufism does. Just as we Sunnis have some sides that need to be whittled down and reshaped, so do the Alawis. Some people have made special research regarding the Alawis. Looking at their observations, the Alawis definitely enrich Turkish culture. In my opinion, that culture shouldn't be viewed from a single, def-

---

[117] Oral Çalislar, "Fethullah Gülen'le Röportaj," *Cumhuriyet*, August 20–26 1995.

[118] Alawi (also Alawite and Alevi): One who loves and is connected to 'Ali. Those who love him are divided into two groups: sincere and candid followers, and political supporters. The first group love him for his virtuous, exalted character, piety and austerity, and because he is a member of the Prophet's family (Ahl al-Bayt). Alawism is not a sect nor a school. It started as a Sufi order based on the love of Ahl al-Bayt. Its historical progress is as follows: Timur took 30,000 Turkish captives to Iran after defeating the Ottomans in the Çubuk War (near Ankara). There, they joined the Sufi order of Sheikh Ali (a.k.a. Sheikh of Erdebil). Timur freed them upon the Sheikh's demand, which dramatically increased their connection to the Sheikh. Some returned to Anatolia, and the Sheikh kept in touch with them. They gradually became known as Alevis and later on lost touch with the sheikhs in Iran. Nevertheless, due to the Sheikh's influence, they thought Anatolia's Sunnis did not love the Ahl al-Bayt adequately. This caused tension and eventual conflict. The Alevis did not attend the Ottoman madrasas or similar educational institutions, and so their culture remained largely oral. Turkey's Alawis differ markedly from Syria's Alawites (Nusayris), who go to the extent of deifying Ali.

inite perspective; rather, it should be considered from different viewpoints.

The Alawis have developed different modes of thought during different periods, which has cost them a lot. If we put this aside and together forge anew the unity necessary for becoming one nation and establishing fraternity, I think our culture will naturally progress. In other words, an opportunity for enriching each other will be born. Mutually probing each group's inner worlds and spiritual depth for the sake of mutual benefit is another dimension. For the sake of this unity and enrichment, they should open up to the Sunnis. In the current state, this matter is still open to exploitation by some groups.

Q: Alawi culture seems to have a rich history.

A: Alawi culture is based on oral traditions. Therefore there are different groups of Alawis in Turkey, ranging from those who sincerely desire to follow the way of the Prophet's family to those who are atheists. To establish the common ground for the Alawi culture and creed, we should resort to their written tradition. We should review the works of their forerunners. If they regard such persons as Yunus Emre,[119] Niyazi-i Misri,[120] Hadji Bektash,[121] and others as the main figures of Alawism, we should look at what they wrote and how they lived. Otherwise, the base for agreement is too slippery and there's hardship in understanding.

---

[119] Yunus Emre (c.1238-c.1320): A poet and Sufi who had a powerful influence on Turkish literature. He was well versed in mystical philosophy, especially that of Rumi, and, like Rumi, became a leading representative of Sufism in Anatolia (but on a more popular level). He was venerated as a saint after his death. His poems, devoted mainly to divine love and human destiny, are characterized by deep feeling. He wrote in a straightforward and almost austere style, and mainly in the traditional syllabic meter of Anatolian folk poetry. His verse had a decisive influence on later Turkish Sufism.

[120] Niyazi-i Misri (1618-94). A Sufi poet and member of the Khalwati order.

[121] Hadji Bektash Wali (1209-71): A foremost Sufi master whose followers later came to be called the Bektashis. This movement acquired definitive form in the 16th century in Anatolia, and spread to the Balkans, particularly Albania.

In addition, Alawi meeting or prayer houses should be supported. In our history, a synagogue, a church, and a mosque stood side by side in many places. This reflects the spirit of Islam and its inclusiveness.[122]

## Sunni–Alawi Tension?

Q: There has been obvious tension between Alawis and Sunnis for some time in Turkey. Why is this?

A: People who visit me frequently know I worry that this issue could turn into conflict, that it could become even more dangerous than the PKK terror. I don't know who used this issue in Sivas. Turkey is treading a very fine line here. I don't know which circles or centers of power are instigating it.

Q: Now there are new issues. For example, like *cem* (gathering) houses (Alawi assembly halls).

A: Forgive me, but there have always been *cem* houses. It's not right to interpret this in a different way or to see it as a new issue. The Sunnis' tension must be brought down, and Alawi citizens must understand that Sunnis never treated them unjustly. In fact, during the early years of the Republic when dervish lodges and dervish hostels were closed down, cem houses were not touched.[123]

## A Gathering House for Alawis

Q: It was reported that in your meeting with Prime Minister Tansu Çiller, you suggested establishing a gathering house for Alawis. What's happening? What's this issue of a gathering house?

A: Sunnis and Alawis are the two sections of Turkish society. If some want these two groups to fight each other, we can make sure that that fist is swung to nothing by keeping one group from fighting the other. I've seen great understanding from Alawi citizens,

---

[122] Nevval Sevindi, "Fethullah Gülen Ile New York Sohbeti."

[123] Özkök, "Hoca Efendi Anlatiyor."

with few exceptions. If necessary, we can make an Alawi meeting house next to a mosque.[124]

## Lesser and Greater Jihad

Jihad is greatly misunderstood by both Muslims and non-Muslims. Gülen analyzes this topic in his *Cihad veya I'la-yi Kelimetullah* (Jihad or Raising the Word of God) and in the answer he gave to a specific question. The following are highlights of his views explained in his book and his answer to the question:

### What Is Jihad?

Derived from the root *j-h-d*, jihad means using all one's strength, as well as moving toward an objective with all one's power and strength and resisting every difficulty. This latter definition of jihad is closer to the religious meaning.

Jihad gained a special characteristic with the advent of Islam: struggling in the path of God. This is the meaning that usually comes to mind today. Jihad occurs on two fronts: the internal and the external. The internal struggle (the *greater* jihad) is the effort to attain one's essence; the external struggle (the *lesser* jihad)is the process of enabling someone else to attain his or her essence. The first is based on overcoming obstacles between oneself and one's essence, and the soul's reaching knowledge and eventually divine knowledge, divine love, and spiritual bliss. The second is based on removing obstacles between people and faith so that people can choose freely between belief and unbelief. In one respect, jihad is the purpose of our creation and our most important duty. If the opposite were true, God would have sent Prophets with that duty.

There is an unbridgeable difference between those who remain behind without a valid excuse and those who continually engage in jihad:

> Not equal are those believers who sit (at home) and are not hurt, and those who strive and fight in the cause of God with

---

[124] Çalislar, "Fethullah Gülen'le Röportaj."

their goods and their persons. God has granted a grade higher to those who strive and fight with their goods and persons
than to those who sit (at home). Unto all (in faith) has God
promised good: but those who strive and fight has He distinguished above those who sit (at home) by a special reward
(4:95).

The Prophet says:

Keeping watch one day to protect the border for God's sake
is superior to this world and everything in it. The small place
that your whip (used in the way of God) occupies in Heaven
is superior to this world and everything in it. An evening or
morning walk made on God's path is superior to this world
and everything in it.[125]

## Types of Jihad

The lesser jihad is not restricted to battlefronts, for this would
narrow its horizon considerably. In fact, the lesser jihad has such a
broad meaning and application that sometimes a word or silence, a
frown or a smile, leaving or entering an assembly—in short, everything done for God's sake—and regulating love and anger according to His approval is included in it. In this way, all efforts made to
reform society and people are part of jihad, as is every effort made
for your family, relatives, neighbors, and region.

In a sense, the lesser jihad is material. The greater jihad, however, is conducted on the spiritual front, for it is our struggle with
our inner world and carnal soul (*nafs*). When both of these are carried out successfully, the desired balance is established. If one is
missing, the balance is destroyed.

Believers find peace and vitality in such a balanced jihad. They
know they will die the moment their jihad ends. Believers, unlike
trees, can survive only as long as they bear fruit. On the contrary,
when a tree stops producing fruit, it dries up and dies.

Observe pessimists, and you will notice that they no longer
struggle or explain the Truth to others. And so God cuts off His

---

[125] *Sahih al-Bukhari*, "Jihad," 142; *Sunan al-Tirmidhi*, "Fada'il al-Jihad," 25.

blessing to them, leaving their interiors dark and hard. But those who pursue jihad always are surrounded by love and enthusiasm. Their inner worlds are bright, their feelings are pure, and they are on the road to prosperity. Every struggle stimulates the thought of yet another one, and thus a righteous circle is formed. As every good deed becomes a vehicle for a new good deed, such people always swim among good deeds. Our hearts are informed of this truth: *And those who strive in Our Cause, We will certainly guide them to Our Paths: For God is with those who do the right* (29:69).

There are as many roads to God as there are creatures. God leads those who struggle for His sake to salvation on one or more of these roads. He opens each road to goodness and protects it from the roads to evil. Everyone who finds His road, the Straight Path, finds the middle road. Just as these people follow a middle path regarding anger, intelligence, and lust, so do they follow a middle way regarding jihad and worship. This means that God has led humanity to the path of salvation.

The lesser jihad is our active fulfillment of Islam's commands and duties; the greater jihad is proclaiming war on our ego's destructive and negative emotions and thoughts (e.g., malice, hatred, envy, selfishness, pride, arrogance, and pomp), which prevent us from attaining perfection. As this is a very difficult and hard jihad, it is called the greater jihad.

During the Age of Bliss, people fought like lions on the battlefield and, when night fell, lost themselves in devotion to God through worship and *dhikr* (remembrance and invocation of Him). These valiant fighters passed their lives in a corner in worship and solitude. They learned this from their guide, the Prophet, a man of the heart who was first in the material and spiritual jihad. He encouraged his followers to ask for God's forgiveness, and was always the first to do so.

Those who succeed in the greater jihad will succeed in the lesser jihad; those who fail in the greater jihad will fail in the lesser jihad. Even if such people obtain some degree of success, they cannot obtain the full results.

'A'isha related:

> One night the Messenger of God asked: "'A'isha, can I spend
> this night with my Lord?" (He was so genteel that he would
> ask for such permission. Nobility and refinement were
> important aspects of his profundity.) I replied: "O Messenger
> of God, I would like to be with you, but I'd like what you like
> even more." The Prophet performed ablution and began
> praying. He recited: *Behold! In the creation of the heavens
> and earth, and the alternation of Night and Day—there are
> indeed Signs for people of understanding* (3:190). He recited
> this verse and shed tears until morning.[126]

Sometimes in order not to wake up his wife, the Prophet would
get up and worship without asking her. Again 'A'isha relates:

> One night when I woke up, I couldn't find God's Messenger.
> My vein of jealousy immediately began to swell. I wondered
> whether he had gone to another wife of his. When I started to
> get up in the dark, my hand touched his foot. He was pros-
> trating on the prayer rug and reciting something. I listened to
> his prayer. He said: "My God, I take refuge in Your compas-
> sion from Your anger and wrath. I take refuge in Your spar-
> ing me from punishment. My Lord, I take refuge in You from
> You (refuge in Your blessings from Your wrath, refuge in
> Your grace from Your grandeur, refuge in Your mercy and
> compassion from Your domination.) I am not capable of
> praising You (properly). You are as You have praised
> Yourself."[127]

This shows the inner depth and the extent of greater jihad in
the Prophet.

In another *hadith*, the Prophet mentioned these two jihads:
"There are two kinds of eyes that will never see the fire of Hell:
those of soldiers who act as guards on battlefields and fronts, and
those who weep because of the fear from God."[128]

---

[126] Ibn Kathir, *Tafsir* ("Âl 'Imran), 190

[127] *Sahih al-Muslim*, "Salat," 22; Haythami, *Majma' al-Zawa'id*, 10:124; *Sunan al-Tirmidhi*, "Da'wat," 81).

[128] *Sunan al-Tirmidhi*, "Fada'il al-Jihad," 12.

The jihad of those who abandon their sleep and act as guards at the most dangerous times is material jihad. Their eyes will not be subjected to the fire of Hell. As for those who do the spiritual and greater jihad and cry for fear of God, they also will not see the torture of Hell. Instead of repeating what others have done, people should have good intentions and implant in their hearts and minds the consciousness of being sincere.

Jihad is a balance of internal and external conquest. Reaching spiritual perfection and helping others do so are points of consideration. Attaining internal perfection is the greater jihad; helping others attain it is the lesser jihad. When you separate one from the other, jihad is no longer jihad. Indolence is born from one and anarchy from the other. However, we expect one Muhammadan spirit to be born. As is always the case, this is possible only by following and conforming to God's Messenger. How happy are those who search for a way to salvation for others as much as they do for themselves. And how happy are those who remember to save themselves while saving others![129]

---

[129] Fethullah Gülen, *Cihad veya I'la-yi Kelimetullah* (Izmir: Nil Yayinlari, 1998); Fethullah Gülen, *Asrin Getirdigi Tereddütler* (Izmir: T.Ö.V. Yayinevi, 1997), 3:186-219.

CHAPTER 3

# Religion and Society

Fethullah Gülen is one of the most influential thinkers in Turkey. He has expressed his views on many modern concepts. Excerpts are given below:

## Science and Knowledge

- Avoiding the physical sciences due to the fear that they will lead to heresy is childish. Seeing them as contrary to religion and faith, and as means of rejecting religion, is prejudice and ignorance.

- Science and technology are beneficial to the extent that they guarantee happiness and help us attain true humanity. If they develop in a way that harms humanity, they become devils who block our road.

- At the beginning of the twentieth century, some shortsighted materialists turned science into an idol and sacrificed everything to it. However, that century's most famous scientist [Albert Einstein] criticized this tendency in a pleasant way by saying: "Science without religion is blind; religion without science is lame." What would they have said if they saw those of today who are both blind and lame?!

- Claiming that the positive sciences have no value is ignorance and bigotry, and rejecting everything else outside their field is crude fanaticism. Realizing that there is still much to be learned signifies the true scientific mentality and sound thinking.

- All of us are travelers, and the worlds are variegated exhibitions rich and colorful books. We were sent to study these books, increase our spiritual knowledge, and uplift others. This colorful and pleasurable journey is a one-time event. For those whose feelings are alert and whose hearts are awake, this journey is more than enough to establish a Paradise-like garden. But for those whose eyes are covered, it is as if they have lived but one breath.

- Those who profoundly ponder about and evaluate nature and the laws of life will see the coquetry of eternal beauty in everything. They hear the consecration of Infinite Power in every sound—from flowers' shining colors to sway-ing tree branches, from frightening thunderclaps to sparrows' harmonious songs. Such people see the traces and works of a Divine source manifested in such phenomena as light and heat, and laws as attraction and chemical reac-tion, and the directing of animate beings.[130]

## The Concept of Science

Flowing to the future like a rapid flood full of energy and vital-ity, and sometimes resembling a dazzling garden, the natural world is like a book offered to us to examine, an exhibition to behold, and a trust left to our safekeeping with permission to benefit from it. By studying this trust's meaning and content, we are to exploit it in a way that benefits future as well as present generations. If we wish, we can define science as the above-envisioned relation between humanity and the world.

Science is humanity's common heritage, not the private prop-erty of a specific nation. Its infancy began with humanity's infancy. When Europe's intellectual culture attained a sufficient maturity, attained in great part through the achievements of non-European nations, the experimental sciences in particular were ripe for a new, comprehensive flourishing through the Renaissance.

While borrowing science from its ancient origins, and then absorbing and appropriating it, Europe did not hesitate to import the ways of developing it. Although the West tends to deny the non-Western origin and transferal of science, its relations with the East did not prevent it from transferring the zeal and resolution necessary for scientific development. Of course, science cannot be borrowed and then "worn" like a medal of success or other symbol of outward show. It has to permeate through the veins of the society in which it develops and functions like a substance of life diffused into the "air" of every new day.

If true science means directing the intelligence toward eternity without expecting any material gain, making a tireless and detailed study of existence to discover the absolute truth underlying it, and

---

[130] Gülen, *Ölçü veya Yoldaki Isiklar*, 2:89-91.

following the methods required to reach this aim, their absence means that science cannot fulfill our expectations. Although usually presented as a conflict between Christianity and science, the Renaissance-era conflicts were mainly between scientists and the Church. Copernicus, Galileo, and Bacon were not anti-religious. In fact, we can say that their religious commitment ignited the love and thought of finding truth.

Before Europe, Islam was the torchbearer of scientific knowledge. The religious thought springing from eternity and the love and zeal arising from that thought, accompanied by the feeling of poverty and impotence before the Eternal Creator, lay behind the great 500-year scientific advance observed in the Muslim world until the close of the twelfth century. The concept of science as based on the Divine Revelation, which drove scientific study in the Islamic world, was represented almost perfectly by the illustrious figures of the time who, intoxicated with the thought of eternality, studied existence tirelessly in order to attain eternity. Their commitment to the Divine Revelation caused Its intellect to diffuse a light that engendered a new concept of science in human spirit.

If that concept of science, approved and appropriated by society as if it were a part of the Divine message and then pursued with the zeal of an act of worship, had not been exposed to the destructive Mongol invasion and the pitiless Crusades from Europe, our world would be more enlightened, have a richer intellectual life, a more wholesome technology, and more promising sciences. I say this because Islam's concept of science was embedded in the aspiration for eternity, the ideal of being beneficial to humanity and responsible for earning the pleasure of God.

The love of truth directs true scientific research. This means approaching existence without any consideration of material and worldly benefit, and observing and recognizing it in its true essence. Those equipped with such love can reach the final destination of their quest. However, those infected with worldly passion, material aspiration, ideological prejudice and bigotry, and those unable to develop any love of truth, will either fail or, worse, divert the course of scientific study and make science a deadly weapon to be used against the best potentials of humanity.

No intellectual activity arising from and directed by worldly passion and egocentricity can be truly beneficial for humanity. If such soul-darkening passions and inappropriate behavior are combined with ideological fanaticism and prejudice, they inevitably will put insurmountable obstacles in the way of reaching the truth and using the results of scientific study to benefit humanity.

Therefore, intellectuals, educational institutions, and the mass media must work to deliver modern scientific study away from the lethally polluted atmosphere of materialistic aspiration and ideological fanaticism and toward true human values. The first step involves freeing minds from ideological superstition and fanaticism, and purifying the soul's carnal desires. This also is the first condition for securing true freedom of thought and engaging in truly beneficial science. Having fought the clergy and corrupt conceptions formed in the name of religion, and having blamed them for regression, narrow-mindedness and fanaticism, scientists should strive to remain free from being the target of comparable accusations.

There is no difference between the intellectual or scientific despotism arising from interest and power seeking, and the ideological fanaticism and restrictive reasoning based on corrupt and distorted religious conceptions and clerical domination. The original name of God-revealed religion always has been Islam, meaning peace, salvation and obedience to God. This is true whether it was taught by Moses or Jesus, or communicated by Muhammad. Islam preaches and propagates courtesy, respect for human values, love, tolerance, and brotherhood.

In addition, many Qur'anic verses encourage the study of nature, which is seen as an exhibit of the Divine Names. It asks people to reflect upon creation and the created and to approach them responsibly. When studied with an open mind, we see that the Qur'an promotes the love of science and humanity, justice and order.

On the comparatively smaller scale of exploiting science and its products for the sake of power and worldly ambition against weaker people, some have used the Qur'an to satisfy their own hatred and enmity. Unfortunately, in the hands of those who want to eradicate Islam, such attitudes have been used to portray Islam as a religion of hatred, enmity, and vengeance.

Islam literally means peace and salvation. The Prophet defined Muslim as one from whose hand and tongue everyone is safe and secure; and mu'min (believer, derived from amn: security and safety), as one who believes in and guarantees security, order, justice, love, and knowledge. Through the light disseminated by Islam, many have dedicated their lives to the happiness of others via self-denial, and many others have resolved to carry humanity toward eternity.

Basing itself on the Qur'an, Islam has established knowledge and its quest on the intention of discovering the meaning of existence so that its adherents can reach the Creator and thereby benefit humanity and all creation, and to combine itself with belief, love, and altruism. This is what we learn from the Qur'an, the Prophet's exemplary life, and the conduct of many who have represented it perfectly in thought and action.[131]

## What We Expect from Science

* Since "real" life is possible only through knowledge, those who neglect learning and teaching are considered "dead" even though they are still alive. We were created to learn and communicate what we have learned to others.

* Right decisions depend on having a sound mind and on sound thinking. As science and knowledge illuminate and develop one's mind, those deprived of science and knowledge cannot reach right decisions and always are exposed to deception and misguidance.

* Those who are truly human continue to learn, teach, and inspire others. It is hard to regard as truly human those who are ignorant and have no desire to learn. It is also questionable whether a learned person who does not pursue self-renewal and self-reform, and so set an example for others, is truly human.

---

[131] Fethullah Gülen, *Yeseren Düşünceler* (Izmir: T.Ö.V. Yayinevi, 1996), 172-78.

- Science and knowledge should seek to discover the nature of men and women and the mysteries of creation. Any knowledge, however scientific, is not true knowledge if it does not shed light on the mysteries of human nature and the dark areas of existence.

- Status and merit acquired through knowledge and science are higher and more continuous than those acquired through other means. This is due to two reasons: Knowledge will enrapture its possessors, when they reach the other world, with the pleasure of the positions acquired while in this world. In addition, it will keep them away from bad morals in this world and cause them to attain many virtues.

- Parents should feed their children's minds with knowledge and science before they become engaged in useless things, for souls devoid of truth and knowledge are fields in which all kinds of evil thoughts are grown and cultivated.

- The purpose of learning is to make knowledge a guide for your life, to illuminate the road to human perfection. Any knowledge that does not fulfill these functions is a burden for the learner, and any science that does not direct one toward sublime goals is just deception.

> Knowledge is to understand the reality of knowledge,
> To understand your own "self."
> If you do not know who you are,
> What is the use of learning?
> — Yunus Emre

- Appropriate language is an inexhaustible source of blessing for the learner. Those who possess such a source are always sought by people, like a source of fresh water, and lead people to the good. Knowledge consisting of empty theories and unabsorbed pieces of learning, which arouses suspicions in minds and darkens hearts, is like a "pile of garbage" around which desperate and confused souls flounder.

- Although science and all branches of knowledge are beneficial to almost everyone, one cannot possibly acquire all of them, for people's life spans and resources are limited. Therefore, learn and use only things that benefit yourself and humanity at large. Do not waste your life.

- True scientists base their study and research on true reports, correct expositions, and scientific experiments. As a result, they have peace of mind and solve their problems easily. However, those who do not know the truth are buffeted constantly by changing goals and methods, and so are always disillusioned.

- People are esteemed and appreciated in proportion to the profundity and content of their knowledge. The knowledge of those who spread gossip and idle talk is nothing more than what they spread. On the other hand, those who use

their knowledge as a prism to perceive things and events, as a light to illuminate "space" to the darkest points, and to reach the most transcendental truths
are truly valuable.[132]

## Regretting Science and Technology

Despite the disasters caused by science and technology, their
mistaken approach to the truth, and their failure to bring happiness,
we cannot condemn them outright and become pure idealists.
Science and technology alone are not responsible for a devalued
humanity, diminished human feelings, and the serious weakening of
certain human virtues, health, and the ability to think. Rather, the
fault lies with scientists who avoid their responsibility, cause science to develop in a materialistic and almost purely scientific
atmosphere, and then let it be exploited by an irresponsible minority. Many threatening conditions probably would not exist if scientists had remained aware of their social responsibility, and if the
Church had not forced science to develop in opposition to religion.

Science can be described as comprehending what things and
events tell us, what the Divine laws reveal to us, and striving to
understand the Creator's purpose. Created to rule creation, we need
to observe and read, discern and learn about our surroundings so
that we can find the best way to exert our influence and control.
When we reach this level, by the decree of the Exalted Creator,
everything will submit to us and we will submit to God.

There is no reason to fear science. The danger does not lie with
science and the new world it will usher in, but with ignorance, irresponsible scientists, and others who exploit it for their own selfish
interests. So what is there to fear from science? Planned acts based
on knowledge sometimes cause bad results, but certainly ignorance
and disorganization *always* cause bad results. Instead of opposing
the products of science and technology, we must use them to bring
happiness to humanity. Herein lies the essence of our greatest problem, for we cannot take measures against the Space Age or delete
people's knowledge of how to make atomic and other more bombs.

---

[132] Gülen, *Ölçü veya Yoldaki Isiklar*, 2:9-14.

Science might be a deadly weapon in the hands of an irresponsible minority. However, we should not hesitate to adopt both it and its products and then use them to establish a civilization in which we can secure our happiness in this world and the next. It is pointless to curse machines and factories, because machines will continue to run and factories to operate. Science and its products will begin to benefit us only when people of truth and belief begin to direct our affairs.

We have never suffered harm from a weapon in the hands of angels. Whatever we have suffered has come from those who still believe that only might is right. This will continue until we build a world on the foundation of faith and science.[133]

## Culture

### Art

• Art is the spirit of progress and one of the most important means of developing feelings. Those who cannot make use of art are unfortunate, and live a numbed, diminished life.

• Art is like a magical key that opens hidden treasures. Behind the doors it opens are ideas embodied and dreams given substantial form.

• Art inspires human beings to travel in the depths of oceans and heavens. By means of art, humanity sets sail for the outer limits of the Earth and sky, and reaches perceptions beyond time and space.

• Art shows the highest goals to human sentiments and feelings, and incites sensitive souls to profound depths. Without art, we would have seen no beauty in the realm of existence where we are allowed to act, and all those great talents and the works they have produced would not have come to surface.

• Art manifests and defines the powers and deepest potentials of the human psyche and soul. Through art, the most profound emotions and ideas, the most striking observations and discoveries, and the most heartfelt desires are preserved as if recorded on a tape, and so gain eternity.

• Through art combined with faith, this once-magnificent world of Islam with its most magnificent places of worship, slender minarets pointing to the realms beyond, sacred designs and intricate patterns carved in marble and

[133] Fethullah Gülen, *Çag ve Nesil* (This Era and the Young Generation) (Izmir: T.Ö.V. Yayinevi, 1997) 115-18.

bearing a distinct message, diverse kinds of calligraphy, brilliant gilding, and embroideries as beautiful and fine as butterfly wings became a gallery of invaluable beauty.

- True knowledge shows itself through art. If one has never produced anything in the name of art, how can we say that he or she knows much?

- The vitality of a person's natural capabilities is closely related to his or her artistic spirit. One devoid of this spirit may be regarded as little different from a corpse.

- Art makes iron more precious than gold, and copper more precious than bronze. Thanks to art, the most worthless metals become more precious than gold, silver, and diamonds.

- Whether one without the spirit of art exists or not, there is no difference. Such people comprise crowds that are of no use, and might even be harmful to themselves, their families, and their nations.

- All the fine arts are eternal gifts of blessed souls to humanity. The products of technology, combined with the spirit of art—clocks and glasses, telecommunication devices that shrink space by conveying sounds and images over unbelievable distances, modern means of transportation—all such tools and objects currently in common use can be the work of and even inspire such sensitive, artistic souls.[134]

## Literature

- Literature is the eloquent language of a nation's spiritual composition, world of ideas, and culture. Those who do not share this "language" cannot understand each other, even if they belong to the same nation.

- Words are one of the best means to transfer ideas. Those who use them skillfully find many followers of the ideas they spread, and so attain immortality through their ideas. Those who cannot do so die without a trace, along with the mental pain they suffered while alive.

- With the material it uses and its particular way of expression, each type of literature is a unique language. Even if everyone understands some of this language, only poets and writers use and speak it with its true meaning.

- Just as gold and silver dealers can evaluate gold and silver, only dealers of words understand literary jewels. An animal will eat a flower lying on the ground, and those who cannot appreciate it will step on it and leave. Only one who is truly human will smell it and place it in his or her lapel or hair.

---

[134] Gülen, *Ölçü veya Yoldaki Isiklar*, 3:104-9.

- High thoughts and elevated topics must be explained with a style that penetrates minds, excites hearts, and is welcomed by spirits. If not, those who keep the letter of words only will see the torn and miserable "clothing" put on the meaning, and thus will not seek the inner jewels.

- Meaning is literature's essential element. Thus words should be kept to a minimum while being rich and full in meaning. Some people explain their thoughts with similes, metaphors, allusions, allusive metaphors, and puns. However, the most meaningful word is to be sought in exuberant, inspired spirits; profound imaginations that embrace all existence; and believing, analyzing, and synthesizing minds able to attain the vision of both worlds and the same truth.[135]

## Poetry

- Poetry is the poetic expression of the universe's hidden beauty and symmetry, and the heart-ravishing, smiling view of existence by sensitive, inspired souls. Among such souls are those whose hearts have become inkpots, and whose ink is the breath of the Holy Spirit.

- Poetry is the sound heard while delving into the beyond, and the moan coming from those so engaged. Its sounds and tunes are sometimes uproarious and sometimes fine, for they depend on the poet's spiritual condition and inner depth. For this reason, poetry's every word and sound can be comprehended fully only if the hearer knows the poet's spiritual state at the time of his or her poem's conception.

- Poetry is born and takes shape according to the belief, culture, and style of thought affecting the poet's view and sensitivity. Only inspiration deepens it and causes it to transcend consciousness. In a heart that is exuberant with inspiration, an atom becomes a sun and a drop becomes an ocean.

- Regardless of how great the role of intelligence and thought is in poetry, the human heart has a deep direction of its own. In Fuzûlî's words: "My word carries the standard before the army of poets."[136] When thoughts growing in the heart put on the wings of imagination, they begin to force the doors to infinity.

---

[135] Ibid., 3:1-11.

[136] Mehmed bin Süleyman Fuzuli (1495-1556): Turkish poet and the most outstanding figure in classical Turkish literature. He is famous for his melodic and sensitive rendition of the great Muslim classic Leylâ ve Mecnun, which recounts the allegorical romance between Majnun (the human spirit) for Layla (divine beauty). He also wrote two collections of poems, one in Azerbaijani Turkish and one in Persian.

- Poetry, like an entreaty, expresses the ups and downs as well as the enthusiasm and sadness of the individual's inner world. To the extent the poet concentrates on exalted truths, the resulting poems become like breaths from beyond. Every supplication is a poem, and every poem is a supplication if it flutters its wings toward infinity.

- A poem that grows in the thought of infinity and flies in the skies of pure thought with the heart's wings and the spirit's strength does not pay too much attention to positive thought. It uses the material, concrete world only as a vehicle to find and catch the abstract.

- Poetry is far more than rhymed speech, for the meaning and way of expression of many non-metrical phrases attract the spirit and awaken wonder and amazement in the heart. Each is a monument of poetry in itself.

- Like every branch of art, poetry is barren and dim if it is not connected to the infinite. The human spirit fascinated with infinite beauty, the human heart obsessed with infinity, and the human conscience longing for the eternal and eternity plead with artists to delve into the beyond. Artists who resist this plea spend a lifetime imitating the external face of things, for they cannot see beyond this curtain of lace.

- A poem that considers form and meaning in the way the relationship between the spirit and body is considered, without sacrificing one to the other, will attain a harmony that everyone will like and find natural. Even the imagination will be unable to suggest a new motif for such a poem.[137]

## Pearls of Wisdom

- Opposing the majority that represents the truth is a mistake. Otherwise, consent is a mistake. It is all right to oppose an engineer in matters of medicine, just as it is all right not to consult a doctor on a construction project.

- Helplessness is not only a lack of strength and power. Many strong and talented people seem helpless, because nobody ever thought to benefit from them.

- Neither "darkness" nor another light can defeat those whose light comes from themselves. Such sources of light will burn throughout their natural lifespan in spite of everything, and will illuminate their surroundings.

- Those who act according to what they have seen are not as successful as those who act according to what they know, and the latter are not as successful as those who act according to their conscience.

---

[137] Gülen, *Ölçü veya Yoldaki Isiklar*, 3:12-23.

- Poverty is not only the lack of money, for it can assume the form of a lack of knowledge, thought, and talent. In this respect, wealthy people who lack knowledge, thought, and talent can be considered poor.

- Glasses are a vehicle for the eyes, the eyes are a vehicle for the mind, the mind is a vehicle for insight, and insight is a vehicle for the conscience. The conscience is an outlet through which the spirit can observe, and a vehicle through which it can see.

- Humanity is a tree, and nations are its branches. Events that appear as heavy winds hurl them against each other and cause them to clash. Of course, the tree feels the resulting harm. This is the meaning of: "Whatever we do, we do it to ourselves."

- Nights are like arenas in which people discover, develop, and prepare for human happiness and serenity. Great ideas and works always developed in the wombs of darkness and were offered to the benefit of humanity.

- The stomach expels food that cannot be digested and has no benefit, and then spits in its face. Time and history does the same to useless people.

- Rust is the enemy of iron, lead the enemy of diamonds, and dissipation the enemy of the spirit. If the first does not cause the latter's decay and ruin today, it will definitely do so tomorrow.

- Every flood originates from tiny drops whose existence and size is negligible. Gradually, it reaches a level that cannot be resisted. A society's body always is open to such floods.

- Even if explaining knowledge and truth to the ill-mannered and inexperienced is as hard as dealing with the mad, enlightened people must do so eagerly.

- Since everyone cannot understand clear truths at the same level, abstraction was abandoned in favor of demonstration, representation, and personification.

- People usually complain of time and space, whereas the fault always lies in ignorance. Time and space are innocent, whereas humanity is ungrateful and ignorant.

- Some sunny, grassy, bright roads adorned with flowers eventually lead to valleys of death, while other steep, thorny paths reach the border of Heaven.

- One of the wisest sayings is: "Each person is hidden under his or her tongue." An even greater one is: "If you want a friend, God is enough; if you want a companion, the Qur'an..."

- We know the act and object of perception, but not the perceiver. The spirit knows; the mind is a vehicle. The spirit sees; the eye is a vehicle.

- If an action results from mental or natural instincts, it is animalistic. If it results from the will or conscience, it is spiritual or human.

- Non-existence is a dreadful nothingness, such an infinite and mind-boggling field that not even one atom of existence can be found there.

- Today, people label the devout as "fanatics." Fanaticism means insisting on false and blind persistence. Insisting on what is right is a virtue, and such behavior by a believer cannot be considered fanaticism.

- Sometimes the sun is manifested in an atom, a flood in a drop, and a book in a sentence. For such profundity, the eye (sight) is as important as the word.

- The pen is a golden channel for the light of thought. This light descends from the mind to the arm, and therefrom to the finger, and finally comes out from the pen.

- Even if the number of blind people increases, they still cannot determine an item's color. Two sound eyes destroy their consensus.

- Every tree is made up of wood. A tree is differentiated by its fruit, and people are differentiated by their piety.

- Every mind is like a separate knife made from the same steel. Any difference among them derives from their sharpness.

- In great and magnificent nations, dervish lodges and even gravestones are ornamented. One can read a nation's concept of beauty and art in its places of worship and on its tombstones.

- Matter has no comprehension, consciousness, feeling, or will. It is comprised only of some laws and particles (used to form things). What an embarrassing mistake it is to count it as the essence of existence.

- True philosophy is only a spiritual and mental struggle (trial, suffering) that appears when God arouses us to seek wisdom.[138]

## Social Concerns

### *Freedom*

- Freedom means that the spirit voluntarily limits itself to nothing but sublime feelings and thoughts, and serves only the principles of goodness and virtue.

- Many people who are actually imprisoned or in chains are free in their conscience and thus do not feel their imprisonment. Many others, however,

---

[138] Ibid., 4:1-9.

inhabit grand palaces and gardens and yet never taste the true meaning of freedom although.

- True freedom is civilized freedom. It wears the diamond chain of religion and morals, and the golden collar of sound thinking.

- True freedom is the freedom of the human mind from all shackles that hinder it from making material and spiritual progress, as long as we do not fall into indifference and heedlessness.

- Freedom allows people to do whatever they want, provided that they do not harm others and themselves and that they remain wholly devoted to the truth.

- Freedom that does not acknowledge religious ideas and feelings, and does not serve as the ground for virtue and morality, is like the desire to scratch one-self. Communities afflicted with this desire eventually become restless and wander off the common road of humanity.

- Those who regard freedom as absolute liberty confuse human freedom with animal freedom. Animals have no moral questions asked of them, and so have no moral constraints. Some people desire this kind of freedom and, if they can, use it to indulge their darkest desires. Such freedom is worse than bestial. True freedom, however, the freedom of moral responsibility shows that one is human, for it motivates and vitalizes the conscience and removes impediments before the spirit.[139]

## Progress

- A nation's development and progress depends upon the intellectual and spiritual training given to the people who live within its borders. A nation whose members are lacking in intellectual and spiritual development should not be expected to develop and progress.

- Nations begin to move backward when they allow once-cultivated fields to be neglected, and turn vineyards and gardens into rubbish heaps. Fertilizing barren soil and then cultivating it so that it becomes a vineyard and a garden is progress. A developed country's lands consist of gardens, its mountains have vineyards, and its places of worship are like magnificent palaces. In contrast, the cities of an underdeveloped country are ruins, its streets are rubbish heaps, and its places of worship are left to decay as moldy halls.

- When something has been improved, it becomes cleaner and brighter, better and more orderly than before. Accordingly, being content with things as they are indicates a lack of effort, while true progress is the realization of development.

---

[139] Ibid., 2:82-84.

• Each forward advancement starts as a concept. Then the mass of people is persuaded to accept it, and finally it is put into practice by those united in heart and mind. Every attempt to progress that is not based on reason and science is futile.

• A nation's people must have the same goal in order to experience national development. A nation cannot develop and progress if some of its members say "black" and others say "white" for the same thing, regardless of how much activity it engages in.

• A community that has not trained its people in a shared tradition eventually splits into different groups based on their different knowledge and upbringing. These groups will be hostile to each other. It is impossibly difficult for such a fractured community to progress.

• Although education is undeniably important for a country's progress, the expected results will never be achieved if the young people are not educated according to the country's traditional values.

• For true and beneficial progress to be made, people must evaluate the present conditions and use the experience of former generations intelligently. If coming generations do not learn from the experience of their predecessors, and if each generation follows its own way, the nation will begin to move backward.[140]

## Culture

• Culture is an important resource that must be used by those seeking to develop their community in the most beneficial and appropriate way. There is a vital link between the cohesion and strength of a community's direction and the authenticity of its cultural resources.

• Culture is a stable mix of such fundamental elements as language, education, tradition, and art, all of which form a community's structure and lifestyle. It is a kind of blindness to ignore the reality that these fundamental elements have (and ought to have) unique features, as well as different characters and temperaments, for they reflect the people to whom they belong. A community that has broken ties with its essential cultural values inevitably loses its identity and collapses as a scattered society.

• The existence of distinct and unique cultures does not mean that there can (or should) not be any intercultural exchange of ideas and people. Rather, it means that each culture should demand a "visa" from a foreign cultural element seeking entrance. Its right of entry should be questioned and granted only after analyzing what effect it might have upon the indigenous culture.

---

[140] Ibid., 2:66-69.

Foreign elements should be "distilled" before being absorbed into the indigenous culture. Otherwise, a cultural and civilizational crisis will occur.

- A distinctive culture evolves in the crucible of true religion, high morality and virtues, and well-digested knowledge. Where religion and morality are opposed and rejected, and ignorance is widespread, a high culture cannot be formed.

- People who seek their own continuance or survival by blindly accepting the culture and civilization of others are like trees upon whose branches are hung the fruits of other trees. They deceive not only themselves, but also lay themselves open to ridicule.

- Cultural values have the same meaning and value for a people as blossoms and fruits have for a tree. A community that has failed to produce a distinctive culture, or has lost or forsaken it, may be likened to a barren tree or to one whose fruit has dropped off. Today or tomorrow, that tree will be cut down and used as wood.[141]

## Civilization

- Civilization does not mean being rich and putting on fine airs, nor does it mean satisfying carnal desires and leading a luxurious, dissipated life. What it really means is being civil and courteous, kind-hearted, profound in thought, and respectful to others.

- Savage people are usually cruel, oppressive and bloodthirsty, as they usually live by plundering ... However, what about those civilized savages equipped with modern weaponry, who are always seeking and finding subtle, deceiving ways of shedding blood?

- Communities based on the cooperation of science and morality always have established true civilizations. For this reason, Western civilization remains paralyzed because it is based mainly on science, and Eastern (Asian) civilizations are not "true" because, in their present conditions, they have no scientific background. The civilization of the future will have to be established upon a combination of Western science and eastern faith and morality.

- Civilization means more than scientific advancement, modern means of transportation, ships, and living in large cities with skyscrapers. While such things may be adjuncts to civilization, it is folly and ignorance to identify civilization with them.

- If a given civilization is not based on morality and virtue and nurtured in the pool of mind and conscience, it is no more than a passing flash of illumina-

---

[141] Ibid., 2:45-48.

tions that serves a couple of rich people and excites some thrill seekers. What a pity for those who are fooled by its blinking lights.

- One becomes truly civilized only when all human virtues and potentialities have been developed to the extent that they become second nature. People who think that civilization means indulging all kinds of desires, and who identify it with outward forms and modern fashions, have no sound judgment and have surrendered to their bodily desires.[142]

## *Nation*

- Individuals who have sincerely resolved to be pillars of their nation never allow themselves to neglect even the smallest matter of concern to it, even though there may be times when they forget about their own problems.

- The nation with the best standing consists of people who are unified on all public matters and respect the majority view. It hardly needs to be said that the nation's people must have received a common education of shared values in religion, language, and historical awareness.

- If we cannot accept the criticism of those we love and who love us, we may lose our friends and remain unaware of our defects.

- Do not remember the promises that others have failed to keep; instead, remember your own promises that you did not fulfill. Do not blame others because they are not doing good to you; instead, remember the chances you missed of doing good to someone else.

- One of the most important things that weakens us as a nation is that we are simple-minded toward those who deceive us while pretending to be our friends. Do not believe every promise, and do not be misled by everyone who gives advice with a smile.

- If people consider cheating and trickery to be prudence and intelligence, their nation is suffering from something like terminal cancer. All that is seen as signs of recovery in such a nation are deceptions, like the swelling of a tubercular gland being taken for healthy growth.

- If the people of a nation can establish relationships as strong as those among family members, their nation will develop quickly. On the other hand, a nation whose people do not love and confide in each another cannot be considered a nation in the true sense of the word, and its future holds no promise.[143]

---

[142] Ibid., 2:85-88.

[143] Ibid., 2:33-35.

## Friendship

- Those who hold their friends in good esteem and treat them with respect gain many defenders and supporters against their enemies.

- Having faithful friends is just as important as satisfying the vital necessities of life. Being among a secure and peaceful circle of friends means finding safety against many hazards and dangers.

- Wise people, upon seeing that a friendship has become damaged, immediately remove the cause of discontent and restore good relations. Even wiser are those who strive to avoid or prevent disagreement with their friends in the first place.

- Love and good relations between friends continue as long as they understand each other, practice self-denial, and make sacrifices within permissible limits. Friendship between those who cannot renounce their interests and preferences for the sake of their friends cannot endure.

- We are loyal and faithful to our friends to the extent we share their troubles as well as their joys. If we cannot weep when they weep and rejoice when they rejoice, we cannot be regarded as faithful friends.

- Those who maintain a friendship with one who has fallen on hard times are true, loyal friends. Those who do not support their friends during their misfortune have nothing to do with friendship.

- Those who tend to disagree and struggle with their friends have few friends. Those who want to have faithful and numerous friends should not disagree with them on trivial matters.

- Friendship pertains to one's heart and its sincerity. Those who think they can gain another's friendship through deception and hypocrisy only deceive themselves. Even if some simple-minded people are taken in by their hypocrisy and flattery, they will not be able to sustain a long-lasting friendship.[144]

## The Perfect Generation

### The Victory of Good and Beauty

- Goodness, beauty, truthfulness, honesty, and being virtuous are the essence of the world. Whatever happens, the world will one day find this essence, and no one will be able to prevent it from happening.[145]

---

[144] Ibid., 1:94-97.

[145] Ibid., 2:112.

## The Happy Future

Life is possible only through hope;
The hopeless are distressed and misfortunate.
— M. Akif

My eyes closed, I imagine the happy future being formed in the "land of my hope." Beauties of every sort coming out from corners of existence run through our houses and streets, and through institutions of education and worship. Reflecting back in the rooms of our houses, they envelop us as a flood of light. Combined with colors, this light forms a rainbow, under which I run continuously to "set it up" in my eyes and soul as an everlasting arch of happiness.

While we pass in a second under a man-made arch, it seems impossible to pass under this heavenly arch (rising) over us. As we run under it, we feel our life united with all of existence in an endless stream. We watch in amusement the things flowing back after a short halt on either side to greet us, and then are replaced by new ones. We are enraptured with the immaterial pleasures coming from that continuous stream of things and intimacy between them and us.

Trees sway gently with the breeze, hills are green and radiant, sheep graze here and skip and bleat over there, and villages lay scattered on slopes and in plains and valleys. We observe with delight how all these contribute to a universal harmony, and comment that one lifespan is not enough to taste all of these pleasures.

These colors and lights and sounds, this liveliness springing from the breast of existence, are reflected in the world of our emotions. We feel as if we are listening to lyrics composed of sweet daydreams and memories flowing in waves. We absorb the vast Book of Nature, which arouses within us spiritual pleasures with its Heaven and Earth and all their contents. It fills us with inexplicable delight and joy, and elevates us to the higher realms of existence.

With each new season, we find ourselves as if waking up from a different death sleep and encountering various colors ranging from violet to green. We feel caressed by breezes conveying the perfume of flowers and fruits and ears of grain.

These tremendous spectacles, which implant in souls the sense of beauty, give some relief even to those pessimists who always see everything through the window of their dark souls and are overwhelmed with evil thoughts and suspicion. As for believers, time streams in them and echoes life's melody in each of their cells. Mornings come upon them with songs of gentle breezes blowing through tree leaves, murmuring streams, twittering birds, and children's cries. The sun sets in their horizon, arousing feelings of love and excitement. Nights take them, in pitches of music, through time's mysterious tunnels and nature's most romantic spectacles.

Every spectacle we observe within the horizon of belief and hope, and every voice we hear, removes all the veils from our souls and takes us through paradisiacal valleys—radiant and soft, pure and serene, and pleasant—in which time acquires infinity. This peace attracts us into fascinating worlds, half-seen, half-unseen, which we have long been watching with the eyes of our hearts, as if from behind a lace curtain.

At this point, when the spirit is enraptured with the pleasure of observing, the tongue is silent, eyes are closed, and ears no longer receive sounds. Everything is voiced with the tongue of the heart. Pure thoughts and feelings envelop people as vapors of joy and excitement, and in the face of such dazzling spectacles, the spirit feels as if it is walking in the gardens of Paradise.[146]

## Toward the World of "Righteous Servants"

Righteous servants will inherit the world. So what are the criteria of righteousness? The righteous heir's first and foremost quality is perfect faith. The Qur'an determines the purpose of humanity's creation as belief in God, which is woven from the threads of the knowledge of God, love, enthusiasm, and spiritual fulfillment.

Only in the light of faith can people, by realizing their essential nature with all its dimensions and the existential aims of creation,

---

[146] Fethullah Gülen, *Yitirilmis Cennet'e Dogru* (Towards the Lost Paradise) (Izmir: T.Ö.V. Yayinevi, 1997), 48-50.

penetrate the inner reality of existence. Lack of belief is a suffocating dungeon. In the view of unbelievers, existence began with chaos, developed in the frightening uncertainties of coincidences, and is speeding toward a terrible end. In this uncertain movement of existence, there is neither a breath of compassion to relieve them, nor a place of security to embrace them in our human desires, nor even a piece of ground to step on.

Believers who know their origin and destination, as well as their responsibilities, see everything clearly and so travel to their destination in utmost security. During their sojourn, they study existence and what lies behind it very carefully. They examine things and events over and over again, try to establish a connection with their surroundings, use the studies of others, and fill in their gaps of their knowledge and experience with untiring research and hope.

Believers have an inexhaustible source of power on which they can rely during their travel: Strength and power belong to God alone. This phrase is a power source, and those who obtain it feel no need for another. Believers who have equipped themselves with it direct their lives toward God in the hope of securing Divine approval. Their abiding optimism enables them to overcome every obstacle and challenge all kinds of worldly opposition.

The second quality of the heir is to overflow with love. People whose hearts are content with belief in and knowledge of God feel, in proportion to the extent of their belief and knowledge, a deep love for humanity and creation. They spend their lives in the colorful fluctuations of universal ecstasy, rapture, and spiritual pleasure.

Today, as in every era, hearts need to be enraptured with love and overflow with zeal so that a new revival can occur. There can be no permanent movement, especially that related to the Hereafter, without love. The Divine love we feel in order to gain God's approval is a boundless and mysterious source of power. Those who want to be heirs should make as much use of it as possible.

We need to look into the origin of existence from the perspective of the Qur'an and the Sunna. Our origin, place in the universe, the Divine purpose for our creation, and the way we should live and our final destination, as described in the Qur'an and the Sunna, are in such a harmony with our thoughts, feelings, and aspirations that we cannot help but be filled with wonder and admiration.

For people of understanding, these two pure sources are a spring of love and enthusiasm, and a means to ecstasy. Those who have recourse to them with pure intention and petitions of needs are not refused, and those who take refuge in them gain immortality. They must do so, however, with the sincerity of people like Imam Ghazali,[147] Imam Rabbani,[148] Shah Waliyullah,[149] and Bediüzzaman Said Nursî. They must approach these sources with the excitement of Gâlib Dede[150] and Mehmed Akif, and turn to them with the conviction and activity of Khalid,[151] 'Uqba,[152] and Salah ad-Din.[153]

---

[147] Al-Ghazali, (1058-1111): Muslim theologian and mystic whose great work, *Ihya' 'Ulum al-Din* (The Revival of the Religious Sciences), made Sufism an acceptable part of mainstream Islam.

[148] Imam Rabbani (Shaykh Ahmad Sirhindi) (1564?-1624): Indian Sufi and theologian largely responsible for reasserting and reviving Sunni Islam in India against the syncretistic religious tendencies prevalent under the Mughal emperor Akbar. He was given the posthumous title: *Mujaddid-i Alf-i Thani* (Renovator of the Second [Islamic] Millennium).

[149] Shah Waliyullah Muhaddith of Delhi (1702-62): The *Mujaddid* of the 12th Islamic century. Some writers call him *Khatam al-Muhadditheen* (the last of the hadith scholars).

[150] Gâlib Dede (Sheyh Gâlib) (1757-99). A Mawlawi dervish, he is one of the last great classical Ottoman poets. He is known primarily for *Hüsn ü Ask* (Beauty and Love), an allegorical romance describing the courtship of a young man (Hüsn [Beauty]) and a girl (Ask [Love]).

[151] Khalid ibn al-Walid (d. 642): One of the two generals who directed the enormously successful Islamic expansion under Prophet Muhammad and his immediate successors: Abu Bakr and 'Umar.

[152] 'Uqba ibn Nafi': An ex-slave who became a commander of the Muslim army and conquered North Africa from Libya to Morocco (c. 663-70).

[153] Salah al-Din (1137/38-93): Muslim sultan, founder of the Ayyubid dynasty, and the Muslim hero who defeated the Crusaders by re-capturing Jerusalem (1187). He is known in the West as Saladin.

Indeed, by combining the love and enthusiasm of those personages with modern methods and styles, we will penetrate into the ever-fresh essence of the Qur'an and arrive at a universal metaphysics.

To turn to sciences with a sensible synthesis of mind, logic and consciousness is the third quality of the generation that will inherit the Earth. This turning, which also will provide a direction for the general inclination of humanity, which is lost among obscure hypotheses, will be a significant step in our liberation.

As pointed out by Bediüzzaman, humanity is increasingly concentrating on science and technology, from which we are deriving our strength. He also pointed out that eloquence and rhetoric will gain momentum and ascendancy, for they will be used to present the products of scientific knowledge to the masses. In fact, we no longer have any other way of escaping from the cloudy atmosphere of illusions enveloping us, or any other way to reach truths and, most importantly, the most manifest Truth. To achieve this, we must re-evaluate science in the light of the Divine Revelation, and become unique representatives of scientific knowledge combined with religious spirit.

Since we have been unable to assign a true direction to science, and thus confused revealed knowledge with scientific theories and sometimes scientific knowledge with philosophy, serious confusion has appeared in scientific thought and scientists have lost considerable esteem. On result is that the younger generations became alienated from their society. After a while, these inexperienced generations lost their religious and moral values, and the whole nation began to decline in thought, ideals, art, and life. Religion and religious people were attacked unceasingly by destructive representatives of non-enlightenment, and evil aspects of modern civilization were propagated. We cannot forget this dark period of history, and those responsible for it always will be remembered in the consciences of people as national and historical criminals.

The fourth characteristic of this generation of heirs is to review and re-evaluate the established views of humanity, life, and the universe. The following points should be considered in this respect:

First, the universe is a book written by God for us to study over and over again. Humanity is a transparent index of all the worlds, a being that can discover the depths of existence. Life is the manifestation of the meanings filtered from that index and book, and reflected by Divine Expression throughout the universe. If humanity, life, and the universe are three aspects of a single truth, each having a genuine color of its own, then a partial approach to them shows our disrespect for humanity in particular, and for creation in general, as such an approach demolishes the harmonious composition of reality.

Humanity must study, understand, and obey the Divine Revelation derived from God's Attribute of Speech. Therefore, we must perceive all things and events to which God gives existence through His Knowledge, Will, and Power. Being the manifestation of the Divine Attribute of Speech, the glorious Qur'an is the spirit of existence and the sole means of happiness in this world and the Hereafter. The "Book of the Universe" is the embodiment of this spirit, and an account of the branches of science originating in it. Thus it is a very important dynamic of both worlds, direct in relation to this life and indirect with respect to the other. For this reason, people who understand both of these books and apply their principles in their lives will be rewarded, while those who do not will meet the consequences of their neglect.

Second, our humanity lies in our feelings, thoughts, and character, which also determine our esteem in the sight of the Creator and the created. Sublime human attributes, depth of thought and feeling, and a sound character are valued by everybody. Those who adulterate their faith and conviction with irreligious thoughts and causes distrust to emerge in their characters will not receive God's support and help nor preserve their esteem and dignity among people. We should not forget that God Almighty and people evaluate people according to their human character, and that those without human values cannot perform great feats even if they appear to be good believers. On the other hand, those distinguished with laudable virtues and a sound character cannot always fail despite their apparent weakness in conforming their lives to religious principles.

Third, an Islamic goal can be achieved only through Islamic means and methods. Muslims must pursue Islamic goals and adopt Islamic methods to attain them. As God's approval cannot be obtained without sincerity and a pure intention, Islam cannot be served and Muslims cannot be directed toward their real targets through diabolic means and methods.

The generation that will become responsible for bringing justice and happiness to the world should be able to think freely and respect freedom of thought. Freedom is a significant dimension of human free will and a key to the mysteries of human identity.

The Muslim world has been under internal and external pressure for centuries. The resulting restrictions placed on our feelings, thoughts, culture, and education have made it almost impossible for anyone to maintain his or her human faculties, let alone realize a renewal and development. In such a climate, one in which it is difficult to live as a common man or woman with human values, a person of true greatness cannot be raised. Only people with weak character, inactive disposition, palsied brains, and paralyzed feelings grow in such climates.

If this is so, we should realize the need to be more tolerant and more altruistic when we move toward a better future. Today more than anything else, we need magnanimous hearts and open, profound minds that respect free thinking, are open to science and scientific research, and can perceive the harmony between the Qur'an and the Divine laws of the universe and life. This requires the existence of a community in which geniuses can flourish. In the past, a single genius could lead a nation toward high objectives. But today, when everything has taken on an incredibly elaborate form and specialization has gained prominence, counsel and collective consciousness have replaced geniuses. This is the sixth point, which should be given due consideration by the generation that aims to give a better shape to the world.

In the latest phase of history, we have not been able to establish a desirable coordination among society's vital institutions. Indeed, modern schools could not save themselves from the influence of modern scholasticism and ideological dogmas, and religious schools closed themselves to science and scientific thought, and so lost the spirit and the power to bring about new formations. The representatives of spiritual training lost their love and enthusiasm, consoling themselves with the virtues and wonders of saints who lived long ago. Consequently, everything was upset, and the "tree of humanity" was convulsed so violently that it nearly toppled. Sadly it seems that until these vital institutions are once again able to perform their real functions and bring forward the wedding of the mind and heart so that the perfect generations of thought, action, and inspiration can emerge, such convulsions will continue.

Finally, this generation should be equipped with mathematical thought, as this implies comprehension of the enigmatic connection between creation and mathematical "laws," and the discovery of the mysterious world of numbers. Without mathematics, the mutual relations between humanity and things cannot be perceived. Like a source of light, mathematics illuminates our way from the universe to life, and shows us the depths of the world of possibilities beyond human imagination, thus enabling us to attain our ideals.

To obtain a full perception of existence, we should follow mathematical laws in all fields: from physics to mathematics, from matter to energy, from body to soul, and from law to spiritual training. This implies the need to adopt both spiritual training and scientific research. The West has used so-called mystical movements to compensate for a true system of spiritual training. But Muslims have no need to search for a foreign system to quench their thirst for spiritual satisfaction. Everything a person need to design his or her life on sound foundations is found in Islam, provided that one understands Islam in its pristine purity and original comprehensiveness.

Lastly, to understand the concept of art that righteous servants should have, we should have a much more developed intellectual capacity, refined feelings, and sensitivity.[154]

---

[154] Fethullah Gülen, *Ruhumuzun Heykelini Ikame Ederken* (While Establishing the Sculpture of Our Spirit) (Izmir: Nil A.S., 1998), 27-37.

## The Leading, Exalted Spirits

The leading, exalted spirits are pure in mind, noble in character, healthy and active, deep-sighted and wise, full of humanitarian feelings toward humanity and of love and compassion for their own people. They are a small group of holy people who were leaders in history. Time is freed from relativity through their messages, and their enlightenment changes the "black holes" of space into halls of Paradise.

They are bound together by a unique worldview and belief in one Object of Worship. Therefore, they are aware of life's goal, are always at "heights," and win victory after victory and honor after honor. When they are occupied with their inner world, with nothing to excite them, they are extraordinarily calm and peaceful. They are so gentle that those who see them regard them as angels. But they are as hard and inflexible as steel when roused to fighting for their ideals. Without tiring, they gallop great distances to overcome all obstacles. They continue firmly on their way, conveying their message until their guide tells them to stop.

They hold fast to their principles, are compassionate toward each other, and faithful to their leader, in whose hands each is like a sword of stainless steel. Dedicated to their cause, they spend their lives seeking God's pleasure by serving their nation and humanity.

Even if their plans are upset, their forces destroyed, and discouraging misfortunes befall them, they are never shaken. With renewed vigor, they set out again in full submission to and total reliance upon God.

When they stand before God, each is so devoted a worshipper that those who see them think they have renounced the world completely. But they thoroughly change when on the battlefield. Although they never think of attacking first, they give no respite to their enemies once the battle begins. Whatever aim they pursue, they continue struggling until that aim is obtained.

They hate the feeling of hatred and repel evil with what is best. They never lower themselves by treating even their enemies meanly; instead, they take great pleasure in welcoming their defeated enemies warmly and gently. They are reasonable and wise in all their acts and decisions. Their insight and discernment allow them to solve even the most intricate problems. As a result, they are able to implant hope and resolution in the hearts of even the most hopeless people. They use all their strength, energy, and ability to help— not to harm—humanity.

Deeply attached to their country and people, they are ready to sacrifice themselves whenever necessary. Any misfortune befalling their people hurts them so deeply that they forget all worldly taste and pleasure. In order to heal the nation's wounds, they unceasingly inspire young people to acquire lofty ideals, try to inculcate in them the spirit of struggle, and to equip them with the belief and resolution that an honorable death is preferable to a humiliating life.

Their belief-based zeal to serve their nation is so deeply implanted in their souls that they are preoccupied with it wherever they are. They are very strong-willed, know how to get along with everyone, and always give priority to national matters over their own personal or family problems.

Their belief and conviction, as well as resolution and excitement, are so formidable in resisting all opposition and every treason that they can surmount every obstacle and overcome every difficulty. Never falling into despair, they abound with hope and energy while trying to stop the world's cruelties and to illuminate the whole universe. While others who live beyond their ambience of peace and happiness drown in a marsh of hopelessness, they strive in the way of founding a new world with an abundance of hope and in directing people to new ways of revival.[156]

## The New Man and Woman

History has carried us to the threshold of a new age open to the manifestations of Divine favor. Despite (or in parallel with) advances in science and technology, the last 2 or 3 centuries have

---

[156] Gülen, *Yitirilmis Cennet'e Dogru*, 12-15.

witnessed a global break with traditional values and, in the name of renewal, an attachment to different values and speculative fantasies. It is our hope, strengthened by promising developments, that the next century will be the age of belief and moral values, an age that will witness a renaissance and revival for the believers.

Among wavering crowds lacking in sound thinking and reasoning, a new type of people will appear. They will rely equally on reason and experience, and give as much importance to conscience and inspiration as they do to reason and experience. They will pursue the perfect in everything, establish the balance between this world and the next, and wed the heart to the intellect.

The coming-to-be of such people will not be easy. All births are painful, but these blessed births will take place and provide the world with a new, brilliant generation. Just as rain pours out of long-gathering clouds and water wells up from underground, so will the "flowers" of this new generation one day appear among us.

These new people will be individuals of integrity who, free from external influences, can manage independently of others. No worldly force will be able to bind them, and no fashionable -*ism* will cause them to deviate from their path. Truly independent of any worldly power, they will think and act freely, for their freedom will be in proportion to their servanthood to God. Rather than imitating others, they will rely on their original dynamics, rooted in the depths of history, and try to equip their faculties of judgment with authentic values that are their own.

They will think, investigate, believe, and overflow with spiritual pleasure. While making the fullest use of modern facilities, they will not neglect their traditional and spiritual values in building their own world.

If changes and reforms are linked to and dependent on unchanging universal values, they may be welcomed eagerly. Otherwise, there will be a plethora of speculative fantasies that are appealing because of their novelty and modernity. Standing on the firm ground of those unchanging values, the new man and woman will always look to the future to illuminate the darkness enveloping the world.

They will be completely truth-loving and trustworthy and, in support of truth everywhere, always ready to leave their families and homes when necessary. Having no attachment to worldly things, comforts, and luxuries, they will use their God-given talents to benefit humanity and plant the seeds of a happy future. Then, constantly seeking help and success from God, they will do their best to protect those seeds from harm, just as a hen protects its eggs. Their entire lives will be dedicated to this way of truth.

To stay in touch and communicate with people's minds, hearts, and feelings, these new men and women will use the mass media and try to establish a new power balance of justice, love, respect, and equality among people. They will make might subservient to right, and never discriminate on grounds of color or race.

These new people will unite profound spirituality, wide knowledge, sound thinking, a scientific temperament, and wise activism. Never content with what they knew, they will increase continuously in knowledge: knowledge of self, of nature, and of God.

Equipped with the good morals and virtues that make one truly human, these new men and women will be altruists who embrace humanity with love and are ready to sacrifice themselves for the good of others when necessary. As they shape themselves in the mold of universal virtue, they simultaneously will strive to illuminate the way of others. They will defend and support what is good and recommend it to others, while seeking to challenge, combat, and eradicate all evils.

These new people will believe that the One gave them life here so that they could know and worship Him. Without discriminating between the Book of the Universe (where the Divine Names are manifested and therefore full of signs to Him and a "stairway" leading to Him) and the Divine Scripture (the translation of the Book of the Universe), they will see science and religion as two manifestations of the same truth.

They will never be reactionary. They will not go after events, for they will be the motors of history that initiate and shape events. With due perception of their age and surrounding conditions, and in devotion to their essential values and utmost reliance on God, they will be in a state of continuous self-renewal.

These new people will conqueror their selves, thoughts, and hearts, and those of others, and will discover the unknown. They will regard any time spent not taking a new step into the depths of the self and the universe as wasted. As they remove, through faith and knowledge, the veils covering the face of reality, they will become even more eager to advance further. With the messages and answers received from the Heavens, the Earth, and the seas, they will continue to journey until they return to their Creator.[157]

## For the Conquest and Dominion of Hearts

Over the last few centuries, humanity has suffered hardship after hardship, traveling around pits of "death." All struggles for deliverance and relief have resulted in new calamities. During this dark period, the personal greed and passions, classes, holding companies, and mafias have controlled communities, not the established governments formally in power. Thus, the only criterion by which people and things are evaluated is their financial buying power.

During such a period, it is natural for people to be esteemed for their wealth, car, and house. Material and financial resources or potentials have precedence over such human virtues as knowledge, good morals, sound thinking, and civility. Wealth may be valued when subjected to knowledge, intellect, courage, honor, and devotion to serving others. But when valued for itself or, worse, when united with greed, it can be a means of brutality.

If people debase their lives by gratifying their animal desires and seeking wealth at all costs, rather than being honest, industrious, and competent, then selfish, ignorant, and cunning people will dominate society. Moral values and human virtues will be

---

[157] Gülen, *Zamanin Altin Dilimi*, 157-60.

excluded, as well as those who combine efficiency with personal integrity—precisely the ones who could be useful to society.

Compared with previous centuries, people may well be wealthier and enjoy more convenience and comfort. However, they are trapped in greed, infatuation, addiction, need, and fantasy much more than ever before. The more they gratify their animal appetites, the more crazed they become to gratify those appetites; the more they drink, the thirstier they get; the more they eat, the hungrier they get. They enter into evil speculations to feed their greed to earn still more, and sell their spirits to Satan for the most banal advantages. And so they break with true human values a little more each day.

Those who spend their energy pursuing ephemeral material advantages waste both themselves and all the nobler, truly human feelings in the depths of their being. They no longer possess the serenity coming from belief, the tolerance and depth of spirit enabled by knowledge of God, or traces of love and spiritual joy. They weigh everything on the scales of material advantage, immediate comfort, and gratification of bodily appetites. They think only of increasing profit, buying and selling, and amusing themselves. If they cannot satisfy their appetites lawfully, they rarely hesitate to resort to unlawful means, however degraded and degrading.

To be delivered from the suffocating world of unbelief and ego-centricity, from shuttling aimlessly between the false modern concepts of thought, action, and life, people should strive to rediscover the true human values lying in the depths of their being. To escape the stress and affliction in the psychological, spiritual, and intellectual dimensions of personal life, as well as the strain and conflict in collective affairs within and between nations, they should reconsider the worth of believing, loving, moral values, metaphysical thinking, and spiritual training.

Believing means knowing the truth to be true, and what and how it is; loving means living that knowledge in one's life. Those who do not believe and love are merely physical entities without true life, like mechanically animated corpses. Belief is the most important source of action, a way to embrace all of creation in spirit; love is the most essential element and a transcendental dimension of true human thought. Therefore, those who seek to build the happy world of the future on foundations of spiritual and moral values should arrive first at the altar of belief, then ascend to the pulpit of love, and only then preach their message of belief and love to others. While seeking to achieve their goals, they should never forget that their influence depends on morality and virtuousness.

Morality is religion's essence, a most fundamental portion of the Divine Message. If being virtuous and having good morals is to be heroic—and it is—, the greatest heroes are the Prophets and then those who follow them in sincerity and devotion. A true Muslim is one who practices a truly universal, and therefore Muslim, morality. Anyone can see that the Qur'an and the Sunna are sets of moral principles. The Prophet, the greatest embodiment of morals, said: "Islam consists in good morals. I have been sent to perfect and complete good morals." The Muslim community always has been the representative of good morality and must be so, since only through morality and virtuousness can it attain eternity. Islamic metaphysics is a means to reach the highest point in morality.

Metaphysical thought is the intellect's or spirit's effort to embrace creation as a whole, to perceive it with all its dimensions. Without this effort, everything breaks into lifeless fragments. Thus the failure of metaphysical thought implies the intellect's death. All great civilizations have developed and come into being in the arms of metaphysical thought. Those who see metaphysics and physics (and other sciences) as conflicting disciplines are unaware of the fact that they are seeing a river and its source as contradictory.

Another dimension of metaphysics perceives creation through love. Here love is identical with perceiving the whole universe, and its contents and events, as a continuous interconnected flux and loving it. Those who find this true love pursue neither wealth nor fame; rather, they find peace in the flames of their love and see their beloved's face amid the ashes of their own existence burned away. They are on an uninterrupted journey from the valleys of "self-annihilation in the existence of God" to the heights of "attainment to permanence through permanence of God." This attainment can come through strict spiritual training.

Spiritual training means directing men and women to the purpose of their creation. Through awareness of our ultimate purpose, people can be freed from bodily pressures and begin a journey into their very essence.

We must change the viewpoint and aspirations of modern people. Having lost their spiritual dynamics and broken with their essential identity, they are victims of their own selves. We hope that if we reinforce our will and resolve through regular worship, and control it through continual self-criticism, Almighty God will help us succeed in this blessed mission. It is our duty to sow the seeds for the brighter Earth of the future. We leave to God Himself, if He wills, to grow each of them into fruitful trees.

We are convinced that, due to conscious effort, this corrupt world will give birth to a new one in which belief and worship will carry the fragrance of peace, security, and love everywhere. We are convinced that future generations will aim at and be favored by the ecstasies of an overflowing love, far beyond any aspirations of money, fame, or high position. This love will originate in conquering hearts, and will be recompensed with the dominion of hearts.[158]

## Victory of the Spirit

Human life is a composite of two distinct powers: the spirit and the flesh. Although they sometimes act in harmony, conflict is more usual, conflict in which one defeats the other. If bodily lusts are indulged, the spirit grows more powerless as it becomes more obedient to those lusts. If one can control the desires of the flesh, place the heart (the seat of spiritual intellect) over reason, and oppose bodily lusts, he or she acquires eternity.

Every part of a spiritually bankrupt country can be likened to a graveyard, no matter how many triumphal arches and statues adorn its thoroughfares. Most people living in such a country are in reali-

---

[158] Gülen, *Yeseren Düsünceler*, 140-45.

ty blind and unfortunate. A world not built on the spirit's breath is a plaything of human violence, and a culture without an ethos that encourages virtue is like an evil sorceress who has ambushed humanity. However, it might be impossible to persuade coarse, insensitive people of these realities, for they ignore everything but their own pleasure, and do not consider their lives connected to the well-being and happiness of others. If only they could perceive the mystery of their own deaths, they might acquire the eternal life of the spirit.

Only those who fill their hearts with the most sublime ideals and love of humanity can lead a spiritual life and acquire eternity in their very selves. These fortunate ones, who grow spiritually alert, transcend their carnal desires and lead those who heed them to victory over the commands of their carnal selves. Only those who overcome their carnal selves can be called powerful and victorious. Those who cannot free themselves from this captivity are liable to defeat, even if they conquer the entire world. We would not call their successful conquest of the world a victory, for their permanent presence in the conquered lands is impossible.

Napoleon, madly esteeming himself the world's sole ruler, slapped knowledge and virtue in the person of the philosopher Michel Ney.[159] I wonder whether he grasped that this failure in spirit was more bitter and humiliating than his defeat at Waterloo. Mustafa Pasha of Merzifon was defeated inwardly before his army was routed at Vienna.[160] This first Ottoman defeat showed itself in the spirit of its commander-in-chief, and then spread far and wide among his forces. He lost his head, and the greatest army of con-

---

[159] Michel Ney (1769-1815): One of Napoleon's best-known of marshals, who pledged his allegiance to the restored Bourbon monarchy when Napoleon abdicated in 1814. Upon Napoleon's return in 1815, Ney rejoined him and commanded the Old Guard at the Battle of Waterloo.

[160] Kara Mustafa Pasa, Merzifonlu (1634-83): Ottoman grand vizier (chief minister) from 1676-83 who, in 1683, led an unsuccessful Ottoman siege of Vienna.

quest yet known experienced flight. Yildirim Bayezid Khan was not defeated in Çubuk, but on the day when he belittled his opponent and hailed himself sole ruler of the world.[161] There have been many others like these...

But we also have positive examples, as follows:

• Tariq was victorious not when he defeated the Spaniards' 90,000-man army with a handful of self-sacrificing valiant soldiers, but when he stood before the king's treasures and said: "Be careful, Tariq. You were a slave yesterday. Today you are a victorious commander. And tomorrow you will be in grave underground."[162]

• Selim I regarded the world as too small for two rulers.[163] He was truly victorious not when he crowned some kings and dethroned others, but when he entered the capital in silence while its people were asleep to avoid their enthusiastic welcome and applause. He also was victorious when he ordered that the robe soiled by mud from his teacher's horse be draped over his coffin because of its holiness.

• The Roman commander Cato was victorious and caused his people to remember him not when he defeated the Carthaginians, but when he handed his horse and command over to the

---

[161] Bayezid I (c.1360-1403): Ottoman sultan (1389-1402) who founded the first centralized Ottoman state based on traditional Turkish and Muslim institutions. His conquests brought him into conflict with the Central Asian conqueror Timur (Tamerlane), who claimed suzerainty over the Anatolian Turkmen rulers and offered refuge to those expelled by Bayezid. During a battle in Çubuk (July 1402), Bayezid I was defeated and captured. He died in captivity.

[162] Tariq ibn Ziyad (d. c.720): The general who led the Muslim conquest of Spain. Musa ibn Nusayr, the Arab conqueror of Morocco, left his general Tariq to govern Tangier in his place. The dispossessed sons of the recently deceased Visigoth king Witiza appealed to the Muslims for help during a civil war. Tariq responded with 7,000 men.

[163] Selim I (1470-1520): Ottoman sultan (1512-20) who extended the empire to Syria, the Hejaz, and Egypt. He raised the Ottomans to leadership of the Muslim world.

Roman emperor.[164] While his army was entering Carthage, he told the emperor: "I fought to serve my nation. My duty is fulfilled, and so I am going back to my village."

To sacrifice one's enjoyment of worldly pleasures has the same significance for human progress as roots have for a tree's growth. Just as a tree grows sound and strong in direct relation to its roots' soundness and strength, people grow to perfection while striving to free themselves from selfishness so that they can live for others.

A holy one's sacred saying signifies the spirit's victory:

> I have known nothing of worldly pleasure in my life of over 80 years. All my life has passed on battlefields, in prisons, and in various places of suffering. There is no torment I have not experienced, no oppression I have not suffered. I neither care for Paradise nor fear Hell. If I see that my people's faith has been secured, I will not object to burning in the flames of Hell, for my heart will change into a rose and a rose garden even as my body is being burnt.

The crowned heads of the future will be those fortunate ones who reach felicity through victories of the spirit.[165]

## Devout Servants

- People of service must resolve, for the sake of their heart's cause, to cross over seas of "pus and blood." When they attain the desired object, they must be mature enough to attribute everything to its Rightful Owner, and be respectful and thankful to Him. Their voices and breaths glorify and magnify God, the Sublime Creator. Such people hold everyone in high regard and esteem. So balanced and faithful to God's Will, they do not idolize those whom they praise for their services. They understand that they are responsible and answerable for work left undone, are considerate and fair-minded to everyone who seeks their help, and support the truth. They are extraordinari-

---

[164] Cato the Elder (234-149 BCE). A wealthy Roman landowner who strongly believed in and symbolized traditional Roman Republican values. He believed that the rural farming life was the best and most virtuous life for a Roman citizen, and that the Greek culture and ways weakened Romans. He was a driving force behind the Roman conquest of Carthage.

[165] Fethullah Gülen, *Buhranlar Anaforunda İnsan* (Understanding and Belief: The Essentials of Islamic Faith) (İzmir: T.Ö.V. Yayinevi, 1997), 43-46.

ly resolved and hopeful even when their institutions are destroyed, their plans upset, and their forces routed. They are moderate and tolerant when they take new wings and again soar to the summits, and are so rational and wise that they admit in advance that the path is very steep. So zealous, persevering, and confident are they that they willingly pass through all the pits of Hell met on the way. They are so faithful to their cause that, deeply in love with it, they willingly sacrifice their lives and whatever they love for its sake. So sincere and humble are such people who never remind others of their successes.[166]

## Heroes of Love

- Only those who overflow with love will build tomorrow's happy and enlightened world. Their lips smiling with love, their hearts brimming with love, their eyes radiating love and the most tender human feelings—such are the heroes of love who receive messages of love from the sun's rising and setting and from the stars' flickering light.

- The anger and fury of the heroes of love, who are distinguished with love in treatment of others, are for discipline. Therefore, they serve to improve others and to bestow benefits upon the community.[167]

## Personal Integrity

- Those who want to reform the world must first reform themselves. If they want to lead others to a better world, they must purify their inner worlds of hatred, rancor, and jealousy, and adorn their outer worlds with virtue. The words of those who cannot control and discipline themselves, and who have not refined their feelings, may seem attractive and insightful at first. However, even if they somehow manage to inspire others, which they sometimes do, the sentiments they arouse will soon wither.[168]

## Ideal Spirits

- Those who strive to enlighten others, seek happiness for them, and extend a helping hand have such a developed and enlightened spirit that they are like guardian angels. They struggle with disasters befalling society, oppose "storms," hurry to put out "fires," and always watch for possible shocks.

- People who sincerely resolve to be pillars of their nation never neglect even the smallest matter of concern about the nation, even though they may sometimes forget about their own problems.

---

[166] Gülen, *Ölçü veya Yoldaki Isiklar*, 1:52-53.

[167] Ibid., 2:108.

[168] Ibid., 2:110.

- The most exalted nation thinks of public works in terms of unity and togetherness, and gives precedence to the people's opinion. Of course, that nation's inhabitants must receive the same training in such matters as religion, language, and historical consciousness.

- If the people of a country consider trickery and deceit to be clever, that nation already has reached an incurable stage of cancer. Not all things seen as improvements in a sick person's body are generally true in all cases, for that would be like saying that swollen areas in a tubercular patient as a sign that the body is gaining weight and getting better.[169]

## Essentials of the Way

- The essentials of this sacred way of serving the truth are preferring the sacred cause over all worldly and animal desires; being so steadfast in truth, once discovered, that you sacrifice all mundane attachments for its sake; enduring all hardships so that future generations will be happy; seeking happiness in the happiness and well-being of others, not in material or even spiritual pleasures; never seeking any post or position; and preferring oneself in assuming tasks while preferring others when receiving wages.

- Those who lead the way must set a good example. Just as they are imitated in their virtues and good morals, so do their bad and improper actions and attitudes leave indelible marks upon their followers.

- Those who represent any stage of the truth must try to embody it with honesty, trustworthiness, consciousness of duty, a high degree of perception, awareness of circumstances, far-sightedness, and absolute chastity. People who hold high office but lack one or more of these virtues have one or more serious defects. This is a clear misfortune for those who follow them.

- We applaud every good deed and attempt made in the nation's name, and stand behind the fortunate people who serve them. We do not retaliate against accusations of deviation and apostasy; nor do we say "amen" to curses and anathema.[170]

## Clarity of Goals and Means

- We must be as precise as possible about our project's goal and object. If we do so, we will not fall between the objectives. In our particular service, we must direct our spirits to a definite aim so that our thoughts will not collapse into a whirl of confusion and make us their powerless playthings.

---

[169] Ibid., 2:33-35, 111.

[170] Ibid., 2:107–8, 117.

- Our objective must be the result of clear thought. We must define our objectives clearly so that we will not be lost in a flood of thoughts. So many ambitious ventures failed to bear fruit or benefit, and indeed left behind hatred and rancor, for their aims and means were unclear.

- The Exalted Creator and seeking His approval must have the foremost place in every activist's perspective. If not, that which is not God can intervene, falsehood can present itself as truth, and whims can show themselves as real ideas. Although this task is being done in the name of a struggle for faith, such an oversight allows many abuses and crimes to be committed.

- As for works undertaken to seek the Almighty's approval—a particle can have the worth of the sun, a drop the worth of the sea, a second the worth of eternity. Therefore, even if the world could be turned into gardens of Paradise by means of which He does not approve, the final result would be nothing, completely worthless. Moreover, those responsible would be questioned about it.

- The worth of means and instruments lies in their ability to realize the desired objective and to do so with ease. Means that cannot do so, and especially those that hinder such progress, are regarded as cursed. Based on this same logic, the world may be cursed insofar as it intervenes between people and their real object in life, but loved and applauded for reflecting the grace of a thousand Glorious Names of the Creator and exhibiting His magnificent works.

- Truth can be established and supported in many ways. Their worth is proportional to how much they enhance our respect for the Creator, the Truth, and make us consider what is right and true. If parents educate their children properly, if a place of worship rouses its community with thoughts of eternity, if a school awakens hope and faith in its pupils, they are serving their purpose and therefore are sacred. If this is not the case, they are no more than devilish traps diverting us from the truth. We may apply the same standards to unions, trusts, political institutions, and societies in general.

- Founders and directors of institutions should remind themselves frequently of why the institutions were established. Doing so will ensure that their work does not stray from its objective, but remains fruitful. Without this in mind, they begin to forget why the houses, hostels, schools, and other institutes were established, and so work against themselves, just like those who forget why they were created.

- Claiming a monopoly on good ideas and asserting that only your side is right are signs of utter dependence on material causality and ignorance of the objective. And feelings of rancor and hatred for those who share the same belief, sentiments, and ideas—is this anything other than a lack of sufficient commitment to the objective and purpose? Ah, those base, self-enslaved ones who imagine that they can administer the universe according to their decayed reasoning![171]

## Avoiding Extremes

• Avoid extremes in thought and action, for it is a lethal poison. Just as it is wrong to seek simplicity and sincerity in poor clothing and a life lived in a miserable house with a few, broken old things, it also is wrong to see sophistication, civilization, and prosperity in the modern style of expensive clothes and other luxuries.[172]

## Consultation

*Ask someone who knows;*
*two lots of knowledge are better than one.*

• Consultation is the first requirement for reaching the right decision. Decisions reached without due reflection or proper consultation usually come to nothing. Individuals and even geniuses who depend only on themselves, who are disconnected from others and unconcerned with their opinions, are at considerable risk of error as compared to those who offer and receive opinions.

• Consultation is the first condition for obtaining good results. Paying attention to the opinions of friends and well-wishers is an important means of avoiding mistakes.

• Wise people know who to consult and how to get the most benefit from their opinions. It is a pleasure to work with such people. Others, however, are so insensitive, thoughtless, and complacent about their own knowledge or ability that they intimidate others into accepting their opinions. Such people are always unbearable to work with.[173]

## Children

• Adam (the first man) and Eve (the first woman) were created together at the very beginning of human existence. This indicates that marriage is natural. Reproduction is the most important purpose of this natural state. A marriage made for reasons other than bringing up new generations is no more than a temporary entertainment and adventure. The children who come into the world through such a marriage are the unfortunate products of a transient emotion.

---

[171] Ibid., 1:36-40.

[172] Ibid., 2:113.

[173] Ibid., 1:28-31.

- A nation's durability depends on educating its young generations, upon their being awakened to national spirit and consciousness and spiritually perfected. If nations cannot raise perfect generations to whom they can entrust their future, their future is dark indeed. The main responsibility for raising such generations falls on the parents.

- Human generations come and go. Those who have attained high levels of spiritual attainment are worthy of being considered human. Those who do not develop their spiritual faculties, due to their low level of education, scarcely merit being called human. They are nothing more than strange creatures, even though they are descended from Adam. And their parents, to whom they are a burden, are unfortunate to have nurtured them.

- When trees are pruned properly, they produce fruit and their growth improves. If they are not pruned properly, they shrivel and become stunted. Given this, should not each person, all of whom possess so many talents and abilities, be given at least as much care as a tree?

- Those who bring children into this world are responsible for raising them to realms beyond the heavens. Just as you take care of their bodily health, so take care of their spiritual life. For God's sake, have pity and save the helpless innocents. Do not let their lives go to waste.

- If parents encourage their children to develop their abilities and be useful to themselves and the community, they give the nation a strong new pillar. If, on the contrary, they do not cultivate their children's human feelings, they release scorpions into the community.

- Parents have the right to claim their children as long as they educate and equip them with virtue. They cannot make such a claim, however, if they neglect them. But what shall we call parents who introduce their children to wickedness and indecency, and cause them to break with humanity?[174]

## Youth

- Those who wish to predict a nation's future can do so accurately by analyzing the education and upbringing its young people receive.

- Desires resemble sweets, and virtues resemble food that is a little salty or sour. When young people are free to choose, what are they likely to prefer? Regardless of this, however, we must bring them up to be friends of virtue and enemies of indecency and immorality.

- Until we help our young people through education, they are captives of their environment. They wander about aimlessly, moved by intense passions and

---

[174] Ibid., 2:52-54.

far away from knowledge and reason. They can become truly valiant young representatives of the national thought and feeling only if their education integrates them with their past and prepares them intelligently for their future.

- Think of society as a crystal vessel, and of its young people as the liquid poured into it. Notice that the liquid assumes the vessel's shape and color. Evil-minded champions of regimentation tell young people to obey them instead of the truth. Do such people never question themselves? Should they not also obey the truth?

- A nation's progress or decline depends on the spirit and consciousness, the upbringing and education, given to its young people. Nations that have raised their young people correctly are always ready for progress, while those who have not done so find it impossible to take even a single step forward.

- A young person is a sapling of power, strength, and intelligence. If trained and educated properly, he or she can become a "hero" who overcomes obstacles and acquires a mind that promises enlightenment to hearts and order to the world.[175]

## Two Great "Swamps" on the Way of the "Heroes of Love"

### Addiction to Comfort

- Every noble cause and truth will gain constancy and a universal identity by its adherents' determination to protect it and their devotion to it. If its devotees are not perceptive, faithful and persevering, what they have embraced eventually will be erased from memory by its determined enemies's hostility.

- Just as stagnant water stinks and putrefies upon losing its fluidity (the source of its life), lazy people who abandon themselves to comfort and ease inevitably begin to rot and become losers. Desire for comfort is the first alarm and sign of death. Those whose sensitivity has been paralyzed cannot hear the alarm or understand the sign, and so they do not heed the warnings and advice of friends.

- Laziness and attachment to ease are among the major reasons for deprivation and humiliation. Inactive people who have abandoned themselves to (indolent) comfort one day will fall so low that they will expect even their basic necessities to be supplied by others.

- Once the extreme addiction of staying at home is added to that of indolent comfort, the "front lines" will be abandoned and people will become cow-

---

[175] Ibid., 2:49-51.

ardly. If this decline is not recognized, and the situation is not handled intelligently and properly, deviation and something horrid will ensue.

- Those who leave the "front" because they are addicted to the comforts of their homes or lust usually encounter the exact opposite of what they expected. They may even lose their nice homes and lovely children! How true are the words of a mother to her son, a commander who did not fight courageously when he should have: "You didn't fight like a man on the battlefield, so now at least sit and cry like a woman!"

- For a human being, change and decay usually are slow and silent. Sometimes even a little heedlessness, a slight straying from the "caravan," can cause a complete collapse and a total loss. However, because such people see themselves as still on the same line and in the same situation, they do not realize that they have plunged to the bottom of a deep well from a minaret-like peak.

- Some people who leave the line of exertion and struggle with a feeling of guilt, which every fugitive and truant is bound to feel, are likely to defend themselves and criticize their friends who continue to serve. It is almost impossible for such people to escape their deviation and return to their original line. Adam recovered his previous rank with a single deed (his confession of fault) after he fell into forgetfulness. In contrast, Satan tried to defend himself, despite the gravity of his sin, and thus fell into eternal frustration.

- People who have lost their resolve, willpower, and endeavor affect the courage and devotional strength of those around them. Sometimes only a little hesitation or reluctance displayed by an irresolute individual causes a shock and loss of hope as great as the death of 100 people. Such a disaster encourages the nation's enemies to attack it.

- The attractiveness of children, family, and worldly property is a seductive and burdensome trial. The successful ones are those determined, resolute, strong-willed, and fortunate people who, every morning and evening, renew from the depth of their hearts their oath of attachment to the truth to which they have devoted themselves.[176]

## Love of Position

- Each individual has the seeds of virtue as well as the potential for evil. Such undesirable characteristics as passion and the desire to show off exist alongside such good qualities as sincerity, altruism, and self-sufficiency. We should take all these qualities into account when considering human nature so that we will not be disappointed.

---

[176] Ibid., 1:41-46.

- It is natural for everyone to entertain a love of status and fame to some degree. If these desires are not satisfied in acceptable ways, those without self-control may harm both themselves and their community. Their ambitions may have to be diverted into harmless channels, otherwise their frustrated and unsatisfied desires will cause harm.

- It may be harmful for some unrefined souls to satisfy their desire for prominence by seeking status. Nevertheless such a pursuit may be a good thing, for it will prevent them from doing greater evil. For example, it is preferable for a singer who wishes to make use of his or her God-given ability to sing hymns rather than obscene songs.

- Sincerity or purity of intention determines the quality of the deed and of the one who performs it, and whether or not God will accept it. However, as it is not easy for everybody to serve the faith with complete sincerity, consideration should be given to whether their good exceeds their evil. Many deeds performed for show and without sincerity should not be judged as absolutely harmful. People sometimes may contaminate their deeds by ego and desire, and may not always be seeking God's approval and repenting of their mistakes. But, we have no right to claim that they are not on the side of the truth.

- If each individual in a group tries to impose himself or herself as the only authority in a certain field, and others imitate them, discipline is destroyed, confusion in engendered, and the community is divided against itself. Ultimately, confusion over who is in charge and the ensuing power struggle between the rulers and the ruled destroys order.

- If the successful members of a government or the efficient executives of a state or institution demand the lion's share of benefits because of their abilities, the government is paralyzed, the state collapses, and the institution descends into chaos. A government subsists on a discipline specific to itself, a state is maintained by its principles, and an army is founded upon structures of command and obedience. Anything contrary to this signifies neglect of those vital elements that traditionally have ensured the cohesion of human societies.

- If only people's hearts were content with what the Sublime Creator bestows upon them! If only they would seek His Divine pleasure! Some self-seeking people turn their backs on the sun's light and are content with the dim light of the lanterns in their hands. With these, however, they will never find the door to eternal light.[177]

---

[177] Ibid., 1:9-14.

## CHAPTER 4

# The Individual and Human Rights

## In the Qur'an, Each Individual Is a Species

We should not fear or feel anxiety about individuals, their development, or their motivation, for the Qur'an sees each individual as a *species* as compared to other *species*. The important thing is the source of the emotions and thoughts that nurture them. When individuals attain a certain way of thinking and understanding and reach a certain horizon, they will realize that it is necessary to live a social life. Developed persons will feel the need to be with others, understand that they should not be alone and that they should not harm other social segments or individuals.

Those individuals educated along these lines, who do not use their rights and freedoms to harm others but to choose others' interests above their own, should be allowed to develop individually. Otherwise, there will be constant judgment and condemnation, oppression and being oppressed, cruelty and victims of cruelty. This is one dimension of the tragic tableau in Turkey today.[178]

## Flourishing of the individual

Q: Your suggestion for the individual to flourish indicates your vision, but it is not so easy to change people's habits.

A: This is because we are descendants of a militarist nation. It has been passed on by our ancestors. In fact, I have asked some friends who know genetics if national characteristics can be inher-

---

[178] Sevindi, "Fethullah Gülen Ile New York Sohbeti," August 1997.

ited from one generation to the next. I did not receive a fully satisfactory answer. Such an inheritance always can be a matter for discussion. It is reflected in Parliament in one way and in the presidency in another way. Its manifestation in the military is very different, for its members represent power and, due to their profession's nature, from time to time their attitude can be rougher. In other social segments, they can remain under this same influence to the extent that is permissible.

Q: Can human rights and freedom be narrowed in the name of democracy?

A: A top authority once said: "This constitution is too broad for us." However, narrowing human rights and freedom cannot be recommended. For a long time we have taken things from outside without asking if they suit us, trying to force ourselves into a particular mold. But our nation, state, and society has some special characteristics. Our nation should be viewed within its own characteristics, since ignoring them only causes alienation and social crises anew, such as those we're living through now.

There are some things that our nation will not relinquish. Our historical and religious dynamics, as well as our essence, must be considered. Take this however you want, but there are some things you just can't throw away. Ignoring these in favor of things developed in a different world and according to that world's criteria, like a ready-to-wear dress, creates problems.

Q: In the end, a religious community (like yours) is a closed system. Is it possible to open up and expand within this closed state? I wonder, is the community's spirit a common identity, or does it permit the individual to develop?

A: Today the community is perceived a little differently. First of all, we are not a religious community. If we're going to call it a *community*—and I feel uncomfortable with this word—it is like this:

For example, Islam strongly recommends its followers to perform the prescribed prayers as a congregation. This recommendation caused the building of mosques in almost every city or town. Islam orders that the Friday noon prayer should be performed in congregation. This caused the building of at least a large mosque in every town. This also causes Muslims to come together five times a day in mosques. Again, Islam commands pilgrimage for those Muslims who can afford it.

These are occasions that naturally bring the Muslim people together. Like these, those who have the same ideas and adopt the same way of serving people and the country come together without any compulsion or ulterior motive. They may have different creeds, worldviews, and political inclinations. This is what you see in when you mention as "your community."

You believe in certain things and put them into words. For example, you say *love*; you say *hatred should be buried* so that it can't be revived; and you believe in the significance of education. People who share these feelings and ideas undertake relevant activities accordingly. If this is called a community, there's no reason to be worried.

The second aspect is that certain thoughts of such communities can become static, which might prevent members from developing their natural talents. What you say is true from this perspective. Coming together in a manner that raises doubts, with the view of doing certain things from the outset, can hinder individual development. Those in the forefront of such communities put a high price tag on their experience. When people serve humanity, seeking titles is a display of disrespect to service, to the nation, and to those who trust them.

Q: Can some people in political parties, religious communities, and other groups overcome these?

A: It's possible, but different thoughts should be free to flourish. Otherwise there can be retrogression in contemporary change and transformation. There can be no radical change, for the innovative spirit will be lost or not come forth. But in addition to protecting the basic line, there's a need for innovative spirits, especially when time flows very fast and developments take place rapidly.[179]

## Some Aspects of Existentialism Are Correct

The idea that we cannot escape easily from this inherited influence should be destroyed. It's very important to think more freely and gain an individual identity. I guess this was the starting point for existentialist philosophy during periods of universal crisis following world wars, where people were swept into mass death. The individual lost everything and was annihilated. The existentialists were definitely right to rebel against the loss of the individual. But they went too far on some points and caused other fallacies. As in every other issue, balance is necessary.[180]

## Humanism

Q: What is Islam's perspective on humanism?

A: Love is one of today's most uttered and needed issues. Actually love is a rose in our belief, a realm of the heart that never withers. Before everything else, just as God wove the universe like lace on the loom of love, the most magical and charming music in the bosom of existence is always love. The strongest relationship among individuals in the family, society, and nation is love. Universal love shows itself throughout the cosmos in each particle's help and support for every other particle.

This is so true that the most dominant factor in the spirit of existence is love. As an individual of the universal chorus, almost every creature acts and behaves in its own style, according to the magical tune it has received from God, in a melody of love. However, this exchange of love from existence to humanity, and from one creature to another, takes place subconsciously, because Divine Will and Divine Willing completely dominate those creatures that have no will (power).

---

[179] Ibid.

[180] Ibid.

From this perspective, people consciously participate in this symphony of love in existence. By developing the love in their true nature, they investigate the ways to demonstrate it in a human way. Therefore, without neglecting the love in their spirit and for the sake of the love in their own nature, every person should offer real help and support to others. They should protect the general harmony that has been put in their spirit, or in respect to the love that has been put into the spirit of existence as a natural law.

Humanism is a manifestation of love that is uttered recklessly today, and so it is adapted easily here and there. Some circles try to impose an abstract and unbalanced understanding of humanism by confusing people about Islam and awakening suspicion in their hearts. It should be difficult to, say, "have pity" on those who are involved in anarchy and terror. It should be difficult to reconcile with humanism the strange behavior of those who murder innocent people or, even more horrible, those who put some supposedly religious people in their forefront and, without even glancing at the people's tears, stand by and watch.

Every believer should follow the Prophet in communicating the truth. They should never give up conveying to people the principles of happiness in both worlds. The Companions, who as a community were a vivid example of the truth embodied by the Prophet, became examples of moderation and balance in love.

Some remarkable people from the fortunate generation that followed the Companions immediately would go to the caliph if they accidentally stepped on a grasshopper to learn what their punishment would be. When we look at the surface of our mosques and minarets that radiate light, we see tiny holes made for the birds to nest, expressions of the depth of our ancestors' love. Our glorious history is fully woven with such tremendously humane acts of protecting animals as well as people.

In the framework of Islam's universal principles, the consideration and idea of love is very balanced. Oppressors and aggressors have denied this love, because just as love and mercy shown to oppressors makes them more aggressive, it also encourages them to violate the rights of others. For this reason, mercy should not be shown to people who threaten universal love. Mercy shown to an oppressor is the most merciless act towards the oppressed. The Prophet said: "Help others whether they are oppressors or victims. You can help oppressors by making them stop their oppression (to others)." It is possible to show mercy to tyrant if they stop acting unjustly.[181]

## Islam as a Religion of Universal Mercy

Life is the foremost and most manifest blessing of God Almighty, and the true and everlasting life is that of the Hereafter. Since we can deserve this life only by pleasing God, He sent Prophets and revealed Scriptures out of His Compassion for humanity. For this reason, while mentioning His blessings upon humanity in *Surat al-Rahman* (the All-Merciful), He begins: *Al-Rahman. He taught the Qur'an, created humanity, and taught it speech* (55:1-4).

All aspects of this life are a rehearsal for the afterlife, and every creature is engaged toward this end. Order is evident in every effort, and compassion resides in every achievement. Some "natural" events or social convulsions may seem disagreeable at first, but we should not regard them as incompatible with com-passion. They are like dark clouds or lightning and thunder that, although frightening, nevertheless bring us the good tidings of rain. Thus the whole universe praises the All-Compassionate.

Prophet Muhammad is like a spring of pure water in the heart of a desert, a source of light in an all-enveloping darkness. Those who appeal to this spring can take as much water as needed to quench their thirst, become purified of their sins, and become illu-mined with the light of faith. Mercy was like a magical key in the Prophet's hands, for with it he opened hearts that were so hardened

---

[181] S. Camci and Dr K. Ünal, *Fethullah Gülen'in Konusma ve Yazilarinda Hosgörü ve Diyalog Iklimi* (The Climate of Dialogue and Tolerance in the Speeches and Writings of Fethullah Gülen) (Izmir: Merkür Yayinlari, 1999), 218-22.

and rusty that no one thought they could be opened. But he did even more: he lit a torch of belief in them.

God's Messenger preached Islam, the religion of universal mercy. However, some self-proclaimed humanists say it is "a religion of the sword." This is completely wrong. They make a great deal of noise when animals are killed or when one of their own is harmed, but are silent when Muslims are massacred in groups. Their world is built on personal interest. It should be pointed out that abusing the feeling of compassion is just as harmful—sometimes even more harmful—than having no compassion at all.

Amputating a gangrenous limb is in fact an act of compassion for the entire body. Likewise oxygen and hydrogen, when mixed in the proper ratio, form a most vital substance: water. When this ratio is violated, however, each element resumes its original combustible identity.

Similarly, it is quite important to apportion compassion and identify who deserves it, for "compassion for a wolf (monster) sharpens its appetite, and not being content with what it receives, it demands even more." Compassion for wrongdoers makes them more aggressive and encourages them to continue. In fact, true compassion requires that such people be prevented from doing wrong. When God's Messenger told his Companions to help people when they were just and unjust, they asked him to explain this seemingly paradox. He replied: "You help such people by preventing them from engaging in injustice." So, compassion requires that those who cause trouble either to be deprived of their means for doing so or to be stopped. Otherwise, they eventually will take control and do as they please.

The compassion of God's Messenger encompassed every creature. An invincible commander and able statesman, he knew that allowing bloodstained, bloodthirsty people to control others would be the most terrible form of tyranny imaginable. Therefore, out of compassion, he required that lambs should be able to live in security against wolves' attacks. He desired, of course, that everyone be guided. In fact, this was his greatest concern: *Yet it may be, if they*

*believe not in this Message, you will consume (exhaust) yourself,
following after them, with grief* (18:6).

But how should he deal with those who persisted in unbelief
and took up arms against him to destroy both him and Islam? He
had to fight such people, for universal compassion encompasses
every creature. This is why, when he was wounded severely at
Uhud, he raised his hands and prayed: "O God, forgive my people, for they don't know."[182]

The Makkans, his own people, inflicted so much suffering on
him that he finally emigrated to Madina. Even after that, the next
5 years were far from peaceful. However, when he conquered
Makka without bloodshed in the twenty-first year of his
Prophethood, he asked the Makkan unbelievers: "How do you
expect me to treat you?" They responded unanimously: "You are a
noble one, the son of a noble one." He then told them his decision:
"You may leave, for no reproach this day shall be on you. May God
forgive you. He is the Most Compassionate."[183] Sultan Mehmed the
Conqueror said the same thing to the defeated the Byzantines after
conquering Istanbul 825 years later. Such is the universal compassion of Islam.

The Messenger displayed the highest degree of compassion
toward believers: *There has come to you a Messenger from among
yourselves; grievous to him is your suffering; anxious is he over*

---

[182] The Battle of Uhud (625): The Muslim army had 1,000 soldiers while the
Makkans had 3,000 soldiers. On the morning of March 23, the Makkan infantry
attacked and was repulsed with considerable loss. As the Muslims pursued, the
Makkan cavalry launched a flank attack when the Muslim archers guarding the
Muslim left abandoned their position. The Muslims were thrown into confusion.
Some made for a fort and were cut down. But Muhammad and the bulk of his
force managed to gain the lower slopes of Uhud, where they were safe from the
cavalry. Due to their losses, the Makkans did not press their advantage and
immediately made for Makka. The Prophet pursued them the following day.
Although there was no clear victor, the Makkans could not respond when the
Prophet followed them.

[183] Ibn Hisham, *Sirat al-Nabawiya*, 4:55; Ibn Kathir, *Al-Bidaya wa al-Nihaya*,
4:344.

*you, full of concern for you, for the believers full of pity, compas-*
*sionate* (9:128). He *lowered unto believers his wing of tenderness*
*through mercy* (15:88), and was the guardian of believers and *near-*
*er to them than their selves* (33:6). When one of his Companions
died, he asked those at the funeral if the deceased had left any debts.
On learning that he had, the Prophet mentioned the above verse and
announced that the creditors should come to him for repayment.

His compassion even encompassed the Hypocrites and unbelievers. He knew who the Hypocrites were, but never identified
them, for this would have deprived them of the rights of full citi-
zenship they had gained by their outward declaration of faith and
practice. Since they lived among Muslims, their denial of eternal
life may have been reduced or changed to doubt, thus diminishing
their fear of death and the pain caused by the assertion of eternal
non-existence after death.

God no longer destroys unbelievers collectively, although He
had eradicated many such people in the past: *But God would never*
*chastise them while you were among them; God would never*
*chastise them as they begged forgiveness* (8:33). This verse refers
to unbelievers regardless of time and place. God will not destroy
whole peoples as long as those who follow the Messenger are
alive. Besides, He has left the door of repentance open until the
Last Day. Anyone can accept Islam or ask God's forgiveness,
regardless of how sinful they consider themselves to be.

For this reason, a Muslim's enmity toward unbelievers is a
form of pity. When 'Umar saw an 80-year-old priest, he sat down
and wept. When asked why, he replied: "God assigned him so long
a lifespan, but he has not been able to find the true path." 'Umar
was a disciple of God's Messenger, who said: "I was not sent to
call down curses on people, but as a mercy,"[184] and:

> I am Muhammad, and Ahmad (praised one), and Muqaffi
> (the Last Prophet); I am Hashir (the final Prophet in whose
> presence the dead will be resurrected); the Prophet of repen-

---

[184] Muslim, *Sahih*, "Birr," 87.

tance (the Prophet for whom the door of repentance will
always remain open), and the Prophet of mercy.[185]

Archangel Gabriel also benefited from the mercy of the Qur'an.
Once the Prophet asked Gabriel whether he had any share in the
mercy contained in the Qur'an. Gabriel replied that he did, and
explained: "I was not certain about my end. However, when the
verse: *(One) obeyed, and moreover, trustworthy and secured* (81:21)
was revealed, I felt secure."[186]

God's Messenger was particularly compassionate toward children. Whenever he saw a child crying, he sat beside him or her and
shared his or her feelings. He felt the pain of a mother for her child
more than the mother herself. Once he said: "I stand in prayer and
wish to prolong it. However, I hear a child cry and shorten the
prayer to lessen the mother's anxiety."[187]

He took children in his arms and hugged them. Once when
hugging his beloved grandsons, Hasan and Husayn, Aqra ibn
Habis told him: "I have 10 children, none of whom I have ever
kissed." God's Messenger responded: "One without pity for others
is not pitied."[188] According to another version, he said: "What can
I do for you if God has removed compassion from you?"[189]

He said: "Pity those on Earth so that those in the Heavens will
pity you."[190] Once when Sa'd ibn 'Ubada became ill, God's
Messenger visited him at home. Seeing his faithful Companion in a
pitiful state, began to cry and said: "God does not punish because of
tears or grief, but He punishes because of this," and he pointed to

---

[185] Ahmad ibn Hanbal, *Musnad*, 4:395; Muslim, *Sahih*, "Fada'il," 126.

[186] Qadi 'Iyad, *Al-Shifa' al-Sharif*, 1:17.

[187] Bukhari, *Sahih*, "Adhan," 65; Muslim, *Sahih*, "Salat," 192.

[188] *Sahih al-Bukhari*, "Adab," 18.

[189] Bukhari, *Sahih*, "Adab," 18; Muslim, *Sahih*, "Fada'il," 64; Ibn Maja, *Sunan*, "Adab," 3.

[190] Tirmidhi, *Sunan*, "Birr," 16.

his tongue.[191] When 'Uthman ibn Mad'un died, he wept profusely. During the funeral, a woman remarked: "'Uthman flew like a bird to Paradise." Even in that mournful state, the Prophet did not lose his balance and corrected the woman: "How do you know this? Even I don't know this, and I am a Prophet."[192]

A member of the Banu Muqarrin clan once beat his maidservant. She informed God's Messenger, who then sent a message to the master. He said: "You have beaten her without any justifiable right. Free her."[193] Setting a slave free was far better for the master than being punished in the Hereafter because of that act. God's Messenger always protected and supported widows, orphans, the poor and disabled even before his Prophethood. When he returned home in excitement from Mount Hira after the first Revelation, his wife Khadija told him: "I hope you will be the Prophet of this community, for you always tell the truth, fulfill your trust, support your relatives, help the poor and weak, and feed guests."[194]

His compassion even encompassed animals. We hear from him: "A prostitute was guided to truth by God and ultimately went to Paradise because she gave water to a poor dog dying of thirst inside a well. Another woman was sent to Hell because she made a cat die of hunger."[195] Once while returning from a military campaign, a few Companions removed some young birds from their nest to caress them. The mother bird came back and, not finding its babies, began to fly around screeching. When told of this, God's Messenger became angry and ordered the birds to be put back in the nest.[196]

---

[191] Bukhari, *Sahih*, "Jana'iz," 45; Muslim, *Sahih*, "Jana'iz," 12.

[192] Bukhari, *Sahih*, "Jana'iz," 3.

[193] Muslim, *Sahih*, "Ayman," 31, 33; Ibn Hanbal, *Musnad*, 3:447.

[194] Ibn Sa'd, *Al-Tabaqat al-Kubra'*, 1:195.

[195] Bukhari, *Sahih*, "Anbiya'," 54; "Musaqat," 9; Muslim, *Sahih*, "Salam," 153; Ibn Hanbal, *Musnad*, 2:507.

[196] Abu Dawud, *Sunan*, "Adab," 164, "Jihad," 112; Ibn Hanbal, *Musnad*, 1:404.

Once he told his Companions that God had reproached an earlier Prophet for setting fire to a nest of ants.[197] While in Mina, some
of his Companions attacked a snake in order to kill it. However, it
managed to escape. Watching this from afar, he remarked: "It was
saved from your evil, as you were from its evil."[198] Ibn 'Abbas
reported that God's Messenger, upon observing a man sharpening
his knife directly before the sheep to be slaughtered, asked him:
"Do you want to kill it many times?"[199]

'Abd Allah ibn Ja'far narrates: "God's Messenger once went
to a garden in Madina with a few Companions. A very scrawny
camel was in a corner. Seeing the Messenger, it began to cry. He
went to it and, after staying beside it for a while, severely warned
the owner to feed it properly."[200]

His love and compassion for creatures differed from that of
today's self-proclaimed humanists. He was sincere and balanced in
his love and compassion. A Prophet raised by God, the Creator and
Sustainer of all beings, for the guidance and happiness of conscious beings—humanity and jinn—and the harmony of existence.
As such, he lived not for himself but for others. He is a mercy for
all the worlds, a manifestation of Compassion.

He eradicated all differences of race and color. Once Abu
Dharr got so angry with Bilal that he insulted him: "You son of a
black woman!" Bilal came to God's Messenger and reported the
incident in tears. The Messenger reproached Abu Dharr: "Do you
still have a sign of *jahiliya* (ignorance)?" Full of repentance, Abu
Dharr lay on the ground and said: "I won't raise my head (meaning he wouldn't get up) unless Bilal puts his foot on it to pass over
it." Bilal forgave him, and they were reconciled.[201] Such was the

[197] Bukhari, *Sahih*, "Jihad," 153; Muslim, *Sahih*, "Salam," 147.

[198] Nasa'i, *Sunan*, "Hajj," 114; Ibn Hanbal, *Musnad*, 1:385.

[199] Hakim, *Mustadrak*, 4:231, 233.

[200] Suyuti, *Al-Khasa'is al-Kubra'*, 2:95; Haythami, *Majma' al-Zawa'id*, 9:9.

[201] Bukhari, *Sahih*, "Iman," 22.

brotherhood and humanity that Islam created between and among once-savage people.[202]

## Human Rights in Islam

Q: Would you explain Islamic viewpoint of human rights?

A:  On the subject of human rights, Islam is as balanced, broad, and universal as possible. Except for those who deserve death, like rebels against the legal administration or murderers, the Qur'an teaches us that killing a person unjustly is a crime against humanity (5:32). Such an appreciation cannot be found in any other religion or modern system, and such a high value has never been given to humanity by any human rights commission or organization. Islam accepted the killing of one person as the killing of all humanity, for the murder of one person gives the idea that any person can be killed.

Adam's son Cain was the first person to shed blood. Although their names are not mentioned specifically in the Qur'an or Sunna, we learn from previous Scriptures that a misunderstanding took place between the two brothers Cain and Abel. The end result is that Cain unjustly kills Abel out of jealousy, thereby opening the era of bloodshed. For this reason, the Messenger said: "No human being is killed unjustly, but a part of responsibility for the crime is laid on the first son of Adam who invented the tradition of killing (murdering) on the Earth."[203]

This event, with an important lesson, is expressed in the Qur'an:

> Explain truthfully to them the news of Adam's two sons: When they each presented a sacrificial lamb, and one was accepted and the other rejected (because of jealousy and ill-intention.) He said: "I swear I'm going to kill you." The other said: "God will only accept from those who are pious." He added: "I swear that even if you reach out your hand to kill

[202] Fethullah Gülen, *Sonsuz Nur* (Prophet Muhammad: The Infinite Light) (Izmir: Nil Yayinlari, 1997), 1:377-97.

[203] Bukhari, "Diyat," 6, Enbiya 1; Muslim, "Kasame," 27.

> me, I will not reach out my hand to kill you. I fear God, the Lord of the Worlds." (5:27-28)

## The following judgment is given:

> On that account: We ordained for the Children of Israel that if anyone slew a person—unless it be for murder or for spreading mischief in the land—it would be as if he or she slew everyone: and if any one saved a life, it would be as if he or she saved the life of everyone. (5:32)

## This is universal and thus valid for all times. Another verse states:

> If someone kills a believer intentionally, his (or her) recompense is Hell, to abide therein (forever): and the wrath and the curse of God are upon him (or her), and a dreadful penalty is prepared for him (or her).

## The Prophet stated:

> Those who are killed defending their property are considered martyrs. Those who are killed defending their blood (life) are considered martyrs. Those who are killed defending their religion are considered martyrs. Those who are killed defending their family are considered martyrs.[204]

All these values have been protected as separate principles in all legal systems. These issues are given importance in the fundamental books comprising our law as *indispensable*. From this perspective, religion, life, reproduction, the mind, and property are basic essentials that everyone must protect. In a sense, Islam approaches human rights from the angle of these basic principles.

Only Islam honors humanity with the title of *God's vicegerent*. No other system or religion does this. In addition, Islam allows humanity the opportunity to intervene with other things due to its superiority with respect to such freedoms as working and initiating. How could a religion that attributes such significance to freedom neglect a person's human rights?[205]

---

[204] Tirmidhi, "Diyat," 22; Abu Dawud, "Sunna," 32.

[205] Camci and Ünal, *Fethullah Gülen'in Konusma ve Yazilarinda Hosgörü ve Diyalog Iklimi*, 223-26.

## *The Rights of Parents*

- The father and mother are two sacred beings who must be respected above everyone else. If you do not respect your parents, you are disobeying God Almighty. Those who treat their parents badly eventually are treated badly by others.

- From the very moment of conception, a growing and developing child is a care and responsibility for its parents. One cannot estimate the depth of attachment and compassion parents feel for their children, or calculate the troubles and hardships they endure because of them. For this reason, respecting parents is a debt of human gratitude as well as a religious obligation.

- Those who value their parents and regard them as a means to obtain God's mercy are the most prosperous in both worlds. Those who regard their parents' existence as a burden or who become weary of them inevitably suffer the most severe hardship in life.

- The more you respect your parents, the greater the respect and awe you feel before your Creator. If you do not feel and show respect to them, this means that you feel no fear, awe, or respect toward God. It is a curious thing today that both those who disrespect God and those who claim they love God disobey their parents.

- Children should respect and obey their parents as much as possible. Parents should give as much importance to their children's moral and spiritual education as they do to their physical growth and health, and should entrust them to the care of the most honorable teachers and guides. How ignorant and careless are those parents who neglect their children's moral and spiritual training, and how unfortunate are the children who experience such neglect.

- Children who are inconsiderate of their parents' rights and disobey them are "monsters derived from a deteriorated human being." Parents who do not secure their children's moral and spiritual welfare are merciless and cruel. Most brutish and pitiless of all are parents who paralyze their children's moral and spiritual development after they have found their way to human perfection.

- Families form a society's foundation. The reciprocal respect of rights and obligations within a family results in a healthy and strong society. When such familial relationships disappear, the society loses its compassion and respect for others.[206]

---

[206] Gülen, *Ölçü veya Yoldaki Isiklar*, 1:98-101.

## *The Rights of Children*

- A child has the same meaning for humanity's continuation as a seed for a forest's continued growth and multiplication. People who neglect their children gradually decay, and those who abandon them to a foreign culture risk losing their identity.

- Children form the most active and productive part of a community after every 30 or 40 years. Those who ignore their children should consider how important an element of their own community's life they are disregarding, and then shudder.

- The vices observed in today's generation, the incompetence of some administrators, and other social problems are the direct result of the conditions prevailing 30 years ago and of that time's ruling elite. Likewise, those entrusted with educating today's young people are responsible for the vices and virtues that will appear 30 years from now.

- Those who want to secure their future should apply as much energy to raising their children as they devote to other problems. While the energy devoted to many other things may go in vain, whatever is spent for raising a young generation elevates them to the rank of humanity. Such people will be like inexhaustible sources of income.

- Those people in our community who are miserable and lost, such as drug addicts, alcoholics, and other dissolute people, were once children. We failed to educate them properly. I wonder whether we are sufficiently aware of the kind of people we are preparing to walk our streets tomorrow.

- Communities that pay close attention to the family institution and their young people's education, as opposed to those who are more advanced in science and technology, will have the upper hand in the future. Communities that neglect the family institution and the young people's education will be crushed by the pitiless wheels of time.[207]

# Women, Marriage, and Polygamy

## *Women*

- Women train and educate children, and establish order, peace, and harmony in the home. They are the first teachers in the school of humanity. At a time when some are in search of a new place for them in society, we would like to remind them once again of the unique position God bestowed upon them.

---

[207] Ibid.

- A house that contains an honorable, well-mannered woman loyal to her home is a corner from Heaven. The sounds and breaths heard there are no different from the musical voices of the young people of Paradise and the bubbling of the *Kawthar* stream in Heaven.

- A woman's inner depth, chastity, and dignity elevate her higher than angels and cause her to resemble an unmatched diamond. A disreputable woman is a false coin, and an undignified woman is a puppet to be ridiculed. In the destructive atmosphere of such women, it is impossible to find either a healthy home or a sound generation.

- A woman awakened to virtues in her inner world resembles a crystal chandelier that, with every movement, illuminates throughout the house. The most important thing a woman should know is social breeding.

- Women often have been used as objects of pleasure, means of entertainment, and material for advertising. However, until now all these unfortunate periods have been a starting point for women to become renewed and find their essence (like nights followed by days).

- In the past, a son was called *makhdum* (servant), and a daughter was called *karima* (pupil [of the eye]). This word expresses a member that is very valuable, as necessary as it is valuable, and as delicate as it is necessary.

- A good woman speaks wisdom, and has a delicate, refined spirit. Her behavior inspires admiration and respect. Familiar looks sense this sacred side of her, and turn instinctive feelings to contemplation.

- Like a flower worn in one's hair, a beautiful woman may receive admiration and respect for a short period. But if she has not been able to get the seeds of her heart and spirit to blossom, she will eventually fade and, like falling leaves, be trampled underfoot. What a sad ending for those who have not found the road of immortality!

- Each woman is a precious, exalted jewel that must not be trampled down and thrown into a sewer. We hope that fortunate generations of future will awaken to knowledge, spirituality, and truth so that women may once again become "the pupil of their eyes."

- Our women are the soundest foundation stone of our national honor and nobility. Their part in forming our long and glorious past is equal to that of the warriors who struggled with our enemies.

- Most champions of women's rights and freedom only excite women with physical pleasure and then stab her spirit.

- Thanks to the good successors she raised and left behind, the home of a spiritually mature woman constantly exudes a scent of joy like an incense burner. The "heavenly" home where this aroma "blows" is a garden of Paradise beyond description.

- A woman whose heart is illuminated with the light of faith and whose mind is enlightened with knowledge and social breeding builds her home anew each day by adding new dimensions of bliss. A dissolute woman who does not know her true self destroys existing homes and turns them into graves.[208]

## Women and Their Rights

Q: What are your ideas about women's rights?

A: This is a very comprehensive subject. From one perspective it's open to debate. It's very difficult to summarize my thoughts on this kind of platform. In one sense we don't separate men and women. In another sense there are physical and psychological differences. Women and men should be the two sides of truth, like the two faces of a coin. Man without woman, or woman without man, cannot exist; they were created together. Adam suffered in Heaven because he had no mate, and then Heaven became a real Heaven when he found Eve. Man and woman complement each other.

Q: If we approach the matter from Islamic perspective...

A: Our Prophet, the Qur'an, and Qur'anic teachings don't take men and women as separate creatures. I think the problem here is that people approach it from extremes and disturb the balance. There are differences on specific points. For example, men usually are physically stronger and apt to bear hardship, while women have deeper emotions; they are more compassionate, more delicate, more self-sacrificing. While looking for a place for each gender in society, we should consider these and other innate differences. God created everything, from sub-atomic particles to human beings, in pairs to form a unity.

Q: Are there examples for the female role?

A: In the social atmosphere of Muslim societies where Islam is not "contaminated" with customs or un-Islamic traditions, Muslim women are full participants in daily life. For example, during the

---

[208] Ibid., 3:67-77.

Prophet's time and in later centuries when the West gave women no place in society, when the West was debating whether or not women had spirits or were devils or human beings, 'A'isha led an army. She also was a religious scholar whose views everyone respected. Women prayed in mosques together with men. An old woman could oppose the caliph in the mosque in a juridical matter.

Even in the Ottoman period during the eighteenth century, the wife of an English ambassador highly praised the women and mentioned their roles in Muslim families and society with admiration.[209]

Q: Can women be administrators?

A: There's no reason why a woman can't be an administrator. In fact, Hanafi jurisprudence says that a woman can be a judge. Maybe some women could explain certain matters more comfortably to a judge of their own gender.[210]

## Women and Men Prayed together at the Mosque

Q: The mainstream of our culture runs from Central Asia. If we recall that, in the Islamic understanding during the Yasawi period,[211] women and men worshipped together and that the Qur'an was read in Turkish until the thirteenth century, why is there an effort to separate men and women in society and in places of worship?

A: Women and men prayed together in mosques during the time of the Prophet. Sometimes a woman would correct the caliph who was giving sermon. For example, in one his sermons Caliph 'Umar warned the Muslims: "Do not pay women in marriage more than 500 dirhams as dowry." A woman in the congregation object-

---

[209] Özkök, "Hoca Efendi Anlatiyor."

[210] Akman, "Fethullah Hoca Anlatiyor."

[211] Ahmad Yasawi (Ahmed Yesevi) (11th century-1166): Sufi poet and early Turkish spiritual leader who had a powerful influence on the development of mystical orders throughout the Turkish-speaking world. He wrote poetry for the people, and his mystical order was a popular brotherhood. His disciples formed many affiliated mystical associations in the Turkish world. His poetry greatly influenced Turkish literature, paving the way for the development of Sufi folk literature.

ed: "O 'Umar! Should we follow the Qur'an or you?" 'Umar asked: "What does the Qur'an say?" The woman replied: "The Qur'an says: *If you divorce a woman in order to wed another, and you have given her a hoarded treasure as dowry, take not the least part of it back* (4:20). Is a hoarded treasure equal to 500 dirhams?" 'Umar replied: "I erred, and the woman spoke the truth."

Time and changing conditions have caused some changes in secondary issues. Women do not have to perform their prescribed prayers in mosques, but if they would like to, they should not be banned if there is no justifiable reason for banning them.

As for the second part of the question, I do not know whether Ahmad Yasawi and his followers recited the Qur'an in Turkish. The Qur'an can be translated into any language, but no translation can reflect the exact meaning of the original. So, in prescribed prayers the original of the Qur'an must be recited, but a person can supplicate to God in any language he or she wishes.[212]

## Women's Covering

Q: Trying to isolate women, it's desired that they wear a *hijab* (a headscarf that completely covers one's hair). Kezban Hatemi says this is not ordered in the Qur'an.[213] Is *hijab* necessary or not?

A: The Qur'an mentions that a woman must cover herself, but it doesn't specify how or in what form this should be done. Dwelling on the form narrows Islam's broad horizon. In fact, it would be a mistake to make a religious costume.

The same thing is true for covering the head. It's a mistake to make this into one of the main principles of Islam and faith. The headscarf isn't one of Islam's main principles or conditions. It's against the spirit of Islam to regard uncovered women as outside of religion. We have so many things in common; we shouldn't be

---

[212] Sevindi, "Fethullah Gülen Ile New York Sohbeti."

[213] Kezban Hatemi: Famous Turkish female attorney at law and wife of Prof. Dr. Hüseyin Hatemi of Istanbul University's Faculty of Law.

divided by details. If we're going to quarrel with one another in the mosque, first let's make peace outside the mosque by giving priority to the spirit or essence of something before its appearance.[214]

## Marriage and the Home

- Marriage is not for pleasure; rather, it is to establish a family, to ensure the nation's permanency and continuation, to save the individual from dispersed feelings and thoughts, and to control physical pleasure. Just as with many other matters related to the basic nature that God has given to each being, pleasure is a payment made in advance to invite and encourage marriage.

- One should not marry for reasons of dress, wealth, or physical beauty; rather, marry for spiritual beauty, honor and morality, virtue and character.

- If a couple wishes to divorce, the most intelligent criteria are of no use to those who did not (or could not) get married for the correct reasons. The important thing is not to escape from the fire in the home with the least harm, but to prevent a fire from ever starting there.

- Some marriages based on logic and judgment were initiated by taking refuge in God. They are so sacred that, throughout a lifetime, they function just like a school, and their "students" guarantee the nation's permanency and continuation.

- Every union made in the name of marriage, but without careful thought, leaves behind crying wives, orphans, and those who wound the family's heart.

- The soundest foundation for a nation is a family in which material and spiritual happiness flows, for such a family serves as a sacred school that raises virtuous individuals. If a nation can make its homes as enlightened and prosperous as its schools, and its schools as warm as its homes, it has made the greatest reform and has guaranteed the contentment and happiness of future generations.

- Nations are based on homes and individuals. If homes are good, the nation is good; if homes are bad, the nation is bad. If only those who want the best for the nation would first work to reform the homes!

- The word home is used according to the people in it. They are considered happy to the extent that they share human values. Yes, we can say that people live humanly with those in their home; a home becomes a home because of its inhabitants.

---

[214] Sevindi, "Fethullah Gülen Ile New York Sohbeti."

- A home is a small nation, and a nation is a large home. One who success-fully manages a home and who has raised its members to a level of human-ity can manage a large organization with a little effort.

- A disorderly house means that its people are slovenly and unhappy. The dirt-iness, disorder, and irregularity of houses, shops, and streets show the local officials' lack of sensitivity.

- What is right is liked and esteemed even if defeated. What is unjust is loath-some and disliked even if victorious.

- What is right is beautiful in character, and the one who is right is sweet. Even if the right falls into the mud, it remains pure and upright. Even if the unjust is washed with musk, it remains impure and repugnant.

- Color and shape may change, but essence does not. Name and title may change, but character does not. Such changes have, and continue to, fool many people.

- Those who oppress the weak are defeated even if they are the victors. Those who are right are victorious even if they lose.[215]

## Marriage Is Based on the Mind and the Spirit

If believers look at their spouses from a different, egotistic viewpoint, it cannot be said that they are marrying for Islam. Marriage is not the purpose of life; it is a means to continue human-ity. Muslims are an ideal representatives of purity and sincerity. Only an act done to obtain God's approval is Islamic. The main basis of the relationship between a man and woman is compassion and lifelong friendship. It is a friendship that does not include only this world, but the next life as well. Satisfying some desires is only a payment given in advance for this relationship in this world.

Marriage is based primarily on the mind and the spirit. It is based on rationality and spiritual conformity or harmony between the spouses, rather than on physical factors. Viewing marriage as an occasion or means to satisfy certain bodily desires, and thereby presenting polygamy as an Islamic way for this, is a purposeful and most abominable misrepresentation of Islam.

---

[215] Gülen, *Ölçü veya Yoldaki Isiklar*, 3:88-93.

Another point here is that at times some things come to the fore and others recede. Some commands can be abandoned for more important ones. There is no fasting during a war, prayer is shortened when one is traveling. If polygamy is considered a stain on Islam and causes people to turn away from Islam, a Muslim does not have the right to practice it.[216]

## Polygamy

Q: I'd like to talk with you about polygamy. This point caught my attention. Some say that since polygamy is permitted by the Qur'an, it must be accepted.

A: God created human beings as noble creatures. We always seek the good and beautiful, but may not always find them. Sometimes when we seek our rights, we encounter what is false. While seeking the truth, we can acquire vain and ugly things. In my opinion, seeking and falling into error while seeking are a part of the road to knowledge and truth. This shouldn't be seen as strange. Maybe stagnation, insensitivity, and not searching and investigating should be viewed as something strange. The dangerous thing is stagnation and insensitivity that kills the development of people's talents.

Over time, we have strayed from certain values. Today we're seeking the truth. While doing this, unfortunately, sides are taken and camps appear. If only this weren't the case. Would that *we* and *they* weren't said. Would that there wasn't the view that we are always right and they are always wrong. Would that we could close the fragmentation of our society's structure inside us, without leaving any trace.

Everyone has a destination of his or her own to go to, and views everything from the perspective of his or her destination. This causes fragmentation, especially in a society that has not evolved intellectually. First of all, we should learn to respect others' views and how to live together in peace.

---

[216] Sevindi, "Fethullah Gülen Ile New York Sohbeti."

Q: There's disagreement on the moral criteria. Isn't this a little odd?

A: There's disagreement because the basis of common morality and thought is not fully understood, or because these are different for everyone. We've not fully comprehended how we can live together despite having different viewpoints on certain subjects. Everyone looks at the issue from one perspective according to his or her own truths. The other side looks with its own truths. Without doubt there are points of truth on both sides. During a certain period, in order to defend themselves, some insistently emphasized marrying four women.

I'd like to talk about the spirit of the issue. First of all, there's no record in the Qur'an or the Hadith that it's a *sunna* to marry more than one woman by means of a religious ceremony. In *Surat al-Nisa* (the Chapter of Women), permission to marry more than one woman under special circumstances is mentioned only as a license or a special condition. But marrying just one woman is encouraged to the extent of being mandatory. Thus, no one can consider marrying four women a matter of fulfilling a *sunna*; they can't claim to have fulfilled any religious law by doing so.

Another side of the issue is this: There is license as well as resolution in religion. Resolution is choosing the difficult side of a matter. Although no one can force you to do it, for example, someone might get up at night and, because of enthusiasm and a heartfelt desire to bow before God, observe a long prayer vigil. This might be done to receive the blessings God will give at that moment. But someone else might choose a small act of worship or one *Kalimat al-Tawhid* (proclaiming God's Unity).

The essence of the matter is this: Be others' advocate and your own prosecutor. We must interrogate ourselves. Thus, acting with resolution means self-questioning, doing the difficult part of a job, choosing the hard way, or being a candidate for the difficult.

License means that God allows something easy for the sake of expansion and comfort. There are Qur'anic verses and *hadiths* on this subject. In Sufism, acting with resolution is essential for those who choose the spiritual life. In religion, those who deem polygamy lawful see it as a license. There can be times when it is necessary, such as during war when many women may be left in a vulnerable position. In order to close roads leading to sin, they must be able to obtain lawful pleasures in a lawful way. Also, widows in need must be considered. Religion doesn't just address this century—it addresses all centuries. Every century takes from religion what suits it and what is necessary. A person determined to draw closer to God and be a good Muslim prefers resolution to license.

Sha'rani, a famous Sufi, said: "Dervishes should act with resolution."[217] On the one hand, people must try Sufism and reason; but on the other hand, they must ask if something is really necessary and if there are conditions for using the license. They must study their choice sincerely and see if it meets with God's approval. Without doing all of these, they will use the full license and show this as a measure for Islam and Muslimness. This is no more than dressing their own faults and human weakness in a religious robe.[218]

---

[217] Al-Sha'rani (1492-1565): Original name 'Abd Al-Wahhab Ibn Ahmad. An Egyptian scholar and mystic who founded the Sha'rawiya Sufi order. He tried to select the best elements from the diverse and often conflicting world of Sufism and of the ulama for its operating principles.

[218] Sevindi, "Fethullah Gülen Ile New York Sohbeti."

CHAPTER 5

# Religion and Politics

## Republic

- Republic means rule based on the people's election and consultation. The first book to teach this principal fully is the Qur'an. Saying that republican rule is contrary to the Qur'an, if done without bad intentions, shows a lack of knowledge. Supporting the republic but refusing to see its source is just plain stubbornness.

- The Prophet did not claim kingship, and his four immediate [political] successors followed his example. Kingship appeared when people grew remote from the Islamic spirit. Eventually this digression became a vehicle for oppression and despotism.

- Based on true freedom and justice, a true republic is an elevated and safe form of government. But it is also an extremely tender system. If this aspect is not considered properly, atheism and anarchy will appear and grow in its heart.

- A true republic is a form of rule by elevated spirits and is the most suitable for humanity's honor. Immature spirits and those with no understanding of the ways to human perfection consider it a mirage, a temporary bower that offers no shelter.

- The republic can be the mother or governess of freedom, for it nurtures and raises generations in love with freedom. It is a government of freedom, virtue, and morality, not a rule of "loose" freedom.

- The republic provides a foundation that elevates us with uplifting values. Later it leaves us alone with our elevated morality and alert conscience. Finally recognizing ourselves as people with willpower, we always think good and virtuous thoughts and follow high human values at home and work.

- As our spirit, which has an innate desire for freedom, rejects all forms of domination, it reacts to any limits to be placed on its freedom of thought, behavior, and expression. For this reason, while a republican government allows individuals broad rights and freedoms, it must educate them as people of elevated morality and virtue, and sound thinking and strong will.

- The republic is obligated to protect its citizens' religious faith, feelings, and thoughts. If its leaders do not do so, but rather hold people in contempt because of their religious feelings and thoughts, violate their rights, and smear their good names, in reality they are holding the republic in contempt and violating all that it represents.

- The republic needs people who identify its principles fully. Its governing body should be dignified and wise, and its works should be fair and just.[219]

## Politics

- Politics is the art of managing a nation's affairs in ways that please both God and people. As long as a government protects people from evil and oppression, it can be considered successful in politics and thus full of promise. If a government does not do so, it can no longer remain in power, and leaves behind turmoil amidst sounds of cursing.

- Good administration and politics are characterized by acknowledging rights, the law's superiority, and consciousness of one's duty, as well as by placing responsible people in crude and difficult jobs and skilled and experienced people in refined and delicate jobs.

- Rather than a government's saying "my nation," it's more important that the nation says "my government." If the nation sees the government as a host of parasites, it means that the body has long ago broken off from the head.

- Government means justice and public order. One cannot speak of government where these do not exist.

- If the officials running a good and virtuous state are chosen because of their nobility of spirit, ideas, and feelings, the state will be good and strong. A government run by officials who lack these high qualities is still a government, but it is neither good nor long-lasting. Sooner or later, its officials' bad behavior will appear as dark spots on its face and blacken it in the eyes of people.

- Public officials should be kind, stay within the law, and have soft hearts. These characteristics will protect their esteem and honor and those of the law and the state. Remember that extreme harshness causes unexpected explosions, and extreme softness causes the rapid breeding of harmful ideas.

- Laws should be effective all the time, everywhere, and for everyone. Those who enforce them should be brave and just so that the masses will have some fear of them, but not to the extent that they no longer trust or feel secure under the law's enforcers.

---

[219] Gülen, *Ölçü veya Yoldaki Isiklar*, 3:32-36.

- Magnificent nations produce magnificent governments. Generations with high spirituality, scientific power, financial opportunities, and broad consciousness, along with those individuals struggling to be "themselves," form magnificent nations.

- Unity of feeling, thought, and culture are essential to a nation's strength; any disintegration of religious and moral unity causes weakening.

- There is a policy for everything. The policy for renewing a nation is to ignore your own pleasure, to feel joy only with the nation's pleasures, and to feel sorrow only with its pain.

- Mature people never make a difference of idea and opinion a means of conflict. However, no one has the right to tolerate understandings and views that separate people into camps and destroy society. Tolerating division means closing one's eye to the nation's extinction.

- People who do not think like you might be very sincere and beneficial, so do not oppose every idea that seems contradictory and do not scare them off. Seek ways to benefit from their opinions and ideas, and start up a dialogue with them. Otherwise, those who are kept at a distance and led to dissatisfaction because they do not think like us will form huge masses that confront and smash us. Even if such dissatisfied people have never achieved anything positive, the number of states they have destroyed is beyond counting.

- People must learn how to benefit from other people's knowledge and views, for these can be beneficial to their own system, thought, and world. Especially, they should always seek to benefit from the experiences of the experienced.

- Those who understand politics as political parties, propaganda, elections, and the struggle for power are mistaken. Politics is the art of management, based on a broad perspective of today, tomorrow, and the day after, that seeks the people's satisfaction and God's approval.

- Power's dominance is transitory, while that of truth and justice is eternal. Even if these do not exist today, they will be victorious in the very near future. For this reason, sincere politicians should align themselves and their policies with truth and justice.[220]

## Democracy Is Irreversible

Q: Turkey has a unique place among other Muslim countries. As a Muslim nation believing in democracy, is Turkey going to be

---

[220] Ibid., 3:37-56.

the only synthesis in the region that makes Islam compatible with democracy?

Democracy is developing. It's a process of no return that must develop and mature. I can't say Darwin's theory of evolution is true, but we undoubtedly experience an evolution of thought in our spirit. Democracy one day will attain a very high level. But we have to wait for the interpretation of time. We have to respect time. The irritability of impatient people shouldn't be incited. In Turkey, both sides are impatient. Turkey is also in a process of proving itself. It's not always right to tell every truth. Truths should be given to society, but if the season is not proper, let's not destroy those truths.[221]

## No Turning back from Democracy

Q: In the famous speech you made at The Foundation of Journalists and Writers, your words "It won't be possible to reverse the process of democracy" attracted a lot of attention. How can Islam live in democracy and vice versa?

A: It's wrong to see Islam and democracy as opposites. In periods when Islam wasn't practiced fully, perhaps it was more backward than today's democracy. For example, human rights were stepped on and despots headed the state. Some enlightened persons have said all this.

Q: Some Islamic groups accuse you of pacifying people.

A: That's not important. Is Islam not full democracy, and is not democracy full Islam? The world favors democracy, but it's still being modified. It's on the way to its real essence. Nobody says that Turkey is a full democracy. What I said is: "We still haven't become democratized. That's why we weren't able to enter the Customs Union." This means that democracy is still being perfected. Democracy is a process; it's not possible to reverse it.[222]

[221] Sevindi, "Fethullah Gülen Ile New York Sohbeti."

[222] Akman, "Fethullah Hoca Anlatiyor."

## Democracy and the Current Situation

Democracy is a system of freedoms. However, because we have to live together with our different positions and views, our freedom is limited where that of another begins. Subjects related to the people's values, some moral norms, the nation's permanency, and the country's unity are not limits to freedoms; rather, they should be seen as criteria for using freedom. Otherwise anarchy will arise, and not even the most basic freedoms can be used in such an environment.

I don't think that it's any easier to live Islam in another country than it is in Turkey. Supposedly there are Islamic regimes in Iran and Saudi Arabia, but they are state-determined and limited to sectarian approval.

Islam is a religion. It can't be called anything else. When the West defeated the Islamic world in military and technology, salvation was sought in politicizing Islam or transforming it into a political system. This resembles a modern version of Khawarij, whereas Islam as a religion is based on enlightening the mind and brightening the heart. Thus faith and worship come first. The fruit of faith and worship is morality.[223]

## Freedom of Thought

Q: You've faced a lot of hardship because of your beliefs. In Turkey, the freedom of expressing one's ideas has not been secured. The eighth article of the Law for Struggle with Terror hasn't been abrogated. What do you think about this issue?

A: Efforts to suppress ideas via pressure or brute force have never been truly successful. History shows that no idea was ever removed by suppressing it. Many great empires and states were destroyed, but an idea or thought whose essence is sound continues to survive.[224]

---

[223] Turgut, "Nurculuk."

[224] Çalislar, "Fethullah Gülen'le Röportaj."

## Secularism

Turkey is a secular state. A state can be secular, but some people say that an individual cannot be secular. In other words, a state is secular because secularism is a legal issue. Unfortunately, for a long time we have perceived secularism as worldliness, as removing religion from society.

Perhaps jurists should consider this subject and develop new definitions, and thus enlighten us. Some people openly say they are Kemalists; others say they are Republicans. Maybe there are others who, although identifying with democracy, say: "Democracy does not fulfil all of my needs. It should be more comprehensive as to encompass all my needs as a human being composed of a body, spirit, and mind."[225]

## Excerpts from the Media

### *Differences Should Not Lead to Separation*

By Professor Dr. Ali Yasar Saribay

Dr Saribay: Fethullah Gülen clearly shows that Islam can have different interpretations. In the coming days, there will be a settling of accounts between populist and radical Islam. I believe that the first group's victory will enable democracy to develop more evenly.

Q: Is the RP using politics as a tool?

Dr Saribay: In a sense, yes. Politics in Turkey is based on protective relationships. Not only religion is misused; Atatürk and the very concept of democracy also are misued. Thus even if it's not their intention, the RP is exploiting religion.

### Becoming a Fashion-Plate

In my opinion, the RP is close to both modernism and postmodernism. Even if it's a common example, Erbakan's wedding was striking. Does Islamic tradition feature a wedding held at a five-star hotel, an Islamic-but-modern bridal dress, and the exchange of

---

[225] Turgut, "Nurculuk."

Rolex watches? This is congruent with becoming modern and natural. There's nothing to reproach here.

Looking from the perspective of post-modernism, in a culture
that gives priority to image, Muslims are not above this. The Islamic
headscarf (*hijab*) fashion, which they themselves call becoming
"Vakkoish," is a typical example.[226] Another indication of the RP's
post-modernism is that everything can easily turn into something
else. A model displaying transparent clothing suddenly starts wearing *hijab*. Her writing a book on Islam 3 days later is accepted quite
naturally.

Q: Is the division between the RP and Fethullah Gülen's movement apparent or real?

Dr Saribay: In my opinion, there are serious differences. The
RP is a political organization; Gülen's movement is a civil organization. Gülen wants Islamic values to become generally accepted,
not to politicize them. If the movement wanted to use Islam for
political purposes, it could swallow the RP.

### The Fethullah Gülen Movement

By developing an interpretation of Islam that is compatible with
human rights and democracy, the Fethullah Gülen movement contributes to the stabilization of Turkey's democracy. Turkey has not
reached this point yet. Thus, if we are going to develop democracy,
where is Islam's place? Islam has represented itself in both the cultural and political arenas—and it should. But a concept of living
side-by-side has been developed in and for democracy over the last
10 years. We're living side-by-side, not together. Living together
means seeing others' existence as legitimate as my own.

Q: Isn't the frequently used term *religious nationalism* one of
the special characteristics of Gülen's movement?

Dr Saribay: Fethullah Hodja stresses that religion, not nationalism, is unifying. According to this approach, if we have a glorious
past, this is mainly due to religion. Secular nationalism, based on an

---

[226] Vakko is an Istanbul fashion store that appeals to the Turkish elite.

ethnic foundation, is divisive. Religious nationalism can play a unifying role, especially in a religiously homogeneous society. However, religion can't be unifying if it is absolutist. As far as I can see, Fethullah Hodja is bringing an interpretation that is not absolutist. This provides conditions for living together.[227]

## A Musical Composition, Not an Analysis

### By Professor Dr. Nur Vergin

(Professor Dr. Nur Vergin is associated with Istanbul University, Faculty of Political Science, Istanbul, Turkey. A political analyst, her main interest is the relationship between state and religion. She also studies the sociological aspects of women in politics.)

The poverty of ideas shaping Turkish political life; the shallowness of the world around us; the empty, hollow, sterile, short-sighted games being played in the name of political struggle and democratic competition; and the display of superficial politics here have both saddened and angered me for a long time. As a Turk I am sad; as a sociologist I am upset.

The roads to Turkey's ability to be governed and to taking its rightful place in history have been blocked (or cut), and its political philosophy and foresight have atrophied. There might be many reasons for this that are unknown to me. Perhaps the reasons for our lack of philosophy should be sought elsewhere. Maybe it is necessary to surmise that the misfortune befalling Turkish political thought comes from other sources. Obviously a trauma occurred and, as a sociologist, I should have diagnosed it.

I wonder if it is only an interesting coincidence that the three great figures of sociology—Karl Marx, Émile Durkheim,[228] and Max Weber—put religion in the center of their thought. The first concentrated on rejecting religion and its negativity as a social

---

[227] Interview by Nilgün Cerrahoglu, *Milliyet*, 8 October 1995.

[228] Émile Durkheim (1858–1917): French social scientist who developed a vigorous methodology combining empirical research with sociological theory. He is considered the founder of the French school of sociology.

factor; the other two dedicated themselves to explaining the impossibility of forming a society without religion.

My investigations led me to Carl Schmitt,[229] a good student of Weber's, and his *Siyasi Ilâhiyat* (Political Theology), translated from German, which I read only a few years later. Schmitt says that all concepts of modern state theory (e.g., sovereignty, obedience to and dependency on the state, allegiance to politics) are secularized religious concepts carried over from theology to state and political theory. His purpose is not to make the politics theocratic, but only to emphasize that subjects exclusive to politics and concepts used in politics have their roots in theology. According to him, an analogy between these two fields must be established if we are to achieve a correct and orderly political philosophy.

By pointing out the conceptual proximity between politics and religion, Schmitt both proves what a close follower of Weber's he was and also opens an enlightening window. In Turkey's case, this window opens on our society's political thought and lack of knowledge about it, in which I share. When I read his words, I understand that ignorance of religion, an ignorance that either is not known or is willfully ignored by academic circles, results naturally in the existing political class' inability to have a flourishing political life on the intellectual plane. Moreover, these circumstances prevent the development of a philosophical perspective related to politics or the conception of a new political model or models.

The worst part of this is that in a society where religious scholars have become this blind and where religious knowledge is so absent, political thought, which is trying to crawl in society, becomes a game with blindfolded players. Forget about the present political structure being strengthened; it cannot even be protected. Turkey's political uncertainty, vague ideas, and current instability prove this.

---

[229] Carl Schmitt (1888-1985): An influential German law professor largely unknown in the English-speaking world. His name is associated with Nazism. His Weimar writings confront the role of modern technology as it finds expression through the principles and practices of liberalism.

Once again the "deep" Turkey comes to help—this time in the light of day in a concrete and vivid form. In Turkey, where it appears that a wall has been built to obstruct the horizons, we have set out on a "tour of the horizons" with a man who is obviously and undeniably a product of love and belief, who has been conceived in Turkey's bosom, protected in its political genius, and raised jealousy.

The interview in *Zaman* that I have been reading for the past 3 days, "A Tour of the Horizons with Fethullah Gülen," appears to us as a sign that the above-mentioned depressive dead-end period is ending and that Turkey's historical and natural style of political thought is producing new shoots. Turkey is learning about today and the future from the analysis of a hodja longing for religion. Hodjaefendi's analysis of our social structure, religious consciousness, and position in the international community are things that maybe we never knew or heard explained in such a simple, profound, and intense way. But they are things we always wanted to hear.

The composition that Turkey has longingly and patiently waited to see has appeared. The analytical ties between faith and the politics it will follow have been established. Turkey has begun to find answers to the questions of who it is, what its direction is, and how it should be.[230]

### Religion and Politics

By Sahin Alpay

(Sahin Alpay was a columnist for *Milliyet* and a visiting professor at Princeton University.)

An enlightened generation of youth, of which I was one, found it hard to understand religion's place in the lives of individuals and societies. Some, myself included, thought that Marxism was the key to Heaven on Earth, that "Religion is the opiate of the people" explained everything. Everything was determined by the "substruc-

---

[230] At the end of Ufuk Turu ("A Tour of the Horizon"—Eyüp Can's interview with Fethullah Gülen), Istanbul, 1996.

ture," namely, production and ownership; the rest was superfluous. Later we began to understand that this was not a real ideology and that we have more needs than just eating, drinking, and reproducing. We began to realize that meaning and needs related to the cultural world were at least as important, and that religion was a cultural code that held societies together.

When our eyes opened a little more, we began to understand that there was a *structure* called *culture,* and that society could not be understood without understanding religion. Great social scientists like the late Sabri Ülgener, whom I mention with deep respect, and Serif Mardin were instrumental in waking us up to the world of meaning and culture. Mardin's works especially helped us see the cultural vacuum caused by a one-party administration.

Meanwhile, we discovered that we couldn't analyze Turkey's politics without considering developing religious communities and *tariqas* that officially do not exist, but which in reality maintain their liveliness. We understood that in Turkey, where modern institutionalization and organization remain behind, that religious brotherhood and solidarity, basic forms of social organization, continue.

Religion is one of the most important elements in our worlds of meaning and culture. Attempting to abolish it is a futile and will boomerang, as many experiments have shown. Religion is not the people's opiate, but it might just be society's mortar.[231]

### Respect for Hodjaefendi

By Sahin Alpay

Even today, the views of many intellectuals on religion, especially Islam, carry the stamp of the late-nineteenth century's Young Turks movement. This movement later turned into the Society of Union and Progress. Some of its leaders, among them Ahmet Riza and Abdullah Cevdet,[232] held religion (in general) and Islam (in par-

---

[231] *Milliyet*, 18 February 1995.

[232] Dr. Abdullah Cevdet (1869-1932): Turkish journalist and co-founder of the Young Turkish movement.

ticular) responsible for the Ottoman Empire's decline. Young Turk leaders defended the Ottoman elite's adoption of Positivism, developed by Auguste Comte (d. 1857) and his followers in France, which put "science in the place of religion" so that the state could modernize. According to them, modernization and Westernization could succeed only by educating people with "true Islam," which meant presenting these concepts as Islamic.

There is a very enlightening study on the Young Turks' view of religion by Sükrü Hanioglu, a professor at Princeton University: *The Young Turks in Opposition: 1889-1902* (Oxford University Press, 1995). It is extremely important and interesting.

The Young Turks' worldview affected the views of both the Society of Union and Progress and the Kemalists. As his book emphasizes, the Young Turks developed the official ideology of the Republic of Turkey. Such a view makes it impossible to differentiate among the variety and forms that Islam has assumed in Turkey, to understand and solve problems, and for religion and politics to find their rightful places. With the help of the freedom and democracy that we have, and the insistence of the people, we are overcoming these shallow perceptions slowly but surely.

In this respect, we cannot ignore the contribution and benefits of Fethullah Gülen Hodjaefendi's recent initiatives. Hodjaefendi is a different "Young Turk," one trying to reconcile Islam with modernism and science.

As far as I can see, Hodjaefendi opposes the use of Islam as a political ideology and a party philosophy, as well as polarizing society into believers and nonbelievers. He calls for those who believe and think differently to respect and tolerate each other, and supports peace and reconciliation. In my opinion, Hodjaefendi's efforts will help us put religion in its rightful place.

According to some secularists, this situation is worrisome. They make several claims: Hodjaefendi is "pretending," that is, he is trying to establish an Islamic state and is lying for the sake of his cause, or he is working secretly. According to some Islamists, there is no need for concern, for there is a division of labor between Necmettin Hodja and Hodjaefendi. They are walking toward the same goal: Necmettin Hodja on the path of politics and Hodjaefendi on that of education. According to conspiracy theory believers, Hodjaefendi is, of course, "working for the state..."

I perceive Hodjaefendi as a man of religion who separates religion from politics, opposes a culture of enmity that can polarize the nation, and contributes to our understanding of Islam with his tolerance. His efforts should be respected.[233]

## Fethullah Gülen's Dinner Table

### By Sahin Alpay

Fethullah Gülen Hodja is respected by a broad Islamic community. He opposes the recent trend of using Islam as a political ideology and dividing society into believers and nonbelievers. Rather, he states that people with different thoughts, beliefs, and lifestyles should be respectful, tolerant, and forbearing toward each other. He is trying to explain to society, through his words and deeds, that differences and problems are solved only through discussion, debate, and dialogue, not through fighting and violence.

Because he has opposed the political use of religion and has contributed to badly needed internal peace in a way becoming to a man of religion, I and many others respect him. His interpretation of Islam is compatible with free democracy. The world should be made aware of this effort.

I visited his community's schools in Uzbekistan and Turkmenistan. With their emphasis on scientific education, these schools are perhaps our most important tie with Central Asia. I participated twice, at the Hodja's invitation, in the large groups attended by fellow journalists. The second was the dinner given on the evening of November 8. It opened with the subject of tolerance and dialogue, which the Hodja frequently emphasizes. In relation to this, I pointed out how the intolerance shown to Deniz Gezmis (a militant left-

---

[233] *Milliyet*, 29 July 1995.

ist political activist) caused a great deal of pain in our society. I said I believed that if Gezmis were alive today, he would share our opinion that different ideas and beliefs must be respected.[234]

## Fethullah Hodja and Politics

By Ali Bayramoglu

The most important special characteristic, as opposed to political Islamic movements declaring war on local Islamic traditions, is that Fethullah Hodja's followers defend these traditions. They interpret Islam based on them and challenge political Islam—perhaps even the spirit of the times. As derivatives of this, his followers accept difference instead of rejecting it, thereby gaining new vitality for Anatolian traditions through civil associations and foundations, and interpret Islam in a way that suits current traditions.[235]

## Followers of Fethullah Gülen

By Ali Bayramoglu

The aspect that first strikes one regarding the followers of Fethullah Hodja is that their basic understanding differs in important respects from political Islamic movements. In fact, there is a serious conflict between them.

Political Islam is essentially a puritanical movement that includes criticisms ranging from Qur'anic interpretation to those directed against the regime, from nationalist factors to daily symbols. This understanding rejects cultural continuity and is closed to every kind of reconciliation. Expressing a fragmented ideology, it is reminiscent of the official ideology. Such an understanding is very effective in Arab countries, and in both globalist and "imported" versions of Islam.

The essential struggle in the Islamic segment of society derives from this traditional point. The peculiarity of the Fethullah move-

---

[234] Ibid., 21 November 1996.

[235] *Yeni Yüzyil*, 13 July 1995.

ment, in contrast to the understanding of political Islam, is that it protects cultural continuity within a religious understanding, and calls for reconciliation by emphasizing such factors as the nation, state, and Islamic traditions.[236]

## Fethullah Hodja and His Community

By Ali Bayramoglu

From the perspective of Islamic movements, the followers of Fethullah Hodja are challenging the spirit of the times. From Algeria and Egypt to Iran and Turkey, the common point of political Islamic movements is declaring war on both Western modernism and local Islamic traditions. Fethullah Hodja's followers oppose this trend. Even more important, they defend these traditions, interpret Islam through them, and oppose political Islam with at least as much power, numbers, and legitimacy as those who follow the other path.

Since they do not resemble Western civil organizations, such social enterprises as educational and social services that are unique to Anatolia are not recognized. However, his followers have gained new life for their activities via traditional foundations, which help legitimize them and represent an important method of linking society's past and culture. It is also an important indication of the culture's requests for unity and modernity.

This breath is legitimizing from a religious perspective. This is equally true for the devout and for those concerned with the importance of interpretation in Islam, its relationship to modern dynamics, and the existence of different interpretations. Thus it presents Islam's pluralistic character. Within this framework, Fethullah Hodja and others who accept the existence of different Islamic and non-Islamic social segments as natural are the only vehicles for adapting Islam to the age, for strengthening Islam once it has been adapted, and for reform based on analogy and interpretation.[237]

---

[236] Ibid., 8 July 1995.

[237] Ibid., 26 August 1995.

## *An Analysis of Ecevit's View on Gülen*

By Tankut Tarcan

In Turkey's shortsighted way of thinking, important events, people, and movements do not receive the scientific analysis they deserve. As a result, and most unfortunately, they are sacrificed to patterns created by ideologies or other interests. For example, we still have produced no serious analysis of Marxism and its philosophical, sociological, and economic facets. Orhan Hançerlioglu, in the absence of any scientific evidence, claims in his *Felsefe Sözlügü* (Dictionary of Philosophy) that dialectical materialism is the only scientific philosophical movement. His claim, again with no supporting scientific proof, that dialectical materialism is scientific and realistic is inconsistent and prejudiced.

Those who opposed communism without critically examining its ideological and philosophical basis behaved in the same way. It can be said that opposing communism based on such popular emotions as the right to private property and the family's sacredness was a banal approach that made it more attractive. Although the Marxist worldview contains very important contradictions on such basic subjects as its epistemology and view of history and events, unfortunately our intellectuals have yet to analyze this point seriously.

Now Turkey is witnessing a drama that appears unimprovable for some: the view of Fethullah Gülen. Beginning with some theses put forth in the name of analyzing Ecevit's views on Gülen, I will analyze this movement briefly from the perspectives of Islam (which it takes as its base), Turkey's sociopolitical and ideological foundations, and its tomorrow.

### An Analysis of a Perspective
According to a *Cumhuriyet* (a left-wing daily newspaper) columnist, Ecevit's view of Gülen is based on these headlines:

• 	Gülen does not represent a Sufi order. He evaluates his group more as a civil organization.

- Gülen does not oppose Atatürk's principles and secularism, as claimed. Rather, his movement prevents the spread of reactionaryism and stops the tendency toward Sufi orders.

- Gülen and his community are serving Turkey with their schools. In particular, their schools in the Central Asian republics have decreased Iran's influence there.

Since the columnist, while criticizing these lead sentences, uses the same arguments as the militant so-called secularists use against the Gülen movement, I will deal with these arguments:

### The Title *Hodjaefendi*

"Let's put everything else aside. Is there such a title as *Hodjaefendi* in Turkey? Representatives of his community use this title for Gülen. Those around him approach him with an air of servanthood. Moreover, those close to Gülen don't deny their connections with the *tariqa*." These lines comprise the most important argument in criticizing Ecevit's views of Gülen. Now let's see to what degree such an argument is true:

One does not need to ask if *hodjaefendi* is or is not an institutionalized Turkish tradition. In Iran, *hujjat al-Islam* and *ayatollah* (a religious leader among Shi'a Muslims; used as a title of respect especially for one who is not an imam) are institutionalized. In Christianity the papacy is an institution; and in the Ottoman State the office of *shaykh al-Islam* was institutionalized. In the literature of the Iranian *madrasa* hierarchy, *hujjat al-Islam* and *ayatollah* are titles like *professor* and *doctor* in modern universities.

Thus, *hujjat al-Islam* is an institutionalized office. Calling Imam Ghazali *hujjat al-Islam* doesn't signify an office, for this title, which means "one proving the truth of Islam" or "the proof of Islam," is not used as a scientific hierarchical name. It was deemed suitable as a title of honor by the people and other scholars because of his knowledge, virtue, and humanity.

In the same way, *hodjaefendi* does not designate a scientific or religious hierarchy. Just as Turks use *brother, sister, aunt,* and *uncle* with others even though there is no biological tie, *hodja* or, more respectfully, *hodjaefendi*, is a form of address or reference used by our people for those whose religious knowledge they respect. It has no institutionalized aspect.

Among students, *ögretmenim* (my teacher) has not been common in Turkey; instead, they use the more easily pronounced *hodja*. Similarly, all sportsmen, including soccer, basketball, and volleyball players, use *hodja* for their technical director, trainer, or even referee. Even though it is contrary to Kemalist reform laws and therefore the constitution, we use *pasha* instead of general, and none of our secular, Kemalist generals object.

### Gülen, Secularism, and Kemalism[238]

Like *reactionaryism* and *secularism*, *Kemalism* brings no ready definition to mind. If we use these terms only to slander people or institutions we do not approve of, with nothing in the name positive values, people will see secularism and Kemalism as purely negative systems. Do we have a common view on nationalism, populism, and reformism based on Atatürk's six principles? Can we defend étatism today? Are we blind to the fact that étatism equals economic backwardness? Why? Because conditions have given precedence to free enterprise. Thus, equating Kemalism with étatism means seeing it as economic backwardness.

If Kemalists are sincere in their ideology, they should define it as behaving in a way required by this age and today's condition, for not doing makes it a means of fanaticism, bigotry, and conservatism. Loyalty should be to goals, not to stereotypes. On this point, no one can accuse Gülen of being unaware of the requirements of the age. Nor can he can be blamed for antisecularism. Everybody knows what he said about Atatürk. Accusing one of "making pretense" assumes that what is in his or her heart is known. Those who see being scientific as superior to everything would find this assumption laughable.

---

[238] Kemalism: The ideology based on Mustafa Kemal Atatürk's six fundamental principles: republicanism (creating the republic), nationalism, populism, étatism, secularism, and revolution. The bases of his policies were enshrined in the Republican People's Party' program of 1931, which was written into the Turkish constitution in 1937.

## Gülen and Reactionaryism

To accuse a movement of being reactionary, we must understand what is meant by *reactionaryism*. Do we mean Islam? The author assumes that all religious training rests on reactionaryism. There can be no more splendid example of reductionism and simplification! What if that education is opposed to reactionaryism, both in its understanding and as a natural necessity of belief?

For example, today Islam is said to be a religion of terror and to encourage terror. However, the Qur'an reserves the heaviest punishments for those who engage in terror and anarchy. It is not Islam's fault if some Muslims are terrorists. Similarly, due to misunderstanding or sociopolitical conditions in some countries, Islam is perceived by the majority as a political ideology. Some have even attempted to use it in that way.

But should those who perceive Islam in exactly the opposite way, as a system for raising virtuous individuals, be placed in this category? To a certain extent they have united Islam, long criticized for being opposed to science, with science that, when stripped of religious spiritual and moral principles, brings as much harm as good to humanity. They have opened schools to prove this, and even used religious feeling to serve science. This has been developed into a thesis.

In the name of our country, I have difficulty comprehending why some are offended by this. Who can object to raising youth who use science and the technology it gave birth to for the good of humanity, scientists respectful of moral principles, administrators who serve people sincerely, and officials and managers who do not steal and abuse their position but rather understand administration to mean serving the people?

## A New Phase

It was wrong to show Fethullah Hodja as an instrument of a state conspiracy, because his interpretations that brought him into opposition with the RP were not produced after the RP danger.

"Everyone will be accepted as they are, and no one will condescend to another because of their religion or lack of religion. No one will be looked down upon because of their way of dressing." Of course the words I quote from Fethullah Gülen create hope and excitement. For a long time people have wanted an organization of social reaction against the RP, which has used religion as a sword and shield for its political work. Trying to claim a monopoly on Islam, the RP has opened the most dangerous kind of division.

The discussion begun by Fethullah Hodja can lead to a much sounder deterrence against religious fundamentalism than that which the state has produced. The door he opened can be a stage on the road to having the chance to live Islam within our own national identity.

The great support he received to save religion from the RP monopoly can cause other parties to take action. We have misunderstood secularism for years. We thought it meant that politics should not show any interest in religion, and so left religion defenseless. This great power, which comprises the foundation of culture, became the plaything of exploiters.

To open the people's way and secure peace and tolerance, religion must be protected by contemporary thinkers and institutions. If developments of the past few days have taught us about this need, how fortunate we are...[239]

## Gülen and Reconciliation

- "Politicizing religion would be more dangerous for religion than for the regime, for such people want to make politics a means for all their ends. Religion would grow dark within them, and they would say: 'We are the representatives of religion.'" This is a dangerous matter. Religion is the name of the relationship between humanity and God, which everyone can respect.

- "Some are harsh in their defense of secularism; others attack secularism and democracy unjustly. Secularism has not been in danger to date, and I don't believe that it will be endangered in the future either.

---

[239] Güngör Mengi, *Sabah,* 16 February 1995.

- "I didn't find the 8-year uninterrupted education system dangerous, as others did. The issue of whether it should be uninterrupted or not can be settled by consensus.

- "As Turkish society has not yet proven its maturity and fully digested democracy, a crisis is occurring. The republic and democracy comprise the foundation for the continuation of Islamic thought. It's a mistake to interpret them as being opposed to Islam.

- "In religion, 95 percent deals with belief; 5 percent deals with rules."

Gülen wants to bring secularists and antisecularists, who have been artificially separated on this issue, together on common ground. He says: "Secularism should not be an obstacle to religious devoutness, nor should devoutness constitute a danger to secularism." If I understand this correctly, this is Fethullah Hodja's aim.

The biggest difficulty being experienced in Turkey, or any Muslim society that wants to politicize Islam, is this: the "conflict between secularism and antisecularism."[240]

### *The Fethullah Gülen Difference*

Fethullah Gülen is an important name in religious circles... Every message he gives is based on tolerance. However, some lump him and his community with political Islamists and try to show him as a reactionary. But he opposes the politicization of Islam and reactionaryism. We should not mix the chaff with the wheat. If we mix him and his community with reactionary groups, we will have been disrespectful to this social segment and have missed the target.

Religion will be damaged greatly by politicization. Despite this, some circles are trying to force its use as political material for state administration. In such a period, Fethullah Hodja is performing a very important duty. Both our Right and Left wings should be aware of this. We should not turn to easy accusations like: "Sir, he's just pretending." It is very clear that Fethullah Hodja is not pretending.[241]

---

[240] Süleyman Yagiz, *Takvim*, 18 April 1997.

[241] Ibid., 3 April 1997.

### *Gülen and Reconciliation*

Gülen stresses religion together with adorning contemporary knowledge or a kind of enlightenment. He indicates that religion never became as great a show as it has today, and urges Muslims to avoid display. Emphasizing that this approach damages the chance for reconciliation in Turkey, he states:

> Politicizing religion is dangerous, but it's more dangerous for religion than for the regime. Actually, it darkens religion's spirit, for religion belongs to everyone. Those who make a claim for religion with political considerations want to make everything an instrument of their politics, political considerations, and political goals. Famous people should be more careful. What they represent in the name of religious feeling and religious thought should not be injured because of their behavior, which can be misunderstood.

My liking Fethullah Hodja and seeing him to an extent as an example derives from his being a sincere man of the heart. Some leave the human heart outside... This means they leave something else outside... Let's understand one another.[242]

## Attitude toward State and Power

### *The Pro-State Attitude*

Q: For the sake of the state, you supported Çiller.[243] You have said to those around you: "When someone in power is unsuccessful they shouldn't be pulled down, as Demirel[244] did to Özal.[245] Demirel

---

[242] Riza Zelyut, *Aksam*, 19 April 1997.

[243] Tansu Çiller (1946- ): On June 25, 1993, she became Turkey's first woman prime minister and the first woman without a family political connection to head an Islamic country. Çiller has served several terms as prime minister.

[244] Süleyman Demirel (1924- ): Politician and civil engineer who has served as prime minister of Turkey seven times, and as president (1993-2000). He pursued a policy of economic growth, despite civil violence and terrorism from extremist factions, inflation, and a trade deficit.

[245] Turgut Özal (1927-1993): Turkish politician, prime minister (1983-89) and president (1989-93). As prime minister, he continued his free-market, Western-oriented economic policies.

shouldn't be pulled down either." Doesn't this approach put you in the position of naturally supporting every governing party?

A: We don't support those in power in any case. The constitution explains how one or a party comes to power and goes. If you don't like their performance, you can use democratic ways. I should remind you that our Prophet said: "You are ruled how you are (according to your belief, worldview, and lifestyle.)" If people want a good government, first they should improve themselves intellectually, morally, and spiritually. Opposing or being displeased with the government should not mean criticizing it bitterly and thereby producing pessimists and an anarchic atmosphere. Nor should it allow opposition to the state and degrading it in the people's view.

Q: OK, you are opposed to using the governing party's mistakes against the government and state as institutions. But doesn't refraining from struggling against these mistakes eventually lead the state to a dead end?

A: Propaganda that is too negative will sabotage the state. The state means authority. It is the final point where a community's diverse trends are united. Therefore it is important; without it anarchy arises. If there is no trust in the state, different conflicts can occur. Islam does not allow anarchy and terror. If there were some anarchic and terrorist activities in the history of Islam, they either took place via foreign powers, hypocrites within the community, or heterodox deviationists. The Sunni majority always refrained from such things.

From this perspective, I'm opposed to both provocative and anarchic movements and activities. From now on I'm going to try and be the same. I was giving sermons at mosques. Some even wanted to bring disorder to the mosque's courtyard, and shouted slogans there. I stopped giving sermons. I haven't given them for 3 years now.[246]

---

[246] Akman, "Fethullah Hoca Anlatiyor."

## Truth–Power and Authority—Justice Relationships

Q: How do you evaluate the relationship between power and justice?

A: According to our criteria, right is might, not the other way around. Arrogant power opposed to common sense and perfected reasoning is rebellious. Those who gain such power try to solve problems by force instead of by intelligence, reason, discernment, dialogue, suitability, or other human values. For this reason, those human values are ignored. For the last century we have been living through such a period.[247]

## Obedience

Q: I guess what you mean by obedience is not obedience to oppression...

A: Absolutely not. The obedience commanded by Islam is not obedience to despotism. Surrender to or bowing before despotism is out of the question. Islamic obedience means accepting and following legal authority, Parliament, a leader, or an administrator. It is conforming to law and order. This is a duty. The duty of rulers is to refrain from abusing their position, rank, and esteem against the people in a despotic way. This relationship should continue in mutual harmony.[248]

Q: In one of your speeches, you drew an unusual picture of the state by beginning with Socrates' philosophy of the state. When you consider all these historical views, what is your own approach?

A: If we approach any issue from the perspective of absolute beauty, we will be critical and suspicious of every system. Regarding such criticizers, Bediüzzaman says: "God forbid, if they live a thousand years they won't find a state that will make them happy," because they're not happy with any administration. Today there are

---

[247] Eyüp Can, "Fethullah Gülen Ile Ufuk Turu," Zaman, August 1995.

[248] Ibid.

just such people at different extremes. They represent this type of understanding perfectly. No one can make them happy. If our Prophet were to appear and they only knew him by what he said, they would criticize him too. If he presented the eternal Qur'anic laws and they didn't know it was the Qur'an, they would criticize it too. If they don't criticize it now, it's because they have faith in it, even though it's superficial.

Q: In this framework, what value do you ascribe to the state?

A: If we approach this issue from a viewpoint of relative beauty and everything from a relative perspective, the state has an essential value. The existence of the state, a system based on certain laws, of course has a value. Although the constitution and laws have some importance of their own in a good or bad administration, the real factor always lies in the administrators themselves. All problems in human life begin and end with human beings. Thus if the state is run by good people, it will be good. If it is administered by even better people, it will be even better. If it is administered by the Rightly Guided Caliphs, it will be perfect. But if now there are no such caliphs and the state is being run by the current administrators, it's better to approach the matter from the viewpoint that it's better to have this state than none at all.

Q: Some claim that you have sanctified the state...

A: If this approach means sanctifying the state, this is my approach. I see the absence of state as anarchy. I see conflict between the army, the governmental board, and the security forces as perilous with respect to our honor, security, and dignity—in short, to our very existence. Law is implemented by authority. If there is no authority, this will be no more than a written document. We should not confound the state, government, Parliament, and even politics as vital institutions for the community's life with those in power. So our criticism of those in power, the governmental board, should not be directed against the institutions they represent.

There is another point here: If criticism is made in the name of destroying without the intention of improving and showing what is better, it is 100 percent harmful. It causes anarchy, pessimism, lack of trust in the state, and finally chaos. If some call this opinion sanctifying the state, they are unaware of the essence of the issue.

Of course, at the head of state I would prefer someone like Abu Bakr (the Prophet's first political successor), who is moral, virtuous, and evolved; whose purpose is to ensure the nation's continuation and life; who thinks not of his own interests but only of the nation's welfare. If this is not possible, there is the religious legal opinion: "Something that cannot be achieved fully should not be abandoned completely." I can't reconcile with any logic the idea that: "If it isn't perfect, we shouldn't accept the imperfect. Let them go to Hell."[249]

## The Frenzy of Power for the Sake of Power

Those who have the power and technological means to satisfy their greed, hate, and vengeance can bring about as much destruction in one day as would have taken a century in the past. They can demolish the most formidable-seeming systems at one go and exchange them for others. They can ruin the most established ideas, place restrictions on long-held beliefs and, supported by the mass media, represent right as wrong and vice versa.

In no period of human history have such moral values as personal honor, religion, family life, and decency been mocked and condemned as relentlessly as they are now. In consequence, we live in an epoch of confusion and chaos. Light and darkness, purity and pollution, virtue and vice, and hope and despair exist side by side or one within the other. In no previous period of history have collapse and reform happened on such a scale or at such speed. Those who opposed this flood of chaos cannot find the opportunity to express or present their alternative standpoints.

Among this age's most visible characteristics are that right is consistently sacrificed for the sake of might, selfish interests replace all other considerations, racial discrimination has a pre-eminent role in determining social attitudes and relations, and force is resorted to

---

[249] Ibid.

as the sole means to resolve national and international conflicts. Power must have its due place in the scheme of things, but if it is considered the single or most effective means of solving problems, why are we endowed with such faculties as reason and compassion? All past social revolutions and military movements that were not based on belief, knowledge, moral values, and sound reasoning failed to endure much beyond their leaders' lifetimes.

Power used in the cause of right and sound reasoning may do some good on the way to resolving problems. However, power always has been a means of destruction when driven by ambition and greed, coarse feelings and ideas. The madness of disposing and increasing power drove Alexander to military ventures in Asia, brought Napoleon's genius to ruin, and made Hitler the most accursed person ever. Despite these lessons, right and intelligence remain under the dominion of power.

Behind the chaotic whirl of damnable ideas and events lies the abuse of power and the over-rating of its usefulness. As a result, human values, reasonableness, and respect for right have been replaced by the resort to force. It seems that chaos will continue until those few having great power submit to the cause of right. Only then will the majority, freed from chaos and confusion, clearly see the world and its events. If they are to survive in a world where only the strong have the right to live, oppressed peoples must free themselves and bring that power under the dominion of right.

While learning lessons from history, we should know how to prepare a desirable future for ourselves. If we are to have hope in the future and not sink deeper into a darker whirl of new, greater confusion, we need altruistic souls who live for others and prefer others' happiness to their own. Only those willing and able to sacrifice themselves for humanity's well-being can save us from today's chaos and confusion.

When light-diffusing ideas, united with love and altruism, are shared by the majority of humanity, the global "storms" now blowing, along with the resulting pain and suffering, will end. When the ideas of heroes of love and altruism, combined with just discipline and balanced freedom, are a determining factor in the global balance, worldwide social crises and massive problems arising from international conflicts will be solved, and the balance between joy and sorrow, happiness and misfortune, will be re-established.

Humanity expect from us—the believers—great efforts to help realize world peace and harmony. Every effort to attain this goal, every movement to support right and truth, is a most blessed step taken toward God. Every such step, regardless of size, plays a part in the new, expected global reform. Such steps may be thought of as drops fallen into our present from the future's blue ocean, where we will enjoy true happiness. We live now upon the dream of that blessed time to come.[250]

## Turkey's Domestic and Foreign Affairs

### His Meetings with Political Leaders

My efforts are for Right–Left and Alawi–Sunni brotherhood.

For years I served as a public official in the Turkish republic, and tried to perform my duties fully. My meeting with political leaders and government members, who hold in their hands the fate of this state and the administration of this nation—which I know to be a part of my own destiny—was regarded as bizarre by some. I have difficulty reconciling this with the attribute, position, and level of these circles.

Everyone knows that republic and democracy are defined, even in primary school books, as the self-rule of the people by their elected representatives. In a democracy, a system with a fully civil character, popular participation in the administration is encouraged to the extreme, as summed up in the saying that the nation owns unrestricted and unconditional sovereignty. I have never even thought of going into the street to demonstrate and openly criticize the system, although democracy permits this when necessary. In fact, as such behavior could lead to anarchy, I always approach it with caution. For this reason, not only as a right but as a responsible citizen, citi-

[250] Gülen, *Yeseren Düşünceler*, 155-58.

zens meeting with political and state leaders, or state leaders and politicians meeting with people from every social segment, should be appreciated and encouraged.

### No Nation without Religion

If such meetings are criticized because I am a retired religious official, remember that the Ministry of Religious Affairs, where I worked for years, is one of the state's most essential institutions. It operates fully within the legal framework of the Turkish republic.

Religion is a most vital factor in a nation's make-up. There has never been a nation without religion. Communism, which tried to eliminate religion through oppression, collapsed into ruins before it. Today, it is a sociological and historical phenomenon that humanity has turned toward religion.

Especially in recent years, Turkey has suffered terror and other activities planned abroad and implemented by those desiring secular–antisecular and Alawi–Sunni conflicts.

### Citizens Should Do What They Can

Everyone agrees that it is a national and historical duty for all citizens to do what they can to prevent activities opposed by all social segments and members of the nation. Of course, this includes everyone from the people to the administrators. In addition, for years some have portrayed Alawis and Sunnis as mutual strangers, and some, unfortunately, have identified the CHP (the Republican Peoples' Party) with atheism.

### Talk with Çetin, Head of the CHP[251]

Long considered impossible, the CHP–DYP (The True Path Party) coalition, which is between left and right wings, has been approved by most in the name of national and political unity. Given this, there is nothing strange about my initiatives in the name of national unity, which is longed for by all, for a warm dialogue among all social segments, for Sunni–Alawi and Right–Left brotherhood, and especially my recent visit to CHP's

---

[251] On Feb. 18, 1995 the Social Democratic Populist Party (SHP) and the Republican People's Party (CHP) merged under the latter's name. Çetin is its leader.

leader Hikmet Çetin. Thankfully, the majority of our media support such initiatives, regardless of their origin. Almost all state and political leaders and intellectuals have expressed their approval and appreciation.

How are we to understand the logic of those who oppose such efforts, who seem to represent a secularism hostile to Islam, Alawism as a completely different religion or system of beliefs, and the CHP as an atheist party?

It is a fact that some schools, incorrectly associated with my name, from the first day have been connected to the National Educational Ministry. No investigation into them has been conducted, even during the last 4 years when the CHP was a governmental coalition partner. The students from these schools have best represented our country worldwide successfully, and were even accepted by the President.

I consider it a duty to make these matters known once again through the media, and I take this opportunity to extend my respects and good wishes to everyone.[252]

## Relations with the Media and Politicians

Q: You were an introverted man of religion. Lately there have been indications that you intend to become more open. Why did you feel the need for this?

A: Actually, due to my profession I have always been close to the public, although perhaps not as much as a media member. Preachers are public people. I began preaching before I was 20 years old. I traveled around the Marmara and Aegean zones of Turkey. For a long time I was a traveling preacher. I was among the people. If being heard, seen, and known mean anything, I was heard, seen, and known. However, the media did not relate my ideas as they were found in my writings and sermons.[253]

---

[252] *Aksam*, 23 June 1995.

[253] Özkök, "Hoca Efendi Anlatiyor."

## Gülen and Politics

Q: Those looking at you from the outside get the impression that you're trying to set up a political organization. Were you ever involved in any political activities?

A: No, I was never involved in any political effort or activity.

Q: Do you vote?

A: Yes, I was able to vote one time. Sometimes I wasn't there for the registration, sometimes I was under surveillance.

Q: Are you opposed to voting for any particular party?

A: Just the opposite. I always said from the mosque pulpits: "Go and use your vote. This is a citizen's right and responsibility. Express your choice. Wherever you want to vote, do so it, but definitely vote." Turkey should get accustomed to it, and so should democracy be established. You'll hear this many times on my previous tape recordings.

Q: Do you have any political aspirations or expectations?

A: Absolutely not. I don't even have the desire to live after this. I have a different kind of understanding. I've met good people and made many friends. I desire either a solitary corner or the other world. But I see myself as a genuine member of this nation, as one of the threads in the lace of this culture. So as long as I live, if I have an opinion about an issue related to it, I won't hesitate to express it.

## Excerpts from the Media

### Ecevit and Fethullah Hodja

Last night I had a brief talk with Bülent Ecevit.[254] I asked about his meeting with Fethullah Gülen. He said that their talk had been very beneficial, and that it had centered on religious, scientific, and philosophical subjects rather than politics.

---

[254] Bülent Ecevit (1925- ): Turkish poet, journalist, and politician who has served as prime minister several times. He is the current prime minister of Turkey.

Quoting from his book, Ecevit pointed out to Gülen: "In your books you indicate that there is no room for doubt in religion and that belief takes precedence. However, for there to be progress in science, there is a constant need for doubt." Gülen shared the same observation. Ecevit also indicates that Gülen and his followers are very beneficial for the development of democracy.

Gülen has another important characteristic. With donations from people close to him, they are opening private schools at a fast pace, especially in the Central Asian Turkic republics. Today 186 high schools and their equivalents have been established there, and there are another 130 in Turkey. These schools provide a high level of science education. For example, a student from Izmir Yamanlar College has become the world physics champion. This success earned him a scholarship from NASA in America.

These schools do not operate like Qur'an courses, as some have claimed. I personally visited two of them in Turkey. They have very modern biology, physics, chemistry, and computer laboratories. Very serious education is being given. The students' dress is no different from that of students at Robert College. The schools in Central Asia are said to be similar. And, the best schools in these countries are those established by those near to Gülen.

This undertaking also made Ecevit very happy. Ecevit said: "I consulted my friends. These schools are very good. According to information I have received, they are increasing Turkey's influence in the Turkic republics at the expense of Iran and Saudi Arabia." We need tolerance and agreement in the world of belief, politics, and science. I consider Gülen's undertakings very successful steps toward agreement and unity in society.[255]

### Yes to Consultation, No to Fatwa

By Ertugrul Özkök

The meeting held in the Prime Minister's residence two weeks ago, on Thursday, didn't surprise me. I've known for a long time

---

[255] Meric Köyatasi, *Aksam*, 18 June 1995.

that Prime Minister Tansu Çiller has been in need of this kind of expansion in her relations. Fethullah Gülen first attracted my attention at the beginning of the 1990s at the time of the "Headscarf issue." I remember very clearly. At that time I had just come to the position of *Hürriyet*'s General Editor. Turkey was experiencing a clash regarding whether or not the headscarf would be free.

The atmosphere was extremely strained. As the General Editor of Turkey's most influential newspaper, I was asking myself the question of how this tension could be decreased.

### Mitigation of Anarchy
Just at that time I realized that a segment of the circles that advocated freedom for women to wear a headscarf had suddenly entered a period of silence. Those circles began to follow a milder policy because of the tension in society created by the headscarf issue. When I investigated the reason for this, I found this answer.

Fethullah Hodja had begun to take a stance to prevent the society from being drawn into domestic anarchy because of the headscarf issue. Later when I talked with these circles, they said that Fethullah Hodja's moderate policy had been very effective in the prevention of further tension.

Now 4 years have passed. I'm asking myself: "Would it be bad if people like Fethullah Gülen intervened in other issues that divide the society with messages of moderation?"[256]

### *It Is Better To Learn*

By Tamer Korkmaz

Taking Fethullah Gülen Hodjaefendi's name as a starting point and calling a segment of devout Muslims *Fethullahçilar* (followers of Fethullah) goes back to a 1986 edition of *Hürriyet*. During July 18–19, 1986, this newspaper published an edition full of extreme mistakes and slanders regarding Fethullah Gülen Hodjaefendi. In news full of lies from beginning to end, including his age, his ideas

---

[256] *Hürriyet,* 14 December 1994.

and marital status, *Fethullahçilar* was used for the first time. (Çetin Emeç, general editor of the newspaper at that time, was the writer of the first news that I mentioned.)

During the 1989 headscarf conflict, Çetin Emeç pointed out the warnings Hodjaefendi made in a sermon. Toward the end of November 1989, he praised Hodjaefendi in an article as "a foremost name in sermons on unity." In short, terms like *Fethullahçilar* and *Fethullahçilik* are names produced by *Hürriyet*'s imagination and don't actually exist. Regarding the Çiller–Fethullah Hodjaefendi meeting, political scientist Nur Vergin commented:

> If Turkey is democratic, those making politics in this country and especially those in the position of ruling the country of course are in a position to please the hearts of millions of citizens and ask their ideas.[257]

### Religion and Politics

By Yavuz Donat

*Tariqas* (Sufi mystical orders) are a reality of Turkey. They existed yesterday, they exist today and they'll exist tomorrow. Those involved in politics in the center–right know this reality, and while establishing internal party balances they don't neglect it. Seeing this as a *concession* is misleading. The word *reconciliation* is perhaps more appropriate.

After September 12, 1980, pressure was put on *tariqas*. Kemal Kaçar, leader of the Süleymanci community,[258] was arrested. Professor Muammer Aksoy acted as his lawyer.[259] Encountering a lot of criticism, Aksoy said: "Making politics while closing one's eyes to the *tarqias'* reality is misleading."

---

[257] *Zaman*, 17 December 1994.

[258] Süleymancilik (followers of Süleyman): A religious movement founded by Süleyman Hilmi Tunahan (1888-1959). His followers are well-known for teaching the Qur'an and their Islamic centers.

[259] Muammer Aksoy: A law professor who became famous during the May 27, 1960, coup and cooperated with the military. His assassin was never caught.

Turkey is a laic republic. However, if the big political parties don't take into consideration "certain balances" and don't hold the conservative masses within their organizations, then with certainty the "extremes" will gain strength.

Özal and Demirel acted politically with awareness of this reality. In the 1970s when the left's vote was climbing to 42%, Ecevit was careful not to fight with religion... There were parliamentarians with strong religious roots in his cadre (for example, Lütfü Dogan). Americans also know "this reality."

In the 1960s, members of the US-financed Peace Corps in Turkey, attempted to make a public survey in 462 villages.

Let's look at a few examples from the questionnaire form:

- Is there a mausoleum or entombed saint nearby that the people visit?
- How many influential sheiks are there in the village and neighboring villages?
- How closely tied to religion are the village people?
- Do young people under the age of 18 fast?
- Does the "aga" (local landlord), "kaymakam" (district official), "mukhtar" (local official) or teacher assist you in religious issues?
- How frequently are official sermons given in your village?
- Are there any non-Muslims in your village?
- How many males go to the mosque on a daily basis?
- Do helpful ideas come from the imam, the "aga" or another eminent person?
- Do women in your village go to the imam's wife or the teacher's wife for advice?

Our political parties aren't curious enough about the Turkish village and villagers to make the survey that the Americans made.[260]

## A Confused Duck Dives in Bottom First

By Oktay Eksi

A "Fethullah Hodja" crisis has arisen in the CHP recently. As is known, during the recent days of the Religious "Bayram"

---

[260] *Milliyet*, 14 December 1994.

(Festive Day) of Sacrifice a man of religion named Fethullah Gülen—perhaps there is a quite broad segment that respects him— visited the Deputy Prime Minister, CHP General Chairman Hikmet Çetin in his home. Gülen wished to make a call of congratulations for the Bayram. Çetin accepted and they talked.

### Did Fethullah Hodja Request Something from Çetin?

No, it's understood from what both sides said that not even the first letter of the word "politics" was pronounced. As a matter of fact, Fethullah Hodja's statement was published in yesterday's newspapers. With a soundly knit logic he said:

> My meeting with the political leaders and members of the administration, who hold in their hands the fate of this state and this nation—which I know to be a part of my own fate— was regarded as bizarre by some. I have to admit that I have difficulty reconciling this with the attribute, position and level of these circles.

The man says: I'm a citizen of this country and a retired official of this government. What's wrong with it? Moreover, the request to meet came from him. And, he was careful enough to choose a religious holiday for this visit, which provides an opportunity for everyone who wants to extend good wishes to another.

### What's Wrong with It?

Would those who criticized Hikmet Çetin have been able to refuse a request for a visit, not from Fethullah Gülen, but from someone who said, "I want to visit you," even if that person had been involved in events that were a disgrace to his society, his family, and humanity? If they refused, wouldn't they fall to a lower position than the other person?

Even if those who have ridiculed for years warnings about laicism now show this sensitivity in the name of laicism, let them know that they're knocking on the wrong door at the wrong place and at the wrong time.[261]

---

[261] *Hürriyet.*

### *Bülent Ecevit and Fethullah Gülen Draw Closer to Each Other*

By Ismet Solak

An important interview made by Eyüp Can with Fethullah Gülen began appearing last Sunday in *Zaman*. Prior to this, Gülen had answered Nuriye Akman's comprehensive questions in *Sabah*.

Those reading Akman's interview saw an interesting portrait of Gülen. One who thought that he was faced with a different person was Bülent Ecevit, DSP chairman. Ecevit stated several times previously that he had followed the interview in *Sabah* and at least found Gülen "interesting." Some time earlier he had talked with Gülen. According to information at hand, this meeting was a meeting between two intellectuals interested in poetry and intellectual issues rather than politics. Ecevit gave Gülen his poetry book and translations he made from the famous Indian poet Tagore.[262]

Ecevit, who had become personally interested in Gülen through Akman's interview and who had met with Gülen, read Eyüp Can's interview, which appeared in *Zaman* all last week, and this time felt close to Gülen in regard to his ideas.

Ecevit, who made a speech Friday evening in Istanbul's Dedeman Hotel at a meeting about foreign affairs held by the "Association for Solidarity in Business Life," made frequent references to this interview. He stated that he "wholeheartedly shared" some of Gülen's ideas. Actually, the feeling was mutual. While Gülen didn't mention any other politician's name in the interview, he mentioned Ecevit's name twice regarding two different issues.[263]

### What Did Gülen Say?

Fethullah Gülen, referred to respectfully as *Hodjaefendi* by his community and sometimes in a derogatory manner as *Hodja* by oth-

---

[262] Rabindranath Tagore (1861-1941): A Bengali poet, short-story writer, song composer, playwright, essayist, and painter awarded the Nobel Prize for Literature in 1913.

[263] *Hürriyet.*

ers, said essentially seven things in his interview that appeared last week in *Zaman*: There is no place for dogma in Islam. Islam is a progressive religion. Just as there are "fanatics" or dogmatists in Islam, there are "laic fanatics" in the laic segments of society (here he quotes from Ecevit). These two segments, which are not sufficiently broad-minded, could turn Turkey into a new Algeria.

Breaking relations with America would leave Turkey isolated. Due to a misunderstanding of Imam al-Ghazali's views, Islam was removed from positive sciences, and this hindered Islam's rise. Moving away from the positive sciences lowered the *madrasa's* academic standards, which then taught only religion and religious subjects. Western and laic public schools taught positive sciences but ignored religious education. Together with being controversial, *Turkish Islam* goes back to Ahmad Yasawi. We owe our current Muslim culture to the Central Asia.

His ideas and activities inside Turkey are also interesting. In Gülen's broad statement, which I have tried to summarize above, he clearly opposes the RP in a totally unexpected way. Speaking in abstract terms without giving names of people and institutions, still he expresses his opposition to the RP by giving its name. He also approves of the Customs Union.

In domestic Turkish policy, which was displaced by the events of September 12th, experienced a huge quake as a result of Özal's striking ideas and applications, and was severely shaken by the USSR's collapse, the dust is slowly settling. In this settling process, the ideas of the "most laic" Bülent Ecevit regarding laicism or Central Asia are very compatible with Fethullah Gülen.

## Turkey's Internal Affairs

### STV and KANAL D

**What Did Gülen Say about the Situation in Turkey?**
Turkey is in a time of tension. Perhaps it's necessary to dwell on why this is so. One influential factor is Turkish society's general structure. No one should get upset, but according to this our society has not yet found its right course.

In an age of enlightenment like that of today, Turkey has not produced that which is required by enlightenment or fully digested democracy. Politics is based more on self-interest. A great thinker of our time has said: "Politics revolving around interest is a monster." I think some people are making a monster out of politics and basing it on self-interest. Turkish society needs reconciliation and agreement. If the powers and those representing power in Turkey would act democratically, we could overcome these troubles. If emotions replace logical judgments and embraced by the media, government officials, or political leaders, many mistakes can be made. Every social segment must be very balanced.

It's dangerous to politicize religion, but even more dangerous for religion than for the regime, because religion belongs to all. Everyone must be able to respect religion and find worldly peace with it, and the heart must be able to attain tranquillity within it. Religion connects God and humanity.

At this moment in Turkey, there is a very serious discussion about whether or not secularism is in danger. If reconciliation is being sought between Islam and secularism, then according to some views of Islam, in fact according to some Qur'anic verses like *Your religion for you, mine for me,* there's no big problem. If secularism is understood as not basing the state on religion, not interfering in religion or in the believers' religious life, and acting in an unbiased way, there's no problem at all. I don't think secularism is in danger now or that it will be in the future.

## Toward Tomorrow's Turkey

Q: Do you see any parallels between your coming into view and Turkey's flight from the "cocoon" it has woven around itself?

A: If the people and government are not ready to step forward, if circumstances are not favorable, you cannot do anything worthwhile. You might encounter some government members who oppose what you've done because of your ideas. But in general, Turkey's internal and foreign policies have begun to change. You can't see your own government as an enemy. This would be a big mistake, for compatibility between the state and the people is a very important factor, especially at this time.

Q: Can it be said that a new image is appearing?

A: I think that developments observed in the political arena and among the people as a whole are a source of hope. What I have seen in my contacts shows that our society sees the new trend as the expression of a collective conscience and collective sentiment, common thoughts and feelings. Until now there has been a different Islamic image. There are efforts to perpetuate and manipulate this image for their own interests. I see that this image is gradually changing, that rulers and people are open to change and renewal.

Q: Where does this mistaken assumption come from?

A: It might be intentional or due to ignorance. Change needs time. Some individuals might act roughly in the name of Islam, but that's still an individual action. People's makeup and way of thinking affects this, but Islam absolutely doesn't allow it. Islam came to give peace and happiness.

Now Islam has the image that if someone doesn't think just like you, he or she can lose his or her head. Everyone must think and live like you. So far, this has been the attitude of the West toward the Islamic world. And this is like a hump on our back. Muslims in Algeria and Sudan have been on trial for terrorism because of this view. A very bad image has been raised. I think that our nation, which has interpreted Islam for 9 centuries in line with the perfect, flexible, broad understanding of love and tolerance in the Qur'an and the Sunna, will remove that hump from Islam's back via its broad vision, consideration, and tolerance.

## Transformation from Paradigm to Enigma

Q: When the paradigm becomes an enigma, does it lead to a common dogmatism?

A: Yes, I think they produce new dogmas against dogmatism. Saying this may bother some friends. Our current problem is a war of dogmas. One dogmatic front is fighting with another dogmatic front. They are tied to rigid things and insist on their own way. Even though they are extremists and in the minority, they affect a broad range of the public. Their voices are loud and effective. The majority, who remain in the middle and are not part of either extreme, should be moderate, for they can balance the extremes and thus continue to push for the tolerance, dialogue, and forbearance that we need today.[264]

## Turkey's Foreign Relations and the Current World Situation

### Foreign Press

> Fethullah Gülen has been interviewed by: *Time, The Wall Street Journal, Le Monde, Eleftheropitia, Rilindia Demokritika, Albania, Rilindia Kosova* newspapers; by journalists from newspapers in Ukraine and Bulgaria; and by NMO, Azerbaijani, Russian, and Kazakhstani television. As an example, we offer the answers to the Bulgarian journalist's questions.

Q: What can be done to establish peace, especially in the Balkans?

A: Non-human creatures, like plants and animals, have common characteristics, whereas every individual person is like a species. Consequently, educators say we must deal with individuals separately and according to their own characters, natures, peculiarities, and abilities. Given this, people are the most difficult creatures to educate and control.

But human beings are also the most honorable and perfect of creatures. In addition to our individual characteristics, our own civilized and social nature force us to live in harmony with other people and the natural environment. Consequently, we can bring our individual characteristics into line with our society's common values and morals, and conform to such social rules as human rights, justice, and mutual respect.

---

[264] Can, "Fethullah Gülen Ile Ufuk Turu."

Nations and countries sharing a common geography, history, and even destiny can be considered a large society. I see the Balkans as such a society. Within each country and as a Balkan society, there are many things in common. By giving sufficient importance to neighborly, friendly, and even brotherly relationships on the basis of such a shared consciousness, they can establish conformity, peace, and harmony.

In an increasingly civilized world that is growing ever-smaller, every type of hostility should be discarded, and respect should be felt for every individual's and nation's freedom to live. Non-interference in each other's internal affairs, assistance, and cooperation should be the norm. Existing and future problems should be solved diplomatically based on mutual goodwill. In addition, internal political matters and anxiety regarding elections should not be tied to international problems, as so often happens today.

Q: How can peace be made and maintained in the Balkans?

A: Two of the most important factors here are education and religion. Religion's unifying and common aspects should replace all the misunderstandings and conflicts that exploit religion and let it be used by others for their own purposes. Education will enlighten people's minds; religion will adorn their hearts with moral values, love of humanity and nature, respect for others, and observance of basic human rights. Artificial factors that separate people and nations should be removed, and aspects unfitting to our human dignity should be eliminated. Success in these areas will leave today's generation and our children a much more livable and happy world, one in which human relationships are brotherly.

## Excerpts from Other Interviews

### China's Position in the World

Q: Do you have any anxiety about China? What do you think about China's position in the world?

A: We don't have any anxiety now about China. I am not certain whether the Chinese people are worried about us. The US has a strong foothold in China. If the Americans arouse anxiety regarding Turks, then the Chinese might become worried. We are trying not to give any reason for anxiety to either front, because we're acting in accordance with a spirit of the Messiah, dialogue, and tolerance in the name of world peace and serenity. We're wondering if we can be a catalyst.

## No Cultural War or Clash of Civilizations

Q: What do you say about the thesis Huntington put forth in his article "Clash of Civilizations"?

A: I don't believe there's going to be a clash between cultures or civilizations. If some people are planning such a thing based on their current dreams and making claims on this subject, and if such a wave has risen and is on its way, then before we suffer such a clash, let's put a bigger wave in front of it and break their wave.

## Relations with the Muslim World and Europe

Q: What do you say about the attitude: "Forget about Europe, and become the leader of the Muslim world in the East. You're not European anyhow."

A: We have one side in common with Europe and one side in common with the Muslim world. Our integration with Europe necessarily will bring the other.[265]

## The European Union (EU) and Turkey

Q: I guess you're not worried that Turkey's entering the EU will open the way to assimilation.

A: I don't approach this matter from the viewpoint of assimilation. Economists and politicians should examine this matter carefully from the perspective of our economy and political issues.[266]

---

[265] Sevindi, "Fethullah Gülen Ile New York Sohbeti."

[266] Akman, "Fethullah Hoca Anlatiyor."

## Turkey and the Customs Union

Q: What about Turkey's entering the Customs Union?

A: I've presented my views on this subject on various occasions. This matter's economical aspect should be discussed and debated thoroughly by experts in this field. If the Customs Union is going to tie our hands, obstruct our trade outside of Europe and in other places, and cause a snag in our imports and exports, then we must consider these issues and decide accordingly. I don't believe it's right to oppose the Customs Union because it might lead to our assimilation. For whatever reason we might enter the Customs Union, assimilation in our part is out of question.[267]

## Relations with the West

Q: How do you see our relations with the West?

A: I don't see any harm in joining the West and Western thought on points where it's necessary and where there's no danger. It's inescapable... God created humanity as an honored creature with intelligence and conscience. Those who do not know Islam are also human beings with intelligence and a conscience. There are things that intelligence, conscience, and being human promise to humanity. As one sage said: "God created humanity as an honorable creature who always looks for goodness and beauty. But sometimes falsehood can be pulled over its head like a cap..." This means that human nature inclines toward goodness and beauty. If we have found our essence, we can get only beautiful things from it. There are many beautiful things to borrow from the West.

Q: But there is hostility toward the West, especially in Islamic circles, in the form of slogans.

A: In the absolute sense, such an unquestionable hostility is an anachronism. Such people will be eliminated by time. Europeans didn't hesitate to borrow from us what they thought they needed. Those who read a little history of science know that before Europe's

---

[267] Çalislar, "Fethullah Gülen'le Röportaj."

Renaissance, a true renaissance took place in the fifth Islamic century in the Muslim world. Scholars like Bîrûnî, Harizmî, Ibn Sina,[268] and many others were translated into European languages. European students poured into Andalusia, a center of learning, for centuries.

As acknowledged by many historians of science, the foundation of Europe's Renaissance was laid in the Muslim world. Some European zealots changed the names of our scholars. For example, Ibn Sina was "latinized" into Avicenna, and Ibn Rushd became Averroës.[269] Fair Western writers admit this. I don't see any harm in taking things the West has developed. We can get them and make further advancements.[270]

## Relations with Central Asia, the Islamic World, and the West

Q: Is the Central Asian corridor going to carry Turkey to the West, the Middle East, and the Pacific?

A: Yes. You expressed it very well. The important thing is for that corridor to open, and, with God's will, a corridor free of time and space will open. As stated in the old expression "A road will open from heart to heart," this will be realized on the planes of feeling, thought, and faith. At the same time, it will allow Turkish society to become integrated with the West in a harmless way. In this sense, we should discuss the possible harm from such integration with Europe. For example, we should dwell on the possible economic harm of entering the Customs Union. But we also will benefit in other ways from integration.

---

[268] Ibn Sina (Avicenna) (980-1037): Turkish physician and the most famous and influential Muslim philosopher–scientist. He was particularly noted for his contributions to Aristotelian philosophy and medicine. He wrote *Kitab al-Shifa'* (Book of Healing), a philosophical and scientific encyclopaedia, and the *Canon of Medicine*, a very famous medical treatise.

[269] Ibn Rushd (Averroës) (1126-98): Influential Islamic religious philosopher who integrated Islamic traditions with ancient Greek thought.

[270] Can, "Fethullah Gülen Ile Ufuk Turu."

## Close Relations with the Pacific Region

It's very important that we join Europe. However, Central Asia is important for Turkish businessmen and entrepreneurs, and mutual cooperation between us will make our competition with the world easier. Maybe some joint ventures will be undertaken, thus providing an opportunity to evaluate our relationship with Europe. The same thing is possible with the Pacific region. We're not bound to anyone; we can use the Pacific region, Central Asia, and Europe. Different alternatives will give us a broader base for bargaining.[271]

## US at the World's Rudder

Q: You've been in the US for a while. How do you describe it? What is its role in the world?

A: Democracy and certain national traditions are well-established in the US. The social mosaic perhaps necessitates this. America is like ancient Babylon. If there weren't a democracy in the sense that Americans understand, establish, and sanctify, its national unity could not be protected. In the current global framework, and with its present position and power, America can control the world.

All the work to be done in the world can be managed from here. In fact, not getting along with America—not necessarily getting its support but not getting along with it as a friend—would make it difficult to do anything anywhere. America still controls the rudder of the world.

Sociologists say that every nation and civilization, just as every individual, has a lifespan. America is no exception. America is a democracy, and democracies fall very slowly, like feathers. The disintegration of despotic regimes, like the Soviet Union, takes place suddenly like a gas explosion.[272]

---

[271] Sevindi, "Fethullah Gülen Ile New York Sohbeti."

[272] Ibid.

## CHAPTER 6

# Dialogue

## Why Dialogue?

- Be so tolerant that your heart becomes wide like the ocean. Become inspired with faith and love for others. Offer a hand to those in trouble, and be concerned about everyone.

- Applaud the good for their goodness, appreciate those who have believing hearts, and be kind to believers. Approach unbelievers so gently that their envy and hatred melt away. Like a Messiah, revive people with your breath.

- Return good for evil, and disregard discourteous treatment. An individual's character is reflected in his or her behavior. Choose tolerance, and be magnanimous toward the ill-mannered.

## Islam Is a Religion of Tolerance

Islam is a word derived from the roots *silm* and *selamet*. It means to surrender, reach, and establish security and mutual safety and accord.

Islam is a religion of security, safety and peace. These principles permeate Muslims' lives. When they stand to pray, they cut their connection with this world, turn to their Lord in faith and obedience, and stand at attention in His presence. Completing the prayer, as if returning back to life, they greet those on their right and left by saying *salaam*: "Remain safe and secure." With a wish for safety and security, peace and contentment, they return to the ordinary world once again.

Giving *salaam* and wishing safety and security for others is considered one of the most beneficial acts in Islam. When asked which act in Islam is the most beneficial, the Prophet replied:

"Feeding others and giving *salaam* to those you know and do not know."

### Jihad and Terrorism

How unfortunate it is that Islam, which is based on this understanding and spirit, is shown by some circles to be synonymous with terrorism. This is a great historical mistake, for wrapping a system based on safety and trust in a veil of terrorism shows that Islam's spirit remains unknown. Seeking Islam's true face in its own sources, history, and true representatives shows that it contains no harshness, roughness, or fanaticism. It is a religion of forgiveness, pardon, and tolerance, as such saints and princes of love and tolerance as Mawlana Rumi, Yunus Emre, Ahmed Yasawi, and Bediüzzaman have so beautifully expressed. They spent their lives preaching tolerance, and each became a legend in his own time as an embodiment of love and tolerance.

Depending on circumstances, jihad is a matter of self-defense or removing obstacles in the path of exalting the Word of God. We can give many examples. For example, as a nation we have struggled valiantly on many fronts to defend our country. Should we have done otherwise with those who sought to occupy our country? Should we have said to them: "You have come to civilize us; it is good you came! Welcome, you have delighted us!"

Of course there are and should be occasions where war is inescapable. However, the Qur'anic verses on jihad that were revealed for particular conditions have been generalized by some short-sighted individuals. While war is a matter of secondary importance, it is given priority as an essential issue. Such people do not understand Islam's true meaning and spirit. Their failure to establish a proper primary–secondary balance leads others to conclude that Islam advocates malice and hatred in souls, whereas true Muslims are full of love and affection for all creation. Regarding this, how apt is the following couplet:

Muhammad was born out of love,
What can be born out of love without Muhammad!
Love is the essence of creation.

The Pride of Humanity was a man of love and affection. One of his names was *Habib Allah* (the Beloved of God). In addition to meaning one who loves, *habib* means one who is loved, one who loves God and is loved by God. Sufi masters like Imam Rabbani, Mawlana Khalid,[273] and Shah Waliyullah state that love is the ultimate station of the spiritual journey.

God created the universe as a manifestation of His love for His creatures, especially humanity, and Islam became the fabric woven out of this love. In the words of Bediüzzaman, love is the essence of creation. Just as a mother's love and compassion allows a surgeon to operate on her sick child to save his or her life, jihad allows war, if needed, to preserve such fundamental human rights as the right to life and religious freedom. Jihad does not exclusively mean war, although some claim that that is its only meaning.

Once a friend said to me: "Without exception and regardless of faith, you meet with everyone, and this breaks the tension of Muslims. But it is an Islamic principle to love what or who must be loved in the way of God and dislike what or who must be disliked in the way of God." Actually this principle is often misunderstood, for in Islam all of creation is to be loved according to the rule of loving in God's way.

"Disliking in the way of God" applies only to feelings, thoughts, and attributes. Thus, we should dislike such things as immorality, unbelief and polytheism, not those who engage in them. God created humanity as noble, and everyone shares in this nobility to a certain degree. His Messenger once stood up out of respect for humanity as the funeral procession of a Jew passed by. When reminded that the deceased was a Jew, the Prophet replied: "But he's a human being," thereby showing the value Islam gives to human beings.

---

[273] Mawlana Khalid al-Baghdadi, (d. 1827): Naqshbandi master considered the *mujaddid* (revivifier) of 13th Islamic century. The Khalidi order, a new Naqshbandi branch, arose under his leadership and had acquired a large following by the end of the nineteenth century.

This shows how highly our Prophet respected each person. Given this, the involvement of some self-proclaimed Muslim individuals or institutions in terrorist activities does not lie in Islam. The reasons should be sought in themselves, their false interpretations, and other factors and motives. Islam does not support terror, so how could a Muslim who truly understands it be a terrorist?

Within this framework, if we exclude certain periods and individuals, the Turks' interpretation of what Islam allows to be interpreted is correct and positive. If we can spread globally the Islamic understanding of such heroes of love as Niyazi-i Misri, Yunus Emre, and Rumi, if we can extend their messages of love, dialogue, and tolerance to those thirsty for this message, everyone will run toward the embrace of love, peace, and tolerance that we represent.

Islam's definition of tolerance is such that the Prophet prohibited verbal abuse. For example, Abu Jahl died before embracing Islam despite the Prophet's efforts. His unbelief and enmity toward the Prophet was such that he deserved the title *Abu Jahl*: Father of the ignorant and impudent. His untiring opposition to Islam was a thorn in the side of Muslims.

Despite such hostility, however, the Prophet always warned his Companions against disparaging Abu Jahl. Once in an assembly of Companions where Abu Jahl's son Ikrima was present, the Prophet admonished a Companion who was heard insulting Abu Jahl: "Do not hurt others by criticizing their fathers." Another time, he said:

> "Cursing your mother and father is a great sin." The Companions asked: "O Messenger of God, would anyone curse their parents?" The Prince of Prophets replied: "When someone curses another's father and the other curses his father in return, or when someone curses another's mother and the other does the same in return, they will have cursed their parents."[274]

While the Prophet of Mercy was inordinately sensitive when it came to respecting others, some Muslims today justify their abra-

---

[274] Muslim, *Sahih*, "Iman," 145; Tirmidhi, *Sunan*, "Birr," 4.

sive behavior on the basis of religion. This shows that they do not understand Islam, which has no place for malice and hatred.

The Qur'an strongly urges forgiveness and tolerance. In one verse, it says of pious people: *They swallow their anger and forgive people. God loves those who do good* (3:134). In other words, Muslims do not retaliate when verbally abused or attacked. If possible, as Yunus says, they act as if they had no hand and tongue to respond or heart to resent. They swallow their anger and close their eyes to others' faults. The words selected in the verse are very meaningful. *Kezm*, translated as *swallowing*, means swallowing something like a thorn that cannot be swallowed; *kzm* means someone who has swallowed his wrath. Again verse, while mentioning the characteristics of believers, says: *And if they pass by futility, they pass by it with honorable avoidance* (25:72).

When we look at the exalted life of God's Messenger, we see that he always practiced the precepts presented in the Qur'an. For example, a Companion once repented of a sin and admitted: "I am guilty of fornication. Whatever my punishment is, give it and cleanse me." The Prince of Prophets said: "Go back and repent, for God forgives all sins." Another time, a Companion complained to him about someone who had stolen his belongings. But at the punishment was about to be carried out, the Companion said: "I have changed my mind and do not want to pursue my case. I forgive this individual." The Prophet asked: "Why did you bring this matter to court? Why didn't you forgive him from the outset?"

When such examples are studied from their original sources, it is clear that the method used by those who act with enmity and hatred, who view everyone else with wrath, and who blacken others as infidels is non-Islamic, for Islam is a religion of love and tolerance. A Muslim is a person of love and affection who avoids every kind of terroristic activity and who has no malice and hatred for anyone or anything.[275]

[275] Camci and Ünal, *Fethullah Gülen'in Konusma ve Yazilarinda Hosgörü ve Diyalog Iklimi*, 104-10.

- The most distinctive feature of a soul overflowing with faith is to love all types of love that are expressed in deeds, and to feel enmity for all deeds in which enmity is expressed. To hate everything is a sign of insanity or of infatuation with Satan.

- Accept how God treats you. Make it the measure by which you treat others, so that you may represent the truth among them and be free of the fear of loneliness in either world.

- Remember that you travel the best road and follow the Prophet, an exalted guide. Be mindful that you have his guidance through the most perfect and expressive revelation. Be fair-minded and balanced in your judgment, for many people do not enjoy these blessings.

## Prophetic Definitions of *Ideal Believer* and *Ideal Muslim*

A prophetic *hadith* makes the following statements: "The Muslim is one from whose tongue and hand other Muslims are safe and sound. The emigrant is one who leaves behind and abandons those things God has prohibited."[276]

Let's analyze this *hadith*. Notice the presence of the definite article *al* (the) before *Muslim*. This gives the meaning that ideal believers, entering an atmosphere of safety and security, have so immersed themselves in that atmosphere that they harm no one with their hands or tongues. This refers to true and ideal Muslims who leave their mark on all minds, not those who appear or claim to be so, or whose birth certificate reads "Muslim." We understand this from the article, which points to a specific, definite one. This is derived from the grammatical rule: "When something is described with a definite article, the item's highest and most perfect condition is indicated." So, when "the believer" is said, the first thing that comes to mind is the most perfect meaning of "believer," and that is what is meant in the *hadith*.

This fine grammatical point can be learned only at a school or from a teacher. Having such a lesson was out of the question for God's Messenger, because he was unlettered. Thus, he was not speaking on his own but was relaying what the Eternal Teacher was

---

[276] Bukhari, *Sahih*, "Iman," 4.

making him say. For this reason, all subtle grammatical points are found in his expressions and declarations without error.

Let's return to the above *hadith*: True Muslims are such people of safety and trust that Muslims can rely on them without doubt or suspicion. They can entrust a family member to such people without fear, for that person will be absolutely safe from the Muslims' hand or tongue. If they attend a gathering together, the person can leave in full confidence that no one will gossip about him or her or that he or she will have to listen to gossip about others. Such Muslims are as sensitive to the dignity and honor of other people as they are to their own. They do not eat; they feed others. They do not live; they enable others to live. They will sacrifice spiritual pleasure for others. I derive all these meanings from the fact that the definite article also means *hasr (*restrained, devoted to one purpose).

### Security and Muslims

There is also a play on words in this expression. The word *Muslim* and the verb *selime* both come from the root *silm*. Due to the similarity between some of the letters, this is a partial play on words. However the modes of these two words are separate. This similarity and dissimilarity reminds us of another meaning: For Muslims, every matter occurs in line with *silm* (security), *selamah* (safety), and Muslimness. They have been seized by such a divine attraction that all of their actions occur around this powerful center.

They greet everyone with *salaam*, thereby placing love for themselves in everyone's heart.[277] They end their prayers with *salaam*. All people, jinn, angels, and conscious creatures receive their *salaam*. They exchange greetings with invisible creatures. Until now no one has spread this act of giving *salaam* as much as the Muslims.

Islam is practiced and secured by performing such principal duties as fasting, giving alms, performing hajj (pilgrimage), and making the profession of faith. This means opening your sail in the sea of safety and security by obeying the command: *Enter safety*

---

[277] Bukhari, *Sahih*, "Iman," 20; Muslim, *Sahih*, "Iman," 63

*wholly* (2:208). Those who throw themselves into that sea emanate safety and Islam under every condition. No one sees anything but goodness in the actions and behavior of such people.

### Why Hand and Tongue?

As in every statement of our Master, every word in this *hadith* was chosen carefully. Why were the hand and tongue mentioned? Of course there are many subtle points related to this choice. A person can harm someone in two ways: either directly or indirectly. The hand represents presence (directly), and the tongue represents absence (indirectly). People attack others directly (gossip) or indirectly (ridicule). True Muslims will never engage in such activities, because they always act justly and generously.

The Prophet mentioned the tongue before the hand because one can retaliate for what is done with the hand. However, the same is not always true for damage done indirectly through gossip or slander. Thus, such action can easily cause conflict between individuals, communities, and even nations. Dealing with this type of harm is relatively more difficult than dealing with that caused by the hand. And so the Prophet mentioned the tongue before the hand. On the other hand, the value of Muslims before God is indicated. Being a Muslim has such a great value before God that other Muslims control their hands and tongues concerning them.

Another important moral dimension of Islam is that Muslims keep at bay things that will harm others, whether physically or spiritually, and that they do their best not to harm others. Forget about giving harm; every segment of a Muslim society must represent safety and security. Muslims are true Muslims to the extent that they carry within themselves a feeling of safety and their hearts beat with trust. Wherever they are or live reveals this feeling that derives from *al-salaam*. They wish safety when leaving, adorn their prayers with greetings, and give *salaam* to other believers when they leave God's presence. In all probability, it is unthinkable that people who pass their entire lives in such an orbit of *salaam* will enter a path contrary to the basic principles of safety, trust, soundness, and worldly and other-worldly security and harm either themselves or others.

Let's look at these points deriving from its spirit: True Muslims are the most trustworthy representatives of universal peace. They travel everywhere with this sublime feeling, which is nourished deep in their spirits. Contrary to giving torment and suffering, they are remembered everywhere as symbols of safety and security. In their eyes, there is no difference between a physical (direct) or a verbal (indirect) violation of someone's rights. In fact, in some cases the latter is considered to be a greater crime than the former.

If Muslims commit some of these sins, they are still Muslims. We cannot consider them as being between faith and denial. As in every matter, in the matter of faith and Islam one should aim high and seek perfection rather than being satisfied with remaining a common believer. These are only a few of the many things miraculously compressed into this *hadith*.[278]

- Take note of and be attentive to any behavior that causes you to love others. Then remind yourself that behaving in the same way will cause them to love you. Always behave decently, and be alert.

- Judge your worth in the Creator's sight by how much space He occupies in your heart, and your worth in people's eyes by how you treat them. Do not neglect the Truth even for a moment. And yet, "be a man or woman among other men or women."

- Only those who do not use their reason, or who have succumbed to plain stupidity and desires of the flesh, are convinced that believers might harm them. Apply to a spiritual master to stir up your heart, and fill your eyes with tears.

## Handless to Those Who Hit, Tongueless to Those Who Curse

(A talk given at the breaking-of-the-fast meal given by the Foundation of Writers and Journalists, February 11, 1995, at the Polat Renaissance Hotel.)

Honorable ministers and parliamentarians, enlightened people of the world of art, members of various religions, and esteemed guests: I greet you with my most sincere *salaam* and hope that this night will be beneficial for all of us. I'm one of those who made

[278] S. Camci and Ünal, *Fethullah Gülen'in Konusma ve Yazilarinda Hosgörü ve Diyalog Iklimi*, 127-31.

arrangements for this evening. And I admit this at every opportunity. However, I had a little bit of difficulty in participating in this meeting, because although everyone observes the fast during the month of Ramadan, in my case the fast holds me. I have a serious diabetes problem. Only 2 or 3 hours after the fast is over do I begin feeling a little normal. For this reason, I had hoped that I would be forgiven if I did not attend this evening. But I was wrong. So for my friends' sake and yours, I am attending the meeting and am in your presence. I give you my respects once again.

From the day the Foundation of Writers and Journalists was established until now—even if things were not always as we wished—we can say that you always have organized important activities. But somehow I could never participate fully in any of them. For this reason, I cannot claim a share in their success.

This foundation has performed important services. It brought world-famous soccer players here for aid to Bosnia. Every year it has brought together special groups like you on various platforms, preparing for at least an exchange of ideas. Regardless of our views and thoughts, it has suggested on which idea we can come together. As a result, we have seen with our own eyes that there's no reason to fear one another, and that all people can meet with whomever they want. If we have not come together until today, it means that we have been hung up on our mistaken conjectures and neglected an important human responsibility.

The foundation is known in Turkey mainly as a representative of tolerance. In fact, it has identified itself with tolerance. Whenever it is mentioned, immediately after that tolerance is mentioned as well. In fact, the envy aroused by the foundation's image has caused several alternative organizations to appear. Now they are singing the same tune. For this reason, I believe that tolerance is going to spread faster to the grassroots, diffuse throughout the country and, as an artist friend said, we'll walk head to head, heart to heart, and hand in hand toward "happy tomorrows," God willing.

Actually, what the foundation or alternative groups have done regarding this issue is to bring out a quality that already exists in the spirit of our noble nation. Until today there were certain obstacles, and this quality could not be reached and brought out. However, in addition to jihad, which is inaccurately explained and understood, there are activities designed to raise humanity to a level of real humanity. In other words, in the essence of explaining beauty and goodness there is the idea of removing obstacles between people and God. If the foundation has removed the obstacles preventing this precious quality from appearing in our people's spirit, then it has accomplished a very important duty.

When the Prophet was dying and about to pass on to the next world, he stated: "I place in your trust the People of the Book, the Christians and Jews." When 'Umar was in the throes of death due to a dagger wound, he warned: "I place the minorities among us in your trust. Fear God regarding them and treat them justly."

After defeating the enemy at Malazgirt, the Turkish commander Sultan Alp-Arslan hosted the military chiefs and ruler of the rival state in his tent.[279] He then had them conveyed safely to their capital, Constantinople (now Istanbul), escorted by some of his officers. In Jerusalem, the commander and ruler Sultan Salah ad-Din Ayyubi went at night to the tent of Richard, the commander of the Crusader army, to cure his wounds—despite the fact that Richard's forces had killed thousands of Muslims.

We are the children of a culture that produced such people. We are the heirs of the culture that has the world's broadest, most comprehensive, and most universal tolerance. This understanding and view is spreading today like waves in the sea, and reaching the four corners of the Earth. I fully believe that the coming years will be years of tolerance and love. In this framework, we're going to give the world a lot and receive a lot. Let alone fighting with our own

---

[279] Battle of Malazgirt (or Manzikert): This battle, fought in 1071, pitted the Byzantine Emperor Romanus IV Diogenes against the Seljuq Turk Sultan Alp-Arslan. The emperor's defeat resulted in the Seljuq conquest of most of Anatolia. Alp-Arslan (1030-72) inherited the Seljuq territories of Khorasan and western Iran, went on to conquer Georgia, Eastern Anatolia, and much of Asia Minor (from the Byzantines).

people, we will not even be fighting with other cultures, civilizations, or people of other beliefs and worldviews. Issues leading to argument and opposition will be resolved completely, and once again understanding the power of love, we'll open our hearts to everyone with love and compassion. With God's help, we'll realize the important matters of dialogue and tolerance, which today's world needs so much.

When I saw Izzettin Dogan,[280] I remembered a *hadith*. Mentioning a group in Nehrivan that was hoping to ambush him, "Ali said: "It would have been unjust for us to attack them before they attacked us." We are a society nurtured by the culture of such commanders. At a time when we are in great need of it, with God's grace, every social segment will stand up for tolerance and dialogue, and the good things born from this will spread even faster than hoped for in every direction.

Maybe I'm going to take too much of your time, but I cannot proceed without mentioning the anxiety I feel. Turkish society, which has been wrung by internal conflict, was awaiting tolerance just at this time. Upon finding it, when one step toward it was made with this view, it responded with three steps. But it also is obvious that certain weak and marginal persons, who by ranting and raving demonstrate their own weaknesses and try to show themselves as strong by being destructive, will lie in ambush to attack tolerance and attempt to destroy the bridges to dialogue. We'll face great tests after this. Our nation, which already has passed through many trials, will face these future tests by means of solidarity among individuals, and will overcome every obstacle in the path to social harmony. God reveals in the Qur'an: *I swear, We are going to test some of you with others* (6:53).

What we are seeking is very valuable. The goal of tolerance and dialogue that we want to reach will cost a lot. Just as it is not easy to achieve such precious and expensive things, it is difficult to pro-

---

[280] Izzettin Dogan, chairman of the Cem Foundation, which was established by Alawi citizens of Turkey. He currently is a professor of international law in Galatasaray University, Istanbul.

tect them once they've been achieved. Attaining social harmony through dialogue and tolerance is a matter of achieving two valuable things in order to realize a third. God is going to test us in different ways so that we will realize how great this value is and, accordingly, for us to stand up for it. We're going to endure all these trials and say:

> If harshness comes from God's Majesty
> Or generosity from His Grace,
> Both are delights to the soul.
> Pleasing are both His blessings and His wrath.

We must be as if "handless to those who hit us and tongueless to those who curse us." If they try and fracture us into pieces even fifty times, still we are going to remain unbroken and embrace everyone with love and compassion. And, with love toward one another, we will walk toward tomorrow.

I wish for this happy evening to be an occasion for mercy and forgiveness. I greet you all with my deepest respect. To preserve your credit, honor, and love, love for the sake of the Truth, hate for the sake of the Truth, and be openhearted toward the Truth.[281]

- Do not allow your carnal self to be a referee in any contention, for it will rule that everyone but you is sinful and unfortunate. Such a judgment, according to the word of the Prophet, the most truthful, signifies your destruction. Be strict and implacable with your carnal self, and be relenting and lenient toward others.

## Contacts with Various Social Segments

Q: What was the first thing you saw as a result of contacts you made with various social segments?

A: I saw that there are countless people with whom we have countless things in common to share. There are so many things we have in common to emphasize. Instead of struggling with each other over our differences, instead of exaggerating and deepening them, we should emphasize our common points. Kurdish–Turkish, Sunni–Alawi, right wing–left wing—let's not use such differences

---

[281] Gülen, *Ölçü veya Yoldaki Isiklar*, 1:9-14.

as subjects of debate. Let's insist on ideas that will lead us to dialogue. We have as great a need for a big leap to greatness as we do
for unity and solidarity. Let's not get bogged down by small things
and lose our way.[282]

## We Must Struggle (Make Jihad) for Tolerance

Q: As a method, has tolerance been useful in Turkey, where
there's a cultural clash? How can peace be attained?

A: Some well-established customs and behavior can be eliminated only gradually. Some sociologists and psychologists see our
Prophet's greatness here. Eliminating the bad morals and characteristics of wild and primitive tribes in such a short period of time
seems to be a miracle. Tolerance already exists in our people's spirit. Everyone in society, from artists to academia, must insist on this
trait's surfacing. Hostility doesn't disappear immediately. Here, a
very important task falls to the media. We have to be careful,
because it's easy to destroy but difficult to mend.

Restoration will not take place immediately. A change of feelings and an increase in trust, a change in perspective, and everything settling into its rightful place will take a long time. Society has
to uphold tolerance. If we don't announce jihad for anything else,
we should announce it for tolerance.

Q: People don't like differences and are biased against them.
There is a desire for others to be just the way oneself is. All fronts
in Turkey want this.

A: You're very right. Maybe this is what we're trying to overcome with the spirit of tolerance. Different positions mean different
understandings. Once you accept that, you can benefit from others'
thoughts and ideas.

Western thought has some very beneficial aspects. For example, systematic thinking is and must be a believer's attribute. A
believer cannot always be a believer in every attribute. If this is a

---

[282] Can, "Fethullah Gülen Ile Ufuk Turu."

believer's attribute, those believers who don't have it are carrying an attribute that doesn't issue from belief. Whether you're a Christian, a Jew, a Buddhist, or of another creed, if you have that attribute you're carrying a believer's attribute. There's a very fine point here: At least in this world, God treats people according to their attributes. Thus your attributes and behavior are important.

For example, I'm amazed by one thing here in America. There's a perfect and functioning system. In the hospitals, all doctors handle everyone's problems all at once and don't hurt you. I saw at least 20 doctors and 30 nurses at the hospital. Their faces don't look anything like the cross faces of some of our doctors. They behave warmly and sincerely with smiles on their faces. This is a believer's attribute. If other believers spends all their time in the mosque but lacks a believer's attributes and doesn't grasp the spirit of the matter, they cannot succeed in the worldly life. I think this is very important.

### Like Mawlana's Compass
On the one hand, believers are people of enthusiastic love; in fact, more a pole of attraction. Or beyond that, with their rapture like a Pascal, a Bergson,[283] a Muhyiddin Ibn al-Arabi, and Mawlana Rumi, a whirlpool whose depth we can't fathom. On the other hand, when such people are open to others, they are like people striving after a purpose.

Using Rumi's expression, such a person is like a compass with one foot well-established in the center of belief and Islam and the other foot with people of many nations. If this apparently dualistic state can be caught by a person who believes in God, it's most desirable. So deep in his or her own inner world, so full of love... so much in touch with God; but at the same time an active member of society.[284]

---

[283] Henri-Louis Bergson (1859-1941): French philosopher who developed a humanistic philosophy of process to counter positivism. He was awarded the Nobel Prize for Literature in 1928.

[284] Sevindi, "Fethullah Gülen Ile New York Sohbeti."

## Activities for Dialogue

> (In order to promote dialogue and internal peace within the Turkish community, The Foundation of Journalists and Writers has organized and continues to organize many activities. What follows is only a few of them with their repercussions in the press.)

### The Ramadan Dinner at the Polat Renaissance Hotel

> (This dinner was held on February 11, 1995. Excerpts from the after-dinner speeches are given below.)

- It was an extremely wonderful night. If the media contains a strand of thought that upholds journalism and writing and that conforms to basic Islamic commands and prohibitions, but which doesn't forget the contemporary age, then our nation can become renewed in a powerful way. (Professor Abdulkadir Karahan, Istanbul University)

- Being here with you at this blessed Ramadan dinner and seeing this beautiful unity and togetherness and splendor has touched me very deeply. As people of the arts, we have a rather sensitive nature. We all know that nations stand on their own feet to the extent that they are tied to their cultural values, traditions, languages, and religions. (Necla Akben, folk singer)

- Everyone has seen at this blessed Ramadan dinner table how our people, in whose yeast love and tolerance, mobilize when the opportunity is presented. I thank the Foundation for its efforts to spread Turkey's national unity and solidarity both at home and abroad. (Köksal Toptan, former minister of education)

- I congratulate the Foundation members who organized this wonderful night. Actually there's only one thing to say in face of this tableau, and it has been said already by previous speakers. I wish for unity, solidarity, and well-being from God. (Yalim Erez, industrialist, former minister of industry)

- I am proud to be among such wonderful friends. Thank you all. I thank the Foundation of Writers and Journalists for realizing the great Yunus Emre's call made 7 centuries earlier: "Come, let's be together, let's make things easier, let's love and be loved; the world doesn't remain with anyone." (Ali Talip Özdemir, former mayor of Bakirköy and minister of the environment)

- Because journalists and writers usually find themselves in the frontline of courts, I was amazed when I saw this meeting. It can be seen as a model of a multicolor, multivoice, pluralistic Turkey that we all desire. (Professor Mehmet Altan, university lecturer and columnist for *Sabah*)

And in the words of Fethullah Gülen Hodjaefendi:

I feel very happy to attend such a meeting where people who have exchanged Ramadan greetings with love have come together. I attended this meeting to express my respect for the feelings of its arrangers, those who were invited, and those who actually came. This distinguished group, which has really touched me, in fact enchanted me, can nourish our hopes and enliven our hearts.

Even though I don't have the right, I'm a member of this foundation. My friends ordained it and so I bowed to their will over my own and agreed to join. I ask God that they, together with similar organizations, will be able to bring together different social segments, which resemble parts of a crystal chandelier scattered here and there, and thereby reconstruct a dialogue that has disappeared and renew an atmosphere of tolerance.

More than ever before, our different social segments need to be welded together in order to pursue cooperation and agreement. If we accomplish this, we will have achieved a very important goal. Actually, our noble nation is open to this spiritually. But the media has to do this, via television and radio, so that everyone will accept others as they are. No one should be accused because of their belief, or reproached because of their religion or lack of it. I believe that the media will do this.

Turkey is surrounded by enemies. Given this, we cannot afford to argue among ourselves. Moreover, as a great man said, we must temporarily forget some focal points of controversy between Christian spiritual leaders and us and seek dialogue with them. Savages (forgive me for using this term) accomplish something by hitting and fighting, while noble and enlightened spirits believe they will realize their goals by thinking and talking. I think we have left the period of brutality far behind. Victory in civilization and acceptance of the truth will be accomplished through persuasion. I believe that the visual and literal media will do this.

I apologize for these inadequate and unbecoming words. May the Ramadan of those who celebrate it be blessed. I congratulate your "Night of Power," and may your holidays be blessed. I offer my respects.

## *Gülen's Surprising Ramadan Dinner*

By Mehmet Barlas

While practicing and interpreting Islam, I guess we have made mistakes. Otherwise, in Turkey where 99 percent of the population is Muslim, would the participation of people with different political views and from social groups in Fethullah Gülen's Ramadan dinner have created such bewilderment?

Whether we like it or not, we have placed Islam on one side of the political polarization. Now when people of the same religion but representing different political views and social segments come together at dinner, we are confused.

Necmettin Erbakan and RP members and then other prominent politicians must pay attention to this reality. The primitive Republicans who present Islam as an antithesis to secularism must do the same. By making every social event a subject for fighting and polarization, we can never protect our peace or unity.

### Always Fighting?

Because we don't consider the universal dimensions of secularism–Islam relations when we speak of Turkish democracy's future, such phrases as "being like Iran" and "resembling Algeria" always enter the conversation. We have to forego half-enlightened distortions and prejudices, especially on the subject of religion.

First, let's be sure that... The religion of countries and religion's basic nature can't be changed. There are countless examples of this.... For sensible Muslim Turks who know history, it doesn't take 1,000 years to remove religion from the arena of conflict.[285]

## *Valentine's Day and Fethullah Gülen*

By Ayse Önal

When I was invited to the Ramadan dinner given by the Foundation of Writers and Journalists, like Fehmi Koru I thought it

---

[285] *Sabah*, 14 February 1995.

would be for fifty or sixty people. However, from the moment I entered the Polat Renaissance Hotel, it was clear that, in regard to those attending and the arrangements, this type of dinner had not been seen before in Turkey.

Several women had been invited to this religious community dinner. Some were strikingly dressed; others were covered. At Hodjaefendi's request, Professor Nur Vergin and journalist Nuriye Akman gave short speeches. He called Vergin to his table from her seat at a table of journalists. Just as this led to an increased attack against him in *Cuma*'s latest issue, it also was perceived as a challenge to Islamic groups that don't share his views on women.[286] Vergin's call for others to "take in your new co-religionist" led to journalists making a "neo-Muslim" joke among themselves.

The evening's surprise began after dinner, when *Zaman*'s owner Alaaddin Kaya invited journalists, protocol guests, and Fethullah Hodja to drink tea in a small room. The young reporter from Channel 6, entering the private tea meeting after great effort and asking Fethullah Hodja if he had ever celebrated Valentine's Day, created an unusual atmosphere. But regardless of how much he perspired and rubbed his legs together under the table in embarrassment, he patiently explained that he favored every kind of love, although he had never celebrated such a day.

Regarding his interviews that appeared in the media many years after he started his service, Gülen commented: "Those who thought I was important understood that even if I were a flame, I could burn only within my reach, that I wasn't very important, and that they had gotten excited for no reason."[287]

### Ramadan Dinner with the Literary People

By Professor Ayhan Songar

On Saturday February 11th, more than 1,000 writers, members of the arts, and scholars met at a Ramadan dinner in the

---

[286] *Cuma:* A Turkish magazine that usually favors radical views on Islamic issues.

[287] Aksam, 15 *February* 1995.

Polat Renaissance Hotel. A wonderful thing about Ramadan is that it brings together friends of the heart at such a dinner. As the time to break the fast drew closer, everyone was very quiet, as if not to disturb the moment's sanctity. Talking was done in whispered tones. Only the sweet sound of a *nay* (flute) from the loudspeakers filled the hall and added exhilaration to our hearts. It was as if Rumi was there, and the *nay* was "complaining of separation."

However, this time it wasn't a meeting of separation but the good news of unity and solidarity. The Foundation of Writers and Journalists was formed for this purpose. As Fethullah Hodja was going to express nicely in his speech, it was the wish of all present that this meeting would be a "point of uniqueness."[288]

### "World Peace Ramadan Dinner" at the Hilton Hotel

"Don't let the bridge of tolerance be destroyed."

(This dinner was held on January 27, 1996. Related newspaper articles are given below.)

### Fethullah Hodja's Ramadan Dinner

By Sakir Süter

I was at the Foundation of Writers and Journalists' traditional Ramadan dinner. The organization was flawless. But after everyone had been seated, I noticed some empty tables in the Hilton Hotel Convention Hall. Out of curiosity, I investigated the matter. I learned that the Foundation directors had taken precautions against "surprise guests" by arranging extra tables so that no one would be left without a seat. The "empty places" were due to this meticulous organization.

This Foundation continues to maintain its importance due to the "spiritual directorship" of Fethullah Gülen Hodja, who takes its very seriously. This is why he attended yesterday's dinner despite the serious discomfort caused by his diabetes.

---

[288] *Türkiye*, 14 February 1995.

Finally Fethullah Hodja came to the podium. He pointed out that the Foundation had assumed a leading role in making important advances in the name of tolerance, and that the number of similar foundations with the same purpose had increased.

"Despite advances in the atmosphere of social tolerance, a marginal group still spoils social peace by screaming and shouting to make it appear that they are strong." He was warning us to stay alert: "After this, traps will be set for tolerance. They're going to try to destroy the bridges. And it appears that after this we will face some serious tests."

After drawing this tableau, Fethullah Hodja continued: "We're going to endure this test. With the slogan 'handless to those who hit us and tongueless to those who curse us,' we're going to walk toward tomorrow by embracing everything with love and compassion and by loving each other."

His speech and the evening were ending when newspaper reporters seeking "a little bit of politics" began asking questions. They were pulling him toward a field that he always tries to avoid: "You didn't attend the Ramadan dinner at the Prime Minister's Residence..." Fethullah Hodja indicated that he had attended no political dinners to date: "I'm also not planning to attend any after this." It seems to me that the reason why RP members feel uncomfortable with Fethullah Hodja is hidden in these "finely tuned" words...[289]

### A Criterion Viewing the World from Turkey

By Associate Professor Nabi Avci

To be truthful, I think that intellectuals, businessmen, and bureaucrats from the National Education and Foreign Affairs ministries should evaluate Hodjaefendi's educational and cultural advances, especially those directed toward the Central Asian republics, both carefully and fairly. These advances clearly show how Turkey should view the world.

---

[289] *Aksam*, 29 January 1996.

Another important point is his independent approach to daily politics and politicians. It would be a mistake to reduce his expression *Turkish Muslimness* to a national axis with an interpretation going beyond what was intended. I understand this expression to mean that Islam will blossom differently in different areas and different cultural atmospheres, as it has done so until now. I interpret this as a sign of the multicolored, multidimensional richness of the Muslim peoples.[290]

## Ramadan Dinner at the Hilton Hotel

(This dinner was held on January 27, 1997. Related newspaper articles are given below.)

### Banquet of Tolerance

By Ali Acar

On Tuesday evening, January 27, 1997, Fethullah Gülen, chairman of the Foundation of Writers and Journalists, gave a Ramadan dinner. Held in the Hilton Hotel Exhibition Hall, it was more a banquet of tolerance and love than of food.

Even the representatives of Christianity were very impressed. Their views, which they summarized as "mosque and church side by side," were later explained as: "We're all on the same ship. If it leaks, we'll all sink together." Speaking on behalf of theater artists, Gazanfer Özcan began his speech by saying: "Today is my birthday." Weeping, he had difficulty completing his talk. This flood of feelings affected people from almost all social segments.

Fethullah Hodja, who suffers from diabetes, did not want to speak due to the effects of fasting and an above-300 blood sugar count. However, unable to turn away from everyone's insistence, he mounted the podium. After dinner, a small group of politicians and journalists gathered around him and discussed recent events.[291]

---

[290] At the end of Can, "Fethullah Gülen Ile Ufuk Turu."

[291] *Yeni Yüzyil*, 29 January 1997.

### *The Fethullah Gülen Reality*

By Memduh Bayraktaroglu

Everyone taking a breath in this country should accept that there is a Fethullah Gülen reality in Turkey. This reality is growing like an avalanche... It is a reality that brings me together at the same point with Cengiz Çandar, Gülay Ertok and Hilmi Yavuz. Its name is said to be love of humanity.

Or, in short: LOVE... Last night I witnessed this tremendous power at the traditional Ramadan dinner held by the Foundation of Journalists and Writers at the Hilton Hotel... After dinner I listened with my heart beating with excitement and enthusiasm...

One who doesn't retort those who curse him... One who does not strike those who strike him... One who forgives those who slander him...

Like Yunus Emre—loving all creatures for the sake of the Creator... Without becoming enshrouded in darkness... Without appearing as an enemy of Atatürk...

His face is clean-shaven...A shining heart... People—those who govern and the governed—need to see this reality...[292]

### *What We Thought at the Iftar*

By Riza Zelyut

I was invited to a breaking-the-fast dinner (*iftar*) Monday evening at the Hilton Hotel. The dinner was given by the Foundation of Writers and Journalists, which has attracted attention in recent years by its members' extraordinary contributions to enlivening the atmosphere of dialogue and tolerance in Turkey. It is under the spiritual chairmanship of Fethullah Gülen. Although it has invited me to many of its activities, until now I hadn't accepted any. That evening at the Hilton, I found the beautiful, warm, and sincere atmosphere that I had expected.

---

[292] *Aksam*, 30 January 1997.

Having developed an understanding that gives importance to religious motifs, this Foundation brought about an atmosphere that didn't make me feel like a stranger. It presented to us a gentleness and contemporaneousness that said to an Islamic society: "This is what we should be like."

Chairman Latif Erdogan uttered two sentences that startled me. He spoke in a way as if to mean: "We view as normal the attitude of those who don't know Islam and who oppose it. Actually, what we should dwell upon is how those who say they know Islam have brought it to an unrecognizable state."

I arrived at the hall a short time before the dinner began. When I saw that Hüseyin Dede, general director of the Cem Foundation, was there, I asked to be excused from my table and went to his side. A little later, I saw Professor Izzettin Dogan. It was interesting that the Alawis weren't forgotten.[293]

### Gülen's Ramadan Dinner

By Özlem Öztürk

"Until now I had never attended any political party's dinner. I declined because of my diabetes. I don't know with what ideas this dinner was planned. I didn't plan this matter with them."

This was Gülen's explanation of why he didn't accept Erbakan's invitation. When asked about some sheikhs arriving at Erbakan's dinner in Mercedes, he asked: "Is there a rule that people in turbans and long robes can't ride in Mercedes? These people buy these cars to ride in. You don't have to wear a turban to be rich. This type of clothing isn't my style, but is a special costume needed to ride in a Mercedes?"[294]

---

[293] *Aksam*, 29 January 1997.

[294] *Milliyet*, 29 January 1997.

## *The Weeping Man*

By Bekir Coskun

Fethullah Gülen, who didn't attend Erbakan's Ramadan dinner for Muslim community leaders, gave a dinner that received wide press coverage. Christian and Jewish community leaders also attended... There also were theater artists, journalists, representatives of foreign embassies, including some socialists and Alawi *dede*s (elderly leaders)... Out of respect for the guests, the prayer before the meal was first read in Turkish and then in English...

Some journalist even called Fethullah Gülen Hodja's dinner a "banquet of tolerance." Especially in these days, which of us doesn't need tolerance and peace?

As a person with watery eyes, I now understand better why Fethullah Gülen cries a lot. Tolerance and peace... Perhaps the future of our nation, which is knotted in these two magical words, can be unknotted with a string of tears... At least crying is the most intense thought...

In my opinion, intelligent Islam should rebel against the unintelligent...[295]

## Hand-in-Hand for Happy Tomorrows

The Foundation of Writers and Journalists celebrated its third birthday at the Lütfi Kirdar International Congress and Exhibition Center (Istanbul), on September 30, 1996. The guests, irrespective of religion, race, or social status, created a tableau of social accord and tolerance, something that Turkey needs. The speakers agreed that tolerance and love are mandatory for not only Turkey, but for the whole world.

In his speech, Fethullah Gülen Hodja said:

> For one or two centuries, our people have been pushed to "swim in separate lanes" with different ideas. Today that

---

[295] *Hürriyet*, 30 January 1997.

period of differences is being experienced. What was to be gained by this? Was it gained? No. We were in friction with one another. We separated in order to solve the problem, but we didn't attain what we expected to. As a result, we lost our own paradise.

## Through the Eyes of the Speakers

* Journalists and writers seek to help others and spread tolerance in society. These two institutions, which take material, spiritual, and intellectual things as essential to all people, have come together in the body of the Foundation of Writers and Journalists and created a very meaningful platform. Social tolerance will spread through the activities of such foundations. (Cemil Tunç, minister of state)

* Celebrating its second year with the theme of "Tolerance" last year, this year the foundation has fulfilled a basic need by emphasizing "Hand-in-Hand for Happy Tomorrows." Humanity is the main axis in a state based on law. It is contrary to humanity and a law-based state to direct people with dogmatic values or force them in a particular direction. (Ismail Kahraman, minister of culture)

* People can't help fighting among themselves. We should know our Creator and ourselves and love all creatures for the sake of our Creator. This foundation is a result of harmony, brotherhood, and helping others, all of which its supporters have sought, faithfully and enthusiastically, to make current. Today we see the *baraka* (blessing) and result of joint efforts for two years. (Riza Akçali, MP, former minister of the environment)

* While there are people hung on electric poles all over the world, and while elsewhere rocks are answered with bullets, we should be grateful for the environment we're living in and think seriously about who prepared it. Amidst thousands of identities, we all share a common one: We are in a position to walk hand-in-hand towards this superior identity. (Professor Toktamis Ates, university lecturer and columnist for *Cumhuriyet*)

* This tableau here shows that we have begun to walk hand-in-hand. We came together 3 years earlier. Our achievements so far show that our tomorrows are going to be happier. We have taken important steps in the name of tolerance. (Professor Nur Vergin)

### *Agreement without Conflict*

While Samuel P. Huntington's "clash of civilizations" thesis is being debated, a contrary movement aimed at dialogue is growing slowly. The "Hand-in-Hand for Happy Tomorrows" conference, organized by the Foundation of Writers and Journalists and attended by members of three religions as well as people of religion, scholars, and media representatives, was this effort's first harvest. The Phanariot Greek Patriarch Bartholomeos I was applauded for his speech. His words regarding Fethullah Gülen were taken as a tangible indication that reconciliation can be attained without having to live some painful experiences.

### Multicolored Mosaic

The participation of Georges Marovitch (the Vatican's Istanbul representative), Kati Pelatre (the Catholic community's spiritual leader), Isa Karatas (spokesman for Turkey's Protestant Presbyterian community), and Fotis Ksidas (the Greek chief consulate) created a multicolored mosaic. Speakers' words were full of tolerance and very appreciated. Üzeyir Garih stated: "At this moment, people are being trained here to love one another and form relationships with each other."

Patriarch Bartholomeos I said: "Fethullah Gülen Hodja and I love each other very much. He is an example of harmony and tolerance for all of us, a model of high values for all humanity." Gülen remarked: "We didn't accept each other internally, so we lost our paradise." The words of both religious leaders indicated a point of coming together.[296]

### *A Special Night*

By Taha Kivanç [Fehmi Koru]

After the meeting, when I asked people "Who was the most unusual guest at the dinner?" I got very different answers. One was surprised by the presence of Banu Alkan, the "local Aphrodite," who came on her own. Another mentioned Emel Sayin, who came with a friend. Perihan Savas also came. I saw Mustafa Keser, too, leaning on a chair listening to what others were saying.

For some, the most interesting guest was Phanariot Greek Patriarch Bartholomeos I. Others noticed members of the Jewish community: Istanbul M. P. Cefi Kamhi, businessmen Üzeyir Garih,

---

[296] *Zaman*, 2 October 1996.

and Alber Bilen. Prominent businessmen Feyyaz Berker and Rona Yircali were mentioned as "surprise names."

Meetings of the Foundation of Writers and Journalists are enriched by Fethullah Gülen Hodjaefendi's participation. Due to previous activities, his messages have been long-standing current topics. This time, Phanariot Patriarch Bartholomeos I's presence and his words: "We love Hodjaefendi very much," probably made positive reverberations outside the country as well as in our press.

Hodjaefendi was rumored to be very ill. Several speakers remarked on this. When guests saw that he spoke with difficulty regarding a recommendation that "associations and foundations for tolerance should be opened in every corner," they became concerned about his health. Apparently, he had a serious cold.[297]

### For Happy Tomorrows

By Tahir K. Makal

With his sensitive heart, his productive and contemplative brain, and his works and actions, Fethullah Gülen Hodjaefendi is this age's Mawlana Rumi. Wherever you go in the Turkish–Islamic world, you encounter one of his works or activities. You will see his schools diffusing light in many places as far as Moldavia's Gagzeli free district, Azerbaijan, Turkmenistan, and Kazakhstan. Fethullah Hodja is an important spokesman for national problems, too. His lessons at the mosque contain rich examples in a language that believers can understand, and his approach to Turkey's problems is moderate. Rumi was also like this. He conversed with state officials, who would visit him, and was close to them.

Three years old, the Foundation of Writers and Journalists continues its successful activities under the presidency of Latif Erdogan. Last night it celebrated its anniversary in the Lütfi Kirdar Congress Center. The topic of last year's meeting was "Tolerance." This time, the meeting was held around the main idea of "Hand-in-Hand for Happy Tomorrows." More than 2,000 people attended.

---

[297] *Zaman*, 2 October 1996.

The event was arranged along modern lines... The guests comprised Turkey's mosaic. People from various religions and lines of thought were tolerant, loving, and respectful of each other. We held hands for happy tomorrows...

The foundation enabled us to experience a beautiful evening. May its horizon be broad and its road illuminated; let's remain in advanced, contemporary tolerance and enlightenment.[298]

## *Tolerance Awards Found Their Owners*

By Muhammed Pamuk

### Tolerance Hosted at the Çiragan Palace

The year 1995, declared "Tolerance Year" by UNESCO, was supported by Turkey. The Foundation of Writers and Journalists presented its 1995 Tolerance Awards last night (January 4, 1996) in a magnificent ceremony.

In the well-attended ceremonies, everyone was given an olive branch. Foundation members on duty and members of the jury pinned red carnations, which represented Hazrat Ali, on their collars. The jury was composed of Dr. Agah Oktay Güner, Ali Coskun, Hülya Koçyigit, Kamran Inan, Latif Erdogan, Mustafa Çalisan, Professor Nilüfer Göle, Togay Bayatli, and Zülfü Livaneli.

It was decided to give 14 people awards in 10 different branches. Fethullah Gülen, honorary president and foundation board member, was given a bouquet of roses for his contributions to creating an environment of tolerance in Turkey. Coming to the podium at the guests' insistence, he stated that:

> It's useless to look somewhere else for it with its true depth and dimensions. The tolerance in our characters is the thought of Rumi and Yunus Emre. If we can grasp the spirit of Habib Allah's (Prophet Muhammad) words in Islam, we'll understand the basis of our religion. I truly believe that this world, which has lost its balance, will understand the truth after it hits its head left and right. I beg God that the coming years be built on love and tolerance, not hatred, malice, anger, and violence.

---

[298] *Orta Dogu*, 2 October 1996.

The biographies of the award recipients were shown to the audience in a slide display.[299]

## Tolerance Awards Found Their Holders

By Murat Batmankaya

The 1995 Tolerance Awards designated by the Foundation of Writers and Journalists were presented to recipients in a ceremony at the Çiragan Palace last night. Guests from many different social segments attended, including members of Parliament and the arts. The person receiving the most attention during the evening was Fethullah Gülen.

Speakers included Riza Akçali (former minister of the environment), Melih Gökçek (mayor of Ankara), Ertugrul Günay (former CHP MP), Nail Güreli (president of the Journalists' Association), Hasan Cemal (journalist), Orhan Gencebay (singer), and Sevket Demirel (businessman). All expressed their views on tolerance by quoting from Yunus Emre, Ahmed Yesevi, and Mawlana Rumi.

Before presenting the awards, which included the media, science, thought and the arts, a slide show describing the award fields. The jury consisted of Agâh Oktay Güner, Ali Coskun, Hülya Koçyigit, Kamran Inan, Latif Erdogan, Mustafa Çalisan, Nilüfer Göle, Togay Bayatli, and Zülfü Livaneli. After making their evaluations, the honorees were announced:

- Columnist: Taha Akyol and Cengiz Çandar
- Media/TV: Toktamis Ates and Abdurrahman Dilipak.
- Media/Journalism: Münire Acim
- Arts: Baris Manço, Kutsi Ergüner, and Fehmi Gerçeker
- Diplomacy: Isik Sadik Ahmet
- Science: Mehmet Aydin
- Nature and Environment: Hayrettin Karaca
- Family: Perihan Savas
- Help to the Handicapped: Müjdat Gezen and R. Tayyip Erdogan
- Sports: Fatih Terim

---

[299] *Yeni Safak*, 6 January 1996.

Baris Manço pointed to his long hair as an example of Turkey's tolerance. Müjdat Gezen apologized to the handicapped for misunderstandings regarding his following their lives closely. Toktamis Ates joked that although he had not made his student Abdurrahman Dilipak a Kemalist, he had not become an advocate of the Shari'a either. Cengiz Çandar stressed that the responsibility the award brought with it was more important than the award. Ertugrul Günay indicated that by declaring 1995 a "Year of Tolerance," UNESCO actually wanted to cover up it intolerance to Muslim countries.

At the ceremony's end, a special award was presented to Fethullah Gülen, honorary president and member of the foundation's board of directors.[300]

### *Enough!*

By Süleyman Yagiz

We are in a period when it is a mistake to look constantly at problems from an ideological perspective, because this is a fixed idea and an obsession. Do not misunderstand. The fixed idea is not ideology; rather, every event is looked at through ideological glasses. I want to point this out specifically. Tolerance is a necessity in our country's conditions. We do not have the luxury of living angry with one another, nor should we. No one has the right to exclude anyone else. Tolerance requires forbearance toward opposing parties. In this respect, we should not see tolerance, reconciliation in society, and social harmony as uniformity.

For example, Toktamis Ates (columnist for the leftist *Cumhuriyet*) and Abdurrahman Dilipak (columnist for *Akit,* which favors radical views on Islam) sharing the same award, and Fethullah Gülen shaking hands with Ates in the awards ceremony are, in my opinion, steps forward. We should be able to congratulate those contributing to this progress.[301]

---

[300] *Hürriyet*, 6 January 1996.

[301] *Takvim*, January 8, 1996.

## *Enmity toward Tolerance Is a Confession of Narrow-mindedness*

By Arslan Bulut

Creating a foundation of tolerance among intellectuals carries priority from Turkey's perspective. Because Turkish intellectuals have split into three distinct groups, they have developed their own different concepts and no longer understand each other.

Some people, who have been made columnists only because they belong to a certain ideology, have sharply criticized those— both followers of the same and of other ideologies—who approach others with tolerance. They do so because when a foundation of tolerance is born, there will be no work for people of poor quality. Those who have achieved position and interests because they adhere to an ideology, but who have no talents or works, will be unemployed.

What would happen if worthy people in the three groups respected one another, even if they did not accept each other's ideas? Before anything else, they would see that they are not opposed to one another, but side-by-side one another. In this situation, everyone would benefit from the other's positive ideas. Those who develop negative thoughts would have to forego such an approach.[302]

### *Awards for Reconciliation*

The Encouraging of National Reconciliation Awards was made at ceremonies organized by the Foundation of Writers and Journalists on December 24, 1997. Its honorary chairman is Fethullah Gülen, widely known as Fethullah Hodja. The Night for Encouraging National Reconciliation, held at the Hilton Convention Center and hosted by Professor Mim Kemal Öke, began with singing the Independence March and everyone standing at attention.

---

[302] *Aksam*, 9 January 1996.

After a video display entitled *We're One Family*, the awards were presented: Hülya Koçyigit, Gülay Göktürk, Riza Zelyut, Nevval Sevindi, and Sahin Özer in the Media–Arts category; Istanbul University Theological Faculty Dean Professor Nuri Öztürk, Professor Nilüfer Göle, Professor Halil Inalcik, Professor Ihsan Dogramaci, and singer Sezen Aksu's father Sami Yildirim (founder and principal of the Private Yamanlar College) in the Education–Culture category; and Professor Serif Mardin, who received an award in this category but could not attend due to ill health.

Türk-Is General Chairman Bayram Meral, as well as businessmen Üzeyir Garih and Nihat Gökyigit, were presented awards in the Business World category, as were businessman Sakip Sabanci and Aydin Dogan, owner of the *Hürriyet* and *Milliyet* newspapers, respectively (they were not able to attend). In their places, awards were accepted by Sabanci Holding General Secretary Ertügrul Ergöz and *Hürriyet* executive council member Yasar Eroglu.

Chairman of the Turkish Parliament Hikmet Çetin and DSP General Chairman and Deputy Prime Minister Bülent Ecevit, who were deemed worthy of awards in the Politics category, did not attend due to government budgetary meetings. The award to the former chairman of the Turkish Parliament, Mustafa Kalem, was accepted by his wife. The "Man of the State" award was presented to Süleyman Demirel.

### Ilicak's Words
Journalist–writer Nazli Ilicak, who presented the award to Professor Öztürk, stated:

> I see the Turkish President's presence here as an effort to correct an ugly mistake. The Honorable Demirel's presence here is in the nature of an answer to those in Ankara speaking inappropriately. Our distinguished Hodja is a person with a very refined spirit, and even the smallest thing hurts him very much. For this reason, he offered to turn over the schools connected to him to the Ministry of National Education. Even if he gives them, we won't agree to it. Perhaps these words written to me in a letter by the Honorable Demirel from Zincirbozan will explain everything better: "Even in its weakest form the moon is pointed to and it is said: 'There it is.'"

Her words: "Esteemed Hodja, despite everything, you're still on your feet," received loud applause. President Demirel appeared to be very emotional at this time.[303]

### The Republic Is Not at Stake

By Ihsan Yilmaz and Özlem Öztürk

Indicating that he did not see political Islam as a danger in Turkey, Fethullah Gülen said: "Even those people to whom political Islam was ascribed implemented secular and democratic republican principles when they came to power." Answering the questions of journalists at the National Reconciliation Awards ceremonies, Gülen stated that Islam does not separate political and nonpolitical. He continued:

> The thing called Islam is derived from the Qur'an. Turkey has always been 98% Muslim. In such a country, searching for political and nonpolitical Islam is not right. We put some things forward without thinking. At a time when we're seeking reconciliation, we're weakening tolerance and dialogue.

Stating that he is ready to turn over the schools connected to his community if the government wants him to do so, he said:

> The Ministry of National Education controls these schools. If there were a danger of reactionaryism, they would have said so. I don't know 80% of the founders of these schools. Among supporters there are Jews and Christians.

Giving messages of unity that night, Demirel remarked:

> I support activities that solidify the Turkish nation's unity and solidarity like this evening's program. If some among you are trying to cause difficulties, oppose them. Regardless of which belief or ethnic root you come from, this is your country and state. You're all equal. You've paid your dues. I commend these activities. This ceremony was very educational. I accept this award on behalf of Turkey's indivisible unity, the happiness of the Turkish nation, and living in peace.[304]

---

[303] *Aksam*, 26 December 1997.

[304] *Milliyet*, 27 December 1997.

## *Reconciliation Is a Virtue*

By Riza Zelyut

Last night at the Hilton Hotel, while looking at the people who had come together from different social segments, I felt that I had seen the magnificent tableau of Turkey's next step. And in this tableau I saw once again the distinct color of President Süleyman Demirel's essential portrait.

As an Alawi writer, I thought of the weight of the responsibility of my accepting a "National Reconciliation Award" from a group that takes its place in the right-wing of the Sunni social segment. A journalist brother wanted to rebuke me based on prejudice from the old-fashioned, imported leftist–rightist polarization. To his question "What are you doing here?" I gave the following multidimensional answer:

- One: My place is wherever reconciliation can be found.
- Two: Prejudice blinds people.
- Three: Moreover, if prejudice includes polarization, it darkens a person's heart.
- Four: Bringing up events from the past benefits no one.
- Five: Someone thinking like that yesterday can think the same today. The idea that "whatever a person is at age 7, he or she is the same at age 70" is incorrect, according to social psychology. This idea means that education does not benefit people. For this reason, no one has the right to condemn another with stereotyped ideas or say that he or she is bad because he or she used to think such and such.
- Six: It's time to say "good-bye" to divisive, provocative, and polarizing concepts imported in the past. Judging today according to leftist–rightist concepts is a means of salvation for people who cannot see development and change.
- Seven: Regardless of what President Süleyman Demirel did or said in his past political life, he is the "man of the state" in my heart today. It's good to follow in his tracks.
- Eight: Fethullah Gülen is a spiritual guide for a social segment that is very sensitive to religion. If this guidance is open to tolerance and dialogue and to creating national harmony, why shouldn't I shake his extended hand? How long are we going to nurture and grow the old enmity in our hearts? What did this polarization gain us to date, and what will this race to create rivals gain us after this?

The Foundation of Writers and Journalists is truly taking on a leading role with efforts that can be an example to other organizations. Instead of being suspicious and looking for criminal factors like detectives just because Fethullah Gülen is behind these people, let's try and take a lesson from them. If they have brought an important cause like national reconciliation to the country's agenda, let's support them instead of digging a well in front of them.

Those who consider Islam as identical to the Welfare Party (RP) also identify Fethullah Hodja and the world and the religious views of those people with the RP. Due to this incorrect assessment, every person who is sensitive to religion is branded with the RP stamp and pushed to one side. Only those who have been saved from the enslavement of their own fears understand that this is not the reality.

When you look at Fethullah Hodja and their attachment to him, you see how much importance they give to educating people.[305]

### Ramadan and New Year's Eve

#### By Taha Akyol

Celal Dogan is Gaziantep's leftist mayor. During our university years we fought a lot; he was on the left and I was on the right. Now we are very good friends.

The only city government the Left did not lose (in the elections) is Gaziantep, and the reason is Dogan's success. After congratulating me on the phone for Ramadan and New Year's Eve, he remarked: "As a city government, we hung illuminated messages between the minarets for Ramadan, and for New Year's Eve we lit up the city. We celebrated both Ramadan and New Year's Eve on lighted billboards. Gaziantep is shining…"

That's great… Why should one light or celebration be the enemy of "the other"? Let everyone celebrate as they like, and light lights as they like… And live as they like…

---

[305] *Aksam*, 26 December 1997.

But we are in a period of polarization. The meeting of the Ramadan illuminated messages and the New Year's Eve lights becomes even more meaningful in such a period. Our rough political culture reveals itself in phrases like "smashing and eliminating," closed fists, and shouts of "May he be damned!"

Regardless of his aim, an Istanbul mayor should have avoided saying "minarets as bayonet, mosques as barracks..." Regardless of his aim, a Supreme Court chief should have refrained from saying "those barking with spoiled blood, spoiled milk, handicapped brains and spirits..."

The words "making no concessions," which we like so much, have a different connotation in our political culture. Putting acceptance of each other aside, if we do not make concessions, how are we going to reach reconciliation and become a harmonious society?

Philosophy Professor Macit Gökberk writes:

> The philosophy of the English enlightenment developed in a calm atmosphere of investigation; the French enlightenment was a philosophy of conflict from the beginning. This ... was due to the ideas it brought creating a harsh opposition to the social-political structure left over from the Middle Ages...[306]

Tolerance is the condition for social harmony in our age. In our time, liberal and reconciliatory values are necessary for every ideology, every subculture, and even the law! In our age one of the most important factors of a "nation" is the unity of individual citizens with liberal rights!

President Demirel's accepting a plaque from Hodjaefendi, who has rendered education a great service, was very appropriate. The President should attend the opening of an Alawi meeting hall and a whirling dervish ceremony... He should listen to a Kurdish song from a Kurdish folklore group.

Just as Ramadan's not being in conflict with New Year's Eve is something wonderful, all moderate and reconciliatory values are

---

[306] *The Evolution of Philosophy*, 66.

also wonderful... I wish our motherland Turkey Happy New Year and happy tomorrows![307]

### Reconciliation and Tolerance

By Nazli Ilicak

I received so many telephone calls and fax messages regarding the speech I made at the Foundation of Writers and Journalists that it's impossible to answer them individually. For this reason, I want to thank everyone in my column. Some circles have again, unfortunately, interpreted this sincere and unaffected talk as "enmity toward the military."

It is not becoming for journalists to talk about themselves in their columns, but there is benefit in underscoring everything one more time. I'm a nationalist. I've always taken pride in the Turkish soldier's success. I've stood up for the Turkish Armed Forces. If today I'm going from court to court and giving testimony to prosecutors due to the claim that I have insulted the army, since I have not changed, this means that something in Turkey has changed.

Also, no one should look for a calf under an ox. The speech I made at the evening for reconciliation was a call for accordance. Of course, accord will be reached around true and beautiful things.

### Call for Harmony
The following is what I said at that night:

> I see the Honorable Demirel's being here among us as an effort to correct an ugly mistake. In some circles biting rumors are being produced regarding the service to others for which Fethullah Gülen Hodjaefendi has taken the lead. Demirel's presence is in the nature of an answer to those who are speaking inappropriately.

> Gülen Hodja is extremely sensitive. Unbecoming talks hurts and grieves him. For this reason, he said he is going to turn over the schools. Esteemed Hodja! Even if you donate those schools, we will not allow it. Esteemed Hodja! I want to address you with one sentence that Demirel wrote to me from

---

[307] *Milliyet*, 1 January 1998.

Zincirbozan: "Even if the moon is in it's weakest moment as a new moon, in fact, even if there is an eclipse of the moon, it is still pointed to and said: 'There it is.'"

Do not feel sad that your cause might become weak. That cause continues to enlighten many hearts. Is a solar or lunar eclipse permanent?

## And Letters

For the attitude of the quiet majority to be better understood, I would like to print some of the thank-you letters:

- Your giving support—even if it's moral support—to the esteemed Fethullah Hodja, who for many years has devotedly worked day and night for his country and nation, and your helping to increase the love and enthusiasm of him and his friends is a great service to the noble Turkish Nation...

- With this brave speech, I believe you've made a service equal to the educational institutions that have proven themselves inside and outside of the country. May God increase the number of sincere and struggling people who think like you...

- Last night my wife and children and I watched your speech on social reconciliation with tears in our eyes... You became a fresh breath for hundreds of thousands of warriors of love who don't expect the slightest thing from anyone in this world, who only seek God's approval, who love and extend their hands to all creatures for the sake of the Creator, who are struggling to raise a generation that can enable the state to become an eternal one and who are willing to be a doormat for this cause...

## Call for Tolerance

I published some of these letters from ordinary citizens to make their voice heard. Listen to this voice and to pious people's chests full of fear. It seems almost as if they are waiting for rains of wrath that can fall at any moment. Come and let's try and understand each other. Let's disperse the clouds of doubt that have come between us. All beautiful people of the Turkish nation, come and let's embrace each other.

Perhaps it is a divine coincidence that the New Year begins on the first day of Ramadan. Different lifestyles and beliefs can melt in one crucible. Roads going in different directions can even cross.

The Qur'an commands:

> And spy not on each other, nor speak ill of each other behind their backs...O humanity! We created you from a single (pair) of a male and female, and made you into nations and tribes that ye may know each other. (49:12–13)

> Let not some men among you laugh at others: It may be that the (latter) are better that the (former)... Nor defame nor be sarcastic to each other. (49:11)

The Qur'an commands accord and tolerance. Thus the Turkish nation can overcome discord and easily find the true path.[308]

### *Applause to Gülen from the Heart*

By Jefi Kamhi

Actually, I would have expected nothing else from Fethullah Hodja. He is following the path of his ancestors in a way that becomes them. For centuries Turks have shown all people love and respect. They did not bring religious war or oppression in their wake; rather, they enabled people to gain their freedom. Even in the Balkans. The other day I went to Hungary. They always praise Turks. I went to Romania. Turks are met there with the same love.

I have been following his tolerance initiatives, which I applaud. We can hold these beautiful social values in a way worthy of the world. Great catastrophes that happened elsewhere and events that occurred in Germany cannot be erased for thousands of years and are always in the news. Nothing can be erased from history. Gülen's activities should be applauded. If my ancestors had not seen that tolerance from the Ottomans and Turkey, I would not be alive.[309]

### *Turkish Renaissance*

By Seref Oguz

A word can stop a war; a word can cause decapitation
A word can turn poisonous food into butter and honey.

---

[308] *Aksam*, 28 December 1997.

[309] *Zaman*, 11 March 1998. Former DYP Deputy Kamhi is a prominent Jewish businessman.

This is the prescription for dialogue put forward by Yunus Emre, this region's and this tradition's great man. Dialogue is necessary, essential, and the preface of the Information Age. At the National Reconciliation awards ceremony organized by the Foundation of Writers and Journalists, we saw one more time how thirsty we are for dialogue as a country and society.

Cracks begin at the point where communication channels are blocked. The same thing condition in a person's body will lead to a crisis and take life away. Dialogue for the society is more important than a person's body. If communication is not kept alive and open among social segments, streets will become lakes of blood, a generation will be destroyed, and the place in which we live will become a Hell on Earth.

Since we are talking about the Information Age, dialogue should be our constitution. In an environment in which all science knowledge accumulated since the beginning of time can be communicated from one place to another in less than a second, you cannot not exist with your old paradigm. You have to open your ears and eyes and comprehend information coming from outside with as little distortion as possible. However, even more important is that you know that to understand the world outside yourself, you must establish a dialogue with it and become harmonious with it.

Unfortunately, results of the World Index of Intolerance does not say good things (about us). In the index, we are in a bad way in the order of "intolerance to neighbors" percentages. A list of descriptions is given regarding neighbors like "sick, addicted to drugs, from another religion, from another sect, sentenced to imprisonment, and of a different ideology" and then the question is asked: "To what degree are you intolerant of such people?" Turkey's scores are at the level of 90% and above; in the countries we imitate, the scores range from 10% to 40%.

If you subtract the Intolerance coefficient from 100, you reach the Tolerance Index. In Turkey, when calculated as above, this index is under 10%. Result: We're at the peak of intolerance.

There is an amazing similarity between the intolerance index and the inflation rate. What really amazed me is the correlation between the tolerance index and the knowledge index. The below-10% tolerance figure is almost exactly the same as the knowledge index.

Tolerance, dialogue, and social harmony... Is it not time for us to include these in our lives? The answer to this question came yesterday from Nevval Sevindi, who received an award at the Reconciliation Night. In her thank-you speech, she said: "I have a goal! It's to establish a national cultural synthesis and realize a modern Turkish renaissance."

Waiting at the threshold, we have remained in the shadow of the West's Age of Awakening. We missed the Renaissance, and come today to an age that presents this opportunity once again. The mortar of a Turkish renaissance is knowledge. This will not turn only the fate of our economy but, at the same time, will make us the master of the global village. Dialogue will bring harmony, and harmony will bring success. As a result of this success, I see not only a Turkish renaissance but also a Turkey as the master of the Information Society.[310]

### Rain of Awards on the Gala
### Night of "Island of Dogs"

The film's themes are the lack of communication, loneliness, deception, and abuse of others' rights resulting from modern city life, as well as themes of nature, environment, and love of animals. The Foundation of Writers and Journalists presented awards for "successful efforts to put into action one's love of nature and animals" to TBMM Chairman Mustafa Kalemli's wife Betül Kalemli, Professor Ismet Sungurbey, Professor Zafer Ayvaz, Nergis Yazgan (president, Association for the Protection of Natural Life), Dr. Ilhan Gökgöl, Faruk Yalçin, Esin Elingür, Ediz Hun, Nevzat Ceylan, Türkan Akalin, and Nurten Akoral.[311]

---

[310] *Milliyet*, 27 December 1997.

[311] *Zaman*, 29 December 1996. The event was held on December 28, 1996.

## *In the Midst of Loneliness*

### Halit Refig Explains

I did not make a film addressing youth. The subject of the film is old age, a period when we come face to face with death. As Orson Welles said in that famous song: "I know what it means to be young, but do you know what it means to be old?"

*Island of Dogs* is not an action film. There are no heroes with superhuman powers. In fact, the hero is weak, powerless, and clumsy. Refig says: "I don't believe that people have divine powers." He adds: "This film might be interesting for people who have come to the stage of thinking about life." Saying that he always felt close to Fethullah Gülen's community, Refig concluded: "I've never been shown by the intellectuals of the left the closeness that I've seen from the Nur community and other conservative groups."[312]

### We Are in a Period of Empty Commotion

Refig: One sentence in the film reflected the beyond: "Explain the truths that people aren't aware of..." The film's name is *Island of Dogs*, but it represents nature as a microcosm. The dogs symbolize nature's animate creatures. If there can be harmony among all these, then real harmony can be dreamed about. The seed of this film was a dream. While making it into a scenario, I wanted to maintain its dream characteristic. Dreams are irrational; they are ridiculous when you look at them externally, but are open to interpretation. A dream doesn't reveal itself openly.

Kuyas: But reality is stronger. You're subconsciously a rich director. Your personal films are more powerful. It's as if you've limited your personality a little for the sake of social engagement. What do you say?

Refig: I'm aware of what you've said.[313]

---

[312] *Orta Dogu*, 8 January 1997

[313] *Milliyet*, 8 January 1997.

## *Dialogue among Civilizations*

### By Ismail Bezirci

As another dialogue attempt, the "Dialogue among Civilizations" congress was organized by the Foundation of Writers and Journalists.

Indicating that the attending scholars are experts in their fields, Professor Mim Kemal Öke said that participants will include Professors Barbara Stowasser, Robert Royal, and Richard Longorne (USA); Professor Johannes Kalter (Germany); M. E. Yapp (England); Professor Thomas Michel (Italy); and Gilles Kepel (France). The 2-day congress will be held in the Lütfi Kirdar Congress Hall.[314]

## *Dialogue among Civilizations Congress*

### By Zeynep Çuhaci

The congress organized by the Foundation of Writers and Journalists, known for its closeness to Fethullah Gülen's community, began yesterday at the Istanbul Hilton Hotel.

The Vatican Ankara Representative, Pierre Luigi Celata; the Chairman of the Board of Catholic Spiritual Affairs, Pellat Lui; the Head of the Syriac Catholic Community, Yusuf Sag; the Head of the Ancient Syriac Orthodox Community, Samuel Akdemir; Kirkor Damatyan, the head priest representing the Armenian Orthodox Patriarch; the Vatican Istanbul Representative, Georges Marovitch; representatives of the Komsaua and Jewish Community; and representatives of the Metropolitan Greek Patriarch attended the congress to discuss "interreligious dialogue."

Fethullah Gülen was unable to attend due to his illness.[315]

---

[314] *Yeni Safak.*

[315] *Yeni Yüzyil.*

## *Islam Is Civilization*

By Firat Gülver

The "Dialogue Among Civilizations" congress was a meeting place for people from political, scientific, business, and art circles, as well as for representatives of various religions. It emphasized that dialogue is necessary if people are going to get to know each other and reach agreement. The event, sponsored by the Foundation of Writers and Journalists and Park Holding, began at the Istanbul Hilton Hotel.

Making the opening address, Professor Mim Kemal Öke said that its purpose was to abandon the idea of accepting mistakes for the sake of reconciliation and to oppose the status quo. He said:

> We believe that with an open heart and a hand extended in friendship, we can solve problems beyond accepting one another in different positions and cultural identities. Even if we can't solve them, we can fulfil the responsibility of being a global society and discuss them in a civilized manner in such forums as this.

After Professor Öke's address, the ANAP Istanbul M.P. Yilmaz Karakoyunlu and Ali Coskun each made a speech.

In his talk, Presidential Consultant Mustafa Basoglu pointed out that recently the press has contained ideas depicting Islam as the target of a local struggle. He said:

> Some people are trying to depict Islam as a system of thought, belief, and religion that must be feared. Islam is the last religion sent by God to His servants. God wouldn't send a thing to His servants that should be feared, fought over, or that would give trouble to people. We have differences of belief. No one should fear Islam. Rather, it should be accepted as an important element that allows people to live together in peace. Believers will believe, and unbelievers will continue on their way according to their own belief.

Ankara Mayor Melih Gökçek said that some groups, both inside and outside of Turkey, persist in asserting that Islam has no place in a democracy. He said he hopes that the congress' beautiful tableau will be an example for some media personalities who have tried to create enmity among people every day for the past 6 months.

Georgetown University Professor Barbara Stowasser maintained that the flow of history shows a mutually constructive and productive interaction among civilizations, not a clash. She said: "At any rate, the clash is not of civilizations but of interests and power, even if these conflicts are shown as cultural symbols."

Professor Mehmet Aydin, dean of 9 Eylül University's Theological Faculty, said that dialogue should be made on three levels:

> First, cultures, civilizations, and people should be made known. A large part of today's conflict proceeds from ignorance. Different social segments should get to know each other. The root of conflict in Turkey is ignorance. Because social segments didn't get to know each other and didn't try to know each other, because they were afraid that the idols in their heads would be destroyed, and because they didn't want to change their decisions, they remain closed to learning. A closed state doesn't give birth to dialogue. Second, dialogue should be considered on a critical level. An exchange of knowledge isn't enough. Knowledge has to be criticized and passed through a critical strainer. Third, members of different cultures and religions digest what they learn and make it a part of their lives.

In the afternoon session, Professor Thomas Michel from the Interreligious Dialogue Council, and Professor Johannes Kalter from Stuttgart's Linden-Museum each presented a paper. Professor Süleyman Hayri Bolay, chairman of Gazi University's Philosophy Department, and Professor Ilber Ortayli held a discussion.[316]

### Observing the Religious Festival
### (Ramadan 'Id al-Fitr, 3 February 1998)

Scenes that Turkey has yearned for took place last night at the Plaza Cevahir Hotel in a "congratulating the religious festival" ceremony organized by the Foundation of Writers and Journalists.

---

[316] *Türkiye.*

## Hodjaefendi: "We Have To Tolerate Each Other"

The night's guest of honor, Fethullah Gülen Hodjaefendi, touched on the importance of social accord. He said:

> Yesterday our society was in ignorance, poverty, and conflict. While entering a new age, we haven't yet fully escaped from these. We've made important progress in science and technology, and our businessmen have begun the process of overcoming poverty. Unfortunately, we haven't achieved the same success when it comes to eliminating conflict. The reality of intolerance, imposition of some ideas, and oppression of thought continue to a certain degree.... We had prestige in our region for a long time. We must regain our prestige and, without disappointing those who expect great things of us, assume our place in the balance of nations. For us to build a paradise in our region, great responsibilities await our "architects" of ideas and "workers" of thought.

## Other Speakers

• Looking around, I see people here from every social segment. I ask: What has brought us here? What has brought our Christian, Muslim, and Jewish brothers together? Just as in Konya, where Mawlana Rumi has attracted hundreds of millions, there is a man here who speaks with love and attracts us, namely Fethullah Gülen. This esteemed man speaks to us about love. It's love that has brought us here today. For this reason, I'm praying for him. He needs all our prayers. This man is a great example for the world. Some ask what's behind this man. He has only one weapon: love of God. (Georges Marovitch, Vatican Istanbul representative)

• People from every religion and profession are congratulating each other on this "holiday." People should love one another and God. By bringing us together here, you have given priority to our loving one another. In this respect, I'd like to thank the Honorable Hodjaefendi and the directors of this foundation. (Üzeyir Garih, businessman from Turkey's Jewish community)

• Deputy Chief Rabbi Ishak Haleva, Head of the Jewish Community, Rifat Sabanve, and the Representative of the Greek Patriarch, Konstantin Haisdani, congratulated Hodjaefendi on the holiday and thanked him.

• Harmony is fundamental to Islam. Religious festivals are days on which we return to our essence. In this respect, it is desirable that those days be lived 365 days a year in people's hearts, not just a few days each year. During this time, the winds of war are blowing over our country and region. However, tonight we are in the midst of a very different atmosphere. It's as if there were no such winds. As long as we preserve this unity, the winds of war will not easily affect us. (Halit Refig, film director)

- Being among you has made me very happy. I'd like to quote poets: Hayalî said: "The secret of making a thousand Ka'bas is a heart's humbling itself." Sultan Aziz's mother remarked: "Prophet Muhammad was created from love. What can be created from love without Prophet Muhammad?" God willing, we will be crowned with a Turkey that is full of love, affection, and smiling faces. (Ahmet Kabakli, columnist and literary figure)

- Religious festive days are days that we all live with enthusiasm. On these days hearts soften. Mercy and love open bud by bud and branch by branch on these days. Hoping that the atmosphere of Ramadan and all religious festive days will be reflected throughout the year, I wish that such days will be a vehicle for social harmony. (Ali Müfit Gürtuna, deputy mayor of Istanbul Metropolis)

CHAPTER 7

# Interfaith Meetings and Activities

(Selections from Fethullah Gülen's speeches and interviews
on interfaith dialogue)

## The Necessity of Interfaith Dialogue:
## A Muslim Perspective

### Introduction

Today, people are talking about many things: the danger of war
and frequent clashes, water and air pollution, hunger, the increasing
erosion of moral values, and so on. As a result, many other concerns
have come to the fore: peace, contentment, ecology, justice, tolerance, and dialogue. Unfortunately, despite certain promising precautions, those who should be tackling these problems tend to do so
by seeking further ways to conquer and control nature and produce
more lethal weapons. Obscene material is spread through the mass
media, especially the Internet.

At the root of the problem is the materialist worldview, which
severely limits religion's influence in contemporary social life. The
result is the current disturbed balance between humanity and nature
and within individual men and women. Only a few people seem to
realize that social harmony and peace with nature, between people,
and within the individual only can come about when the material
and spiritual realms are reconciled. Peace with nature, peace and
justice in society, and personal integrity are possible when one is at
peace with Heaven.

Religion reconciles opposites that seem to be mutually exclusive: religion–science, this world–the next world, nature–Divine
Books, the material–the spiritual, and spirit–body. Religion can

erect a defense against the destruction caused by scientific materialism, put science in its proper place, and end long-standing conflicts among nations and peoples. The natural sciences, which should act as steps of light leading people to God, have become a cause of unbelief on a previously unknown scale. As the West has become the main base for this unbelief, and because Christianity has been the religion most influenced by it, dialogue between Muslims and Christians appears to be indispensable.

The goal of dialogue among world religions is not simply to destroy scientific materialism and the destructive materialistic worldview; rather, the very nature of religion demands this dialogue. Judaism, Christianity, and Islam, and even Hinduism and other world religions accept the same source for themselves, and, including Buddhism, pursue the same goal. As a Muslim, I accept all Prophets and Books sent to different peoples throughout history, and regard belief in them as an essential principle of being Muslim. A Muslim is a true follower of Abraham, Moses, David, Jesus, and all other Prophets. Not believing in one Prophet or Book means that one is not a Muslim. Thus we acknowledge the oneness and basic unity of religion, which is a symphony of God's blessings and mercy, and the universality of belief in religion. So, religion is a system of belief embracing all races and all beliefs, a road bringing everyone together in brotherhood.

Regardless of how their adherents implement their faith in their daily lives, such generally accepted values as love, respect, tolerance, forgiveness, mercy, human rights, peace, brotherhood, and freedom exalted by religion. Most of them are accorded the highest precedence in the messages brought by Moses, Jesus, and Muhammad, as well as in the messages of Buddha and even Zarathustra, Lao-Tzu, Confucius, and the Hindu scholars.

We have a Prophetic Tradition almost unanimously recorded in the Hadith literature that Jesus will return when the end of the world is near. We do not know whether he will actually reappear physically, but what we understand is that near the end of time, values like love, peace, brotherhood, forgiveness, altruism, mercy, and spiritual purification will have precedence, as they did during Jesus' ministry. In addition, because Jesus was sent to the Jews and because all Hebrew Prophets exalted these values, it will be necessary to establish a dialogue with the Jews as well as a closer relationship and co-operation among Islam, Christianity, and Judaism.

There are many common points for dialogue among devout Muslims, Christians, and Jews. As pointed out by Michael Wyschogrod, an American professor of philosophy, there are just as many theoretical or creedal reasons for Muslims and Jews drawing closer to one another as there are for Jews and Christians coming together.[317] Furthermore, practically and historically, the Muslim world has a good record of dealing with the Jews: There has been almost no discrimination, and no Holocaust, denial of basic human rights, or genocide. On the contrary, Jews always have been welcomed in times of trouble, as when the Ottoman State embraced them after their expulsion from Andalusia.

### Muslim Difficulties in Dialogue

Christians, Jews, and others may face internal difficulties in dialogue. I would like to make a brief survey of certain reasons why Muslims find it hard to establish dialogue. The same reasons are responsible for the present misunderstanding of Islam.

According to Fuller and Lesser, in the last century alone far more Muslims have been killed by Western powers than all Christians killed by Muslims throughout history.[318] Many Muslims tend to produce more comprehensive results, and believe that Western policies are designed to weaken Muslim power. This historical experience leads even educated and conscious Muslims to believe that the West is continuing its 1,000-year-old systematic aggression against Islam and, even worse, with far more subtle and sophisticated methods. Consequently, the Church's call for dialogue meets with considerable suspicion.

---

[317] Ismail R. Faruqi, *Ibrahimi Dinlerin Diyalogu* (trans.) (Istanbul: 1993), 51–53.

[318] Graham E. Fuller and Ian O. Lessler, *Kusatilanlar-Islam ve Bati'nin Jeopolitigi* (trans.) (Istanbul: 1996), 41–42.

In addition, the Islamic world entered the twentieth century under the direct or indirect European domination. The Ottoman Empire, the defender and greatest representative of this world, collapsed as a result of European attacks. Turkey followed the Muslim peoples' struggles against foreign invasions with great interest. In addition to this, internal Turkish conflicts between the Democratic Party and People's Party in the 1950s led to Islam's being perceived by conservatives and some intellectuals as an ideology of conflict and reaction and a political system, rather than as a religion primarily addressing one's heart, spirit, and mind. Perceiving Islam as a party ideology in some Muslim countries, including Turkey, contributed to this impression. As a result, secularists and others began to look upon all Muslims and Islamic activities as suspect.

Islam also is seen as a political ideology, for it was the greatest dynamic in the Muslims' wars of independence. Thus it has become identified as an ideology of independence. Ideology tends to separate, while religion means enlightenment of the mind together with belief, contentment, and tranquillity of the heart, sensitivity in conscience, and perception through real experience. By its very nature, religion penetrates such essential virtues as faith, love, mercy, and compassion. Reducing religion to a harsh political ideology and a mass ideology of independence has erected walls between Islam and the West, and has caused Islam to be misunderstood.

Christendom's historical portrayal of Islam also has weakened Muslims' courage with respect to interfaith dialogue. For centuries, Christians were told that Islam was a crude and distorted version of Judaism and Christianity, and so the Prophet was considered an imposter, a common or ingenious trickster, the Antichrist, or an idol worshipped by Muslims. Even recent books have presented him as someone with strange ideas who believed he had to succeed at any cost, and who resorted to any means to achieve success.

### Dialogue Is a Must
Interfaith dialogue is a must today, and the first step in establishing it is forgetting the past, ignoring polemical arguments, and giving precedence to common points, which far outnumber polem-

ical ones. In the West, some attitudinal changes can be seen in some intellectuals and clerics toward Islam. I must particularly mention the late Massignon, who referred to Islam by the expression: "The faith of Abraham revived with Muhammad." He believed that Islam has a positive, almost prophetic mission in the post-Christian world, for: "Islam is the religion of faith. It is not a religion of natural faith in the God of the philosophers, but faith in the God of Abraham, of Isaac, and of Ishmael, faith in our God. Islam is a great mystery of Divine Will." He believed in the Divine authorship of the Qur'an and Muhammad's Prophethood.[319]

The West's perspective on our Prophet also has softened. Together with Christian clerics and men of religion, many Western thinkers besides Massignon, like Charles J. Ledit, Y. Moubarac, Irene-M. Dalmais, L. Gardet, Norman Daniel, Michel Lelong, H. Maurier, Olivier Lacombe, and Thomas Merton express warmth for both Islam and for our Prophet, and support the call for dialogue.

Also, what the final declaration of the Second Vatican Council, which began the process of dialogue, said about Islam cannot be ignored. This means that the attitude of the Catholic Church toward Islam has now changed. In the second period of the Council, Pope Paul VI said:

> On the other hand, the Catholic Church is looking farther, beyond the horizons of Christianity. It is turning towards other religions that preserve the concept and meaning of God as One, Transcendental, Creator, Ruler of Fate and Wise. Those religions worship God with sincere, devotional actions.

He also indicated that the Catholic Church commended these religions' good, true, and humane sides:

> The Church reaffirms to them that in modern society in order to save the meaning of religion and servanthood to God—a necessity and need of true civilization—the Church itself is

---

[319] Sidney Griffith, "Sharing the Faith of Abraham: The 'Credo' of Louis Massignon," *Islam and Christian—Muslim Relations* 8:, no. 2 (1997); "Thomas Merton, Louis Massignon, and the Challenge of Islam," *The Merton Annual*, vol. 3 (1990).

going to take its place as a resolute advocate of God's rights on man.

As a final result, the written statement entitled "A Declaration Regarding the Church's Relations with non-Christian Religions," which was accepted at the Council, declared that:

> In our world that has become smaller and in which relations have become closer, people are expecting answers from religion regarding mysterious enigmas in human nature that turn their hearts upside down. What is man? What is the meaning and purpose of life? What is goodness and reward, what is sin? What is the source and point of suffering? What is the path to true happiness? What is death, what is the meaning of judgement after death and receiving the fruits of what one has done on earth? What is the mystery surrounding the beginning and end of existence?

After stating that different religions attempt to answer these questions in their own ways, and that the Church does not reject altogether the values of other religions, the Council encourages Christians to have dialogue with members of other religions:

> The Church encourages its children, together with believing and living as Christians, to get to know and support with precaution, compassion, dialogue and co-operation those who follow other religions and to encourage them to develop their spiritual, moral and socio-cultural values.[320]

Another important point is that Pope John Paul II admits in his *Crossing the Threshold of Hope* that (despite Muslim neglect and carelessness), it is still the Muslims who worship in the best and most careful manner. He reminds his readers that, on this point, Christians should take Muslims as their example.

In addition, Islam's resistance to materialist ideologies and its important role in the modern world has amazed many Western observers. The observations of E. H. Jurji are very significant here:

---

[320] Suad Yildirim, "Kiliseyi Islam ile Diyalog Istemege Sevkeden Sebepler (The Reasons Encouraging the Church to Have Dialogue with Islam)," *Yeni Ümit*, 16:7.

In its self-respect, self-maintenance, and realistic zeal, in its
fight for solidarity against racist and Marxist ideologies, in its
vigorous denunciation of exploitation, as in the preaching of
its message to a wayward, bleeding humanity, Islam faces the
modern world with a peculiar sense of mission. Not confused
and not torn apart by a mass of theological subtleties, nor
buried beneath a heavy burden of dogma, this sense of mission draws its strength from a complete conviction of the rel-
evance of Islam.[321]

Muslims and the West have struggled with each other for
almost 1,400 years. From the Western perspective, Islam has threat-
ened and opened many Western doors, facts that have not been forgotten. That said, the fact that this struggle is leading Muslims to
oppose and resent the West will never benefit Islam or Muslims.
Modern transportation and mass communication have turned the
world into a global village in which every relationship is interactive.
The West cannot wipe out Islam or its territory, and Muslim armies
can no longer march on the West.

Moreover, as this world is becoming even more global, both
sides feel the need for a give-and-take relationship. The West has
scientific, technological, economic, and military supremacy.
However, Islam possesses more important and vital factors: Islam,
as represented by the Qur'an and Sunna, has retained the freshness
of its beliefs, spiritual essence, good works, and morality as it has
unfolded over the last 14 centuries. In addition, it has the potential
to blow spirit and life into Muslims, numbed for centuries, as well
as into many other peoples drowned in the swamp of materialism.

Just as religion has not yet escaped the onslaught of unbelief
based on science and philosophy, no one can guarantee that this
storm will not blow even stronger in the future. These and other factors do not allow Muslims to view and present Islam purely as a
political ideology or an economic system. Neither do they allow
Muslims to consider the West, Christianity, Judaism, and even other
great religions like Buddhism from a historical perspective and
define their attitude accordingly.

---

[321] Abu'l-Fazl Ezzati, *Islam'in Yayilis Tarihine Giris* (trans.) (Istanbul: 1984), 348.

When those who have adopted Islam as a political ideology, rather than a religion in its true sense and function, review their self-proclaimed Islamic activities and attitudes, especially their political ones, they will discover that the driving force is usually personal or national anger, hostility, and similar motives.

If this is the case, we must accept Islam and adopt an Islamic attitude as the fundamental starting point for action, rather than the existing oppressive situation. The Prophet defined true Muslims as those who harm no one with their words and actions, and who are the most trustworthy representatives of universal peace. Muslims travel everywhere with this sublime feeling that they nourish deep in their spirits. Contrary to inflicting torment and suffering, they are remembered as symbols of safety and security. In their eyes, there is no difference between a physical and a verbal violation, such as backbiting, false accusation, insult, and ridicule.

Our beginning point must have an Islamic basis. Muslims cannot act out of ideological or political partisanship and then dress it in Islamic garb or represent mere desires as ideas. If we can overcome this tendency, Islam's true image will become known. The present, distorted image of Islam that has resulted from its misuse, by both Muslims and non-Muslims for their own goals, scares both Muslims and non-Muslims.

Sidney Griffith points out one important fact of how the West views Islam: In American universities, Islam is not taught as a religion in theological schools but as a political system in the political science or international relations departments.[322] Such a perception also is found among Westernized segments of the Islamic world and non-Muslims in Asia and Africa. Strangely enough, many groups that have put themselves forward under the banner of Islam export and actually strengthen this image.

---

[322] Sidney Griffith, *Zaman*. He is director of the Institute of Christian Oriental Research in The Catholic University of America and a sincere supporter of Islam–Christian dialogue.

## Islam's Universal Call for Dialogue

Fourteen centuries ago, Islam made the greatest ecumenical call the world has ever seen. The Qur'an calls the People of the Book (Christians and Jews primarily):

> Say: "O People of the Book! Come to common terms as between us and you: that we worship none but God; that we associate no partners with Him; that we take not, from among ourselves lords and patrons other than God." If then they turn back, say you: "Bear witness that we are Muslims (surrendered to God's Will)." (3:64)

This call, coming in the ninth year of the Hijra, begins with the *la* (no!) in the statement of faith *La ilaha illa Allah* (There is no god but God). More than a command to do something positive, it is a call not to do certain things, so that followers of the revealed religions could overcome their mutual separation. It represented the widest statement on which members of all religions could agree. In case this call was rejected, Muslims were to respond: *Your religion is for you; my religion is for me* (109:6) That is, if you do not accept this call, we have surrendered to God. We will continue on the path we have accepted and let you go on your own path.

Elmalili Hamdi Yazir, a famous Turkish Qur'anic interpreter, made the following interesting observations regarding this verse:

> It has been shown how various consciences, nations, religions, and books can unite in one essential conscience and word of truth, and how Islam has taught the human realm such a wide, open, and true path of salvation and law of freedom. It has been shown fully that this is not limited to the Arab or non-Arab. Religious progress is possible not by consciences being narrow and separate from each other, but by their being universal and broad.[323]

Islam gave this breadth of conscience, this broad path of salvation, and this law of freedom to us as a gift. Bediüzzaman Said Nursî explains this broadest scope of Islam from a contemplative observation he had in the Bayezid Mosque in Istanbul:

---

[323] Elmalili Hamdi Yazir, *Hak Dini Kur'an Dili* (The Qur'an, the Tongue of the True Religion) (Istanbul) 2:1131-32.

Once I thought about the pronoun "we" in the verse: *You alone do we worship, and You alone we ask for help* (1:5), and my heart sought the reason why "we" was used in place of "I." Suddenly I discovered the virtue and secret of congregational prayer from that pronoun "we."

I saw that by doing my prayer with the congregation at the Bayezid Mosque, every individual in the congregation became a kind of intercessor for me, and as long as I recited the Qur'an there, everyone testified for me. I got the courage from the congregation's great and intense servitude to present my insufficient servitude to the Divine Court.

Suddenly another reality unveiled itself: All of Istanbul's mosques united and came under the authority of the Bayezid Mosque. I got the impression that they confirmed me in my cause and included me in their prayer. At that time I saw myself in the earthly mosque, in circular rows around the Ka'ba. I said: "Praise be to the Lord of the worlds. I have so many intercessors; they are saying the same thing I say in my prayer and confirming me."

As this reality was unveiled, I felt I was standing in prayer in front of the blessed Ka'ba. Taking advantage of this situation, I took those rows of worshippers as witnesses and said: "I witness that there is no god but God; again I bear witness that Muhammad is God's Messenger." I entrusted this testimony to faith to the sacred Black Stone. While leaving this trust, suddenly another veil opened. I saw that the congregation I was in was separated into three circles.

The first circle was a large congregation of believing Muslims and those who believe in God's existence and Unity. In the second circle, I saw all creatures were performing the greatest prayer and invocation of God. Every class or species was busy with its own unique invocation and litanies to God, and I was among that congregation. In the third circle I saw an amazing realm that was outwardly small, but in reality, large from the perspective of the duty it performed and its quality. From the atoms of my body to the outer senses, there was a congregation busy with servitude and gratitude.

In short, the pronoun "we" in the expression "we worship" pointed to these three congregations. I imagined our Prophet, upon him be peace and blessings, the translator and propagator of the Qur'an, in Madina, from which he was addressing humanity, saying: *O humanity! Worship your Lord!* (2:21).

Like everyone else, I heard his command in my spirit, and like me, everyone in the three congregations replied with the sentence: "You alone do we worship."[324]

## How to Interact with Followers of Other Religions

In the Qur'an God says: *This is the Book; wherein there is no doubt; a guidance to those who fear God* (2:2). Later it is explained that these pious ones are those: *Who believe in the Unseen, are steadfast in prayer, and spend out of what We have provided for them; and who believe in what is sent to you and what was sent before you, and (in their hearts) have the reassurance of the Hereafter* (2:3-4). At the very outset, using a very soft and slightly oblique style, the Qur'an calls people to accept the former Prophets and their Books. Having such a condition at the very beginning of the Qur'an seems very important to me when it comes to starting a dialogue with the followers of other religions.

In another verse God commands: *And discuss you not with the People of the Book, except with means better (than mere disputation)* (29:46). This verse describes what method, approach, and manner should be used. Bediüzzaman's view of the form and style of debate are extremely significant: "Anyone who is happy about defeating an opponent in debate is without mercy." He explains further: "You gain nothing by such a defeat. If you were defeated and the other was victorious, you would have corrected one of your mistakes." Debate should not be for the sake of our ego, but to enable the truth to come out. Elsewhere it is stated: *God forbids you not, with regard to those who fight you not for (your) Faith nor drive you out of your homes, from dealing kindly and justly with them: for God loves those who are just* (60:8).

According to some, several verses harshly criticize the People of the Book. In reality, such criticism is directed against wrong behavior, incorrect thought, resistance to truth, the creation of hostility, and undesirable characteristics. The Bible contains even stronger criticisms of the same attributes. However, immediately after these apparently sharp criticisms and threats, very gentle

---

[324] Said Nursi, *Mektubat* (The Letters) (Istanbul), Mektup 29, Nükte 6.

words are used to awaken hearts to the truth and to plant hope. In addition, the Qur'an's criticism and warning about some attitudes and behavior found among Jews, Christians, and polytheists also were directed toward Muslims who still indulged in them. Both the Companions and expounders of the Qur'an agree on this.

God-revealed religions strongly oppose disorder, treachery, conflict, and oppression. Islam literally means "peace," "security," and "well-being." Naturally based on peace, security, and world harmony, it sees war and conflict as aberrations to be brought under control. An exception is made for self-defense, as when a body tries to defeat the germs attacking it. Self-defense must follow certain guidelines, however. Islam always has breathed peace and goodness. Considering war an accident, it established rules to balance and limit it. For example, it takes justice and world peace as a basis, as in: *Let not the hatred of others to you make you swerve to wrong and depart from justice* (5:8). Islam developed a line of defense based on principles that protect religion, life, property, the mind, and reproduction. The modern legal system also has done this.

Islam accords the greatest value to human life. It views the killing of one person as the killing of all people, for a single murder engenders the idea that any person can be killed. Adam's son Cain was the first murderer. Although their names are not specifically mentioned in the Qur'an or Sunna, we learn from the Bible that a misunderstanding between Cain and Abel resulted in Cain unjustly killing Abel in a jealous rage. And thus began the epoch of spilling blood. For this reason, one *hadith* records the Messenger of God as saying: "Whenever a person is killed unjustly, part of the sin for murder is credited to Adam's son Cain, for he opened to humanity the way of unjust killing."[325] The Qur'an also states that one who kills a person unjustly in effect has killed everyone, and one who saves another in effect has saved everyone (5:32).[326]

---

[325] *Sahih al-Bukhari*, "Diyat," 2; "Enbiya," 1; Muslim, "Kasame," 27.

[326] *Sahih al-Bukhari*, "Diyat," 2.

## Love, Compassion, Tolerance, and Forgiving:
## The Pillars of Dialogue

Religion commands love, compassion, tolerance, and forgiving. Therefore, I would like to say a few words concerning these fundamental universal values.

Love is the most essential element in every being, a most radiant light, a great power that can resist and overcome every force. It elevates every soul that absorbs it, and prepares it for the journey to eternity. Those who make contact with eternity through love work to implant in all other souls what they receive from eternity. They dedicate their lives to this sacred duty, and endure any hardship for its sake. Just as they say "love" with their last breaths, they also breathe "love" while being raised on the Day of Judgment.

Altruism, an exalted human feeling, generates love. Whoever has the greatest share in this love is humanity's greatest hero, one who has uprooted any personal feelings of hatred and rancor. Such heroes continue to live even after death. These lofty souls, who daily light a new torch of love in their inner world and make their hearts a source of love and altruism, are welcomed and loved by people. They receive the right of eternal life from such an Exalted Court. Not even death or Doomsday can remove their traces.

Love, the most direct way to someone's heart, is the Prophets' way. Those who follow it are not rejected. Even if some reject them, far more others welcome them. Once they are welcomed through love, nothing prevents them from attaining their goal.

Everything speaks of and promises compassion. Therefore, the universe can be considered as a symphony of compassion. A human being must show compassion to all living beings, for this is a requirement of being human. The more people display compassion, the more exalted they become; the more they resort to wrongdoing, oppression, and cruelty, the more they are disgraced and humiliated. They become a shame to humanity. We hear from Prophet Muhammad that a prostitute went to Paradise because out of compassion she gave water to a dog dying of thirst, while another woman went to Hell because she allowed a cat to starve to death.

Forgiving is a great virtue. Forgiveness cannot be considered as separate from virtue, or virtue as separate from forgiveness. Everyone knows the adage: "Mistakes from the small, forgiveness from the great." How true this is! Being forgiven means a repair, a return to an essence, and finding oneself again. For this reason, the most pleasing action in the Infinite Mercy's view is activity pursued amidst the palpitations of this return and search.

All of creation, both animate and inanimate, was introduced to forgiveness through humanity. Just as God showed His Attribute of Forgiveness through individual human beings, He put the beauty of forgiving in their hearts. While the first man dealt a blow to his essence through falling, which is somehow a requirement of his human nature, God's forgiveness gave him a hand and elevated him to the rank of Prophethood.

Whenever people have erred, mounting on the magic transport of seeking forgiveness and surmounting the shame of personal sin and the resulting despair, they attain infinite mercy and overlook the sins of others. Jesus said to a crowd of people eager to stone a woman: "Let one who is without sin cast the first stone." Can anyone who understands this binding, fine point even consider stoning someone else when he or she is also a likely candidate for being stoned? If only those unfortunate ones who demand that others pass a certain litmus test could understand this!

Malice and hatred are the seeds of hell scattered among people by evil. In contrast to those who encourage such evil and turn the land into a pit of Hell, we should carry forgiveness to those whose troubles are pushing them into the abyss. The excesses of those who neither forgive nor tolerate others have made the past one or two centuries the most horrific of all time. If such people are to rule the future, it will be a fearful time indeed. Thus the greatest gift today's generation can give to its children and grandchildren is to teach them how to forgive, even in the face of the crudest behavior and most upsetting events. We believe that forgiveness and tolerance will heal most of our wounds only if this celestial instrument is in the hands of those who understand its language.

Our tolerance should be so broad that we can close our eyes to others' faults, show respect for different ideas, and forgive everything that is forgivable. Even when our inalienable rights are violated, we should respect human values and try to establish justice. Even before the coarsest thoughts and crudest ideas, with a Prophet's caution and without boiling over, we should respond with a mildness that the Qur'an calls "gentle words." We should do this so that we can touch other people's hearts by following a method consisting of a tender heart, a gentle approach, and mild behavior. We should have such a broad tolerance that we benefit from contradictory ideas, for they force us to keep our heart, spirit, and conscience in good shape even though they teach us nothing.

Tolerance, which we sometimes use in place of respect and mercy, generosity and forbearance, is the most essential element of moral systems. It also is a very important source of spiritual discipline, and a celestial virtue of perfected men and women.

Under the lens of tolerance, the believers' merits attain a new depth and extend to infinity; mistakes and faults shrink into insignificance. Actually, the treatment of He Who is beyond time and space always passes through the prism of tolerance, and we wait for it to embrace us and all of creation. This embrace is so broad that a prostitute who gave water to a thirsty dog touched the knocker of the "Door of Mercy" and found herself in a corridor extending to Heaven. Due to the deep love he felt for God and His Messenger, an alcoholic suddenly shook himself free and became a Companion of the Prophet. And, with the smallest of Divine favors, a murderer was saved from his monstrous psychosis, turned toward the highest rank, which far surpassed his natural ability, and reached it.

We want everyone to look at us through this lens, and we expect the breezes of forgiveness and pardon to blow constantly in our surroundings. All of us want to refer our past and present to the climate of tolerance and forbearance, which melts and transforms, cleans and purifies, and then walk toward the future without anxiety. We do not want our past to be criticized, or our future to be darkened because of our present. All of us expect love and respect, hope for tolerance and forgiveness, and want to be embraced with feelings of liberality and affection. We expect tolerance and forgiveness from our parents in response to our mischief at home, from our teachers in response to our naughtiness at school, from the innocent victims of our injustice and oppression, from the judge and prosecutor in court, and from the Judge of Judges (God) in the highest tribunal.

However, deserving what we expect is very important. One who does not forgive cannot expect forgiveness. We will see disrespect to the extent we have been disrespectful. One who does not love is not worthy of being loved. One who does not embrace humanity with tolerance and forgiveness will not receive forgiveness and pardon. One who curses others can expect only curses in return. Those who curse will be cursed, and those who beat will be beaten. If true Muslims would continue on their way and tolerate curses with such Qur'anic principles as: "When they meet empty words or unseemly behavior, they generously pass them by" and "if you behave tolerantly and overlook their faults," others would appear to implement the justice of Destiny on those cursers.

### The Last Word
- Those who want to reform the world must first reform themselves. In order to bring others to the path of traveling to a better world, they must purify their inner worlds of hatred, rancor, and jealousy, and adorn their outer worlds with virtue. Those who are far removed from self-control and self-discipline, who have failed to refine their feelings, may seem attractive and insightful at first. However, they will not be able to inspire others in any permanent way, and the sentiments they arouse will soon disappear.

- Goodness, beauty, truthfulness, and being virtuous are the essence of the world and humanity. Whatever happens, the world will one day find this essence. No one can prevent this.

## Tolerance and Dialogue in the Qur'an and Sunna

The Qur'an always takes forgiveness and tolerance as basic principles, so much so that "servants of Mercy" are introduced as: *And the servants of (God) Most Gracious are those who walk on the Earth in humility, and when the ignorant address them, they say: "Peace"* (25:63); *Those who witness no falsehood, and, if they pass by futility, pass by it with honorable avoidance* (25:72); and *And*

*when they hear vain talk, they turn away therefrom and say: "To us
our deeds, and to you yours"* (28:55).

The general gist of these verses is that when God's special servants encounter meaningless and ugly words or behavior, they say
nothing unbecoming but rather pass by in a dignified manner. In
short: *Everyone acts according to their own disposition* (17:84) and
so displays their own character. The character of heroes of tolerance
is gentleness, consideration, and tolerance. When God sent Moses
and Aaron to a man with claims to divinity like the Pharaoh, He
commanded them to behave tolerantly and *to speak softly* (20:44).

The Prophet's life was in an orbit of forgiveness and forbearance. He even behaved in such a manner toward Abu Sufyan, who
persecuted him throughout his lifetime. During the Conquest of
Makka, even though Abu Sufyan said he still was not sure about
Islam, Muhammad said: "Those who take refuge in Abu Sufyan's
house are safe, just as those who take refuge in the Ka'ba are safe."
In respect to refuge and safety, Abu Sufyan's house was mentioned
with the Ka'ba. In my humble opinion, such tolerance was more
valuable than giving tons of gold to Abu Sufyan, a man in his sev-
enties in whom egoism and tribalism had become ingrained.

In addition to being commanded to take tolerance and dialogue
as his basis while performing his duties, the Prophet was directed to
which points he could hold in common with the People of the Book
(Jews and Christians):

> Say: "O People of the Book! Come to common terms as
> between us and you: That we worship none but God; That we
> associate no partners with Him; That we erect not, from
> among ourselves, lords and patrons other than God." (3:64)

Another verse, which has not been abrogated, orders those
whose hearts are exuberant with belief and love to show forgiveness
and tolerance even to those who do not believe in the afterlife:

> Tell those who believe to forgive those who do not look for-
> ward to the Days of God: It is for Him to recompense (for
> good or ill) each people according to what they have earned.
> (45:14)

Those who consider themselves addressed by these verses, every guardian of love who dreams of becoming a special servant of God just because they are human beings, those who have declared their faith and thereby become Muslims and perform the mandated religious duties, must behave with tolerance and forbearance and expect nothing from the other party. They must have the approach of Yunus: not striking those who hit them, not replying in kind to those who curse them, and not holding any secret grudge against those who abuse them.[327]

## Dialogue with Jews and Christians

Believers determine their attitudes according to their faith. If the message is put across as it should be, I believe that a very good environment for dialogue can emerge in Turkey and throughout the world. Thus, as is true for every subject, we should approach this issue as indicated in the Qur'an and by the Prophet.

At the beginning of the *Surat al-Baqara*, God says: *This is the Book; in it is sure guidance, without doubt, to those who fear God* (2:2). These pious ones then are identified as those: *Who believe in the Unseen, are steadfast in prayer, and spend out of what We have provided for them; and who believe in the Revelation sent to you and sent before your time, and (in their hearts) have the reassurance of the Hereafter* (2:3-4). Using a very soft and slightly oblique style, the Qur'an calls people to accept the former Prophets and their books. Having such a condition at the very beginning of the Qur'an seems very important to me when it comes to establishing dialogue with Jews and Christians.

In another verse God commands: *And don't dispute with the People of the Book, except with means better (than mere disputation)* (29:46). In this verse, the Qur'an describes the method and approach we should use and the manner we should display. Bediüzzaman's words has some extremely significant words to say about this: "Those who are happy about their opponent's defeat in

---

[327] Camci and Ünal, *Fethullah Gülen'in Konusma ve Yazilarinda Hosgörü ve Diyalog Iklimi*, 116-18.

debate have no mercy." He explains: "You gain nothing by defeating someone. If you were defeated and the other person was victorious, you would have corrected one of your mistakes."

Debate should not be for the sake of your ego, but to enable the truth to appear. When we look at political debates in which the only thought is to beat the other person, there can be no positive result. For the truth to emerge in a debate of ideas, such principles as mutual understanding, respect, and dedication to justice cannot be neglected. As a Qur'anic rule, this can only take place in a good environment for dialogue.

Reading 29:64 further, we notice the condition *unless it be with those who inflict wrong (and injury).* Wrong is mentioned: *It is those who believe and confuse not their beliefs with wrong—that are (truly) in security, for they are on (right) guidance* (6:82). According to the Prophet's interpretation, polytheism is equal to unbelief in the sense of contempt for the universe. The greatest wrong or oppression is silencing all the tongues in one's conscience that express God. It also means doing injustice to and oppressing others, and insisting on having one's way. As wrong or oppression includes both polytheism and unbelief, it is a greater sin. Every polytheist or unbeliever may not be a wrongdoer in the sense outlined above. However, those who oppress others, arm themselves in the name of committing evil, and violate others' rights and God's justice must be confronted within the law's framework.

When dealing with People of the Book who are not oppressors, we have no right to behave violently or to think about how to eliminate them. Such behavior is non-Islamic, contrary to Islamic rules and principles, and even anti-Islamic.

In *Sura Mumtahana*, it is stated: *God forbids you not, with regard to those who fight you not for (your) faith nor drive you out of your homes, from dealing kindly and justly with them: for God loves those who are just* (60:8). This verse was revealed when Esma asked the Prophet if she should meet with her polytheistic mother, who wanted to come from Makka to Madina to see her daughter. The verse suggests that such a meeting would be perfectly acceptable, and that she also could do good for her. I leave it to your understanding as to what approach should be used towards those who believe in God, Judgment Day, and the Prophets.

Hundreds of Qur'anic verses deal with social dialogue and tolerance. But care must be taken to establish balance in forbearance and tolerance. Being merciful to a cobra means being unjust to the people it has bitten. Claiming that humanism is more merciful than Divine Mercy disrespects mercy and violates others' rights. Thus it is not necessary to refrain from making God known in the search for tolerance and dialogue. In truth, except for certain special cases, the Qur'an and Sunna always advocate forbearance. The shielding canopy of this tolerance extends not only to the People of the Book, but in a sense to all people.[328]

## Jews and Christians in the Qur'an

Some assert that expressions in the Qur'an regarding Christianity and Judaism are very sharp. Great care should be taken when approaching this subject. There is a rule in *tafsir* (Qur'anic commentary): In order to conclude that a verse refers to a particular people, it must be established both clear and historically that the verse in question refers to them exclusively.

Approaching the matter from this angle, the verses condemning and rebuking the Jews and Christians are either about some Jews and Christians who lived in the time of the Prophet Muhammad or their own Prophets, such as Moses and Jesus, or those who deserved such condemnation because of their wrong beliefs or practices. For example, at the beginning of *Surat al-Baqara*, after praising the believers for some of their praiseworthy attributes and acts, the Qur'an says:

> Surely, the unbelievers: it is the same whether you warn them or not, they will not believe. God put a seal on their hearts and ears, and over their sight is a veil. For them is a mighty torment. (2:6)

---

[328] Ibid., 151-54.

This verse is about, first of all, stubborn unbelievers who lived during the Prophet's lifetime and insisted on unbelief. The Prophet, the Companions, and the unbelievers themselves knew who was meant. In the second degree, it includes all unbelievers, regardless of time or place, who show the same type of resistance against the Qur'an's enlightening rays. So, this sharp criticism is, first of all, about those whom the relevant verses refer to directly, and others of the same attitude. It is not definite that they pertain to all Jews and Christians from that time until now.

Second, that style is due to the incorrect interpretation of Judaism and Christianity and its implementation in the lives of some self-proclaimed Jews and Christians. More precisely, that style was used in the Qur'an because they used religious thought and belief as a cause and material for hostility. Rather than individual Christian and Jews, the Qur'an goes after wrong behavior, incorrect thought, resistance to the truth, creation of hostility, and non-commendable characteristics. The Bible contains even stronger statements against the same attributes. Even if the expression seem sharp to some, immediately after appropriate warnings and threats come very gentle words to awaken hearts to the truth and to plant hope in them.

In addition, the Qur'an's criticism and warning regarding some of these attitudes and behaviors of non-Muslims also were made about Muslims whose faith did not prevent them from engaging in the same behavior. Both the Companions and expounders of the Qur'an agree on this matter.[329]

## Do Islam and Orthodox Christianity Contribute to Relations between Turkey and Bulgaria?

First of all, religions are meant to unite people separated by misunderstandings. Islam and Orthodox Christianity have many common aspects and few differences. Both believe in God, Prophets, angels, the afterlife, and holy books. All Muslims believe in Jesus and the Virgin Mary. Many moral and legal principles are

---

[329] Ibid., 155-56.

the same. Thus, any conflict between these two religions is due to misunderstanding or exploitation for political or other purposes.

The Qur'an states: *Come, let's unite on a common word: worshipping God, not assign Him any partners. Abandoning Him, some of us should not make Lords some among us over others* (3:64). In this call, a divisive matter is mentioned and a warning is given: Don't leave God due to misunderstandings or other reasons, and beware of those who use religion to divide. When there are hundreds of common bridges between us, it is mistaken to stress a few differences. When people really understand such things, Islam and Orthodox Christianity will contribute positively to relations between these two countries.[330]

## Repercussions from the Fethullah Gülen–Patriarch Bartholomeos I Meeting

### While "Civil" Religions Are Meeting

By Hadi Uluengin

The meeting of Fethullah Gülen Hodjaefendi, a distinguished man of religion and civil community leader, and the Phanariot Orthodox Patriarch Bartholomeos I carries historic significance. This conversation should be taken note of immediately.

First of all, it's necessary to thank the Honorable Patriarch for relying on his common sense and making an offer to meet, and the Esteemed Hodjaefendi for showing the wisdom to accept this offer. This meeting means the crowning of the Divine message calling for tolerance among religions and mutual association, which are mentioned in all sacred books.

Such a theme gains a special significance, especially now when fundamentalism in every religion ignores the above message, and intolerance is displayed among religions. It stands up for God's word. In this respect, the Gülen–Bartholomeos I meeting takes on a universal dimension.

---

[330] Interview with Bulgarian journalists.

However, there is a "national" dimension in this theme. First of all, the coming together (outside of protocol) of a Muslim religious community leader with a member of the Christian clergy is a source of pride for our country, which rose on the rich heritage of a multi-religion empire.

A new historic step is made in the process of peace. Moreover, there is no reason why the Patriarchate, which functioned universally during the Ottoman period but later assumed a national identity, should not resume its universality. Claims like Athens politically controls the Patriarchate are not compatible with the truth. The Patriarchate represents the Greeks in the Ottoman State, not the Greeks in modern Greece.

The Gülen–Bartholomeos I contact comprises the first meeting since the founding of the Republic of a civil Islamic community leader with a Christian religious leader. This historic meeting between two esteemed and distinguished men of religion brings the glad tidings of tolerance and civilian sovereignty.[331]

### *The Patriarch and Fethullah Hodja*

By Cengiz Çandar

I felt happy when I read in yesterday's *Zaman* about the meeting between Fethullah Gülen Hodjaefendi and the Greek Orthodox Patriarch Bartholomeos I. *Zaman* gave the news and a picture of the Patriarch together with Fethullah Hodja under the headline: "A Step Toward Interfaith Dialogue." They did not forget to mention that the Patriarch requested the meeting ...

One reason-but not the most important—why I was happy was my indirect connection with this meeting... Last year when a witch's kettle was boiling, especially in the Islamic media regarding the Patriarch and the Patriarchate, they were searching for dialogue but could not decide with whom to meet. In one of my discussions with Patriarchate officials, I fervently recommended that they "definitely meet with Fethullah Hodja," who is at the head of those rep-

[331] *Hürriyet*, 11 April 1996.

resenting the "Islam of the people" in Turkey. Once when Fethullah Hodja visited *Sabah* for some reason, I mentioned the Patriarch's idea to him. I saw that Hodjaefendi, a "person of dialogue," responded positively to this idea.

Naturally, I felt good when I saw the *Zaman* headline: "A Step Toward Interfaith Dialogue," which pointed out that the meeting had taken place and that there had been negative views in the press regarding the Patriarch and the Patriarchate. The meeting's location also was interesting: The Istanbul Polat Renaissance Hotel. This hotel belongs to Adnan Polat, Fethullah Hodja's "fellow-citizen from Erzurum" who happens to be an Alawi. The famous 1994 Ramadan dinner, a vehicle for Hodjaefendi presenting his "reconciliatory personality" to the public, also was held at this hotel.

It is interesting that during this meeting, this symbolic dimension was not neglected. Holding such a meeting at that place is more important than the meeting's content, regardless of what was discussed. In addition to the tolerance among religions dimension, it holds great value for tolerance in the general sense or, in other words, in respect to the culture of tolerance in Turkey.[332]

### A Historic Meeting

By Femhi Koru

Fethullah Gülen Hodjaefendi surprised everyone and met with the Phanariot Greek Patriarch Bartholomeos I at Istanbul's Polat Renaissance Hotel. The two religious leaders discussed subjects related to Turkey's welfare and spiritual life. For 3 days, newspapers and television have stressed the meeting's symbolic value.

Gülen also surprised everyone by extending the hand of friendship to Bartholomeos I. This comprises a full test for the Phanariot Patriarchate and the Patriarch. If he understands that this hand represents the Anatolian Muslim people and makes a sincere effort to fulfill the duty that has required self-sacrifice from the other party, not only will he increase his power in the world, but he also will

---

[332] *Sabah*, 7 April 1996.

make a tremendous contribution to universal peace. If he wants to hold this within the boundaries of a public relations maneuver or a method for appearing sympathetic, he will have prepared the way for disappointing developments in both areas.

I believe that with the good will of both parties, this historic encounter will be the beginning of broad and productive efforts. Is it that hard to end the difficulties of Turks in Western Thrace or open a mutual educational institution that will implant the tolerance mission in Greece? We know that the Patriarch does not represent Athens, but still we cannot refrain from hoping that he will use his prestige on the Greek politicians who come to kiss his hand.

This meeting is a first step toward the dispersal of centuries-old suspicions regarding the Patriarchate in Turkey. We believe that the parties who showed the courage to take this step will be able to use their influence in much simpler matters.[333]

### *Jesus-like Attitude*

By Mehmet Ali Bulut

I feel a deep affection for Fethullah Hodja. Due to his efforts on truth's behalf in the struggle between truth and falsehood, I believe it is a duty of faith and conscience to feel love for him and take my place in his ranks. In every age and time in the midst of grace, there are guides representing our Prophet. Unless the Islamic community shows the same allegiance to them as the Companions showed to the Prophet, they do not live their faith fully.

Of course, it cannot be said that everyone who comes forth as a guide has assumed this duty to the same degree. If that were the case, Islam would not be in its present state. In this age of conflict, disaster, and destruction, many guides have appeared to serve Islam. Each has tried to enlighten the Islamic community with the light he radiated. Like moths flying to the closest light, every believer has run to the closest light.

---

[333] *Zaman*, 8 April 1996.

Some moths turn to the brightest light. I believe I have done that. I feel that the flame lit by Bediüzzaman (Said Nursî) is the brightest one. Many people fell into that flame and burned, but Fethullah Hodja, because he is a candle himself, took light from the enlightened thought and, with the illumination of that light, became a source of light himself. This is my view of him.

I believe that his associates are sincere enough to reflect the *hadith*: "Among my community will be a group acting on the truth in every period until the end of the world." I fully believe that he and his community generally manifest the essence of this *hadith*.

But together with this, I have to say that I was amazed by the awards ceremony held by the Foundation of Writers and Journalists, of which he is the spiritual leader. I do not think anyone has the right to be more royal than the king. I say that this is too much tolerance, because tolerance means seeing the other party without fault. And in my opinion, this does not conform with Islam's honor.

Fethullah Hodja displays a Jesus-like attitude. According to Muslim belief, at the end of time Islam's ascension will occur through Jesus, for Jesus will come and follow the Mahdi.[334] This means that the aspects of God's religion, Islam, that were particularly represented by Jesus will be dominant. It seems that Fethullah Hodja is giving indications of this temperament. At any rate, we are the community of the end times, and we have difficulty comprehending exactly what any action means.[335]

### The Messianic Mission Attributed
### to Jesus Christ toward the End of Time

by Ali Ünal

Some of the first converts to Islam were subjected to the severest persecutions in Makka. They bore them patiently and never

[334] Mahdi (lit.: divinely guided one): A messianic deliverer who will fill the Earth with justice and equity, restore true religion, and usher in a short golden age before the end of the world.

[335] *Yeni Sayfa*, 8 January 1996.

thought of retaliation, as the Qur'an ordered Prophet Muhammad to call unbelievers to the way of God with wisdom and fair preaching and advised him to repel the evil with what was better and to respond to the sins and faults of his enemies with forbearance and forgiveness. Eventually the intolerance of the Makkan polytheists compelled the Muslims to abandon their homes and property in Makka and emigrate to Madina where they could live according to their beliefs, and where the full social and legal dimensions of Islam could evolve in peace. But the hostility of the Makkans continued and in Madina itself, the Muslims became the targets of Jewish conspiracies. Also, since the Helpers, the native believers of Madina, had to share, although willingly, everything they had with their emigrant brothers, all the Muslims suffered privations.

In such strained circumstances, God Almighty permitted them, because they had been wronged and driven from their homes unjustly, to fight against their enemies.

The Battle of Badr was the first major confrontation of the Muslims with the enemy forces. Although outnumbered, the believers won a great victory. Until then—if we do not accept the opinions of some Qur'anic interpreters that *Sura Muhammad*, which contains regulations about how to treat prisoners of war, was revealed before *Surat al-Anfal*—no Divine commandment had been revealed about how the captives should be treated. The Muslims did not even know whether they were to kill the enemy on the battlefield or take them as prisoners. After the battle, the Prophet consulted, as he always did where there was no specific Divine commandment, with his Companions on this question.

Abu Bakr said: "O God's Messenger, they are your people. Even though they did you and the believers great wrong, you will win their hearts and cause their guidance if you forgive them and please them." However, 'Umar said: "O God's Messenger, they are the leading figures of Makka. If we kill them, unbelief will no longer be able to recover to oppose us. So, hand over to each of the Muslims his closest kin. Hand 'Aqil over to his brother, 'Ali to kill. And his son, 'Abd al-Rahman, to Abu Bakr, and ....[so on]."

God's Messenger turned to Abu Bakr and said: "You are, O Abu Bakr, like Prophet Abraham, who said: *He who follows me is of me, and he who disobeys me—but You are indeed Oft-Forgiving, Most Compassionate* (14:36). You are also like Jesus, who said: *If You punish them, they are Your servants. If You forgive them, You are the All-Mighty, the All-Wise*" (5:118). Then he turned to 'Umar and said: "O 'Umar, you are like Noah, who said: *O my Lord! Leave not even a single unbeliever on earth!* (71:26). You are also like Moses, who said (of Pharaoh and his chieftains): *Our Lord, destroy their riches and harden their hearts so that they will not believe until they see the painful chastisement"* (10:88).

## Humanity and Religion

The episode just mentioned above from the early history of Islam illustrates an important aspect of the nature of humanity in relation to the mission of Prophethood and religion in human life.

A human being is a "tripartite" being composed of the spirit, the carnal soul and the body. These three elements are so closely inter-related that neglecting one results in failure to achieve perfection. A human being has accordingly been endowed with three essential faculties, namely the spiritual intellect, reason and will. During his/her lifetime, he/she experiences a continual inner struggle to choose between good and evil, right and wrong. The motor of this struggle is the will, as directed by reason. However, human reason can be swayed by carnal desires, personal feelings, interests and such emotions as anger and rancor, so it needs as its guide the spiritual intellect. The spiritual intellect, including conscience, is the source of moral values and virtues.

Historically it is the Divinely-revealed religions that have determined what is right and wrong on the authority of their Revealer, namely God, and of the character of the Prophets who conveyed first Revelation.

Because of his/her worldly nature, a human being can be too obedient a servant of his/her lusts. When such people as are captive to their lusts gain enough power to rule over their fellows, they light fires of oppression on the Earth and reduce the poor and the weak to slaves or servants. Human history is full of such instances. However, as God is All-Just and never approves oppression, He sent His Prophets in certain phases of that history in order to guide and correct the individual and collective life of humanity.

All Prophets came with the same doctrine, the fundamentals of which are believing in One God, Prophethood, the Resurrection, Angels, Divine Scriptures and Divine Destiny and worshipping God. All Prophets also conveyed the same moral principles. In this sense, all the Divine religions are one and the same. However, the flow of history through some epochs varying in cultural, geographical, social and economic conditions required different Prophets to be sent to each nation and certain differences to be made in the acts and forms of worship and in the subdivisions of the law—until such time as these conditions allowed Prophet Muhammad to be sent and the religion completed. After this, in its essentials, religion sufficed to solve all the problems humanity will encounter until the end of time and is applicable in all conditions.

### Moses, Jesus, and Muhammad

Islam, as the last, universal form of the Divine religion, orders its followers to believe in all of the Prophets. Being a Muslim also means being a follower of Jesus and Moses and of all the other Prophets at the same time.

The Qur'an declares:

> The Messenger believes in what has been revealed to him by his Lord, and so do the believers. They all believe in God and His angels, His Scriptures and His Messengers: "We make no distinction between any of His Messengers"—and they say: "We hear and obey. Grant us Your forgiveness, our Lord; to You is the journeying." (2:285)

Since, due to their historical conditions, the messages of all the previous Prophets were restricted to a certain people and period, certain principles had prominence in those messages. Also, God bestowed some special favors on each Prophet and community according to the dictates of the time. For example, Adam was favored with knowledge of the "Names," that is, the keys to all branches of knowledge; Noah was endowed with steadfastness and perseverance; Abraham was honored with intimate friendship with God and being the father of numerous Prophets; Moses was given the capability of administration and exalted through being the direct addressee of God; and Jesus was distinguished with patience, tolerance and compassion. All Prophets have some share in the praiseworthy qualities mentioned, but each of them surpasses, on account of his mission, the others in one or more of those qualities.

When Moses was raised as a Prophet, the Israelites were leading a wretched existence under the rule of the Egyptian Pharaohs. Because of the Pharaohs' despotic role and oppression, slavery was ingrained in the Israelites' souls  and had become a part of their character. To reform them, to equip them with such lofty feelings and values as freedom and independence, and to rebuild their character and free them from subservience to the Pharaohs, Moses came with a message containing stern and rigid rules and measures. This is why the Book given to Moses was called the Torah, meaning Law. As a requirement of his mission, Moses was a reformer and educator of somewhat unyielding and stern character. Therefore, it was natural for him to pray in reference to Pharaoh and his chieftains: "Our Lord, destroy their riches and harden their hearts so that they will not believe until they see the painful chastisement."

In the time when Jesus came, the Israelites had abandoned themselves to worldly pleasures and led a materialistic life. Qur'an 9:34 states that the common people and even the rabbis and scribes consumed the goods of others in vanity and barred people from God's way. They exploited religion for worldly advantage:

> You see many of them vying in sin and enmity and how they consume the unlawful; evil is the thing they have been doing. Why do the masters and rabbis not forbid them to utter sin, and consume the unlawful? Evil is the thing they have been doing. (5:62-3)

The Gospels relate a similar sentiment attributed to Jesus:

> You snakes, how can you say good things when you are evil, for the mouth speaks of what has filled the heart. A good person brings good things out of his/her treasure of good things;

a bad person brings bad things out of his/her treasure of bad
things. (Matthew 12:34-5)

> Take care: be on your guard against the yeast of the Pharisees
> and Sadducees. The teachers of the law and the Pharisees are
> the authorized interpreters of Moses' Law. So you must obey
> and follow everything they tell you to do; do not, however,
> imitate their actions, because they don't practice what they
> preach. They tie onto people's backs loads that are heavy and
> hard to carry, yet they aren't willing even to lift a finger to
> help them carry those loads. They do everything so that peo-
> ple will see them. . . They love the best places at feasts and
> the reserved seats in the synagogues; they love to be greeted
> with respect in the market-places and to have people call
> them 'Teacher'. . . How terrible for you, teachers of the Law
> and the Pharisees. You hypocrites. . . You give to God one
> tenth of the seasoning herbs, such as mint, dill and cumin, but
> you neglect to obey the really important teachings of the
> Law, such as justice and mercy and honesty. These you
> should practice, without neglecting the others. (Matthew,
> chapters 23, 13, and 12)

When Jesus was sent to the Israelites, the spirit of the Religion
had been dwindled away and the Religion itself reduced to a device
for its exponents to rob the common people. So, before proceeding
to put the Law into effect, Jesus concentrated on faith, justice,
mercy humility, peace, love, repentance for one's sins and begging
God's forgiveness, helping others, purity of heart and intention and
sincerity:

> Happy are those who know they are spiritually poor: The
> Kingdom of heaven belongs to them. Happy are those who
> mourn: God will comfort them. Happy are those who are
> humble: They will receive what God promised. Happy are
> those whose greatest desire is to do what God requires: God
> will satisfy them fully. Happy are those who are merciful to
> others: God will be merciful to them. Happy are the poor in
> heart: They will see God. (Matthew 5:3-10)

As for Prophet Muhammad, he has all the qualities mentioned
above, except being the father of Prophets. In addition, because of
the universality of his mission, he has the distinction of being like
Moses in that he is a warner and established a Law and fought with
his enemies, and like Jesus in that he is a bringer of good news who

preached mercy, forgiveness, helping others, altruism, humility, sincerity, purity of intention and moral values of the highest degree. We should remember that the Qur'an declares that God sent the Prophet Muhammad as a mercy for the whole of creation.

Islam presents God, before all other Attributes and Names, as All-Merciful and All-Compassionate. This means that God mainly manifests Himself as the All-Merciful and All-Compassionate, and that His wrath and punishment are displayed because the individual attracts it via his or her sins and wrongdoing. But God is the All-Forgiving, and forgives most of His servants' sins: *Whatever misfortune befalls you, is for what your own hands have earned and for many (of them) He grants forgiveness* (42:30).

Prophet Muhammad had the mission of both Moses and Jesus. It is evident from the historical episode mentioned at the article's beginning that among the leading Companions, Abu Bakr represented the mission of Jesus, and 'Umar represented the mission of Moses. Since Islam must prevail to the end of time, it requires its followers to act, according to circumstances, sometimes as Moses and sometimes as Jesus.

### The Messianic Mission of Jesus Christ toward the End of Time

We see in the reliable books of Hadith many sayings of Prophet Muhammad that Jesus will come back to the world before the end of time and practice the law of Islam. Although those Traditions have so far been interpreted in different ways, it cannot be wrong to interpret them as meaning that, before the end of time, Islam must manifest itself mostly in that dimension of it represented by Jesus. That is, the main aspects of the prophethood of Jesus must be given prominence in preaching Islam. These aspects are:

*Jesus always traveled.* He never stayed in one place, but preached his message on the move. To preach Islam, it "missionaries" must travel or emigrate. They must be the repenters, worshippers, travelers (in devotion to the cause of Islam and to convey it), bowers, prostraters, commanders of good and forbidders of evil, and observers of God's limits. For them there is good news (9:112).

*Mercy, love, and forgiveness had the first place.* Jesus was a bringer of good news. Therefore, those who have dedicated themselves to the cause of Islam must give prominence to these and, never forgetting that Prophet Muhammad was sent as a mercy for all the worlds and the whole of existence, must convey good news to every place and call people to the way of God with wisdom and fair exhortation. They must never be repelling.

The world today needs peace more than at any time in history, and most of its problems arise from excessive worldliness, scientific materialism and the ruthless exploitation of nature. Everyone talks so much of the danger of war and environmental pollution that peace and ecology are the most fashionable words on people's tongues. But the same people wish to remove those problems through further conquest and domination of nature.

The problem lies in rebelling against Heaven and in destroying the equilibrium between humanity and nature as a result of the modern materialistic conception of, and corrupt attitude toward, humanity and nature. Most people are reluctant to perceive that peace within human societies and with nature is possible through peace with the spiritual order. To be at peace with the Earth one must be at peace with the spiritual dimension of one's existence. This is possible by being at peace with Heaven.

In the Qur'an, Jesus introduces himself as follows:

> I am indeed a servant of God. . . He has commanded me to pray and to give alms as long as I live. And He has made me dutiful to my mother and has not made me oppressive, wicked. (79:31-2)

This means, from the viewpoint of Jesus' promised mission toward the end of time, children will not be dutiful to their parents. Therefore the "missionaries" of Islam in our age must be very careful to show due respect to their parents and elders, in addition to performing their prayers accurately and helping the poor and needy. The Qur'an enjoins:

> Your Lord has decreed that you worship none but Him, and that you show kindness to your parents. If either or both of

them attain old age with you, (show no sign of impatience, and) do not even say "uff" to them; nor rebuke them, but speak kind words to them. (17:23)

One of Jesus' miracles was healing diseases and reviving the dead with God's permission. In other words, the respect for life was very important in his message. The Qur'an attaches the same degree of importance to life: One who kills another wrongly is regarded as having killed humanity; one who saves a life is regarded as having saved humanity. Those dedicated to the cause of Islam must attach the utmost importance to life and try to prevent wars, find cures for illnesses, and know that reviving a person spiritually is more important than healing diseases. The Qur'an declares: *O you who believe! Respond to God and the Messenger, when the Messenger calls you to that which will give you life* (8:24).

## *Dialogue*

### By Professor Niyazi Öktem

The third anniversary of the founding of the Foundation of Writers and Journalists was celebrated on September 30, 1996, at Istanbul's Lütfi Kirdar Congress Hall. They were kind enough to invite me. I am going to try and evaluate this event in relation to tolerance and dialogue.

Scientists, people of religion, members of the arts, and state officials who until recently would never have imagined coming together, shook hands, embraced, and sat side by side. The hall was full. Seated on my immediate right was Refik Erduran, the artist-writer who smuggled the worthy Turkish poet Nazim Hikmet to the Soviet Union. On my left was Professor Nur Vergin, who was raised in Western culture and emphasizes the importance of faith in social life. Professor Toktamis Ates, the unwavering defender of secularism, lovingly embraced Associate Professor Ali Bayramoglu, Professor Nevzat Yalçintas, and people from different places in the political spectrum, all of whom are open to dialogue and tolerance.

I heard that all representatives in the faith mosaic had been invited. Alevi elder Muharrem Naci Orhan; the Vatican's Representative to Turkey, Monsignor Pelatre and his assistant Monsignor Marovitch; and Cefi Kamhi and Üzeyir Garih were all there. The Armenian Patriarch and his deputy, as well as the Syriac community's representatives, had asked me for the address. They must have been invited, but I do not know whether they came or not.

Meanwhile, the distinguished Orthodox Patriarch Bartholomeos I entered the hall. The front rows were full, but some people occupying the seats reserved for protocol immediately got up and gave him a seat. Last year, however, in UNESCO's "Tolerance" meeting organized by representatives of the Ministry of Foreign Affairs, some ministry members had tried to seat him in a rather unpleasant place in the protocol seats. It is impossible not to see the conflict between the state and civilian groups, and not to appreciate the organization of civil groups and their desire for dialogue. A few minutes later, the esteemed Fethullah Gülen entered the hall. He went straight toward Bartholomeos I and, embracing him, sat down beside him. The hall resounded with applause.

There must be something to it if two leaders, in whose communities uncultured and fanatic groups look at each other as "dirty infidel" and "barbarian Turk," can embrace each other. At least, members of society must love and meet each other with understanding. The two leaders spoke at the meetings' end, and gave messages of love and acceptance to each other and the people. They repeatedly stressed the importance of mutual love and behaving with tolerance in the interest of real peace, regardless of which religion, sect, or philosophical trend they follow. Enmity should come to an end. They embraced each other again, and the audience stood up and applauded both leaders for several minutes.

Freedom, democracy, and respect for all human beings are not just Western principles. True Muslims also advocate these principles. They support dialogue, tolerance, and respect for others' beliefs. They seek to implement these concepts in their own lives, and arrange meetings for this purpose. Sure of themselves, they do not fear dialogue. True Westerners and true democrats also are like this. Deviations should be ignored. If both sides have fully assimilated their respective religion or ideology, there is nothing to fear.[336]

## Other Meetings

### *Meeting with the Sephardic*
### *Head Rabbi of Israel*

Israel's Sephardic Head Rabbi Eliyahu Bakshi Doron said that members of Gülen's community could open a school in Israel. Taking a giant step for world peace and dialogue, Fethullah Gülen, honorary chairman of the Foundation of Writers and Journalists, met with the Head Rabbi, the religious leader of the Jews. Gülen previously had met with the Catholic leader Pope John Paul II.

Visiting Gülen at the foundation's headquarters, Head Rabbi Doron spoke with him for approximately one hour. During the visit, he said: "It's necessary to talk about common points among religions. In all religions God is One. It's our duty as men of religion to communicate this message." Saying that he appreciated Gülen's efforts for interfaith dialogue and world peace, Doron stated: "As men of religion we must show peace. Together we must show the world peace and love. The Honorable Gülen is an important person in the Islamic world. For that reason, I wanted to speak with him."

Replying that he appreciated the Head Rabbi's efforts for interfaith dialogue and tolerance, Gülen emphasized that interfaith dialogue should not be misunderstood. Remarking that some groups misunderstand these efforts, he said: "One matter is being misunderstood. It's not a dialogue among religions; it's a dialogue among members of different religions. You can't mix religions and come up with something like Sanskrit." Gülen added that he believes that religion, which has carried important missions in different periods of history, will show its undefeatable power by taking on this mission once again.

When asked if opening a school in Israel was discussed, Gülen replied: "That was always our intention. At any rate there is dia-

---

[336] *Zaman*, 7 October 1996.

logue, contact, and agreement on the state level. There's no problem there. I presented things to the Honorable Head Rabbi that need to be done for our people to come closer together."[337]

[In addition to being interviewed by newspaper and television personalities throughout the world, Fethullah Gülen also gives oral and written interviews to religious or social civil organizations. Within the framework of dialogue, we're presenting as an example the answers he gave to Engelwerkes, a religious organization headquartered in Austria.]

Mr. P. Hanejörg Bitterlich
Moderator des Engelwerkes
Bad Fusch, Austria

Dear Sir:

I thank you for your efforts to develop dialogue among members of the world's great religions. Answers to the questions you were kind enough to ask are presented below.

With deep respect,

Fethullah Gülen

Q: Do you have any connection with the Nur movement?

A: Because describing something or giving it a name makes it easier to introduce, some call our movement the Nur (Light) movement. However, personally I'm not in favor of such a practice, for it causes the impression that we represent a separate and divisive group in society. This is not the case. We're not associated with such a group, nor have we developed such a group.

Coming to your question of whether or not we have anything to do with Nur: As you know, the first verses of Genesis give the impression that *nur* (light) was the first and main thing created. In a

---
[337] *Yeni Yüzyil*, 26 February 1996.

similar way, the Qur'an's *Surat al-Nur*, verse 35, states: *God is the light of the Heavens and the Earth.* In many other places the Qur'an explains that God is our guardian, and that He brought us out of darkness and into light. This is very important from the perspective of how a Muslim thinks or acts, because it is put forward that the most important service we can be given is "enlightenment." While on this topic, we should mention this point.

The "enlightenment" movement spoken of in the last centuries only includes mental enlightenment. Spiritual and moral principles are not mentioned, and the truth that the heart and life can be enlightened only with spiritual and moral values is neglected. Moreover, these values have been ridiculed covertly. But we believe that human existence is too noble for the spiritual and moral dimension to be neglected. Every person should be educated in this respect. Just as no serious enlightenment can occur if this dimension is neglected, peace, harmony, and happiness cannot be established in human life. Real salvation can be realized only by enlightening the mind/intelligence and the heart/spirit.

Q: What are the basic common principles between Islam and Catholicism requiring dialogue?

A: The Qur'an commands us to believe in all the Prophets and the divine Books revealed to them. This means that being Muslim means being a follower of Jesus, Moses, and Abraham.

In addition to the basic principles in Islam and Catholicism that you mentioned, both religions have the same moral principles. Virtue is the fruit of an orderly religious life and training. Muhammad said: "I have been sent only to complete beautiful morality." In Jesus' teachings, love, mercy, forgiveness, and patience are given as basic moral principles. This priority is also Islam's priority. In Islam's formula: *In the name of God, the Merciful, the Compassionate*, God introduces Himself first of all as Merciful and Compassionate. Similarly, in the Qur'an our Prophet is addressed as: *We sent you as a mercy to all of creation.* In addition, in both religions despite some differences in belief based on Catholic interpretation, One God is the essential principle of worship. There are many other common aspects, listing them all here would take a lot of space. Indicating these basic points should suffice.

Q: What are your fields of service?

A: Today in Turkey, works are erroneously attributed to me to facilitate describing and introducing them. In fact, all social segments have contributed to them. They include opening private schools inside and outside of Turkey, building dormitories and youth hostels for students, and also some media services.

Q: Do you favor dialogue with the followers of other religions?

A: We're ready to do whatever we can to establish dialogue and closeness among all nations, in fact, among all people regardless of race, color, belief, thought, or worldview. We believe that especially Muslims and Christians, and undoubtedly members of other religions, will and should cooperate against every kind of anti-religious and anti-human movement.

Islamic sources contain authentic narration that Jesus will return to Earth before Doomsday, and that universal justice will prevail. Some current Muslim commentaries interpret these narrations to mean that when we are close to Doomsday, Muslims and Christians will join hands on basic common points and cooperate against movements opposed to religion, like atheism.

Q: What can we do regarding our common ideals?

A: Such matters can be discussed face to face. With your permission, let me say this much: If there is an intention to work sincerely for a better world, what can be done will become obvious. The most effective path must be to avoid argument and conflict, and always to act positively and constructively.

### *Historic Vatican Meeting*[338]

Belief in God, without associating any partners with Him in His Divinity and Lordship, and worshipping Him are the foundations of

---

[338] This meeting took place on 10 February 1998.

the Divinely revealed Religion that has been the same throughout history with respect to its essentials. This is why the Qur'an states that Abraham was neither a Jew nor a Christian, but one who best exemplified primordial belief in God and total submission to Him. The Qur'an also orders the Prophet to follow the nation of Abraham. But although of the same essence, over time the religion of Abraham has taken three separate forms, which have almost always been in conflict. Simon Jargy writes:

> To try to analyze the historical relations between Islam and Christianity in both their religious and sociopolitical components, is to come up immediately against one preliminary fact: although the three great religions of the monotheist faith came from the same roots, they developed separately from each other. They have not supplemented but rather opposed each other in a perpetual conflict.[339]

Muslims, due to their independence struggles and their tendency to see their problems and solutions as political in nature, have made Islam into an almost-political ideology. The Arab–Israeli conflict has contributed to this. Especially after the so-called Islamic revolution in Iran, Islam was viewed and presented in the West as a religion of conflict, enmity, and violence, and the Iranian revolution as representative of Islam. After the Iron Curtain collapsed, NATO marked out the Islamic world as its potential enemy.

Fortunately, despite historical disagreements and other negative factors, some Muslims, Christians, and Jews have rediscovered that they have much in common: the essentials of belief, faith and trust in God, repentance, truth, purity, chivalry, justice, charity, benevolence, mercy, self-control, chastity, uprightness, respect for others' rights, love, and forgiveness. They also condemn lying, cheating, theft, gambling, usurpation, falsehood, dishonesty, adultery, hypocrisy, injustice, cruelty, pride, ungratefulness, treachery, intemperance, sloth, jealousy, selfishness, hurting others, and violence.

What humanity needs today, more than anything else, is the implementation of these positive values. For this reason, the Qur'an

---

[339] *Islam et Chrétienté* (Geneva: Labor et Fides, 1981), 10.

declares: *Surely, your community is one community and I am your Lord, so worship Me* (21:92), and:

> Say: "O People of the Book! Come to a word common between us and you: that we shall worship none but God, and that we shall not associate any partners with Him, and that we shall not take some of us as lords besides God."' (3:64)

In 1962, the Holy See launched a movement of dialogue between the great religions. The efforts of John Paul II are particularly worthy of mention. He has visited many Muslim countries and, both during such visits and in his *Crossing the Threshold of Hope*, has expressed his feelings and hopes for dialogue. Perhaps the most important and promising response to his call has come from Turkey, when Fethullah Gülen visited him in February 1998.

Like his earlier (and continuing) efforts for dialogue among Turkey's different social strata, a dialogue based on mutual acceptance and respect for the other's identity and building relations on the basis of complete equality, Gülen's meeting with the Pope received a very warm welcome from the Turkish media.

Ankara signaled its approval by having its ambassador to the Vatican, Altan Güven, treat Fethullah Gülen as if he were an official envoy of Turkey. It was only to be expected that, except for a very few small marginal groups of radical Muslims and die-hard materialists, the Turkish media would attach great importance to this meeting. Before and after the event, some TV channels conducted telephone interviews with him. Sociologists, political analysts, and theologians also expressed their views in periodicals, on television, and through interviews they gave to the media. Summary excerpts from some of these views and comments follow:

## Excerpts from the Media

### *Professor Niyazi Öktem*

> (Niyazi Öktem, a professor in Istanbul University's Faculty of Political Sciences, has studied the dialogue between religions and religious schools or sects. He was interviewed by journalist Mehmet Gundem.)

Q: According to you, what do Fethullah Gülen's efforts for dialogue import in Turkey?

A: Economic and ideological differences lie behind the conflicts and clashes in the world. Ideological conflicts originate from the [opposing] sides not knowing each other. Thus, I regard Mr. Gülen's efforts as of great significance, as he calls everyone to accept the other as it is and respect each other's views and identity. His inclusion of international figures in his quest for dialogue means a lot for Muslims [in Turkey] particularly. Especially so in the present circumstances, when both Muslims and Ankara have for so long been rather sensitive [on the issue of] foreigners and representatives of non-Muslim religious communities.

Until Gülen started meeting with those representatives, it was unusual for a Muslim to engage in dialogue with a Christian or Jew. I myself took part in the first Religious Counsel held in 1992 and, together with Ethem Ruhi Figlali, dean of the Faculty of Theology at Mugla University, found it very difficult to include the word *dialogue* in the final declaration. People feared that Christian missionaries would come and poison our people. Why should Muslims convinced of Islam's truth be afraid? Gülen has no such fear, and therefore, as a Muslim with full conviction, opens the doors of dialogue to everyone. He has full confidence in his religion.

Q: Some people in Turkey, albeit few in number, speculate that Mr. Gülen is after power. Do you think that?

A: I can never accept that such an important social phenomenon as dialogue should be reduced to something explicable by conspiracy theories. We have no right to judge anyone by what we produce in our imaginations. Disapproval of an idea or initiative gives no one the right to condemn it. They cannot see the good behind Gülen's attempts at dialogue. We should consider the atmosphere of peace and love that dialogue can engender. Gülen had met with Patriarch Bartholomeos I before. I regarded that meeting as one of the most important events in the [recent] history of the Turkish Republic, for our Muslim and Orthodox citizens had [hitherto] regarded each other as enemies. That meeting has paved the way for a better understanding and coming together. His meeting with the Pope is certainly much more important than that.

Q: Why is that meeting so important?

A: It is of global import. The West has a very negative image of Muslims. In their eyes, Muslims are unproductive, consumers [only], implacable, and inclined to terrorism. And [they see] Islam as the religion responsible for such vices. So, a religious leader's meeting with the Pope at just this time means that he is ready to enter a dialogue with Christians and that Islam is not closed to dialogue. This meeting also contradicts those Europeans who allege that Muslims are too radical to enter a dialogue and offer that as an excuse for not allowing Turkey to join the EU.

Q: Some question Mr. Gülen's status [his worthiness] to meet with the Pope.

A: This is a matter for the Pope. But it seems that the Vatican knows him better than us. The Pope does not accept everyone's request for a meeting, and his appointments are arranged years in advance. Gülen's meeting with the Pope was arranged last year, which shows that the Vatican considers him important.

I regard this meeting as one of the most important events of the twentieth century. Although at first glance it seems to be a simple event, it will have far-reaching consequences, for positive, important changes in world history [often] are started and realized by those wholly dedicated to a cause, not the official actors in state structures. Such people may not have official titles, but they have a power resting upon their followers' love. Gülen has a large following. People agree with him on his initiative. I wish the state would give him greater support. I worry about certain fundamentalist movements in Turkey. Gülen's calls for dialogue make the atmosphere more peaceful and propitious for the coming together of opposing groups. Our ambassador's welcoming him shows that important power centers in the state support him.

Q: Ertugrul Özkök, editor of *Hürriyet,* has said that Fethullah Gülen is becoming an international figure. Do you agree?

A: Yes. Ideologically Turkey is a Western country, but Islam is still a very important social phenomenon. It has long been exploited for political ambitions and so is misunderstood. Gülen and his group give priority to its main elements: love, dialogue, respect for others' rights, and human rights. His movement is loyal to Islam's essence, but this does not prevent its members from understanding contemporary values. They give the society the idea that people can live together regardless of group, faith, or ideology.

Q: Do you agree that religion is becoming increasingly influential in international relations?

A: Religion has been always been influential. However, many intellectuals cannot see this mission of religion. Economics and religion are the two main factors that have roused peoples to war. Why shouldn't we use such a powerful factor to bring about peace? Teaching believers that religion can bring about peace, and that it is not a religious requirement to fight followers of other beliefs, can help eliminate enmity. Also, dialogue between religions can remove the influence of religious differences in international relations.

Q: What do you think about the proposals he made to the Pope?

A: It's very meaningful that Muslims and Christians celebrate the 2,000th anniversary of Jesus' birth. As Jesus has a significant place in the Qur'an and Islam, cities such as Antioch, Ephesus, and Jerusalem mean a great deal to both groups. Gülen suggested to the Pope that they visit those cities together. He proposed that Jerusalem be a city that the followers of the three religions could visit without a visa, and that they hold conferences in different cities. He also proposed opening a university or a theological faculty in Urfa, where scholars from the three religions would teach and students would study.[340] These offers are of great significance for promoting dialogue, peace, and mutual understanding.[341]

---

[340] Urfa: Considered the birth-place of Abraham and where his own people threw him into a fire for daring to challenge their idolatry. It is also an ancient center of Middle Eastern civilizations.

[341] *Zaman*, 15 February 1998.

## *Professor Suat Yıldırım*

> (Suat Yıldırım teaches in Istanbul University's Faculty of
> Theology. He has published many books and is the best-
> known authority on interfaith dialogue. The following is a
> summary of his long article on the Gülen–Pope meeting.)

The twentieth century has seen the Information Age replace the Industrial Age. Huge advances in telecommunications have brought everyone into closer contact. In such a century, ideas can become obsolete very quickly. If this is to be avoided, the idea must be "put in a window" where people can "see" it, so that it can become powerful and influential. The Muslim world lags far behind the West in economic, political, and military power. Even if Muslims wanted to use physical force, they do not have the means to do so.

Despite the advances of science and technology, the Divinely revealed religions will continue to exist. Neither side can remove the other, and this fact means that their followers will have to live together in peace. But more than that, new developments and changes in the world force religions to cooperate against antireligious movements. The Christian West initiated a dialogue after the Second Vatican Council (1962-65). Although the Qur'an made a universal, ecumenical call to dialogue 14 centuries ago, Muslims are reluctant to participate in such a dialogue.

Christianity survived by opposing Islam and resorting to force when necessary. It also imagined that it could survive by distorting Islam's image. To the West, Islam was obscurantist and fanatical, an artful forgery of Judaism and Christianity, and the Prophet was considered an imposter. However, seeing that the Christian world was moving even further away from Christianity, the Second Vatican Council announced one of the most important changes in its history: In the Council's opening speech, Pope Paul VI stressed that although other religions have their imperfections and insufficiencies in, the Catholic Church appreciates their good and right elements.

The Vatican's call to dialogue has not been welcomed by Muslims. This may be due to the following reasons:

- There is no comparable official position or authority to represent Muslims.

- Western colonialism, which lasted for centuries and was supported by Christianity, makes it easy for Muslims to believe that the Vatican has an ulterior political motive for making such a call.

- Muslims have not forgotten the Crusades and so remain on their guard.

- Muslims may see this as a new style of missionary activities.

- This call was made at a time when Muslims did not expect it. The Church was ready, thanks to the extensive studies of Christian Orientalists, to pursue it and counter its possible consequences; the Muslims were not.

Muslims in Turkey have long been indifferent to the Vatican's call to dialogue. While this is partly due to the reasons cited above, a more important reason is that Turkey largely has been closed to such external developments.

It is difficult to approve of such indifference, for, looking at history, we see that the Turks had the closest relations with the West. Around 4 million Turks are living in Europe, and Turkey has a long history of trying to enter the EU. In addition, it would be easy for the West to manipulate the international image of Islam and Muslims against Turkey and other Muslim countries. So, it is up to Turkey as a state, as well as up to Muslim Turks because they are Muslims, to present the true image of Islam and prevent its being misunderstood by ordinary and unbiased non-Muslims.

### Fethullah Gülen's Meeting with the Pope
Fethullah Gülen, a well-known religious scholar, has been identified with efforts for a sincere dialogue within a Turkey torn by division. Except a few radicals on the right and left, his calls for dialogue based on mutual acceptance and respect of each other's identity, have received positive responses from almost all social segments. Since his calls and efforts have attracted a great deal of attention outside Turkey, last summer he organized and attended significant meetings in the US.

Gülen's position as a Muslim scholar in Turkey with a large following makes him an important person. His followers' activities in different fields, especially education, already cover a large area. Almost all communities within Turkey have greeted his calls for dialogue positively, including the representatives of religious communities: the Patriarch of the Turkish Orthodox community, the Patriarch of the Turkish Armenian community, and the Chief Rabbi of the Turkish Jewish community. These facts may have encouraged the Pope to meet with him.

### Fethullah Gülen's Offers

Due to the widespread unfamiliarity with foreign languages and ignorance of basic Islamic beliefs, Muslim Turks have been isolated from the outside world. The European destruction of the Ottoman State after centuries of attacks, as well as Europe's occupation of Turkey following the First World War, make Turkish Muslims very careful when dealing with the Christian West. Thus, it is only natural for them to suspect the Vatican's call for dialogue.

The reaction of certain radicals to this meeting shows that people can still use the Crusades to prevent such a meeting. Others, however few, think that a Muslim religious leader can meet his non-Muslim counterpart only to convert him or her to Islam. It is easy to understand why such people oppose Gülen's offers to the Pope.

Gülen suggested that he and the Pope make joint visits to such historically holy cities as Antioch, Ephesus, and Jerusalem, and hold conferences in various great cities of the world. He suggested that they could open a university or a faculty of theology in Urfa to teach Islam, Christianity, and Judaism, and that Jerusalem be open to visa-less visits by Muslims, Christians, and Jews. These offers are significant steps toward a better understanding among members of these religions. As a religious scholar confident of his belief, fully dedicated to his cause, and of great vision, Gülen does not fear the weakening of Islam by establishing closer contacts with non-Muslims. He opines that past enmities should not hinder dialogue.

### Cooperation against Anti-Religious Movements

Muslims are weaker than Christians in material power. However, they are confident of their belief and have much to offer. Most of our problems come from a materialistic worldview and indifference to the moral values contained and propagated by religions. Muslims and Christians can offer all people, most of whom are ensnared in a corrupt and materialistic civilization, the spirituality and moral values they hold and which can inject a new hope into despairing souls. This is what such unbiased Western thinkers as Olivier Lacombe, Michel Lelong, and Montgomery Watt hope for. They explicitly write that the West, engrossed in materialism and secularism, can return to religion by seeing the power of faith among the Muslims and their submission to God.

So, can we use dialogue to promote Islam's religious, spiritual, and moral values? If one does not see Islam as an ideological and political weapon to be used against rivals or as a means of superiority, if one is not Muslim by name [only], one should be happy with accepting and promoting Islamic values.

### Professor Griffith's Views of Dialogue

During his visit to the US last summer, Fethullah Gülen met with Sidney Griffith, a professor in The Catholic University, Washington, DC. In a subsequent interview in *Zaman*, Griffith expressed his views of dialogue as helping Christians unaware of Islam's truth to get to know Islam. He says that typical Christians think of Islam as belonging only to Arabs. But now, they understand that Turkey is very important with respect to Islam. He continued:

> Many Western historians have not heard of the Crusades. Islam has been taught in the West only in faculties of political sciences. It has been approached as a political phenomenon from the viewpoint of Orientalists. It has not been taught as a religion. This is where the main problem lies.[342]

### Dr. Nevzat Yalçintas

(Nevzat Yalçintas is a member of Parliament.)

Fethullah Gülen's meeting with the Pope in the Vatican is a significant, happy event. The Pope is the spiritual leader of the greatest section of the world's Christians, and a man of extraordinary importance in the international arena. Fethullah Gülen is a sincere Muslim scholar wholly dedicated to spreading Islam's spiritual and moral principles of faith, mercy, love, affection, mutual helping, reconciliation, and respect for others' rights.

---

[342] *Zaman*, 11–12 April 1998.

This meeting between two men dedicated to humanity promises new, happy developments in the arena of interreligious dialogue. The offers made by Gülen to the Holy See are of great significance and should be given due consideration.

Both Muslims and Christians have tried their best to remove atheistic communism, which had no chance of becoming established in Muslim countries, from the world. The Pope's efforts were instrumental in its collapse. Both groups can work together closely in many fields. Thus the meeting in the Vatican is a happy, promising event for Muslims, Christians, and for humanity.[343]

### Professor Mehmet Aydın

> (Mehmet Aydın is dean of Selçuk University's Faculty of Theology. The following is a summary of his report made to the Anadolu Agency, Turkey's official news agency.)

A sincere dialogue between Muslims and Catholics will contribute to world peace. Islam has advocated dialogue with Jews, Christians, Sabeans, and Magians since the beginning of its existence, and the Prophet had several meetings with followers and representatives of these religions. Following their conversion to Islam, the Turks attached special importance to dialogue and contributed a great deal to developing a universal civilization.

Gülen's meeting with the Pope is a continuation of the Turks' historical tolerance toward non-Muslims. I hope this meeting may cause the West to come to understand the universal tolerance of the Turks, which the West has ignored for centuries.[344]

### Hadi Uluengin

> (Hadi Uluengin is a columnist for *Hurriyet*. His comments are summarized below.)

I have never agreed with the Pope on many of his ideas and initiatives, such as banning the pill for birth control and excommuni-

---

[343] *Türkiye*, 11 February 1998.

[344] *Zaman*, 12 February 1998.

cating divorced people. But this does not prevent my acknowledging him as one of the twentieth century's most influential political figures. He made a great contribution to the collapse of the Iron Curtain and the Soviet Union.

Fethullah Gülen, a distinguished religious scholar, met with the Pope and thereby realized a top-level meeting in his search for dialogue and mutual respect. He started this search by meeting with representatives of the Turkish Orthodox and Jewish communities at a time when Islam was being presented [in the West] as a threat, and Huntington's "clash of civilizations" theory was being widely discussed. Gülen's visit to the Vatican is of historic significance.

The existence of his group is a chance for Turkey to end its internal polarization, secularize fundamental religious questions, and open up to the outer world. Some of the worries expressed concerning this group are groundless, and the rest are secondary and quite negligible. The essential points on which we agree are those on which secularists and devout Muslims and sincere followers of other religions can come together. The use of Maoists, who actually have fascist tendencies, in the detestable attacks on this group shows that Gülen and his group are on the right track. ... Many thanks to Fethullah Gülen and his distinguished group.[345]

## Ahmet Tezcan

(Ahmet Tezcan produces programs for a private television channel in Turkey. His comments are summarized below.)

Fethullah Hodjaefendi and Pope John Paul II met at the Vatican. As far as I understand from the newspapers, the dialogue meeting of the two men of religion, turning into cooperation at the recommendation of Fethullah Hodjaefendi, will bear fruit shortly. I want to make two points about this meeting.

First of all, Fethullah Hodjaefendi's recommendations to the Pope:

---

[345] *Hürriyet*, 11 February 1998.

- As Christianity is entering its third millennium, mutual visits should be made to such sacred Middle Eastern places as Antioch, Tarsus, Ephesus, and Jerusalem.

- Efforts should be made to declare Jerusalem an international district so that Christians, Jews, and Muslims can freely visit without limitations or visas.

- With the cooperation of Christian, Jewish, and Muslim leaders, conferences should be arranged in various capitals, beginning in America.

- An independent university should be founded at Harran to meet these three religions' needs. There also should be a student exchange program between the Christian and Islamic worlds.

These are Hodjaefendi's recommendations. If they are realized, cooperative dialogue among these three religions will become more stable, fanaticism will drown, and Turkey will become a global focal point of religions. In particular, the suggestion to make Harran a center of religious knowledge is a magnificent suggestion that will deter the difficulties we're having in the Southeast. It also will contribute to global peace and open the way to healing wounds with "celestial compassion." It should be supported.

Fethullah Hodja did what was expected of him, and made his master happy by being an exemplary "loyal disciple."[346]

## Cengiz Çandar

(Cengiz Çandar is a daily political affairs columnist with *Sabah* and a resident Public Policy Scholar at the Woodrow Wilson Center for International Scholars.)

Several developments have occurred, each of which is closely related to Turkey's future… First, the Fethullah Gülen–Pope John Paul II meeting … a development of extraordinary importance and value … coming just after the Pope's meeting with [Cuba's] Castro.

The Cuba visit, made in front of CNN cameras, proves that the Pope is an international actor worthy of mention. His meeting at the Vatican with Fethullah Gülen immediately after this also brought Gülen into the position of an international actor. From now on, the

---

[346] *Aksam*, 11 February 1998.

international field of legitimacy, from which the regime in Turkey can direct opposition to Gülen's activities inside and outside of Turkey, has ended on its own. At any rate, inside Turkey there is no "foundation of legitimacy" in the public conscience for opposition with this intent. If it continues this path, Turkey will have chosen to be fully a isolationist–totalitarian regime. Those who follow such a path will be assumed to be guilty of having decided to destabilize Turkey or continue to its ongoing instability.

In this respect, the Gülen–Pope meeting is a very important security measure for Turkey's democratization. Indirectly, it is an important contribution toward Turkey becoming a stable country.[347]

## Riza Zelyut

(Riza Zelyut is an Alawi journalist who advocates dialogue.)

Do not say that we are a strange society. Forget it. We jump at the chance to become a part of the modern world, but at the same time brand as "treason to the country" relationships that will provide such union.

To make our name heard in the world, we proudly begin from negative issues. We proclaim as heroes those who go beyond the government's normal operations. We secretly praise those who get mixed up in corruption in other countries. In this case, we see it as our national duty to look for and find fault with those who display a civilized attitude.

Fethullah Gülen Hodja went and met with the Pope. A serious step was taken in developing interfaith dialogue and creating points on which people can find mutual accord. We began shouting: "Who is this Fethullah Hodja? While the huge Turkish government exists, how can this man meet with the Pope? He is trying to save himself because he's in difficulty..." And another attack from the backward wing: "Would a true Muslim ever accept Christians as friends?" Secularists, radical Islamists, and nationalists are all opposed to the meeting. It is as if this poor man sold the country to the Pope.

---

[347] *Hürriyet*, 14 February 1998.

As I said, we do not like positive steps. Why do we need to sit and talk with the Pope? If we are going to address him, it should be with types like Mehmet Ali Agca.[348] We should either hit or burn him… Then we will find inner peace, and our thirst for revenge will be slated… The Vatican is in Rome… The Pope is at the Vatican… He has not escaped anywhere. If there is someone better to have a dialogue with the Pope, let him…

Even if Fethullah Hodja met with the Pope for appearances sake, that is his problem. I find pretence acceptable if it derives from dialogue, tolerance, reconciliation, and the idea of living together.[349]

## Ahmet Turan Alkan

(Ahmet Turan Alkan is a faculty member of the Faculty of Economics and Administration and a columnist for *Zaman*.)

When I read the details of Fethullah Hodjaefendi's meeting with the Pope, I remembered once again how many things the Muslim and Christian worlds have in common, although we think of them as totally separate worlds. I think these common points are truths that are not widely known and taught in the Christian world. Christians quite normally look from their own perspective and accept Jesus as the last prophet, and have developed a harsher historical perspective toward Muslims. In return, we can say that the Qur'an's attitude is not very widespread among us.

We strongly hope that this visit will cause understanding and sympathy to blossom between two neighboring realms. Imagine that these two worlds enter into sincere acquaintance and cooperation with the attributes of not being a servant to anyone but God, not taking any overt or covert partners before Him, being trustworthy, and exalting the truth. What a great step this would be for world peace, and how pleasing it would be to the Creator.

---

[348] Mehmet Ali Agca tried to assassinate Pope John Paul II in St. Peter's Square on May 11, 1981. There still remains some ambiguity over the motives for the attack. Agca was sentenced to life imprisonment in Italy. He was recently extradited to Turkey for trial on several accounts.

[349] *Aksam*, 13 February 1998.

Can you imagine any unmerciful soul who would not be exited by Fethullah Hodja's proposal to establish a university at Harran to meet the needs of the three Abrahamic religions? Close your eyes and imagine that the following kind of university exists. There is a high quality curriculum from the masters level to the post-doctorate. In the corridors, halls, and gardens, Christian, Muslim, and Jewish students and faculty members exchange greetings and have informal, warm conversations. Students attend exchange lessons and seminars as guests, and annual individual or joint scholastic meetings are held. Students are attracted from all over the world. And, these wonderful things occur in the heart of the Abrahamic tradition's motherland. Think that this is realized at Harran. Putting aside this idea's realization, the very idea of which is Abrahamic, and if one day this university takes form, would not giving it Abraham's name make that great spirit happy?

Let's hope that this meeting is the beginning of a permanent and long-lasting atmosphere of understanding. Finally, as Shaykh Sa'di said, human beings are like different bodily limbs. On that great day, all of humanity will be called to account. We have long since forgotten how to think big. We are indebted to those who open a global excitement and perspective in the midst of the many ordinary things surrounding our minds and horizons.[350]

## On His Meeting with the Pope

"I trust in the beauty in humanity's makeup."

Q: At a time when the clash of civilizations theories are being discussed and NATO has declared [the] Islam[ic world] the chief enemy, you call for a worldwide dialogue. What factors urge you to make such attempts?

A: The idea that the world is on the threshold of new clashes is the expectation of those whose power and continued domination depend on continuous conflict. However, as the Qur'an puts it, humanity is a noble creature and in pursuit of good things. While

---

[350] *Zaman*, 14 February 1998.

searching for the good and beautiful, we sometimes may encounter undesirable things. What urges me to call for a worldwide dialogue is humanity's innate nobility and beauty.

Q: Are the relevant commandments or rules of the Qur'an or the Prophet important in your initiatives?

A: The Qur'an urges peace, order, and accord. It aims at universal peace and order, and opposes conflicts and dissension. It is interesting that the Qur'an calls actions acceptable to God "actions to bring peace and order." Our Prophet described fighting in the way of God as the *lesser jihad*, because it is undertaken only to remove obstacles to perfecting people morally and spiritually, and bringing about peace and order in society. The real aim is to perfect people and bring about peace and order. When this cannot be achieved by such desirable ways as education, and when you are exposed to unjust attacks, only then can we undertake the lesser jihad. We must understand it not as a rule, but as the last resort.

Q: What was the process that finally made it possible for you to meet with the Pope?

A: One cannot achieve something positive in an atmosphere dominated by enmity and through reactionary measures. As social and civilized beings, especially now when human values are given prominence even though rather verbally, we can and should solve our problems through dialogue. It is our belief, which also is shared by sociologists and political analysts, that religions will be more influential in the twenty-first century. Islam and Christianity have the largest followings. Buddhism and Hinduism also have considerable followings. Judaism has an influence of its own. If we expect a universal revival toward the end of time, then this requires, as a preliminary condition, that these great religions cooperate on the essentials that they have in common.

We have no doubt about the truth of our values. We urge no one to join us, and I think that no one conceives of urging us to join their religion. The Qur'an made a universal call of dialogue to the followers of other heavenly religions. Unfortunately, however, the cen-

turies following this call saw conflict and quarrels rather than dialogue and mutual understanding. Our time is the time of addressing
intellects and hearts, an undertaking that requires a peaceful atmosphere with mutual trust and respect. At first glance, the conditions
of the Hudaybiya treaty seemed unacceptable to the Companions.[351]
However, the Qur'an described it as an opening, because in the
peaceful atmosphere engendered by this treaty, the doors of hearts
were opened to Islamic truths. We have no intention of conquering
lands or peoples, but we are resolved to contribute to world peace
and a peaceful order and harmony by which our old world will find
a last happiness before its final destruction.[352]

## On the World's Future

### *At the Threshold of a New Millennium*

As every dawn, sunrise, and upcoming spring signifies a new
beginning and hope, so does every new century and millennium. In
this respect, within the wheels of time over which we have no control, humanity has always sought a new spark of life, a breath as
fresh as the wind of dawn, and has hoped and desired to step into
light from darkness as easily as crossing a threshold.

We can only speculate as to when the original man and woman
appeared on Earth, which is equated with the Heavens due to the

---

[351] The Treaty of Hudaybiya was signed in 6 AH between the Prophet and the
Makkan leadership, which sought to block the Muslims' attempt to perform the
minor pilgrimage to Makkah. Under this treaty, the Muslims would be allowed in
next year for 3 days, during which the Makkans would vacate the city. The treaty
also stipulated a 10-year truce, that people or tribes could join or ally themselves
with whoever they wished, and that Qurayshi subjects or dependents who defect-
ed to Madina would be returned. This last condition was not reciprocal, and thus
was opposed in the Muslim camp. However, the following verse was revealed at
this time: *We have given you a manifest victory* (48:1). History bore out the truth
of this verse, for in effect the Quraysh now recognized the Muslims as their
equals, ended their monopoly on the Ka'ba, and gave up their struggle against
Islam. In the newly peaceful atmosphere, people were free to consider the
Prophet's message and join Islam. Several Makkans who would become leading
Muslim personages embraced Islam during this time.

[352] *Aksiyon*, 14 February 1998.

divine art it exhibits, its ontological meaning, and its value largely coming from its chief inhabitant: humanity. According to the calendar we use today, we are at the threshold of the third millennium after the birth of Jesus. However, since time revolves and advances in a helicoidal relativity, there are many ways of measuring time. For example, according to the calendar that currently enjoys global acceptance, we are about to cross the threshold of a new thousand-year period. According to other calendars, we are already in the second half of the sixth millennium (Jewish), the Kali Yuga era (Hindu), and are approaching the end of the first half of the second millennium (Muslim).

But we should remember that this measure of time is relative. While a 100-year period is assumed to be the measure for a century, the idea of a 60-year century, based on the life span of an average person, also is worth mentioning. From this point of view, we are already in the forth millennium after the birth of Jesus, and the third millennium after the hijra (the starting point of the Muslim calendar). I raise this issue due to the spiritual discomfort engendered by the terrifying auguries, especially in the West, believed to be associated with the upcoming millennium.

People live in perpetual hope and thus are children of hope. At the instant they lose their hope, they also lose their "fire" of life, no matter if their physical existence continues. Hope is directly proportional to having faith. Just as winter constitutes one-fourth of a year, so the periods in a person's or a society's life corresponding to winter also are small. The gears of Divine acts revolve around such comprehensive wisdom and merciful purposes. Just as the cycle of night and day builds one's hope and revivifies one's spirit, and every new year comes in expectations of spring and summer, disastrous periods are short and followed by happy times in both an individual's life and a nation's history.

This cycle of the "Days of God," which is centered in Divine Wisdom, holds no fear or pessimism for those with faith, insight, and genuine perceptive faculties. Rather, it is a source of continuous reflection, remembrance, and thanksgiving for those with an apprehensive heart, inner perception, and the ability to hear. Just as a day develops in the heart of night, and just as winter furnishes the womb in which spring grows, so one's life is purified, matures, and bears its expected fruits within this cycle. In this same cycle, God-given abilities become aptitudes and talents, sciences blossom like roses and weave technology in the workbench of time, and humanity gradually approaches its predestined end.

Having stated this general view, which is neither personal nor subjective but rather an objective fact of history, do not think that we welcome either winter or winter-like events, such as sorrow, disease, and disaster. Despite the general fact that disease eventually increases the body's resistance, strengthens its immune system, and drives medical progress, it is pathological and harmful. It is the same with terrestrial and celestial disasters. From a theological and moral point of view, they result from our sins and oppression, which are enough to shake the Earth and the Heavens, and from engaging in deeds declared forbidden and despised by law and ethics (whether religious or secular). Even though they awaken people to their mistakes and negligence; provoke developments in geology, architecture, engineering, and related safety measures; and elevate believers' demolished belongings to the level of charity and the believers themselves to the level of martyrdom, such disasters cause much destruction and harm humanity.

We read in the Qur'an: *Unless God hampered some (of you) with some other (of you), the mosques, monasteries, and synagogues in which God is worshipped would have fallen into ruins* (22:40). In other words, God would be so little known that people, who are inclined not to recognize anything superior to them or believe that they will be questioned in the Hereafter, will go astray completely, thereby making the Earth unsuitable for human life.

There is also the divine decree: *You consider something as evil although it is good for you; you also consider something else as good although it is bad for you* (2:216). For example, war is permissible. Although wars based on specific principles and with the intent to improve the existing situation may have benefits, they should not be demanded, for they leave behind ruined houses, destroyed families, and weeping orphans and widows.

The realities of life cannot be neglected, nor should they be ignored. Human beings are mirrors for God's Names and Attributes, and thus are distinguished from the rest of creation with the honor of being responsible for making the Earth prosperous in His name. If they cannot grasp the wisdom and purposes behind any good or evil sent their way by their Creator, they cannot escape despair and pessimism. For them, as is seen in Existentialist literature, life turns into a meaningless process, existence into a purposeless vacuity, nonsense into the only criteria, suicide into a meritorious act, and death becomes the only inevitable reality.

### Basic Human Nature

After presenting the issues that constitute the basis of this subject, we now discuss or expectations of the third millennium.

Human history began with two people who constituted the essence of humanity and complemented each other. People lived a tranquil life during this time of the original mother and father and the families that descended from them. They were a united society that had the same views and shared the same environment and lives. From that day on, the essence of humanity has remained unchanged, and it will remain so. The realities surrounding their lives, their physical structure, main characteristics, basic needs, place and time of birth and death, selection of parents and physique, innate characteristics, as well as the surrounding natural environment have not changed. All of these require some essential and vital invariable realities and values. Thus, the development and alteration of life's secondary realities should be based on the axis of these primary realities and values, so that life will continue as a worldly paradise under the shadow of Heaven.

We mentioned above some issues that seem harmful and unpleasant. Similarly, there are human traits that appear to be evil at first glance, such as hatred, jealousy, enmity, the desire to dominate others, greed, rage, and egoism. We also have other innate drives and needs that allow our worldly life to continue, such as the need to eat and drink and the drives of lust and anger. All of our drives, needs, and desires should be guided and trained toward the eternal, universal, and invariable values that address the fundamental aspects of humanity. In this respect, the need to eat and drink, and the desire associated with lust and rage, can be tamed and transformed into means of absolute or relative good. Likewise, egoism and hatred can become sources of fine attributes and goodness. Jealousy and rivalry can be transformed into competition in charitable and good deeds. Enmity can be transformed into enmity against Satan, our greatest enemy, and against the feeling of enmity itself and hatred. Greed and rage can become a drive that will force one to perform good deeds without tiredness. Egoism can point out the evil aspects of the carnal soul, thereby seeking to train and purify the soul by not excusing its evil actions.

All negative feelings can be transformed into sources of good by training and struggle. This is how one reaches the level of "the best of Creation," by traveling the way of transformation from a potential human being to a real and perfected human being, to becoming the best symbol, model, and personal representative of creation and existence.

Despite this fact, the realities of human life do not always follow these guidelines. Negative feelings and attributes often defeat people, pulling them under their domination to such an extent that even the religions guiding them to goodness and kindness are abused, as well as the feelings and attributes that are sources of absolute good. At the level of the individual and of humanity as a whole, human life is merely the summation of internal, personal struggles and their external manifestations. These tides make the personal world of the individual, society, and history an arena of battle, struggle, war, oppression, and tyranny. As a result, usually we are the ones who suffer the consequences.

People always receive the fruits of their deeds. In the first period of human history, we lived a happy life as a single society whose members shared their joys and sorrows. But, later on we bound our necks and feet with a rusty yoke composed of chains of oppression due to jealousy, greed, and coveting other's rights and properties. The consequence was Cain's murder of Abel. As a result, we entered the path of disunity. Despite the millenniums coming one after the other like days, seasons and years, this cycle continues.

## The Second Millennium

The second millennium started with the Crusades and then the Mongol invasions of the Muslim world, which was like the heart of the Earth and history at that time. But this millennium was not limited only to the ensuing wars and destruction, and the crimes committed sometimes in the name of religion and sometimes in the name of economic, political and military supremacy. It also witnessed the apex of the Eastern civilization, based on spirituality, metaphysical, universal and eternal values, and Western civilization, based on the physical sciences. Many significant geographical discoveries and scientific inventions also occurred.

However, both civilizations existed separated from each other. This separation, which should not have occurred, was based on the former's retiring from the intellect and science, while the latter retired from spirituality, metaphysics, and eternal and invariable values. As a result, the last centuries of this millennium witnessed disasters that are hard to believe. Due to humanity's growing arrogance and egoism, arising from its accomplishments, we have lived through worldwide colonialism, immense massacres, revolutions that cost millions of lives, unimaginably bloody and destructive wars, racial discrimination, immense social and economic injustice, and iron curtains built by regimes whose ideology and philosophy sought to deny humanity's essence, freedom, merit, and honor. It is partly because of this and partly because of some Biblical auguries that many people in the West fear that the world will be soaked again by floods of blood, pus, and destruction. They are quite pessimistic and worried about the new millennium.

## Our Expectations

Modern means of communication and transportation have transformed the world into a large, global village. Those who expect that any radical changes in a country will be determined by that country alone and remain limited to it are unaware of current realities. This time is a period of interactive relations. Nations and peoples are more in need of and dependent on each other, which causes closeness in mutual relations.

This network of relations, which has surpassed the period of brute colonialism and exists on the basis of mutual interest, provides some benefits to the weaker side. Moreover, due to advances in technology, especially digital electronics, acquiring and exchanging information grows gradually. Thus the individual comes to the fore, making it inevitable that democratic governments respecting personal rights will replace oppressive regimes.

As each individual is like a species with respect to other species, individual rights cannot be sacrificed for society, and social rights should depend on individual rights. This is why the basic human rights and freedoms found in the revealed religions came to be considered by a war-weary West. They will enjoy priority in all relations. At the head of these rights is the right to life, which is granted and can be taken away only by God. Islam accentuates this right: *If one person kills another unjustly, it is the same as if one has killed all of humanity; if one saves another, it is the same as if one has saved all of humanity* (5:32).

Other rights are the freedom of religion, belief, thought, and expression; to own property and the sanctity of one's home; to marry and have children; to communication and travel; and the right to and freedom of education. The principles of Islamic jurisprudence are based on these and other rights, all of which are accepted by modern legal systems: the protection of life, religion, property, reproduction, and intellect. Others include human equality based on the fact that all people are human beings, and the rejection of all racial, color, and linguistic discrimination. All of these will be—and should be—indispensable essentials in the new millennium.

I believe and hope that the world of the new millennium will be a happier, more just, and more compassionate place, contrary to the fears of some people. Islam, Christianity, and Judaism all come from the same root, have almost the same essentials, and are nourished from the same source. Although they have been rivals for centuries, their common points and shared responsibility to build a happy world for all creatures of God make interfaith dialogue necessary. This dialogue has now expanded to include the religions of Asia and other areas. Results have been positive.

As mentioned above, this dialogue will develop as a necessary process, and followers of all religions will find ways to get closer and assist each other.

Previous generations witnessed a bitter struggle that should never have taken place: science versus religion. This conflict gave rise to atheism and materialism, which have influenced Christianity more than other religions. Science cannot contradict religion, for its purpose is to understand nature and humanity, which are each a composition of the manifestations of God's Attributes of Will and Power. Religion has its source in the Divine Attribute of Speech that was manifested as Divine Scriptures (i.e., the Qur'an, the Gospels, the Torah, and others). Thanks to the efforts of both Christian and Muslim theologians and scientists, it seems that this long-standing conflict between science and religion finally will end, or at least have its absurdity acknowledged.

The end of this conflict and a new style of education, fusing religious and scientific knowledge together with morality and spirituality, will produce genuinely enlightened people whose hearts will be illuminated with religious sciences and spirituality. Their minds will be illuminated with positive sciences, characterized by humane merits and morale values, and cognizant of current socioeconomic and political conditions. Our old world will experience an excellent "springtime" before its demise. This springtime will see the gap between rich and poor narrow; the world's riches distributed most justly according to one's work, capital, and needs; the absence of discrimination based on race, color, language, and worldview; and basic human rights and freedoms protected. Individuals will come to the fore and, learning how to realize their potential, will ascend on the way to becoming "the most elevated human" with the wings of love, knowledge, and belief.

In this new springtime, when scientific and technological progress is considered, people will understand that the current level of science and technology resembles the stage when an infant is learning how to crawl. Humanity will organize trips into space as if traveling to another country. Travelers on the way to God, those self-immolators of love who have no time for hostility, will carry the inspirations in their spirits to other worlds. Yes, this springtime will rise on the foundations of love, compassion, mercy, dialogue, acceptance of others, mutual respect, justice, and rights. It will be a time in which humanity will discover its real essence. Goodness, kindness, righteousness, and virtue will form the world's basic essence. No matter what happens, the world will come to this track sooner or later. Nobody can prevent this.

We pray and beg the Infinitely Compassionate One not to let our hopes and expectations come to nothing.

## CHAPTER 8

# Educational Activities

Fethullah Gülen is an educationist. He is an educator of not only mind but also heart and spirit. He is reputed especially for his endeavoring people to establish educational institutions both in Turkey and abroad. In this section you will find his views of education and the educational activities of Turkish entrepreneurs outside Turkey.

## Education from Cradle to Grave

### Introduction

The main duty and purpose of human life is to seek understanding. The effort of doing so, known as education, is a perfecting process though which we earn, in the spiritual, intellectual, and physical dimensions of their beings, the rank appointed for us as the perfect pattern of creation. At birth, the outset of the earthly phase of our journey from the world of spirits to eternity, we are wholly impotent and needy. By contrast, most animals come into the world as if matured or perfected beforehand. Within a few hours or days or months, they learn everything necessary for their survival, as well as how to relate to their environment and with other creatures. For example, sparrows or bees acquire maturity and all the physical and social skills they need within about twenty days; we need twenty years or more to acquire a comparable level of maturity.

We are born helpless as well as ignorant of the laws of life and must cry out to get the help we need. After a year or so, we can stand on our feet and walk a little. When we are about fifteen, we are expected to have understood the difference between good and evil, the beneficial and the harmful. However, it will take us our whole lives to acquire intellectual and spiritual perfection. Our principal duty in life is to acquire perfection and purity in our thinking, conceptions, and belief. By fulfilling our duty of servanthood to the Creator, Nourisher, and Protector, and by penetrating the mystery of creation through our potentials and faculties, we seek to attain to the rank of true humanity and become worthy of a blissful, eternal life in another, exalted world.

Our humanity is directly proportional to our emotions' purity. Although those who are full of bad feelings and whose souls are influenced by egoism look like human beings, whether they really are human is doubtful. Almost everyone can train their bodies, but few can educate their minds and feelings. The former training produces strong bodies, while the latter produces spiritual people.

### Our Innate Faculties and Education

Since the time of Ibn Miskawayh, human faculties or "drives" have been dealt with in three categories: reason, anger, and lust.[353] Reason encompasses all of our powers of conception, imagination, calculation, memory, learning, and so on. Anger covers our power of self-defense, which Islamic jurisprudence defines as that needed to defend our faith and religion, sanity, possessions, life and family, and other sacred values. Lust is the name for the driving force of our animal appetites: *Decked out for humanity is the passionate love of desires for the opposite sex and offspring; for hoarded treasures of gold and silver; for branded horses, cattle, and plantations; and for all kinds of worldly things* (3:14).

These drives are found in other creatures. However, whether in their desires, intelligence, or determination to defend life and territory, these drives are limited in all creatures but humanity. Each of us is uniquely endowed with free will and the consequent obligation

---

[353] Ibn Miskawayh (c.930-1030): Muslim moralist, philosopher and historian. His moral treatise *Tahdhib al-Akhlaq*, influenced by the Aristotelian concept of the mean, is considered one of the best statements of Islamic philosophy. His universal history *Kitab Tajarib al-Umam wa Ta'aqub al-Himam* (Eclipse of the 'Abbasid Caliphate), was noted for its use of all available sources and greatly stimulated the development of Islamic historiography.

to discipline our powers. This struggle for discipline determines our humanity. In combination with each other and with circumstances, our faculties often are expressed through jealousy, hatred, enmity, hypocrisy, and show. They also need to be disciplined.

We are not only composed of body and mind. Each of us has a spirit that needs satisfaction. Without this, we cannot find true happiness and perfection. Spiritual satisfaction is possible only through knowledge of God and belief in Him. Confined within the physical world, our own particular carnal self, time, and place can be experienced as a dungeon. We can escape it through belief and regular worship, and by refraining from extremes while using our faculties or powers. We must not seek to annul our drives, but to use our free will to contain and purify them, to channel and direct them toward virtue. For example, we are not expected to eliminate lust, but to satisfy it lawfully through reproduction. Happiness lies in confining our lust to the lawful bounds of decency and chastity, not in engaging in debauchery and dissipation.

Similarly, jealousy can be channeled into emulation free of rancor, which inspires us to emulate those who excel in goodness and good deeds. Applying the proper discipline to our reason results in the acquisition of knowledge, and ultimately of understanding or wisdom. Purifying and training anger leads to courage and forbearance. Disciplining our passion and desire develops our chastity.

If every virtue is thought of as the center of a circle, and any movement away from the center as a vice, the vice becomes greater as we move further away from the center. Every virtue therefore has innumerable vices, since there is only one center in a circle but an infinite number of points around it. It is irrelevant in which direction the deviation occurs, for deviation from the center, in whatever direction, is a vice.

There are two extremes related to each moral virtue: deficiency or excess. The two extremes connected with wisdom are stupidity and cunning. For courage they are cowardice and rashness, and for chastity they are lethargy and uncontrolled lust. So a person's perfection, the ultimate purpose of our existence, lies in maintaining a condition of balance and moderation between the two extremes relating to every virtue. 'Ali ibn Abi Talib is reported to have said:

> God has characterized angels by intellect without sexual desire, passion, and anger, and animals with anger and desire without intellect. He exalted humanity by bestowing upon them all of these qualities. Accordingly, if a person's intellect dominates his or her desire and ferocity, he or she rises to a station above that of angels, because this station is attained by a human being in spite of the existence of obstacles that do not vex angels.

> Improving a community is possible only by elevating the young generations to the rank of humanity, not by obliterating the bad ones. Unless a seed composed of religion, tradition, and historical consciousness is germinated throughout the country, new evil elements will appear and grow in the place of each eradicated bad one.

## The Real Meaning and Value of Education

Education through learning and a commendable way of life is a sublime duty that manifests the Divine Name *Rabb* (Upbringer and Sustainer). By fulfilling it, we attain the rank of true humanity and become a beneficial element of society.

Education is vital for both societies and individuals. First, our humanity is directly proportional to our emotions' purity. Although those who are full of bad feelings and whose souls are influenced by egoism look like human beings, whether they really are so is questionable. Almost anyone can be successful in physical training, but few can educate their minds and feelings. Second, improving a community is possible by elevating the coming generations to the rank of humanity, not by obliterating the bad ones. Unless the seeds of religion, traditional values, and historical consciousness germinate throughout the country, new bad elements will inevitably grow up in the place of every bad element that has been eradicated.

A nation's future depends on its youth. Any people who want to secure their future should apply as much energy to raising their children as they devote to other issues. A nation that fails its youth, that abandons them to foreign cultural influences, jeopardizes their identity and is subject to cultural and political weakness.

The reasons for the vices observed in today's generation, as well as the incompetence of some administrators and other nation-wide troubles, lie in the prevailing conditions and ruling elite of 25 years ago. Likewise, those who are charged with educating today's young people will be responsible for the vices and virtues that will appear in another 25 years. Those who wish to predict a nation's future can do so correctly by taking a full account of the education and upbringing given to its young people. "Real" life is possible only through knowledge. Thus, those who neglect learning and teaching should be counted as "dead" even though they are living, for we were created to learn and communicate to others what we have learned.

Right decisions depend on having a sound mind and being capable of sound thought. Science and knowledge illuminate and develop the mind. For this reason, a mind deprived of science and knowledge cannot reach right decisions, is always exposed to deception, and is subject to being misled.

We are only truly human if we learn, teach, and inspire others. It is difficult to regard those who are ignorant and without desire to learn as truly human. It is also questionable whether learned people who do not renew and reform themselves in order to set an example for others are truly human. Status and merit acquired through knowledge and science are higher and more lasting than those obtained through other means.

Given the great importance of learning and teaching, we must determine what is to be learned and taught, and when and how to do so. Although knowledge is a value in itself, the purpose of learning is to make knowledge a guide in life and illuminate the road to human betterment. Thus, any knowledge not appropriated for the self is a burden to the learner, and a science that does not direct one toward sublime goals is a deception.

But knowledge acquired for a right purpose is an inexhaustible source of blessings for the learner. Those who possess such a source are always sought by people, like a source of fresh water, and lead people to the good. Knowledge limited to empty theories and unabsorbed pieces of learning, which arouses suspicions in minds and darkens hearts, is a "heap of garbage" around which desperate and confused souls flounder. Therefore, science and knowledge should seek to uncover humanity's nature and creation's mysteries. Any knowledge, even "scientific," is true only if it sheds light on the mysteries of human nature and the dark areas of existence.

- The future of every individual is closely related to the impressions and influences experienced during childhood and youth. If children and young people are brought up in a climate where their enthusiasm is stimulated with higher feelings, they will have vigorous minds and display good morals and virtues.

- Although it is fundamental that girls be brought up to be delicate like flowers and mild and affectionate educators of children, due attention must be given to making them inflexible defenders of truth. Otherwise, we shall have transformed them into poor, impotent beings for the sake of delicacy and mildness. We must not forget that female lions are still lions.

## Family, School, and Environment

People who want to guarantee their future cannot be indifferent how their children are being educated. The family, school, environment, and mass media should cooperate to ensure the desired result. Opposing tendencies among these vital institutions will subject young people to contradictory influences that will distract them and dissipate their energy. In particular, the mass media should contribute to young people's education by following the education policy approved by the community. The school must be as perfect as possible with respect to curriculum, its teachers' scientific and moral standards of teachers, and its physical conditions. A family must provide the necessary warmth and quality of atmosphere in which the children are raised.

In the early centuries of Islam, minds, hearts, and souls strove to understand that which the Lord of the heavens and the Earth approves. Each conversation, discussion, correspondence, and event was directed to that end. As a result, whoever could do so imbibed the right values and spirit from the surrounding environment. It was as if everything was a teacher to prepare the individual's mind and soul and develop his or her capacity to attain a high level in Islamic sciences. The first school in which we receive the necessary education to be perfected is the home.

The home is vital to raising of a healthy generation and ensuring a healthy social system or structure. This responsibility continues throughout life. The impressions we receive from our family cannot be deleted later in life. Furthermore, the family's control over the child at home, with respect to other siblings and toys, continues at school, with respect to the child's friends, books, and places visited. Parents must feed their children's minds with knowledge and science before their minds become engaged in useless things, for souls without truth and knowledge are fields in which evil thoughts are cultivated and grown.

Children can receive a good education at home only if there is a healthy family life. Thus marriage should be undertaken to form a healthy family life and so contribute to the permanence of one's nation in particular, and of the human population in general. Peace, happiness, and security at home is the mutual accord between the spouses in thought, morals, and belief. Couples who decide to marry should know each other very well and consider purity of feelings, chastity, morality, and virtue rather than wealth and physical charm. Children's mischief and impudence reflect the atmosphere in which they are being raised. A dysfunctional family life increasingly reflects upon the child's spirit, and therefore upon society.

In the family, elders should treat those younger than them with compassion, and the young should show respect for their elders. Parents should love and respect each other, and treat their children with compassion and due consideration of their feelings. They must treat each child justly and not discriminate among them. If parents encourage their children to develop their abilities and be useful to themselves and the community, they have given the nation a strong new pillar. If they do not cultivate the proper feelings in their children, they release scorpions into the community.

- Good manners are a virtue and are greatly appreciated in whomever they are found. Those with good manners are liked, even if they are uneducated. Communities devoid of culture and education are like rude individuals, for one cannot find in them any loyalty in friendship or consistency in enmity. Those who trust such people are always disappointed, and those who depend upon them are left, sooner or later, without support.

**The School and the Teacher**

A school may be considered a laboratory that offers an elixir that can prevent or heal the ills of life. Those who have the knowledge and wisdom to prepare and administer it are the teachers.

A school is a place of learning about everything related to this life and the next. It can shed light on vital ideas and events, and enable its students to understand their natural and human environment. It also can quickly open the way to unveiling the meaning of things and events, thereby leading a student to wholeness of thought and contemplation. In essence, a school is a kind of place of worship whose "holy people" are teachers.

Real teachers sow the pure seed and preserve it. They occupy themselves with what is good and wholesome, and lead and guide the children in life and whatever events they encounter. For a school to be a true institution of education, students first should be equipped with an ideal, a love of their language and how to use it most effectively, good morals, and perennial human values. Their social identity must be built on these foundations.

Education is different from teaching. Most people can teach, but only a very few can educate. Communities composed of individuals devoid of a sublime ideal, good manners, and human values are like rude individuals who have no loyalty in friendship or consistency in enmity. Those who trust such people are always disappointed, and those who depend upon them are sooner or later left without support. The best way of equipping one with such values is a sound religious education.

A community's survival depends on idealism and good morals, as well as on reaching the necessary level in scientific and technological progress. For this reason, trades and crafts should be taught beginning at least in the elementary level. A good school is not a building where only theoretical information is given, but an institution or a laboratory where students are prepared for life.

Patience is of great importance in education. Educating people is the most sacred, but also the most difficult, task in life. In addition to setting a good personal example, teachers should be patient enough to obtain the desired result. They should know their students very well, and address their intellects and their hearts, spirits, and feelings. The best way to educate people is to show a special concern for every individual, not forgetting that each individual is a different "world."

School provides its pupils with the possibilities of continuous reading, and speaks even when it is silent. Because of this, although it seems to occupy only one phase of life, school actually dominates all times and events. For the rest of their lives, pupils re-enact what they learned at school and derive continuous influence therefrom. Teachers should know how to find a way to the student's heart and leave indelible imprints upon his or her mind. They should test the information to be passed on to students by refining their own minds and the prisms of their hearts. A good lesson is one that does more than provide pupils with useful information or skills; it should elevate them into the presence of the unknown. This enables the students to acquire a penetrating vision into the reality of things, and to see each event as a sign of the unseen world.[354]

## Educational Services Spreading throughout the World

### Why Education?

Many things have been said and written about education. We will approach this subject from three interrelated angles: human–psychological, national–social, and universal.

We have been under the serious influence of contemporary Western thought, which undoubtedly has many superior aspects, for several centuries. However, it also has some defects stemming especially from the historical period it passed through and the unique conditions it created. In the Middle Ages, when Europe was living under a theocratic order ruled by the Church or Church-appointed monarchs, it came into contact with the Islamic world, especially

---

[354] A summary from Gülen's articles published in *Sizinti*, March 1981–June 1982, nos. 26-41.

through Andalusia and the Crusades. In addition to other factors, this opened the door for the Renaissance and Reform movements. Together with such other factors as land shortages, poverty, the drive to meet growing needs, and some island nations like England being naturally inclined to sea transportation, it also led to overseas geographical discoveries.

The primary drive in all of these developments was to satisfy material needs. As the accompanying scientific studies developed in opposition to the Church and medieval Christian scholasticism, Europeans were confronted with a religion–science conflict.[355] This caused religion to split off from science and many people to break with religion. This development eventually led to materialism and communism. In social geography, humanity was faced with the most striking elements of Western history: global exploitation, unending conflict based on interest, two world wars, and the division of the world into blocs.

The West has held the world under its economic and military control for several centuries. In recent centuries, its religion–science conflict has occupied many intellectual circles. Enlightenment movements beginning in the eighteenth century saw human beings as mind only. Following that, positivist and materialist movements saw them as material or corporeal entities only. As a result, spiritual crises have followed one after another. It is no exaggeration to say that these crises and the absence of spiritual satisfaction were the major factors behind the conflict of interests that enveloped the last two centuries and reached its apex in the two world wars.

As possessors of a system of belief with a different history and essence, we have some basic things to give to the West, with whom we have deep economic, social, and even military relationships, and to humanity at large. At the head of these are our understanding and view of humanity. This view is neither exclusive to us or subjective; rather, it is an objective view that puts forward what we really are.

---

[355] This opposition was due to two factors: the Catholic Church refused to come to terms with new scientific discoveries and concepts, and the emerging new middle class wanted to be free of religion's disciplining rules.

We are creatures composed of not only a body or mind or feelings or spirit; rather, we are harmonious compositions of all of these elements. Each of us is a body writhing in a net of needs, as well as a mind that has more subtle and vital needs than the body, and is driven by anxieties about the past and future to find answers to such questions as: "What am I? What is this world? What do life and death want from me? Who sent me to this world, and for what purpose? Where am I going, and what is the purpose of life? Who is my guide in this worldly journey?"

Moreover, each person is a creature of feelings that cannot be satisfied by the mind, and a creature of spirit, through which we acquire our essential human identity. Each individual is all of these. When a man or a woman, around whom all systems and efforts revolve, is considered and evaluated as a creature with all these aspects, and when all our needs are fulfilled, we will reach true happiness. At this point, true human progress and evolvement in relation to our essential being is only possible with education.

To comprehend education's significance, look at only one difference between us and animals. At the beginning of the journey from the world of spirits that extends into eternity at the earthly stage, we are weak, in need, and in the miserable position of waiting for everything from others.

Animals, however, come to this world or are sent as if they have gained perfection in another realm. Within 2 hours or 2 days or 2 months after their birth, they learn everything they need to know, their relation with the universe and the laws of life, and possess mastery. The strength to live and the ability to work that it takes us 20 years to acquire is attained by a sparrow or a bee in 20 days. More correctly, they are inspired with them. This means that an animal's essential duty is not to become perfect through learning and evolving by gaining knowledge or seeking help through showing its weakness. Its duty is to work according to its natural ability and thus actively serve its Creator.

On the other hand, we need to learn everything when we come into this world, for we are ignorant of the rules of life. In fact, in 20 years or perhaps throughout our whole life we still cannot fully learn the nature and meaning of life's rules and conditions, or of our relationship with the universe. We are sent here in a very weak and helpless form. For example, we can stand on their feet only after 1 or 2 years. In addition, it takes us almost our whole life to learn what is really in our interest and what is not. Only with the help of social life can we turn toward our interests and avoid danger.

This means that our essential duty, as a creation that has come to this passing guesthouse with a pure nature, is to reach stability and clarity in thought, imagination, and belief so that we can acquire a "second nature" and qualify to continue our life in "the next, much more elevated realms." In addition, by performing our duties as servants, we must activate our hearts, spirits, and all our innate faculties. By embracing our inner and outer worlds, where innumerable mysteries and puzzles reside, we must comprehend the secret of existence and thus rise to the rank of true humanity.

The religion–science conflict and its product, materialism, have seen nature, like humanity, as an accumulation of material created only to fulfill bodily needs. As a result, we are experiencing a global environmental disaster.

Consider: A book is the material manifestation via words of its "spiritual" existence in the writer's mind. There is no conflict between these two ways of expressing the same truth and contents in two different "worlds." Similarly, a building has a spiritual existence in the architect's mind, "destiny or pre-determination" in the form of a plan, and a building in the form of material existence. There is no conflict among three different worlds' ways of expressing the same meaning, content, and truth. Looking for conflict is nothing more than wasted effort.

Similarly, there can be no conflict among the Qur'an, the Divine Scripture, (coming from God's Attribute of Speech), the universe (coming from His Attributes of Power and Will), and the sciences that examine them. The universe is a mighty Qur'an deriving from God's Attributes of Power and Will. In other words, if the term is proper, the universe is a large, created Qur'an. In return, being an expression of the universe's laws in a different form, the Qur'an is a universe that has been codified and put on paper. In its true meaning, religion does not oppose or limit science and scientific work.

Religion guides sciences, determines their real goal, and puts moral and universal human values before them as guidance. If this truth had been understood in the West, and if this relationship between religion and knowledge had been discovered, things would have been different. Science would not have brought more destruction than benefit, and it would not have opened the way for producing bombs and other lethal weapons.

Claims are made today that religion is divisive and opens the way for killing others. However, it is undeniable that religion, especially Islam, has not led to the last several centuries of merciless exploitation, especially the twentieth century's wars and revolutions that killed hundreds of millions of people and left behind even more homeless, widows, orphans, and wounded. Scientific materialism, a view of life and the world that has severed itself from religion, and a clash of interests caused such exploitation.

There is also the matter of environmental pollution, which is due to scientific materialism, a basic peculiarity of modern Western thought. Underlying pollution's global threat is the understanding, brought about by scientific unbelief, that nature is an accumulation of things that have no value other than meeting bodily needs. In fact, nature is much more than a heap of materiality or an accumulation of objects: It has a certain sacredness, for it is an arena in which God's Beautiful Names are displayed.

Nature is an exhibition of beauty and meaning that displays such profound and vast meanings in the form of trees taking root, flowers blossoming, fruit producing taste and aroma, rain, streams flowing, air breathed in and out, and soil acting as a wet-nurse to innumerable creatures. Thus, it makes a person's mind and heart like a honeycomb with the nectar that it presents to one's mind, which travels around like a bee, and to one's judgment and faculty of contemplation. Only the honey of faith, virtue, love of humanity and all creatures for the sake of the Creator, helping others, self-sacrifice to the extent of foregoing the passion of life to enable others to live, and service to all creation flow from this honeycomb.

As stated by Bediüzzaman, there is an understanding of education that sees the illumination of the mind in science and knowledge, and the light of the heart in faith and virtue. This understanding, which makes the student soar in the skies of humanity with these two wings and seek God's approval through service to others, has many things to offer. It rescues science from materialism, from being a factor that is as harmful as it is beneficial from both material and spiritual perspectives, and from being a lethal weapon. Such an understanding, in Einstein's words, will not allow religion to remain crippled. Nor will it allow religion to be perceived as cut off from intelligence, life, and scientific truth and as a fanatical institution that builds walls between individuals and nations.

### Serving Humanity through Education

Thanks to rapid developments in transportation and communication, the world has become a global village. Nations are exactly like next-door neighbors. However we must remember, especially in a world like this, that national existence can be ensured only by protecting each nation's specific characteristics. In a unified mosaic of nations and countries, those that cannot protect their unique characteristics, "patterns, and designs" will disappear. As with all other nations, our essential characteristics are religion and language, history and motherland. What Yahya Kemal, a famous Turkish poet and writer, expressed with deep longing in *The Districts without the Call to Prayer* was our culture and civilization that was brought from Islam and Central Asia and kneaded for centuries in Anatolia, Europe, and even Africa.

A related matter is the following. Among the people there is a saying: "A neighbor is in need of his/her neighbor's ashes." If you have no ashes needed by others, no one will attach any value to you. As mentioned above, we have more to give humanity than we have to take. Today voluntary or non-governmental organizations have founded companies and foundations and are serving others enthusiastically. The mass acceptance of the educational institutions that spread all over the world, despite the great financial difficulties they have faced, and their competing with and frequently surpassing their Western peers in a very short period of time, should be proof that what we have said cannot be denied.

As the Turkish people, we have accumulated many problems over the past several centuries. At their base lies our mistaken concentration on Islam's exterior and neglect of its inner pearl. Later on we began imitating others and surmised that there was a conflict between Islam and positive science. We did this despite the fact that the latter are no more than discoveries of Divine laws that manifest God's Attributes of Power and Will, and which are a different expression of the Qur'an coming from God's Attribute of Speech. This neglect, in turn, led to despotism in knowledge, thought, and administration; a hopelessness leading to disorder encompassing all individuals and institutions; confusion in our work; and not paying attention to the division of labor.

In short, our three greatest enemies are ignorance, poverty, and internal schism. Knowledge, work-capital, and unification can struggle against these. As ignorance is the most serious problem, we must oppose it with education, which always has been the most important way of serving our country. Now that we live in a global village, it is the best way to serve humanity and to establish dialogue with other civilizations.

But first of all, education is a humane service, for we were sent here to learn and be perfected through education. Saying: "The old state of affairs is impossible. Either a new state or annihilation," Bediüzzaman drew attention to solutions and the future. Saying that "controversial subjects shouldn't be discussed with Christian spiritual leaders," he opened dialogues with members of other religions. Like Jalal al-Din al-Rumi, who said: "One of my feet is in the center and the other is in seventy-two realms (people of all nations) like a compass," he drew a broad circle that encompasses all monotheists. Implying that the days of brute force are over, he said: "Victory with civilized persons is through persuasion," thus pointing out that dialogue, persuasion, and talk based on evidence are essential for those of us who seek to serve religion. By saying that "in the future humanity will turn toward knowledge and science, and in the future reason and word will govern," he encouraged knowledge and word. Finally, putting aside politics and direct political involvement, he drew the basic lines of true religious and national service in this age and in the future.

In the light of such principles, I encouraged people to serve the country in particular, and humanity in general, through education. I called them to help the state educate and raise people by opening schools. Ignorance is defeated through education; poverty through work and the possession of capital; and internal schism and separatism through unity, dialogue, and tolerance. However, as every problem in human life ultimately depends on human beings themselves, education is the most effective vehicle regardless of whether we have a paralyzed social and political system or one operating with a clockwork precision.

### Schools

After the government allowed private schools, many people voluntarily chose to spend their wealth on serving the country, instead of passing on to the next world after a frivolous existence. In fact, they have done so with the enthusiasm of worship. It is impossible for me to know about all of the schools that have been opened both here and abroad. Since I only recommended and encouraged this, I do not even know the names of many of the companies that opened them or where the schools are located.

However, I have followed this matter to a certain extent in the press and in the series of articles by such worthy journalists as Ali Bayramoglu, Sahin Alpay, and Atilgan Bayar. Schools have been opened in places ranging from Azerbaijan to the Philippines and from St. Petersburg (the capital of Czarist Russia) and Moscow (the capital of communist Russia), and, with the help and reference of our Jewish fellow citizen and prominent businessman Üzeyir Garih, in Yakutsky. These schools have been opened in almost all countries, except for those like Iran that don't give their permission.

Writers and thinkers who have visited them state that these schools are financed by Turkish voluntary organizations. In many or all of them, student fees are an important part of this financing. Local administrators contribute sizable assistance by providing land, buildings, principals, and teachers when necessary. The teachers, who are dedicated to serving their country, nation, and humanity and have found the meaning of life to be in serving others, enthusiastically work for a small salary.

Initially, some of our foreign mission officials were hesitant to give their support, for they did not really understand what was going on. Today, however, most of them support the schools. In addition to Turkey's last two presidents, the late honorable Turgut Özal and the honorable Süleyman Demirel, as well as former Chairman of the Parliament Mustafa Kalemli and former Minister of Foreign Affairs Hikmet Çetin, showed their support by actually visiting the schools.

It is appropriate here to present Ali Bayramoglu's observations. A journalist who has visited many of these schools, he states:

> These schools don't give religious education or encompass educational activities with a religious environment, as is assumed. They have been established on the model of Anadolu high schools, with superior technical equipment and laboratories.[356] Lessons are given within the curriculum prepared by the Ministry of National Education. Religious subjects are not even taught. In fact, journalist Ali Bulaç, who visited these schools, related his impression that the toilets were purposely not kept sparkling clean to avoid the idea that praying might follow cleanliness. Activities take place within the framework of each country's current laws and educational philosophy. For example, in Uzbekistan, after students learn Turkish and English in the preparatory class, they study science in English from Turkish teachers and social subjects in Uzbek from Uzbek teachers. Giving religious knowledge or religious education is not the goal."

---

[356] Anadolu high schools is the term for the state-run schools in which scientific subjects are taught in English.

Local administrators are just as sensitive to secularism, or even more so, than the Turkish government. It has been explained by our enlightened journalists like Alpay, Bayar, and many others in a way similar to Bayramoglu's observations, that these countries do not feel the slightest concern for their future regarding these schools. In fact, speaking at the opening ceremonies for the school in Moscow, the Head of the Moscow National Education Office said: "There are two important events in Russia's recent history. One of these is Gagarin's landing on the moon. The other is the opening of a Turkish school here." He described this as an historic event.

For some, this life consists of the few days passed in this earthly guesthouse, and with the goal of completely fulfilling the ego's desires. Other people have different views, and so give life a different meaning. For me, this life consists of a few breaths on the journey that begins in the world of spirits and continues eternally either in Heaven or, God forbid, Hell.

This life is very important, for it shapes the afterlife. Given this, we should spend it in ways designed to earn eternal life and gain the Giver of Life's approval. This path passes through the inescapable dimension of servanthood to God by means of serving, first of all, our families, relatives, and neighbors, then our country and nation, and finally humanity and creation. This service is our right; conveying it to others is our responsibility.

## On Education and Turkish Educational Activities Abroad

### Traditional Education and Leadership in Modern Education

Q: As one raised in traditional educational institutions, how did you become a pioneer in modern educational institutions inside and outside of Turkey?

A: First let me clarify it that I'm not a pioneer in anything. In my childhood I wasn't able to think of anything outside the influence of the system in which I was raised. I don't know if what a school gives a child allows for questioning the system. In my opinion, the formal education system in Turkey has never been promising. Muallim Naci has a very good book.[357] He compares state schools with *madrasas*, and claims that the old, worn-out *madrasas* still are more advanced in some ways than state schools.

Q: You mentioned the separation of positive sciences from religious sciences. Is this separation applicable to the *madrasa* as well?

A: Yes. This separation began in very early periods at the Nizamiyah *madrasas*.[358] For this reason, some researchers blame Imam Ghazali, who struggled against Peripatetic philosophy. However, at that time philosophy and experimental sciences were studied together. His stance against philosophy affected the sciences, as well as those based on rationalism and their methods of thought. Imam Ghazali openly stated that he was not criticizing the scientific findings of the philosophers he opposed, and that these were not harmful to religion. However, his struggle against this type of theoretical knowledge caused a certain damage in the Islamic world of that time, because it was misunderstood as a stance against positive science and philosophy. Those who opposed positive science, who had made themselves known from time to time, began to make their presence felt more acutely.

Q: Was this separation implemented under the Ottomans?

A: For example, in the Ottoman period the Qadizade group dismissed positive science from the *madrasa* curriculum. The Qur'an frequently refers to natural phenomena in relation to principles of belief and appointing certain times for the daily prescribed prayers, fasting, and pilgrimage. But after a certain period, the *madrasa* closed its ears to such Qur'anic expressions. Although God says in the Qur'an: *Our signs and proofs will be shown to them externally and internally*, research and investigation of things and events were not done thoroughly. Bediüzzaman's approach views the universe

---

[357] Muallim Naci (d. 1893): Turkish literary figure who criticized the mere imitation of Western literary forms and defended classical Turkish literary forms.

[358] State-supported schools (*madrasas*). Those personally patronized by Seljuqid Vizier Nizam al-Mulk were called Nizamiyahs.

and truths of creation as pointing to God, His existence and Unity, and points out that other tenets of faith should be studied just as much as the Qur'an. Scholars forgot (or ignored) that the Qur'an comprises the basis of physics, chemistry, mathematics, and astrophysics, and that half of a believer's responsibility is to study natural phenomena.

Q: Doesn't Bediüzzaman say that the consequences of not studying the Book of the Universe or the Qur'an are different?

A: Yes, he indicates that studying these two books is meritorious, and that not studying them is sinful. The punishment for not studying the Book of the Universe well is given in this world, whereas the punishment for not studying the Qur'an generally is given in the afterlife. This shows that these two books are two faces of the same truth. Very few people expressed this point, and then only indirectly. Bediüzzaman, however, insistently emphasized this. On the one hand, we have the Book of the Universe. On the other hand we have the Qur'an, a guidebook and a translation that enables us to understand the universe, to move safely amidst its corridors, and to walk comfortably in the tide of events without stumbling and banging into things. In addition, there is the esoteric truth of discovering and seeing the universe's vastness in our own conscience. I think these are the triad of our civilization.

Our Prophet declared: "A time will come when the Qur'an is in one valley and humanity in another." This has happened. We must rediscover the valley where the Qur'an is and walk in its light. The spirit of the *madrasa* education and the spirit of the modern education can come together. They can make a new marriage, and the mind's radiance and the heart's light can be reunited. With their union and integration, the student's zeal will take wing and fly.

Q: Did the *madrasa* throw out only positive science?

A: No. At the same time it threw out Sufism, which we can call Islam's spiritual life. It restricted itself to religious sciences, and so everything stagnated. Objects and events were evaluated from a narrow perspective of the universe.

## Catastrophes in Our Intellectual Life
Q: What is your opinion of Islamic thought today?

A: There are several great catastrophes here. One is closing the Islamic education institutions to positive science. This was true for the *madrasas*, partially for the Imam–Hatip secondary schools, and completely for the theological faculty. They also are closed to Islam's spiritual life. Islam's unifying spirit has disintegrated. Some were contented with telling the lives, especially "miracles" of past saints in the name of Sufism; others regarded a superficial study of religious sciences as acquiring all of Islam; and a third group, based on scientific materialism, rejected Islam in all its aspects.[359]

## From *Madrasa* to University

In recent years, those who respect Fethullah Gülen's views on education have launched a great education campaign inside and outside of Turkey. As a result, around 200 educational institutions were opened abroad alone. These schools, stretching from China to the Adriatic Sea, were equipped with all the wonders of modern technology. Schools and preparatory courses for the university education have become hearths of learning, where students displayed their success and won many first-place awards.

Turkish entrepreneurs from almost all walks of life pioneered in schools, colleges, and universities. Fethullah Gülen only gave advice to these charitable businessmen. To those who said: "We're going to build a mosque in our country," he replied: "I'd like to see a school beside it." In fact, in most places he recommended building a school instead of a mosque.

Fethullah Hodja explains his views of Turkish entrepreneurs' opening schools within Turkey and abroad:

> All problems start and end with people. The most effective vehicle for a well-functioning and (almost) defect-free social system, or for the grave and beyond, is education. Just as education and teaching are the most sacred professions, the

---

[359] Can, "Fethullah Gülen Ile Ufuk Turu."

best service to a country or a nation is made through education. Our Prophet esteemed teaching more than another way of serving people.

Recent developments in communication have made the world a globalized village. Our continued existence, and especially our becoming a country with some say in the existing balance of power, is only possible through alliances with our neighbors and the countries with whom we have much in common.

Establishing natural alliances and being surrounded by a circle of friends rather than enemies would benefit Turkey. In such a framework, I would also support opening schools in Armenia and Israel, if so permitted.

As for my relationship with the schools that have been opened, there is a lion in everyone's heart—a purpose hidden in one's nature since birth. This purpose can be different for everyone. When I was 12 or 13 years old and studying in Erzurum, I had a book in one hand and a map in the other. I would ask: "My God, how can we become a country whose problems have been considerably solved?"

I have never even thought of having a house, children, or a car. You can't oppose natural laws: water flows, condenses at 100°, and freezes at 0°. If there is such a characteristic in my nature, and if it's not harmful, what could be more natural than for this seed to flourish?

I grew up with the desire and objective to serve my country. If now this service can be realized through education, my interest in education is as natural as the flow of water, the rising and setting of the sun, and the activity of the world. But I have no power, capital, or army—only an unstoppable love and enthusiasm for service. All I can do is explain this, tell those who will listen, and suggest. Such service to others resembles a "bazaar of those seeking God's approval."[360]

## Schools

Q: That's just the point I wanted to come to. It is said that every day, schools belonging to you are being opened and that this is a kind of organization. This, too, is making a lot of people think.

---

[360] Turgut, *Yeni Yüzyil*, 27 January 1998.

A: Wherever I go I make some suggestions. Without being discriminatory, I tell our citizens: "Open university preparatory courses and raise the level of our people." (In a foreign country) I told some people who had come to listen to a teacher from Turkey:

> Stay here. Prepare your children for attending a university. Let them study sciences. If the level of general culture and education isn't high enough, open university preparatory courses. Put your means together. A world that is becoming globalized will bring certain things with it. For example, small trades and small business are going to disappear. Build big business enterprises.

Q: But what do you think about the fact that those who open schools are all people close to your views?

A: I talk with everyone. I am sorry to say that the government doesn't have a special policy on this issue. I met with some fellow citizens about this, and so a chance was born to end this nightmare. It was understood that private schools are very beneficial. Through encouragement, some people who came to perceive the importance of quality began opening private schools. But some thought that they were my followers or sharing my opinions on all subjects.[361]

## Relationships with Education and Media Organizations

Q: You say you are poor. But we know that everywhere in Turkey you have special courses, schools, universities, a daily newspaper, and a television channel.

A: I have no organic or material connection with any of them. My only worldly possessions are the clothes I wear and my bed sheets. I donated all of my books to a foundation.

Q: OK. How is it that you can do what the government cannot? And for what objective? On top of this, for example, children attending your school in Tiflis (now Tbilisi, capital of Georgia) aren't even Turkish or Muslim. What's your aim?

---

[361] Özkök, "Hoca Efendi Anlatiyor."

A: The schools are not mine. I'm a poor man with nothing more than the clothes on my back. Behind the institutions you mention are many people and companies from almost all walks of life regardless their worldview, beliefs, and lifestyles. If they wish, they sometimes ask for my advice.[362]

## Educational Service in Asia

Q: What are your expectations from the schools abroad?

A: We hope that our understanding of Islam and Turkish culture will provide for the conditions for a mutual, vital dialogue in the world. I think we're at a fateful point of history. Actually, the expected friendship has developed to a large extent among the students. The indigenous peoples and governments must be pleased with the schools the Turkish entrepreneurs have opened; they must have left a good impression. For example, the Yakutian principal expelled the Turkish teachers from the technical school because of jealousy but later sent a message: "Come back, and you can open any kind of technical school you want under your own management." However, I don't know whether they opened such a school. Yakutia is far away...

Q: I saw many of the schools the Turkish people have opened in Central Asian countries. How do you inspire people with this ardency and enthusiasm?

A: There are different factors. In fact, our people have a spirit of enterprise. But in order to display this, they have to believe. If someone like me even whispers something like a bee's buzzing, the collective conscience can become active immediately.

What I have done is only to encourage people. I believe that the cooperation between Turkey and Central Asia will be beneficial to both parties and also will contribute to regional and global peace. People from diverse walks of life have responded to my call. They really believed. I believed once more in the precious quality of a nation's spirit.

---

[362] Çalislar, "Fethullah Gülen'le Röportaj."

Turkey is a well-established state. Democracy is, at least, in the process of settling down. Instead of dreaming about unity that currently seems impossible with people and countries who look down on us and see themselves as better Muslims than us, I found it more beneficial to turn toward people who have been looked down upon and oppressed for years, even centuries, and who are closer to us in many respects.

Q: Actually, these are things politicians should have done but didn't.

A: Everything takes place in accordance with Destiny. When there's a conjuncture where the apparently necessary means and causes, human free will and decision and Divine Destiny are agreed and united on a thing, surprising and only dreamed-of things can take place.

Q: An ideal is necessary...

A: What will we lose if we open up to Central Asia? Ours is a civil initiative, even though we do nothing against the state's will. The indigenous people of the countries where schools are have trusted their Turkish brothers and sisters and given them a sincere welcome.

I have been looking forward to a better world resembling Paradise, where humanity can live in peace and tranquility. Our world is tired of war and clashes. It direly needs mercy, affection, spiritual well being, and peace more than air and water. I believe that people in every country are ready for such a world. For example, we made an offer to the Greek government: "Don't be afraid of us. Come and open a school in Turkey, send your children here, we'll take care of them and give them scholarship. In return, we'll send you students and open a school in any city you wish."

Our efforts and enterprises are completely for humanity's sake. In a world becoming more and more globalized, we are trying to get to know those who will be our future neighbors a little earlier. Telecommunication and transportation systems are going to make us all like people in the same room.

**Social Sciences**

Q: Mathematics and sciences are given the most weight in schools that appear to be related to you. In a country as rich as Turkey is in social and cultural fields, why don't those schools give enough importance to the social sciences and encourage students to study them? Their importance has been recognized in the world, and in today's evaluation there's no other road.

A: When Turkey was knocked out by its adversaries technologically, it was decided to turn all superior minds in this direction so that they would study physics and chemistry and transfer high technology to Turkey as soon as possible. But it seems that some who gave priority to the social sciences also will be among those who will manage the future.

Q: The world is producing great architects of thought. Why doesn't Turkey produce a leader?

A: Raising a leader is tied, in part, to respect for free thought. A seed has the strength to sprout in the soil's bosom and grow. If the air is beneficial to growth and if it reaches water, the sapling will grow taller. People are like that. There shouldn't be any pressure. People should be able to express themselves. People, even geniuses, are not directed to their essential capabilities. This system must change. Students should choose what they want to study. Both high school and the university need this flexibility. An untalented, incapable team is controlling this nation's destiny.[363]

## Any Political Aims?

Bulgarian journalists: Your activities in the field of education have led to rumors that you have political aims. What are your comments?

Gülen: Humanity is very different from other creatures. It possesses such unique characteristics as consciousness, the ability to learn and speak, and feelings of responsibility. In addition, believers seek to gain eternal life in Paradise. We can attain real humani-

---

[363] Sevindi, "Fethullah Gülen Ile New York Sohbeti."

ty, fulfill our responsibility, and obtain eternal happiness through faith in God and service to others. Our Prophet said: "The person most beloved by God is the one who has faith in Him and is beneficial to others." 'Ali, who has an important place in our religion, said: "Muslims are your brothers in religion, and non-Muslims are your human brothers."

We are all human. Today everyone and every organization is working for some specific goal. I serve other people in a way appropriate to myself within the framework of my beliefs. As stated above, human beings are the most honorable of creatures. Those who want to increase their honor should serve this honorable creature. As regards international relations and humanity, one of the most important factors here is to eliminate factors that separate people, such as egoism, self-interest, and discrimination based on color, race, belief, and ethnicity. When idealized, these can cause conflict and be exploited by big powers. Education can uproot these evils.

Also, education is the most effective and common tongue for relations with others. We are trying our best to do this; we have no other intention. I would prefer a million times over to gain permanency in this transient life with faith and service to others and to gain eternal happiness, rather than ruling this world, even if it united with others and became a single state.

## Impressions

### *Children: Either to School or the Mountains*

By Nevval Sevindi

There is a great educational campaign underway in Van. Among the youth that manage to get an education, you can even find top winners in the university exam.

#### The Power of Love Overcame Terror
Bahattin Karatas, who laid the foundation of the Private Serhat High School, ran around like crazy for 8 years leaving no place unvisited. When he became the general director of Serhat's com-

plex of schools, he turned over the school principalship. However, when the children see him, they still applaud him wildly and fall over with love.

Bahattin speaks Kurdish, Arabic, and Farsi (Persian) in addition to Turkish. He knows the region very well, and is very experienced and tried. Saying that "the greatest enemy of humanity and the East is ignorance, poverty, and schism," he explains his interesting experience with two PKK students who came to school. Speaking Kurdish, he established a close relationship with them and listened to their problems. He gave them something to eat and drink and a place to sleep.

However, for 15 days these two boys became very unruly. They broke windows and destroyed furniture. Later on, it came out that their purpose was to make the principal angry and, after being beaten or thrown out, they would say: "Turks treat us like this." However, being treated in such a loving way finally caused them to admit: "They told us so many negative things that we hated you. We came to burn the school, but we couldn't. We're going to go back and spit in their faces. You'll hear the noise all the way from Van!"

For the first time in Van's history, a female student earned enough points to be admitted to the Hacettepe Faculty of Medicine (Ankara). The problem of not allowing girls to continue their education was entrenched. To convince their parents, the girls held discussions. As a result, girls' high schools were opened. They all came to our discussions held in the cultural center. Their excitement warmed our insides a little as we sat in the ice-cold cultural center.

### The Letter That Made Us Weep
Kamil Satir, the regional coordinator, explains:

> We don't see the East as second-class. We print every document on first-quality paper. In the history of Van, no one had qualified for the second level of the university exam. When the first student from the Çaglayan Preparatory Course won entrance to Bilkent University (Ankara), everyone went crazy. Last year we were unable to accept 200 students because of insufficient accommodation. Our consciences are still suffering from this.

I have never seen such intelligent children as those from Van. We even prepared a world champion. Our teachers cover the students in the dormitories at night. There are desks in the students' rooms, and they can study as late as they want. We put students who get along well with each other in the same room, and let them study and participate in recreational activities together. Here it's necessary to provide dormitory facilities, because some students come from Yüksekova, Hakkari (a town in southeastern Turkey).

We saw many who wanted to go to the mountains (as terrorists). In Mus, one parent fell down at the door and cried: "If you don't take my child, he is going to go to the mountains. Two of my sons died; let me give this one to you so he can be saved. I have two oxen. I'll sell one of them and be your slave!"

One student from Cizre (a town in southeastern Turkey) wrote in a letter: "I always saw Turks as our enemy until the Preparatory Course opened. I liked all of you a lot. If you had come here before, maybe there wouldn't have been any terror. My uncle went to the mountains; maybe he wouldn't have gone."

When I read the letter, I felt weak inside and my tears fell like snowflakes, as did Kemal's words. "Who is going to give account for those who previously joined the terrorist organization and became lost? Sirnak and Silopi need these preparatory courses. Please open them immediately."[364]

## *A Religious Scholar: Fethullah Gülen*

### By Cenk Koray

In his Altunizade (Istanbul) residence, we ask him: "Are you making religious pretense?" If he were, would he admit it? But the answer he gave was interesting. He reminded us of the *hadith* of our Prophet: "Those who deceive are not from us." This is a binding answer. If tomorrow or another day he displays behavior other than his behavior of today or if he asserts ideas other than today's ideas, these words will have to be thrown in the trash can.

---

[364] *Yeni Yüzyil.*

It is impossible to imagine that a person who so fears God and so loves the Prophet would pretend and risk being rejected by the Prophet. He is very emotional. When the Prophet's name is mentioned, his eyes become tearful. If he is acting, no one else could get an Oscar. Gülen has handled a job that would be difficult for even the president. While cardinals wait in line for months at the Vatican to see the Pope, he struck up a friendship with the Pope. What opened this door? Answer: Love for humanity.

When Gülen is mentioned, one thinks of unbelievably sincere manners, genuine humility, and tolerance as great as the oceans. I visited the schools opened by Turkish entrepreneurs in Moscow, St. Petersburg, Almati, Merv, and Ashkabad. Russian, Turkmen, and Kazakh students read poetry in Turkish. They are educated with the most modern means. In my opinion, instead of binding these schools to the Ministry of National Education, we should allow Gülen to administer the state schools in Turkey! A flower is not easily grown in a swamp. We are trying our best to pull up the flowers, make them fade and destroy them! What a shame!

In the future, Turkey's greatest public support is going to come from students studying in those schools beyond our borders. A Russian official succinctly stated the essence of this work: "There are two important events in Russian life: One of these is Yuri Gagarin's being sent into space before the Americans, and the other is the opening of these schools." If foreigners are thinking like this, what are we doing?[365]

## Fethullah Hodja's Profile

### By Ali Bulaç

Fethullah Hodjaefendi easily refers to the Islamic sciences, has a distinct style, and knows the heritage of Islamic historical thought, knowledge, and art. He also is close to the actual problems of today's world. Moreover, he is developing a vision of world politics, Turkey's current situation, and the general shape that Turkey,

---

[365] *Aksam,* 13 March 1998.

the region, and the world will take in the coming period. This can be considered the profile of a true intellectual–scholar.[366]

## *Fethullah Gülen and the Schools*

By Hulusi Turgut

## What Does Fethullah Gülen Say?

Fethullah Gülen, the originator of the idea to open elite educational institutions, made the following comments:

> The human factor lies at the base of all our problems, for all problems begin and end with people. Education is the best vehicle for a defect-free (or almost free) well-functioning social system or for a good life beyond the grave. In this respect, just as teaching is the most sacred profession, the best service to one's country or nation is education.
>
> When I was studying at Kursunlu/Erzurum around the age of 12 or 13, I would have an Arabic book in one hand and a map in the other. I would ask: "God, how can we save young generations from being wasted? How can we be a country without any problems unsolved?" As a child I would make plans for this. I grew up with these dreams. I never had any other goal in life, or thought of having a nice house, children, and a car.
>
> You can't oppose natural law. Water will flow, boil at $100°$, and evaporate; it will freeze at $0°$ and become ice. If my nature contains a special characteristic that doesn't harm others, what is more natural than for it to flourish? As a person who grew up with the feelings and goal of serving my country and nation, and if this service passes initially through education, my interest in education is as natural as water flowing or the sun rising and setting.
>
> I have no power, capital, or army. I only have an unobstructable love and enthusiasm for serving others. I can explain this only to those who will heed my advice and make recommendations. At any rate, this kind of service is like a "bazaar for God's approval."
>
> Turkey can't be cut off from the world. When it is cut off, it is like a branch broken off from a tree–it can't live, and so will

---

[366] At the end of Can, "Ufuk Turu."

dry up. Turkey must be integrated with the world. In such integration, the foremost countries with which we can establish sincere bonds and closeness are those of Central Asia. In one way we are a branch from the same shoot, and so I directed my friends toward that region. Maybe this is just dreaming.

Loyal Turkish people supported this idea, and schools were opened in Central Asia. Some of them are now self-supporting. If we hadn't supported them until now, it wouldn't have been possible to take this operation there. We had an opportunity and tried to take advantage of it by believing in it and being conscious of our responsibility.

Turkey needs enlightenment. We need to give direction to our friends. Those who built mosques wanted to open Qur'an courses beside them. I said: "Mosques are wonderful; we have the greatest respect for them. However, it would be better if you open a school." Our country needs distinguished and well-trained technicians and social scientists. From the outset I have tried to make suggestions to my friends. I was never actively involved in these efforts. I never asked for a house and home in this world. I used my friends' trust in me like a credit card for educational services. I did all this with the good will of my friends."

## Opening Up

Fethullah Gülen used the collapse of the Berlin Wall (November 1989) and the Soviet Union (1991) to good advantage. He wanted to direct his audience to the former Iron Curtain countries. There were Turks in Central Asia, related nations in Caucasus, and former Ottomans in the Balkans. He advised his audience to go to Central Asian countries in a sermon he gave in the Süleyman mosque in Istanbul in November 1989.

On January 11, 1990, the first convoy of 11 people entered Georgia through the East gate and reached Batum (Georgia). After spending 2 days in this coastal town in the Ajara region, they went to the capital, Tiflis, where they made friends. Muslim villages in Georgia were very happy to see their Muslim brothers from Turkey after 70 years.

A new group of businessmen set out on May 28, 1990. They went through Batum, Tiflis, Kazan, and Gence to reach Baku. The friendship formed 6 months earlier bore fruit on this trip. The Georgians and Azeris welcomed them very warmly.

**Three New Countries**

The 37-member Turkish caravan passed from Azerbaijan to Uzbekistan, and from there to Kazhakstan and Tajikistan. Contacts and impressions gave much better results here. This second journey was a great success.

These new republics gained their independence in 1992. After being formally recognized by the Republic of Turkey, the problems associated with students coming from those regions ceased, and they could pursue their education in our country. After they returned home, they informed their people of Turkey's greatness and wonderful aspects. They played a role in removing obstacles to future Turkish colleges that would be opened in their countries.

Turkish entrepreneurs already had decided to open up to the outside at the recommendation of Fethullah Gülen. Many people formed companies in different cities. They set out to search for new possibilities in Central Asian countries.

**Özal's Last Act Was to Visit the Schools**

The late Turgut Özal traveled to the Balkans and then to the Central Asian Turkish republics in the spring of 1993. He returned exhausted from the Balkans. In fact, he had difficulty walking on the street and praying in the mosques during his trip of the newly independent Muslim countries. Minister of State, Serif Ercan tried to help him by supporting his arm when he got up from the prayer rug and when he climbed stairs.

Özal was going to begin his trip to Central Asia on April 5, 1993. He wanted to set out with a large delegation, intending to take some people with private invitations. This was to be his last trip, for on April 17, 1993, 24 hours after he returned, Özal passed away.

Özal supported the Central Asian schools as if they were his own. When a problem developed in Uzbekistan, he met with the President Islam Karimov in his last visit. Karimov explained his concern, and Özal replied that he guaranteed them. The matter was settled. The cold atmosphere warmed up and trust was renewed. Özal displayed the same attitude in other countries.

## Owners of the Schools

Companies were established in Turkey to open schools, which now have spread over five continents. These companies applied to the Turkish National Education Ministry and received permission to open these schools. After that, the army of teachers that would serve was selected. Totaling over 4,000 today, teachers were chosen from Turkey's most distinguished universities. All of them were between 22 and 35 years old, had received a high quality of scientific training, and had learned perfect English.

Some of these companies are: Çag Ögretim Isletmeleri A.S., Selale A.S., Eflak A.S., Kazak Turk Liseleri Genel Müdürlügü, Sebat A.S., Silm A.S., Taskent Egitim Sirketi, Serhat Egitim Ögretim ve Saglik Hizmetleri A.S., Tolerans Vakfi, Ufuk Egitim Vakfi, Toros Egitim Hizmetleri Turizm ve Ticaret A.S., Karaçay Çerkes Toros Egitim Hiz. Tur. Ve Tic. A.S., Palandöken Egitim Ögretim Hiz. A.S., Dunae 94 Sti., Özel Burg A.S., Dostluk Yurdu Dernegi, International Hope Ltd. Company, Balkanlar Egitim ve Kültür Vakfi, S.C. Lumina SA Sirketi, Gülistan Egitim Yayin ve Ticaret Ltd. Sti., Sema Egitim Ögretim Isletmeleri A.S., Türkiye Saglik ve Tedavi Vakfi, Yayasan Yenbu Indonesia Vakfi.

## Azerbaijan

Turan Öztoprak, a graduate of the Istanbul Technical University, manages the General Directorship of Azerbaijan's Turkish high schools. Explaining the work, he states:

> We are educating close to 2,000 students in our schools. Even though our schools are still very young, they have very high standards. In the 1994 World Biology Olympiad held in Varna, Bulgaria, our students won two gold, one silver, and one bronze medal. Another group won the world championship in the Biology Olympiads. Again, in the 1994 World Environment Project Competition, our students earned high marks.
>
> After all this, I can say that our students are among the best in Azerbaijan. Our doubts have been left behind. When our

school was being opened, we had some anxious moments, as is the case whenever a new school is opened somewhere. We think that's natural, because a country is entrusting its children, its most valuable possession and future, to you. However, Azerbaijani state officials supported us from the beginning.

Azerbaijan, bothered by radical movements, is in a critical position. Its officials investigated us and had their doubts dispelled. The system became stable, and people began to trust each other. Our students' success on a world scale crowned this work."

## Turkish Tradition Brought Peace to Families in Kyrgyzstan

If we begin by saying that: "Turkish schools in Kyrgyzstan united broken families," you would of course ask how they did so. Kyrgyz families were not broken up because of duty in distant places, but by divorce and abandonment. It's a very difficult task, but the Turkish teachers succeeded.

Yücel Bozkurt, General Director of the Kyrgyz Turkish schools, begins by saying: "I'm from a family of social democrats. I'm also a social democrat and a follower of Atatürk." He gives some interesting information. Let's listen to him:

In Kyrgyzstan, especially among Russian families, the divorce rate is high. Generally the men abandon the home, leaving the women and children to their fate. There were children from broken homes like this among our students. We trained them according to Turkish customs and traditions. We talked about family togetherness, and instilled in them a love for their parents and other siblings. They all became like us. They truly learned love and respect. Later on we reconciled the parents, which became a source of great joy for us. During the last year we reconciled 30-35 families. The mother and father came together under one roof.

In these regions, when children reach a certain age they leave the family and sever ties with their parents. As their children don't look after them, they spend their old age alone. I hope that from now on our students in Kyrgyzstan will show interest in their parents throughout their lives.

People become addicted to alcohol and cigarettes at a very young age. We try to turn our students away from this road by holding conferences on the health hazards of such addictions. We make cooperative efforts with their parents, and have obtained very good results.

## Turkish Colleges in Afghanistan

Today, there are four Turkish colleges in Afghanistan. Mustafa Yilmaz Aydin, a graduate of Erzurum's Atatürk University, is general director of these educational institutions. With 50 teachers like himself, Aydin performs his duty in Afghanistan. Let's listen to his words on the life and death work conditions there:

> We have four schools in Afghanistan, two of which are in Sherberghan and Meymene. War is continuing in the country full force. Winters are very severe. As there is no fuel, schools are on vacation throughout the winter. We continue lessons during the summer. There is no glass in the windows, and there are no desks in the classrooms. Students sit on bullet crates. There are no notebooks or pencils. We loaded everything from teaching materials to student desks, from books to building materials, in short, everything from thread to needles on trucks and trailers and brought them to Afghanistan. Philanthropic people from Istanbul took the lead in this task. We repaired buildings and planted our flag in the modern school. Two of our schools are colleges. English in the medium of instruction, although we also emphasize Turkish. Due to the war, our school in Meymene is closed now. We have 350 students. Among the students there are Uzbek, Turkmen, and Hazara Shi'ite children.

> In this unending war, most of us have remained prisoners of war. But this didn't last long. The conditions of war continue with all their horror. However, our education programs continue without faltering. Some time previously, our former ambassador Bilge Cankoray visited our schools. In spite of all the negative conditions, we are happy because of the service we are giving here.

## Turkmenistan

Turkish entrepreneurs entered Turkmenistan in 1992. Within 5 years, the Baskent Egitim Company established twenty educational institutions in this brother country. The Turkish colleges passed a 2-year trial period. In 1992 Turgut Özal, who opened the Turkmen-

Turk High School that resembles the Anadolu high schools in Turkey, examined the curriculum and system's quality for student placement. The results became a reference for future schools. Seyit Embel, coordinator of Turkmenistan's educational institutions, gives important information regarding the interest they have received.

According to him:

> Today we have 20 educational institutions in Turkmenistan. The last five came about as a result of the desire of Turkmenistan's President Turkmenbashy. He liked our educational system and its successful students very much. When our schools reached 15, he asked President Demirel to open new ones. Our President relayed the matter to us, and we said: "At your command."

> In our schools there, we teach Russian and English, and Turkish in both the Turkmen and the Turkey dialects.

> Most of the schools in Turkmenistan are similar to the Anadolu high schools. One of these schools is the International Turkmen–Turkish University. A total of 3,757 students are being educated in these schools. Our student body contains young people from eight different countries. During a visit, President Turkmenbashy told us: "You are bringing out Turkmenistan's real wealth. History will write about you.'"

> Turkmenbashy, who followed the progress of the Turkish colleges for 3 years, sent this message to the first graduation ceremony: *I sincerely congratulate you on the occasion of the Turkmen-Turkish Colleges' first graduation ceremonies. I wish the graduates a bright future and happiness. Don't ever forget that you are the offspring of Korkut Ata, Oguz Han, Köroglu, Sultan Sancar, Yunus Emre, Mahmutguli, and thousands of great men like them. Stand up for the spirits of these heroes who wrote ineffaceable pages in history.*

> *From the first days of our independence and sovereignty, the Republic of Turkey and its people have extended a brotherly hand to Turkmenistan. I proudly emphasize that the success attained in our country during the years of independence and neutrality was accomplished with the special support of our Turkish brothers, whose language, religion, and path is one with ours. This support can be seen more openly in the*

*knowledge and good manners given to the rising generation. The successful activities of 15 Turkmen-Turkish educational institutions in our country and thousands of Turkmen youth being educated in the Republic of Turkey are bright examples of this support.*

**Turkmen Students World Champion**
In Turkmenistan, we have brought up champions. Two years ago in the World Biology Olympiad, held in Ukraine, Turkmenistan won two gold and two bronze medals. As a team we won first place.

We give education on par with world standards. Our students have lessons in Turkmen, Turkish, English, and Russian. Actually the Turkmen government has created a high educational standard. They give great importance to science. This year in the World Mathematics Olympiad, Turkmenistan won one gold and three bronze medals.

## Kazakhstan
At this time, more than 5,000 students are studying in the educational institutions established by Turkish entrepreneurs in Kazakhstan. Students learn perfect Turkish and English. Graduates from the best universities in Turkey are serving as teachers.

## Two Hundred Turkish Teachers in Uzbekistan
Uzbekistan gained its independence on September 1, 1991. One year later, businessmen from Bursa arrived. Representatives of Bursa's Silm Corporation received positive results from their talks with Uzbekistan's national education authorities. Mutual agreements were made and signed. First, the Tashkent Boys' High School was opened.

After Özal's visit to Uzbekistan, the sign to "continue service" was given to Silm. With a special ruling by the Uzbek Council of Ministers, the number of Turkish colleges was increased to 18 all at once. During these 6 years, the Turkish educationists and Turkish businessmen have had great success. They opened schools resembling the Anadolu and science high schools. Today, Turkish educational institutions have 3,500 students and have become the favorite schools in Uzbekistan.

## Mongolia

Young Turkish teachers entered Mongolia on August 31, 1994, before the Turkish Government went in. Mongolia is actually our "motherland." The *Orhun Kitabeleri*, the first written work to use the name Turk, was found in this country.

Called *Ötüken* in Turkish history, Mongolia became an area of settlement during the Neolithic Age. This land later served as a homeland for the Hungarians, Turks, and Tartars. Around 1,300 years ago, migrating Turks established the first Turkish state: the Göktürk Empire. It was finally rediscovered by our fellow citizens.

Turkish entrepreneurs who wanted to open schools here set out with 27 young teachers. They took everything with them, from teaching materials to chalk, Turkish and English textbooks and medicine. Under Suat Toprak, who acted as coordinator, six Turkish schools were opened. Schools under the administration of General Director Hüseyin Karakus gained a reputation in Mongolia. Through these schools, geographically distant Mongolia drew close to Turkey. Visiting these schools on September 13, 1995, Turkish President Demirel was met by Mongolian children singing the Turkish national anthem.

Karakus gave this information regarding the schools: "Today in Mongolia around 50 Turkish teachers are educating approximately 500 students. There are 38 Mongolian teachers. Some Turkish businessmen took over the bread market there."

## Pakistan

While the imperialists fixed their eyes on our land during the War of Independence, implemented the Sèvres plan, and tried to break us into pieces, some sincere friends in distant lands tried their best to send us financial aid even though they were having economic difficulties. These were the Indian Muslims who had not yet gained their own independence. Last year, the Pakistanis celebrated their 50th year of independence. We are enthusiastically preparing this year for the celebration of our Republic's 75th anniversary. Our public-spirited people went to this brother country and opened four schools at once.

### Bosnia-Herzegovina

Esref Demir, principal of the school opened in Bosnia, explains:

> On one of our visits, President Aliya Izzetbegovich of Bosnia-Herzegovina told us: "My paternal grandmother was an Istanbul lady from Üsküdar." Yes, we have many people close to us in Bosnia. Many Bosnians speak Turkish. In our schools, we teach Turkish in the dialect of Turkey. Last year we brought 150 students to Turkey to study Turkish and English in Istanbul.

### Rumania: School in Bucharest United Families

In 1994, some Turkish businessmen entered Rumania, home to many Turks. The doors of this friendly country were opened by Turkish President Süleyman Demirel's letter to Ion Iliescu, the Rumanian president at that time.

These schools are the property of S.C. Lumina SA. The name of the educational institutions is "Liceul International." The first college was opened in Constanza, where there are many Turks; the second was opened in the capital city of Bucharest. Sahin Durmaz, a graduate of the Istanbul Technical University's Mechanical Engineering Department, is in charge of the general directorate of these educational institutions.

Durmaz relates:

> There are 362 students studying in our schools here. Administrative and assistant personnel, as well as 42 teachers, have come from Turkey. There are 150 Rumanian personnel. Our Constanza school has 84 Rumanian Christian students and 58 Turks. In the Bucharest High School, there are 100 are Rumanian and 6 Turkish students, and 2 children of an Indonesian diplomat.

> Children of members of the Turkish Embassy attend the Süleyman Demirel Primary School, which was opened in 1996. In addition to a kindergarten class, there is an 8-year program. Of 112 students, 59 are Turkish. Our businessmen in Rumania have entrusted their children to us.

> We opened this school at the request of the wives of Turkish businessmen working in Rumania. Families were being split

up. Mothers educating their young children in Turkey frequently asked us to open a primary school in Rumania. We
felt we had to meet their demand. There are three interesting
students in this school: children of a Greek family. This family came to our school, examined it, and was very pleased.
They entrusted their children to us without hesitation.

Our students come from many different nations. For example, the children of diplomats and businessmen from
Czechoslovakia, Indonesia, the Congo, South Africa, India,
and Iran are studying under our roof. In addition to
Rumanian, we teach Turkish and English.

## Albania

If we say that the most unusual of our schools are the Turkish
schools in Albania, I guess we would not be too far from the truth.
Why? Because one of these schools is located in Tiranë's War
Academy Headquarters. There's more. Physics professor Recep
Meidani, who was teaching at this school until very recently, is now
Albania's president.

Ibrahim Aydogan, a graduate of the Ankara Technical
Education Faculty, is general director of the educational institutions
in Albania. Aydogan gives a lot of interesting information. He says:

We received a lot of attention after we opened our first school
in Albania. Girls and boys were studying together, but as
candidates increased we began to encounter difficulties. At
that time, the father of three of our students was the Minister
of Defense. His three daughters were attending our school.
We visited him and told him that we were looking for a
school building. He sent us to the Commander of the War
Academy, who said: "We have a lot of empty buildings.
Choose the one you want." They showed us 5 or 6 buildings.
We liked the four-story one.

Perhaps for the first time in the world, we opened a civil
school in military facilities. We settled into the building. The
children began training at the same time as the soldiers.
While the students studied inside, the soldiers were receiving
armed training outside.

Our diplomats in Tiranë heard about this. In fact, Chief
Consul Metin Bey was amazed. He asked: "How did you
manage this?"

In the Mehmet Akif Boys' High School, there are 230 boarding students; the Girls' High School has 250 boarding students. Also, the Turgut Özal Primary School has an enrollment of 450 students.

## Universities Are Increasing in Number

The number of universities and colleges opened by Turkish entrepreneurs in various countries increases every day.

### Qafqaz University, Azerbaijan

Beginning educational activities in 1993, this university now has 750 students. There is a preparatory class there, and subjects are taught in Turkish and English. Students are given an entrance exam. Every year approximately 7,000 students apply, but only 10 percent are accepted. Some receive scholarships. Caucasia University offers engineering, economics, administrative science, open education, and theological faculties.

### International Black Sea University in Georgia

There are 157 students this year at the Black Sea University. Classes are taught in English. Students coming from the Russian Federation, Azerbaijan, Turkmenistan, and Turkey are taught by Georgian academicians.

### International Turkmen–Turkish University

Opening for the 1994-1995 school year, this university gives education in English, Turkish, Turkmen, and Russian. It has 420 students, and features active faculties of economics, administrative science, education, and engineering. Education is given in four languages in the preparatory class. There are modern girls' and boys' dormitories for the university's students. Currently, there are 123 Turkish students studying at this university.

### Süleyman Demirel University in Kazakhstan

Opened in 1996 by Turkish President Süleyman Demirel and Kazakh President Nursultan Nazarbayev in a magnificent ceremony, this university has English and economics departments. A broader structure is planned for the coming years. Also, 53 students are studying in the Turkish Language and Literature Department opened in the Al-Farabi State University.

*Chain of Higher Education Institutions*

The following schools are being added to universities and higher education institutions: Alada University (Kyrgyzstan), the Mogul–Turk Construction Technical School of Higher Learning (Ulan Bator, Mongolia), Pak–Turk International School and College (Pakistan; institution of higher learning in Islamabad), the Yari Islamic Institute of Higher Learning (Bulgaria), the Derbent Humanitarian Institute (Daghestan; 5 years, including preparatory class), Economics–Administrative Sciences Faculty and Orientalism Faculty (preparatory and 5 years), the London Meridian College (United Kingdom; a 2-year program after high school).[367]

## What Is the Purpose of Schools?

By Sahin Alpay

I knew that Fethullah Gülen is opposed to political Islam. I had some information about the schools opened upon his recommendation in Turkey. But I had no knowledge of the schools opened abroad. In the interview he gave to Eyup Can in *Zaman*, Gülen said that the schools opened in Central Asia blocked fundamentalist trends in those countries.

On my visit to Uzbekistan I saw that a secular, democratic education is given in the schools run by Turkish companies. Mahmut Bal, the general coordinator, says that the curriculum used is the same as that used in Turkey's Anatolian high schools. The teachers working in these schools are young and graduates of the best universities in Turkey.[368]

### I Am Writing What I Observed

By Ali Bayramoglu

The Central Asian schools are not run by a central financial institution. Entrepreneurs came from various Turkish cities and

---

[367] *Yeni Yüzyil*, 15 January–4 February 1998.

[368] *Milliyet*, 31 October 1996.

opened schools in different cities. The teachers, whose teaching is top quality, graduated from the best universities in Turkey.

The schools do not give religious education. Religion is taught, but none of the teachers have been educated in theology. With their well-equipped labs and curriculum, the schools follow the pattern of the Turkish Anadolu high schools. Girls do not cover their heads. The purpose is not to introduce religion as a set of norms, but to raise students according to universal moral standards.[369]

### Two Hundred Schools from Albania to Mongolia

By Atilgan Bayar

Although I know the liberal structure of Fethullah Gülen's community, I thought that in Central Asia I would see religious education and organized efforts to expand the community. My visit changed this prejudice. I now know that the schools are not financed and run by a single company. Many entrepreneurs from various cities have opened different schools. For example, schools in Tashkent are opened and run by businessmen from Bursa, while some businessmen from Erzurum opened schools in Samarkand.

I visited the Turkish Embassy in Tashkent and asked Ahmet Sevgi, our education advisor there, about the schools. He said that the Turkish schools in Uzbekistan give secular education according to the principles of the Republic of Turkey.

When I visited the schools, I was amazed at what I saw. Most of the young teachers were graduates of the best Turkish universities such as Bogaziçi, Marmara and ODTÜ (Middle East Technical University). The show prepared by girl students in Tashkent Private Girls' School affected me very much. They were speaking English, Uzbek, and Turkish very well.

Turgut Özal was loved very much in Turkmenistan. Whoever we encountered and talked to, told us how much he or she loved him.

---

[369] *Yeni Yüzyil*, 31 October 1996.

The best Turkish school in Asghabat is the Private Turgut Özal Turkish–Turkmen High School. It has modern language and computer labs. Students learn mathematics, physics, chemistry, biology, computer, history, art history, geography, history of religions, philosophy, logic, sociology and psychology, the history of Turkmenistan, gym, music, and painting. Scientific subjects are taught in English, while the others are taught in Turkmen.[370]

## Fethullah Gülen is Progressive in Education

### By Üzeyir Garih

As far as I saw, these schools are giving secular education. I visited many of them to see whether they are Muslim missionary institutions established on Islamic standards and pursuing an Islamic unity. I saw that they are not. Students are raised very well.[371]

## Fethullah Gülen and Lenin

### By Mehmet Altan

In Moscow, I visited Lenin's mausoleum. According to me, this was a contradiction, for I went there to visit the schools opened by Turkish businessmen.

The students in Turkish schools are being educated in English, Russian, and Turkish. They are boarders. The teachers, all of whom are very young, graduated from good universities in Turkey. We encountered children singing Turkish pop songs. Two mothers in St. Petersburg told us that they preferred those schools because they were giving education in English protected students against evil habits.[372]

---

[370] *Hürriyet*, 1 November 1996.

[371] *Hürriyet*, 4 November 1996. Garih is a businessman from Turkey's Jewish community.

[372] *Sabah*, 22 January 1998.

CHAPTER 9

# A Teacher of Minds
# and Hearts

Most people know Fethullah Gülen as an activist or for his endeavors to strengthen the bonds between people. However, perhaps more than any dimension of his character or being, he is a teacher of minds and a guide of spirits. The following are only some selections from his writings and interviews. They are provided to give readers a glimpse of the theoretical aspect of how he educates minds, hearts, and spirits.

## Sufism and Its Origin

Sufism (*tasawwuf*) is the path followed by Sufis to reach the Truth: God. While this term usually expresses the theoretical or philosophical aspect of this search, its practical aspect is usually referred to as "being a dervish."

### What is Sufism?

Sufism has been defined in many ways. Some see it as God's annihilating the individual's ego, will, and self-centeredness and then reviving him or her spiritually with the lights of His Essence. Such a transformation results in God's directing the individual's will in accordance with His Will. Others view it, as a continuous striving to cleanse one's self of all that is bad or evil in order to acquire virtue.

Junayd al-Baghdadi (d. 910), a famous Sufi master, defines Sufism as a method of recollecting "self-annihilation in God" and "permanence or subsistence with God." Shibli summarizes it as always being together with God or in His presence, so that no worldly or otherworldly aim is even entertained. Abu Muhammad Jarir describes it as resisting the temptations of the carnal self and bad qualities, and acquiring laudable moral qualities.

There are some who describe Sufism as seeing behind the "outer" or surface appearance of things and events and interpreting whatever happens in the world in relation to God. This means that a person regards every act of God as a window to "see" Him, lives his life as a continuous effort to view or "see" Him with a profound, spiritual "seeing" indescribable in physical terms, and with a profound awareness of being continually overseen by Him.

All of these definitions can be summarized as follows: Sufism is the path followed by an individual who, having been able to free himself or herself from human vices and weaknesses in order to acquire angelic qualities and conduct pleasing to God, lives in accordance with the requirements of God's knowledge and love, and in the resulting spiritual delight that ensues.

Sufism is based on observing even the most "trivial" rules of the Shari'a in order to penetrate their inner meaning. An initiate or traveler on the path (*salik*) never separates the outer observance of the Shari'a from its inner dimension, and therefore observes all of the requirements of both the outer and the inner dimensions of Islam. Through such observance, he or she travels toward the goal in utmost humility and submission.

Sufism, being a demanding path leading to knowledge of God, has no room for negligence or frivolity. It requires the initiate to strive continuously, like a honeybee flying from the hive to flowers and from flowers to the hive, to acquire this knowledge. The initiate should purify his or her heart from all other attachments; resist all carnal inclinations, desires, and appetites; and live in a manner reflecting the knowledge with which God has revived and illumined his or her heart, always ready to receive divine blessing and inspiration, as well as in strict observance of the Prophet Muhammad's example. Convinced that attachment and adherence to God is the greatest merit and honor, the initiate should renounce his or her own desires for the demands of God, the Truth.

After these [preliminary] definitions, we should discuss the aim, benefits, and principles of Sufism.

Sufism requires the strict observance of all religious obligations, an austere lifestyle, and the renunciation of carnal desires. Through this method of spiritual self-discipline, the individual's heart is purified and his or her senses and faculties are employed in the way of God, which means that the traveler can now begin to live on a spiritual level.

Sufism also enables individuals, through the constant worship of God, to deepen their awareness of themselves as devotees of God. Through the renunciation of this transient, material world, as well as the desires and emotions it engenders, they awaken to the reality of the other world, which is turned toward God's Divine Beautiful Names. Sufism allows individuals to develop the moral dimension of one's existence, and enables the acquisition of a strong, heartfelt, and personally experienced conviction of the articles of faith that before had only been accepted superficially.

The principles of Sufism may be listed as follows:

- Reaching true belief in God's Divine Oneness and living in accordance with its demands.
- Heeding the Divine Speech (the Qur'an), discerning and then obeying the commands of the Divine Power and Will as they relate to the universe (the laws of creation and life).
- Overflowing with Divine Love and getting along with all other beings in the realization (originating from Divine Love) that the universe is a cradle of brotherhood.
- Giving preference or precedence to the well-being and happiness of others.
- Acting in accord with the demands of the Divine Will—not with the demands of our own will—and living in a manner that reflects our self-annihilation in God and subsistence with Him.
- Being open to love, spiritual yearning, delight, and ecstasy.
- Being able to discern what is in hearts or minds through facial expressions and the inner, Divine mysteries and meanings of surface events.
- Visiting spiritual places and associating with people who encourage the avoidance of sin and striving in the way of God.

Advocate of Dialogue: Fethullah Gülen

- Being content with permitted pleasures, and not taking even a single step toward that which is not permitted.

- Struggling continuously against worldly ambitions and illusions, which lead us to believe that this world is eternal.

- Never forgetting that salvation is possible only through certainty or conviction of the truth of religious beliefs and conduct, sincerity or purity of intention, and the sole desire to please God.

Two other elements may be added: acquiring knowledge and understanding of the religious sciences, and following a perfected, spiritual master's guidance. Both of these are of considerable significance in the Naqshbandiyah Sufi order.[373]

## The Horizon of Hope: Spiritual or Metaphysical Thought

The modern Western worldview is said to be founded almost entirely on materialistic notions that exclude or even deny the spiritual or metaphysical dimensions of existence. This is a controversial point, but many so-called Muslim intellectuals who blindly imitate and import what they see as Western, despise and reject their societies' traditional modes of thinking and living. This is largely because they no longer have any awareness of the spiritual dimension of existence and life. Indeed, those who reduce existence to matter and think only in physical terms can hardly perceive and understand what is metaphysical and spiritual. Moreover, since those who can only imitate are more radical in their borrowed attitudes than their originators, and since imitation often obscures reality, those so-called intellectuals become more radical in rejecting what is spiritual and metaphysical, and lack adequate knowledge of matter and what is material.

Since the spiritual, metaphysical dimension requires us to go beyond our sensations and instincts into deep and vast horizons, materialists neither understand nor like it. In other words, they restrict their thinking only to what they can perceive and experi-

---

[373] Fethullah Gülen, *Kalbin Zümrüt Tepeleri* (Emerald Hills of the Heart: Key Concepts in the Practice of Sufism) (Izmir: Nil Yayinlari, 1994), 1-5. Naqshbandiyah: A Sufi order found in India, China, Central Asia, Turkey, and Malaysia.

ence. Deceiving themselves and others that existence consists only of its material dimension, they present themselves as true intellectuals.

Despite their claims and the assertions of their Western counterparts, it is difficult to accept that Western scientific thought, although primarily materialistic, has always been separate from spirituality and metaphysics. Modern Western civilization is based on the trinity of Greek thought, Roman law, and Christianity. This latter, at least theoretically, contributes a spiritual dimension. The West never completely discarded Platonist thinking, although it failed to reconcile it with positivistic and rationalistic philosophy. It also has not pretended that such thinkers as Pascal and J. Jeans never existed, or excluded Bergson's intuitivism. Bergson, Eddington, J. Jeans, Pascal, Bernhard Bavink, and Heisenberg are just as important in Western thought as Comte, Darwin, Molescholt, Czolba, and Lamarck. Indeed, it is hard to find an atheist scientist and philosopher before the mid-nineteenth century.

In contrast, metaphysical thought and spirituality have been discarded almost entirely by many Muslim intellectuals. In the name of certain notions reduced to such simplistic slogans as *enlightenment, Westernization, civilization, modernity,* and *progress,* metaphysical thought and spiritual life have been denigrated and degraded. Such slogans also have been used to batter traditional Islamic values.

We use *the horizon of hope* to mean travelling beyond the visible dimension of existence, and considering existence as an interrelated whole in the absence of which things and events cannot be perceived as they really are. Nor can its essence and relation with the Creator, as well as the relation between Him and humanity, be grasped. Scientific disciplines that conduct their own discourse largely in isolation from each other, and the prevailing materialistic nature of science that has compartmentalized existence and life, cannot discover the reality of things, existence, and life.

When such investigations are seen in medicine, for example, people are viewed as being composed of many discrete mechanisms. The consequences are easy to see: Existence is stripped of its meaning and connectedness, and is presented as discrete elements consisting only of matter. However, the only way to fully comprehend and value life and existence is to experience existence through the prism of spirit and metaphysical thinking. Neglect of this way means forcing reason to comment on things beyond its reach and imprisoning intellectual effort within the confines of sense-impressions. But when we heed the sound of our conscience or inner world, we perceive that the mind is never content and satisfied with mere sense-impressions.

All the great, long-lived, and inclusive modes of thinking developed upon the foundations of metaphysics and spirituality. The whole ancient world was founded and shaped by such sacred texts such as the Qur'an, the Bible, the Vedas, and the Upanishads. Denying or forgetting such anti-materialistic Western thinkers, scientists, and philosophers as Kant, Descartes, Pascal, Hegel, and Leibniz means ignoring an essential strand of Western thought.

We can only imagine a new, better world based on knowledge or science if we look at the concept of science through the prism of metaphysics. Muslims have not yet developed a concept of science in its true meaning, namely, one derived from the Qur'an and Islamic traditions molded mainly by the Qur'an and the Prophet's practice. The application of science or technology by an irresponsible, selfish minority has engendered more disasters than benefits.

If Muslims want to end their long humiliation and help establish a new, happy world at least on a par with the West, they must replace old-fashioned positivistic and materialistic theories with their own thoughts and inspirations. Aware of their past pains and troubles, they must exert great efforts to define and then cure them.

A true concept of science will join spirituality and metaphysics with a comprehensive, inclusive view affirming the intrinsic and unbreakable relation between any scientific discipline and existence as a whole. Only a concept embracing the whole in its wholeness can be called truly scientific. Seeing existence as discrete elements and trying to reach the whole from them ends up in drowning amid multiplicity. By contrast, embracing the whole and then studying its parts in the light of the whole allows us to reach sound conclusions about the reality of existence.

Spirituality and metaphysics also provide art with their widest dimensions. It fact, art only attains its real identity through spirituality and metaphysics. An artist discovers humanity's inner world, with all its feelings, excitement, expectations, frustration, and ambition, and its relations with the outer dimension of existence. It then presents them in forms suitable to the medium being used. Art expresses our inner essence, which is in continuous movement to return to its source. In other words, artists unite the inspirations flowing into their spirit from things and events, from all corners of existence. Bringing together all noumena and phenomena, they then present things to us in their wholeness.

Remember that the most important source of science, thinking, and art, even virtues and morality, is metaphysics. All of existence can be perceived with a sound mode of thinking based on pure metaphysics. This allows us to view all of existence as a whole, and to travel through its deeper dimensions. Without spirituality and metaphysics, we cannot build a community on sound foundations, and such a community must beg continuously from others. Communities that lack sound metaphysical concepts are subject to identity crises.

To build a new, happy world wherein human virtues and values are given due prominence and are effective in shaping policies and aspirations, all people, regardless of religion, must rediscover and reaffirm the spirituality and metaphysics taught in the God-revealed religions.[374]

## The Culture of the Heart

Q: You frequently refer to *ma'rifa* (knowledge of God) as heart *culture*.

---

[374] Gülen, *Yeseren Düşünceler*, 155-58.

A: Knowledge of God does not consist of abstract knowledge; in its true form, it is transformed into love. We cannot remain indifferent to someone in whom we believed and then grew to know well. After belief and knowledge comes love, the crown of belief in God and knowledge of Him. Love is open to everyone according to his or her level. Love, which seeks to deepen itself, always travels on the horizon of "increase," asking: "Isn't there more?"

Sacred knowledge increases, giving rise to increasing in love, which causes knowledge to increase still further. Thus a virtuous circle is formed. Love increases not only in the name of knowledge, but also in the name of love. Gedai said: "The more I put my finger in the honey of love, the more I burn; give me some water." Universal light appears in the hearts of those who drink this water, and the way to eternal life becomes illuminated thereby.

Q: Your book *Kalbin Zümrüt Tepeleri* (translated as Key Concepts in the Practice of Sufism) is based on contemplation and ecstasy and is also heavily Sufistic in style ...

A: I tried to bring the matter to that point. Islam's spiritual life should be considered from the approach of the Companions. Imam Rabbani says: "We are reviving the Companions' path." However, reviving the Companions' path was accomplished fully by Bediüzzaman. Now it's unthinkable that such an action of renewal could be far from Islam's spiritual life. Like monks at night, the Companions lived a life in love with worship. Is it possible to remain blind to their inner lives?

### Risale-i Nur, Sufism, and *Kalbin Zümrüt Tepeleri*

Q: Some people claim that the *Risale-i Nur* is far removed from Sufism. Is this true?

A: No. If the *Risale-i Nur* were to be squeezed, you'd see Islam's spiritual life and the Sufi truth dripping from it. I think the mistake here is due to mixing Sufism with dervish orders (*tariqa*). Sufism is Islam's inner life; dervish orders are institutions established in later centuries to represent and live this life. The orders can be criticized. In fact, the Kadiris say: "Audible or loud recitation is better than the Naqshis' silent recitation." The Naqshis, who prefer silent recitation, say: "Since in the Sufi way everything is basically related to heart, it's not necessary to publicize it by loud recitation." But no one gets upset about these differences. Bediüzzaman pointed this out in the *Risale-i Nur*.

Q: Can you give some examples?

A: For example, in his *Mathnawi al-Nuriya*, Bediüzzaman says: "Transcend your animal life, get free from corporeality, and attain the degree of the life of the heart and spirit." Symbolically he pointed to the life of the heart and spirit. At the same time, in the *Talwihat* he elaborately explains the uses and risks of following a dervish order. Every institution may have some defects. Such warnings don't mean that he opposed them. Various orders try to represent our Prophet's example in their lives and inner worlds. It is natural that different understandings and interpretations have appeared.

*Kalbin Zümrüt Tepeleri* expresses an inadequate person's feelings and thoughts in a weak style. Actually, as a theme, these matters can always be written in the light of the *Risale-i Nur*. In later periods of his mission, for example, in *Lahikalar* he emphasized the importance of attaining the highest degree of asceticism, piety, and sincerity.[375]

Sufism is the way of being God's "friend." In the general sense, everyone is God's friend. Those who perform their prescribed religious duties and refrain from major sins are God's friends. But when we say "friend" in a particular way, it takes on its own definition. To become candidates for that definition, our heart must be enlivened and our spirit polished. Just as we use our feet for travelling, we also must use our heart and spirit. This is possible by traveling on the "emerald hills of the heart" guided by innermost, more refined faculties. Making this journey may be

[375] The books of communications between Bediüzzaman and his students, as well as among the students themselves.

considered as a requirement of being respectful of the divine truths manifested in the universe.[376]

## The Journey beyond Being

O God, Most High:

We behold what You have laid out before us, Your most original and striking works made in the most perfect form, to which You invite our gaze. We behold things and events that, in their interrelation, are the most brilliant and well-proportioned of Your dazzling pictures. The manifestation of all Your beauties draws from nature's bosom a variety of colors unfolding as if in a book of art. Bearing witness to You by Your Pen's writing, and in accordance with the Book You wrote with it, our spirits have taken wing. We have seen the source of all things in the light of Your Names. Voices and music of celestial harmonies are heard everywhere, and our hearts are ravished by the mystery of the sacred archetypes, the fountain of all things.

Through the eye of the heart, we have grasped the essential identity between the kernel of belief and the *touba* tree in Paradise, (into which that kernel will grow). We have risen to make a journey extending far into the realms beyond being. On this journey, Your holy Book has guided our spirits by setting out a vision of Your Names and Attributes and leading to eternity. You have described the journey to Yourself, mapped it out in minutest detail, and pictured it in the *mi'raj* (Ascension) of Your holy Servant, peace and Your blessings be upon him, his miraculous ascent through the Seven Heavens to Your Presence. That journey is possible to anyone who has knowledge of You through his or her spirit. If we have gone too far in touching the latch of the gates of Your mysteries, we ask forgiveness for the discourtesies of our coarse, immature souls, which are ignorant of rules and proprieties.

O Creator, Most High and Most Beautiful, Who brought us into this existence and allowed us to feel the infinite pleasure thereof.

---

[376] Can, "Fethullah Gülen Ile Ufuk Turu."

You have opened to us vast worlds as a book. You have made our consciousness the shore at which Your Divine mysteries lap, and so enabled us to have a sense of them. If You had not unfolded these magnificent worlds to us as in a book, if You had not disclosed Yourself to us, according to our capacity to understand, by sending Prophets, we would not have known You at all.

If You had not established connections between nature and our inner experiences, and endowed us with an innate perception by means of which we might arrive at true knowledge and true gnosis, we could never hope to know Your Divine Essence or anything sure about You. How, then, could we have felt admiration for Your Path? We are Your bonded servants. The recurrent flashes reflected in our consciousness are rays from Your Existence. Whatever we own is entirely by Your gift and favor. We declare this once more, confessing that we are Your obedient slaves who never look for release; rather, we long to renew our bonds.

O Ruler of hearts, on the remembrance and meditation of Whom hearts are fixed, we strive to determine the ways leading to Your Presence and the windows opening upon Your Existence. Sometimes we seek by delving into the reality of things and events, and sometimes by relying upon our intuition. Our goal is to communicate what we receive from You to those whose hearts are sick and whose minds are barren, and to remain faithful to the sublime truths that have been shown there in the clearest possible way.

No doubt we have committed errors and indulged our fancies and whims, for we have not been able to offer the most manifest truths in their essential purity. If we have made mistakes, we made them while seeking You and trying to guide others. If we have made mistakes, we have made them on the way to You. But a mistake is still a mistake. With broken hearts, spirits doubled up, and necks in chains, we appeal to Your generous judgment. We make this confession in the knowledge that Your unbounded Mercy always overcomes Your Wrath.

It is not becoming for Your humble slaves, especially those You have favored, to commit mistakes. Yet since they do, graciously permit me to remark that mercy and forgiveness are becoming most of all to You.

O Ruler of my heart. To the Ruler belongs the royal manner that befits Him, just as servitude befits a slave. If You forgive us, we should wish to study the book of Your universe anew so as to pay attention to the voices that tell of You. We should wish to witness the signs of Your Existence, and to be enraptured by the songs about You, so that we may reach Your holy realm. By Your Graciousness, assist those who are in need![377]

## Love

- Love is one of the most subtle blessings that the Most Merciful One has bestowed upon humanity. It exists in everyone as a seed. This seed germinates under favorable circumstances and, growing like a tree, blossoms into a flower, and finally ripens, like a fruit, to unite the beginning with the end.

- As a feeling, love penetrates into our inner being through our eyes, ears, and heart. It then swells like water behind a dam, grows like an avalanche, or engulfs our very being like a flame. It starts to subside only when it results in union. The flame goes out, the reservoir empties, and the avalanche melts away.

- Love is a natural and essential aspect of our being. But when it is transformed into "true love"—love of the Creator—it acquires its true nature and color, and later becomes "pure" pleasure at the threshold of union.

- One's heart is a receptive port for Divine manifestations. Your love of the Creator and yearning to return to Him is the clearest sign of your being loved by God.

- Love is the most direct and safest way to human perfection. It is difficult to attain the rank of human perfection through ways that do not contain love. Other than the way of "acknowledging one's innate impotence, poverty, and reliance on God's Power and Riches, and one's zeal in His way and thanksgiving," no other way to truth is equal to that of love.

- Love is a mount that, bestowed upon us by God, carries us toward the Paradise we've lost. No one who has ridden this mount has ever been stranded on this road, although we sometimes find people on this celestial mount walking on the roadside due to some boastful words they utter because of their intoxication from joy. However, this is a matter between them and God.

---

[377] Gülen, *Ölçü veya Yoldaki Isiklar*, 1:1–8.

- Neither the "flames" of the world nor the fire of Hell can "burn" those who already have been "burnt to ashes" by love. Those who burn with the fear of Hellfire while in this world will not go to Hell. The final abode of those who feel secure against Hellfire will most probably be Hell. Those who burn here in the flames of love and suffer Hell on earth by struggling against their carnal selves and the world will most certainly not be subjected again to the same suffering in the Hereafter.

- Love makes us forget our own existence, and annihilates our existence in the existence of our beloved. It therefore requires the lover always to want the beloved, and thus to dedicate himself or herself, without expecting any return, completely to the desires of the beloved. This is, according to my way of thinking, the essence of humanity.

- In the way of love, even a slight imagined inclination of the lover to someone or something other than the beloved means the end of love. Such an inclination is forbidden. Love continues as long as the lover sees the beloved in everything around him or her, and regards every beauty and perfection as the manifestation of the beloved. If this is not the case, love dies.

- Lovers cannot imagine any opposition, no matter how small, to the beloved. They cannot endure to see the beloved veiled by something that causes Him to be forgotten. Moreover, lovers regard as futile any speech not about the beloved, and any act not related to Him as ingratitude and disloyalty.

- Love means the heart's attachment and the willpower's inclination toward the beloved. It also means the feelings' being purified of anything or anyone else other than the beloved, and all the lover's senses and faculties being turned to and set on the beloved only. Every act of the lover reflects the beloved: his or her heart always beats with yearning for the beloved; his or her tongue always murmurs the beloved's name, and his or her eyes open and close with the beloved's image.

- Seeing the beloved's traces in the blowing wind, the falling rain, the murmuring stream, the humming forest, the dawning morning and the darkening night, the lover comes alive. Seeing the beloved's beauty reflected in everything around him or her, the lover becomes exuberant. Feeling the beloved's breath in every breeze, the lover becomes joyful. Feeling the beloved's occasional reproaches, the lover moans in sorrow.

- Lovers who awaken to the dawn of the beloved's signs find themselves engulfed by a flood of flames. They burn therein, never desiring to escape this pleasant "hell." They are like volcanoes ready to erupt, and their groans are like lava that burns everything it touches.

- One should not confuse true love with the feeling felt for members of the opposite sex. Such love, although sometimes transformed into true love, is deficient, temporary, and without inherent value.

- It is impossible to express love with words, for love is an emotional state that can be understood only by the lover.

- Lovers are intoxicated with their love, admiration, and appreciation of the beloved. Only the trumpet announcing the Day of Judgment will bring lovers to their senses.

- Only true love will end the pain caused by being ephemeral, and extinguish the "flames" in which the afflicted "burn." True love will cure all apparently incurable pain and disease, and answer the cries of the modern world.

- If we do not plant the seeds of love in the hearts of young people, whom we try to revive through science, knowledge, and modern culture, they will never attain perfection and free themselves completely from their carnal desires.[378]

## The Balance between the Physical and the Spiritual

- True life is lived at the spiritual level. Those whose hearts are alive, conquering the past and the future, cannot be contained by time. Such people are never excessively distressed by past sorrows or anxieties of the future. Those who cannot experience full existence in their hearts, and thus lead banal, shallow lives, are always gloomy and inclined to hopelessness. They consider the past a horrifying grave, and the future an endless well. It is torment both if they die and if they live.

- Establishing a sound relationship with a long, great past and a long, better future depends on having a proper understanding of your heart's and soul's vitality. The fortunate ones live at this level and fully understand this life. They see the past as our ancestors' great tents and thrones, the future as roads leading toward the gardens of Paradise. While sipping inspiration from their inner conscience as if from the fountain of Kawthar,[379] they pass on from the guesthouse of this world. The unfortunate ones, those who cannot reach such a level of understanding and endeavor, lead lives that are worse than death. Their deaths are a hell of darkness upon darkness.

- There is a mutually supportive and perfective relation between one's actions and inner life. We call this relation a "virtuous circle." Attitudes like determination, perseverance, and resolve illuminate one's inner conscience, and the brightness of this inner conscience strengthens one's will-power and resolve, stimulating him or her to ever-higher horizons.

- Those fortunate ones whose actions reflect their spirit's obedience always seek to please the Creator and humanity, and continue to acquire praisewor-

[378] Ibid., 3:57-66.

[379] A river in Paradise.

thy virtues. Their *qibla* pointer always points to the same *mihrab*,[380] and their progress indicator always shows the same route. Although some straying may occur every once in a while, a truly sincere remorse and a heartfelt penitence will melt the consciousness of sin from their hearts and souls. After this, they will resume their roads, often with renewed vigor.

- Those fortunate ones who fulfill their duties meticulously and thoroughly, who attend carefully to every little detail, enjoy orderliness, harmony, and devotion to duty in their outer worlds. At the same time, they increase the pure light of their inner worlds and, on the wings of their prayers, attain a few times each day the rank of angels.

- This understanding and balance in human hearts, that is, the inward experience and meticulous practice of religion alongside a love and yearning for eternity, over time was replaced by dull formalism and mysticism that made us lazy. Since that time, those two ominous groups have regarded their own inspirations, which are no more than a firefly's light, as equal to the Revelation's bright and varied brilliance. They block our way to new horizons of thought, and darken the horizons of our aspirations by spraying fumes and dust onto our enlightened path.

- By way of summing up, we may characterize soldiers of truth as having a toughened structure, like tempered steel, that can withstand all pressures and assaults. Their intellect can combine, like an expert chemist, the Divine Word and all current knowledge in a pot and thereby obtain new syntheses. Their spirits have been perfected in the same crucible that perfected such spiritual masters as Mawlana Rumi and Shaykh Jilani. They are so modest that they see themselves as just ordinary people among others. Finally, their altruism has reached such a level that they can forget their own needs and desires for the sake of others' happiness.[381]

## Those Who Are Making Merry Today

- Those who do not increase in dedication to worship of God as they grow older are unfortunate, for they are making a loss at a time when they could be making a profit. If they understood this, they would weep for what they finds amusing today.[382]

---

[380] *Qibla*: The direction in which a Muslim turns to when praying. The individual is its beginning point, and the Ka'ba, located in Makka, is its end point. *Mihrab*: An architectural feature found in every mosque to indicate the direction in which Muslims must turn when praying.

[381] Gülen, *Ölçü veya Yoldaki Isiklar*, 1:9–14.

[382] Ibid., 2:115.

## The Whirlpool of Egotism

•   The trust of ego granted to humanity is a sacred gift given to us so that we can find and know the greatest truth. But this gift should be abandoned as soon as it has served its purpose. If not, the ego will become so big that one day it will swallow its owner. Taking it as a unit of comparison, we must, on one hand, know the Sublime Creator and the infinity of His Power, Knowledge, and Will. On the other hand, we must realize that He has nothing to do with any fault and deficiency. Given this, we will melt our ego in the fire of Divine knowledge and love. We will see with the Exalted Creator's existence, and think, know, and breathe with Him.

•   There are some whose egotism derives from knowledge, while in some others it appears because of wealth and power, or because they boast of their intelligence or beauty. As none of these attributes are our personal property, every claim is considered a vehicle for and an invitation to the true Property Owner's anger. Such claims have resulted in the destruction of these haughty spirits.[383]

## Life, Human Character, and Virtue

•   When an animal dies, it is forgotten and its burial place is lost. However, this is not the case with people. Are people who do not preserve the memories and tombs of their ancestors aware that they reduce them to the rank of animals? Respect for the dead is a security granted to the living for their own future.

•   One of the most important ways to conquer people's hearts is always to seek an opportunity to do good deeds to them. Once such an opportunity appears, make use of it without delay. Would that we could set our hearts on always doing good to others!

•   Good morals and sound conscience, and good manners and virtues, are like a universally acceptable currency unaffected by changes in the value of other means of exchange. Those provided with such qualities are like merchants with the highest credit, who can do business wherever they want.

•   The more people suffer in life and are conscious of their life, the more profound their feelings become. Those who are unconscious of the meaning of life and events and have experienced no suffering cannot develop their feelings and faculties or feel part of existence.

•   Those with strong willpower and good, sound character will lose none of their virtuous essence, even if they suffer thousands of pains and sorrows and are forced to change their views and ways. What shall we say about those weak ones who, without provocation, change their thoughts and ways every day?

---

[383] Ibid., 1:79-80.

- Ignorance is like a veil drawn over the face of things. Those unfortunate ones who cannot remove this veil will never penetrate into the truths of creation. The greatest ignorance is unawareness of God. If it is combined with arrogance, it becomes a kind of insanity that cannot be cured.

- A sensible person is not one who claims infallibility and therefore is indifferent to others' ideas. Rather, a truly sensible person is one who corrects his or her errors and uses others' ideas in acknowledgement of the fact that human beings are prone to error.

- Life blossoms during childhood. During youth it grows through inward tension and spiritual struggle on the way of truth. During old age it holds its vital energy with the desire to reunite with the beloved ones who have passed away already. How wretched it is for atheists, who experience life sometimes as comedy and sometimes as tragedy, and thereby stifle the instinct for ardent hope and gratitude in humanity.[384]

## Humility

- The humble and modest are highly regarded by the created and the Creator. The haughty and self-conceited, who belittle others and put on arrogant airs, are always disliked by the created and punished by the Creator.

- Self-conceit shows a lack of sensibility and maturity. Those who are more reflective and spiritually mature attribute whatever gifts they may have to the Creator, the Most High, and devote themselves to Him with humble gratitude.

- Humility is a sign that people has become truly human. One sign of humility is that such people do not change after obtaining a high position or wealth, learning or fame, or whatever is publicly esteemed. If any of these circumstances causes them to alter their ideas, attitudes, and behavior, they cannot be regarded as having attained true humanity or true humility.[385]

## Humanity

- When interacting with others, always regard whatever you find pleasing and displeasing as the measure. Desire for others what your own ego desires, and do not forget that whatever conduct displeases you will displease others. If you do this, you will be safe from misconduct and bad behavior, and will not hurt others.

---

[384] Ibid., 2:118-23.

[385] Ibid., 1:86-87.

- Considering that favors received make you feel a liking, affection, and attachment for those who bestow the favor upon you, you should understand how to make others like you, and feel affection and attachment for you. It is said that "people are the slaves of the favors done to them." Therefore, doing others a favor and being good to them is a reliable defense against any harm that may come from them.

- Maturity and perfection of spirit is being just in your treatment of others, especially with those who have done you an injustice. Answer their evil with good. Do not stop doing good even to those who have harmed you. Rather, treat them with humanity and nobility, for harming someone is brutish behavior. Returning evil with evil implies a deficiency in character; returning good for evil is nobility.

- There is no limit to doing good to others. Those who dedicate themselves to humanity's good can be so altruistic that they sacrifice their lives for others. However, such altruism is a great virtue only if it originates in sincerity and purity of intention, and if it does not define the "others" by racial preference.

- Our humanity and nobility are directly proportional to our closeness to friends and our maintenance of these friendships. Talking of nobility and kindness without expressing warmth and intimacy in relationships is mere assertion. Doing good in return only for good received, or sometimes ceasing to do good to others to punish them implies moral imperfection and immaturity.

- It is a sign of great generosity and goodness to others if you ignore some of their faults, improprieties, or bad manners, and tolerate their imperfections. Prying into others' affairs and finding fault is rude and uncivil, and publicizing such affairs is unforgivable. Declaring them to the other's face is a severe blow to the bonds of unity between people, a blow from which, sadly, it is almost impossible for friendship to recover fully.

- Those who regard even the greatest good they have done for others as insignificant, while greatly appreciating even the least favor done to themselves, are perfected ones who have acquired the Divine standards of behavior and found peace in their conscience. Such individuals never remind others of the good they have done for them, and never complain when others appear to be indifferent to them.[386]

## Human Beings

- Each individual is equipped with sublime emotions, has a natural disposition toward virtue, and is fascinated with eternity. Even the most wretched-looking person has a rainbow-like atmosphere in his or her spirit comprised of the thought of eternity, love of beauty, and virtuous feeling. If people can devel-

---

[386] Ibid., 1:90-93.

op these most basic, inherent elements of their being, they can rise to the highest ranks of humanity and attain eternity.

- People are true human beings not in the mortal, material aspect of their existence, but rather in their spirits' attraction to eternity and their efforts to find it. Thus, those who disregard their innate spiritual aspect and concentrate only on their physical existence never find true peace and contentment.

- The happiest and most fortunate people are those who always are intoxicated with ardent desire for the worlds beyond. Those who confine themselves within the narrow and suffocating limits of their bodily existence are really in prison, even though they may be living in palaces.

- Our first and foremost duty is to discover ourselves and then turn toward our Lord through the illuminated prism of our nature. Those who remain unaware of their true nature, and who therefore cannot establish any contact with their Most High Creator, spend their lives like coolies who are ignorant of the treasure they carry on their backs.

- All human beings are essentially helpless. However, they discover an extraordinary competence by depending on the Infinitely Powerful One, which transforms them from a drop into a waterfall, a particle into a sun, and a beggar into a king.

- Our familiarity with the "book" of existence and events, and our establishment of a unity between ourselves and that book, causes sparks of wisdom to appear in our hearts. We begin to recognize our essential nature and obtain knowledge of God through the light of those sparks. Finally, we reach God. To attain this goal, however, we must not set out this (mental) journey with a mind conditioned by atheism and materialism.

- Those who are truly human interact with other living beings in the consciousness of personal duty to them and within the limits of need. Those who abandon themselves to bodily desire and pleasure go beyond what is allowed, and therefore cannot maintain the proper distance or balance between duty and desire.[387]

## Excerpts from the Media

### *A Deep Knowledge of Religion, a Rich Philosophy*

By Prime Minister Bülent Ecevit

Gülen appears to have combined a deep knowledge of religion with a rich philosophical, historical, and artistic culture.

---

[387] Ibid., 2:36-39.

He explains knowledgeably and courageously how the Islamic world became fanatical and weakened as it became more and more remote from science and free thought, how Islamic society was damaged by the narrowing of the *madrasa's* educational scope and religion's exploitation of political power as a vehicle.

At the same time, Gülen reminds us of the tolerant Islamic view based on Sufism's concepts of God and love of humanity. He explains that instead of trying to imitate the Islamic understanding of some backward countries ruled by oppressive regimes, we must develop our own Islamic perspective that reflects our national characteristics and heritage. He says that Islam's universality is not an obstacle to this, and further indicates that Islam is compatible with modernity, democracy, and progress. The Turkish experiment during the republican period proves this.

An important contribution of Gülen's ideas to daily debates and the search for solutions is his emphasis that we can open up to the West without breaking away from our national identity, but that we also must strengthen our ties with Central Asia. Such an emphasis is very appropriate at a time when Europe and Asia are rapidly uniting in a "Eurasia" liaison, when concepts of modernity and globalization are replacing Westernization, and when it is possible for Turkey to serve as a key or a bridge.[388]

### A Dream Rising on Our Horizon

By Ayse Sasa

While reading Fethullah Gülen Hodjaefendi, we sense that the geography of a culture that has been left without a horizon or a dream by a 300 year-long gradual decline is once again on the threshold of a brand new, gleaming, broad-scoped, and universal vital leap forward...

Mixed in a crucible of love, pious asceticism, service to others, unbelievable simplicity and modesty, this resistance climbed and persisted in climbing a very steep mountain throughout this dark

---

[388] At the end of Can, "Ufuk Turu."

period of decline. Without relinquishing for even a second the hope received from God, it swam counter to the flood-like current, and overcame physical and metaphysical barriers with unbelievable patience and spiritual knowledge. Finally, carried over from one generation to the next, this legendary resistance, standing on "Mount Everest," pauses to take a new look at the world. Taking into view the universe's horizon from a 360° perspective, it smiles. When we look at the horizon from this perspective, we share a cosmic dream, broken off from the ancient Earth's garden, a fully universal and peaceful spring dream's breadth, indescribable pleasure, and translucency.

It's the 1,000-year-old collective heritage of the freedom-loving Anatolian people. It carries no defect of malice or prejudice. There's a benevolent stamp of broad tolerance and vast well-being in every atom. In this heritage, which is a product of generations, there is the possibility of choosing a common search by people of many diverse inclinations. If we only consider recent times, a Yahya Kemal, a Kemal Tahir, a Necip Fazil, a Sezai Karakoç, a Cemil Meriç, discovering some parts of this dream, tried to find hope…

In the deep darkness of the twentieth century, the majority of humanity mourned for the Godots who never came, who could never come, whose coming was impossible. In particular the writer of these lines is one who was burned throughout her youth by this type of wake. The last 300 years of human history have seen the drowning, degree by degree in history's deep waters, of the gigantic whole of universal values like a gigantic continent. That huge continent is once again surfacing in the light of day, presenting itself to the horizon of humanity as a healing declaration full of peace and dignity.

On one end, the defense of Bosnia; on another side, the venerable Fethullah Gülen. Humanity has always sensed that it was free, a child of infinity, and close to eternity. I salute the beautiful dream reflected on the horizon.[389]

---

[389] Ibid.

## *A Point Where the Intellectual and Sage Meet*

### By Ahmet Turan Alkan

Fethullah Gülen stands at a point where the intellectual and the sage intersect. While displaying an amazing polyphony of cultural accumulation, his view on things, events, and world affairs reflects a perfect believer's determined and tranquil state. The price of uniting firm faith and mental prowess is very high, and can be paid only by some kind of "suffering." It is our duty to at least respectfully approach a mental activity that has risen to this height.[390]

## *Modernity Made Meaningful by Conservatism*

### By Professor Nilüfer Göle

We who have lived in Turkey during the last 20 years have been in a state of shock. We have been swinging back and forth between the desire to catch up with the new age and to know ourselves; wavering among ambition, anger, and excitement; and trying to open a path by hand between our spirit and the world. We are fighting over our unofficial identity and unclear design.

As long as Turkey does not connect its past and future, tradition and modernity, and itself and the world, in Fethullah Gülen Hodjaefendi's words, without keeping the "metaphysical tension" between these, it will remain destabilized. Violence and anarchy are manifestations of this. Gülen's thought favors individual modesty, social conservatism, and Islam in the founding of civilization. His thought gives examples of modest and tolerant people who have not lost their connection with God, and of the individual worn down by traditional suppression and modern excess.

Contrary to the mental impudence and loneliness of Western individuals, the affection that unites faith and knowledge in the "heart culture" gives us the good tidings of a new door of self-con-

---

[390] Ibid.

fidence being opened. For the first time in Turkey, we are witnessing a deep mixture of conservative thought and liberal tolerance.[391]

## *An Exceptional Place of Integrating Intelligence*

### By Professor Serif Mardin

The primary contribution of Gülen's views is the importance he puts on the tie between faith and environmental conditions. With a distinguished view of such focal points as history, society, and the individual, his relating of faith to religion is hardly ever seen, even among social scientists. With this in mind, the exceptional place of this integrating intelligence becomes even clearer.

The principle that society necessarily brings of "calculating tomorrow's interests now" weakens the community structure. Thus, we should not progress too much on this path. Faith creates a strong basis on this subject, and Fethullah Hodja mentions its consolidating power. We can see a self-sacrifice, now quite rare, in those inspired by his ideas.

Consider the following points that he emphasizes: Knowledge is passed on in a civilization by clear expression and technical terminology. In other words, it is passed on as a general symbol cluster and a practical term. Those who see Islam more as a dogmatic whole do not see this functional characteristic of religion, nor do those who describe the phenomenon of religion in Turkey as a focal point of power.[392]

## *A Will That Can Solve Problems*

### By Professor Toktamis Ates

Gülen discusses how the spiritual make-up and strength lying behind a will that can solve Turkey's problems, which are growing like a mountain, should be. Within this framework, he dwells more on should be rather than what is.

---

[391] Ibid.

[392] Ibid.

Gülen's approach of Turkish Muslimness is one that I have defended for years through writing and speech. I am extremely pleased to share the same view. Also, while reading and listening to him, I happily see that we share the same feelings on many points.

## *The Person Sought by Fethullah Hodja*

### By Arslan Bulut

In recent years, Fethullah Gülen Hodja has been trying to give our society a message. If we think that society is trying to find a way out, that our people are searching again for tolerance, that they're waiting for a contemporary Yunus Emre, we'll have explained just a little of why so much interest is directed toward Fethullah Hodja...

Anyway, reminding us that Prophet Abraham carried the value of a nation when he received revelation, Fethullah Hodja speaks of a person who, carrying the seed of a nation, appears and plays an instrumental role in transforming society and establishing an environment of tolerance. He hopes for this...

Fethullah Hodja is a person like you and me... Abraham was a human being. Prophet Muhammad said he was "the son of a woman who ate dry bread." Yunus Emre was a human being... However, according to how much their intelligence and hearts have evolved, some people's messages allow them to encompass all of humanity in their own minds and hearts. These people who bring messages never die... They are living...

However, the meanings of words change, as does the insight of the human mind and heart. If the words acquire a negative meaning, humanity can go in a negative direction... Fethullah Hodja is seeking a person who will program humanity with words to show tolerance and love to each other, to protect nature, and to wrap Turkey, the Turkish world, and the whole world in a bright green countenance. He does not claim to be that person. He has no such egotism...

He describes a tableau that I, too, yearn for... In that tableau, he mentions intellectuals who see different ideas as a source of enrichment instead of conflict, who can brainstorm in an exchange of ideas devoted to unity and peace in Turkish society and the Turkish world. He says that intellectuals raised in this country can meet on a foundation of tolerance regardless of which idea they have...

One who burns his or her mouth on hot milk will blow on yogurt before eating it.[393] Similarly, when the desired result was not immediately obtained after the last tolerance awards dinner, which led to a big uproar, Fethullah Hodja, without mentioning the meeting or any of its effects, called on intellectuals to draw closer together, as if to say: "If I wasn't able to do it, you do it..."

Reminding him that a structure of economic interests surrounds groups of ideas, I asked how the different ideas of spokesmen for various interest groups could flow into one river. The Hodja stated that it would be difficult for such spokesmen to meet on the same foundation. However, they are a small minority. The majority of people welcome dialogue and tolerance in society. He added that a foundation for tolerance among intellectuals can be established, and that this duty falls directly on them.

Let me take this opportunity to state that I also want to see all intellectuals raised in this country approached with tolerance... I am ready to take any step to move this goal forward.[394]

## An Analysis of Ecevit's View on Gülen

By Tankut Tarcan

### Servanthood

Coming to the assertion that those close to Gülen approach him with an air of servanthood. This has appeared from time to time in the press, and it stems from not understanding how Islam perceives servanthood. *Tawhid* (the rendering of servanthood solely to God) is emphasized more than anything else in Islam. Nothing is to be

---

[393] A Turkish proverb similar in meaning to the English proverb: Once bitten, twice shy.

[394] *Aksam*, 14 January 1996.

avoided more carefully than servanthood to that which is not God. This is one of the important meanings of Islam's basic principle of *La ilaha illallah* (There is no god but God). This principle weighs heavier than anything else in Islam.

The most important requirement of this principle is that no servant is great enough to be worshipped, not even the Prophet. In Islam, faith and belief in God are considered the real sources of all knowledge, power, and wealth. They save a Muslim from being a servant to everything else, other people, interests, and obsessions. It makes each person an individual in the full meaning of the word.

For this reason, Islam never gave precedence to a bureaucratic and institutionalized state structure, as is done today. Instead, by addressing all believers it made society responsible. In other words, it considered the whole matter within the framework of a social contract. This was the main factor in the development of many institutions throughout Islamic history and civilization that today are called *civil organizations*, and which performed many functions now done by modern states. Thus Muslims have never considered a religious leader as a Pope, a cardinal, or a priest, as Christians do. Also, because of this principle, consultation could not be neglected even if it would bring about defeat.

The claim that Gülen's followers approach him with an air of servanthood at most means that the respect shown to him is exaggerated. There is only one answer to this: Not everyone can be a leader, a Prophet, a guide. People excelling in certain points undoubtedly influence others and, despite their wishes (this does not happen by wanting it), can create an aura of respect in their surroundings. Why do Prophets who lived thousands of years ago still influence people in this age of science and technology? Should there not be a psychological and sociological basis for this? Moreover, Gülen's relations with his community are more democratic than the most democratic structures, as far as I have seen.

### Gülen and *Tariqa*
Gülen and the Sufi *tariqas* is a subject that requires a separate and deep analysis. However, most Turkish intellectuals, unfortu-

nately, are just as ignorant of Islam as they are of *tariqas* or Sufism. According to the Qur'an, a Prophet is charged with purifying his followers' minds from incorrect perceptions and prejudices, cleansing their hearts from sin, and either saving them from such negative feelings as rebellion and jealousy or else transforming these emotions into virtues. A Prophet also relays knowledge about the creation and the universe, objects, and events; teaches the Book to his followers; and later provides religious knowledge and wisdom on how and why to raise human beings with superior morality.

Sufism was born as a discipline to purify one's heart of sin and negative feelings so that he or she could be transformed into a monument of virtue. *Tariqas* appeared only 3 centuries later, as this discipline began to be institutionalized. The *tariqa* is an institution; Sufism is a discipline. The *tariqa* has its own principles, hierarchies, and chain of sheikhs; Gülen's movement does not. Opposing Sufism as a discipline is opposing the essence of Islam. You can support or oppose *tariqas* according to Islam, or social or psychological conditions, but you cannot defend *tariqas* according to the current laws of the Republic of Turkey.

### *Understanding Hodjaefendi*

#### By Ahmet Selim

This was not a regular sermon. It resembled a scientific conference. I have difficulty describing it; it was more than that... I listened with great pleasure and reflected. It is as if he were saying: "Perhaps it will be heavy, but you should get accustomed to knowledge and thought on this level."

Assuming that the twentieth century has developed and completed its own character, I say: "Hodjaefendi is a twenty-first century dervish and a meditating sufferer." I am using these specific expressions to describe his state of being, which is an answer to some explanations that were not given, and to his leading others to say: "This is how one should be."[395]

---

[395] *Zaman.*

## *Listening to Hodjaefendi*

### By Ali Ünal

To understand Islamic development and growth, and how Islam rules minds and hearts in its own unique way, we must grasp the relationship between the great Muslim guides and their followers. This is the basic key to understanding the structure of Islamic society.

Human history flows in two wide streams. Those at the head of the "negative" stream are the Pharaohs, Nimrods, Neros, and Shaddads. Just as no one asks for mercy on such tyrants, they are always cursed. On the other hand, Prophets and their followers who have directed the stream of light are always mentioned with mercy. Abraham lived approximately 4,000 years ago, Moses 3,500 years ago, Jesus 2,000 years ago, and Muhammed 1,400 years ago. Billions of people have followed these suns of the firmaments of humanity. In addition, because they followed the path of the Prophets, the Imam Ghazalis, Imam Rabbanis, Bediüzzamans, and thousands of others maintained their predominance during their own lifetimes and for centuries to come, even if they were subjected to partial misunderstanding during their own times.

### Sacred Attraction

One day a student of Ibn Sina, the great mathematician, doctor, and philosopher, said: "Master, proclaim your Prophethood and hundreds of thousands will follow you." Ibn Sina did not reply. Later, he was in the desert with his students on a cold winter day. When it was time to pray the morning prayer, Ibn Sina asked that same student, who was staying with him in his tent, to bring him a pan and pitcher of water so he could make *wudu'* (ritual ablution) for prayer. But the tent was warm and it was cold outside, so the student procrastinated. A little later, Ibn Sina repeated his request, but again there was no response. As he repeated it for the third time without success, the morning call-to-prayer was made from the minaret.

The time was ripe for his answer, and Ibn Sina said:

> You are my student, and I have certain direct rights from you. Until now I have made only one request from you, and you didn't fulfill it. Do you hear the *muezzin* (caller to prayer)? For centuries without complaining about heat or cold, summer or winter, day or night, he and thousands like him have climbed the minaret five times a day to proclaim the name of the Prophet and his Prophethood that they have never seen or had any direct relationship with. Now do you understand the difference between the Prophet and me?

Prophets and those following on their path rule hearts. There is not the slightest coercion or even invitation in this, because religion is innate in human nature and conscience; it is a feeling and a culture that is not easily torn out and thrown away. Religion is the name of the relationship between God, who has placed love in the center, roots, and all cells of existence and creation, and His servants. As this relationship deepens, God loves people and makes them loved by others. Those who do not understand this truth because they have not lived it look for an organizational structure in Muslim communities. They try to find different intentions in the activities of those Muslims who base their lives and behavior on God's knowledge, love, and approval.

Hodjaefendi is the seed of a sublime tree whose branches, leaves, blossoms, and fruit have spread over the world. The actual source of this power is religion; it is the depth of the relationship between God and the guides on the Prophet's path. Even if they do not live this, those who do not comprehend it should say nothing about Muslim communities. There is no place here for knowledge based on practical experiment or physical sensation, or for laboratories. There is nothing for science to say here.

### The Truth Hodjaefendi Presented on STV

The other evening while talking on STV, the real truth that Hodjaefendi presented was this. While explaining about the schools in Turkey and Central Asia and openly refuting various accusations, in essence he said:

> You can't say: "Don't serve people in God's way and don't open schools" to a person who represents the relationship of infinite compassion, mercy, and love between God and each

member of His creation. Service to others is his nature, a
necessity of his make-up. Just as the sun gives warmth and
radiates light, and everything in the world needs the sun's
warmth and light, those who were created mortal but found
immortality in serving others radiate warmth and light
around them in a stronger way than the sun."

Hodjaefendi sacrificed himself once more at this critical point
of introducing the Creator to the created; taking the created to the
Creator; and making peace, love, compassion, mercy, forgiveness,
and tolerance predominate in the country. His sacrifice is like a seed
from a tree sacrificing its material existence underground so that its
branches, leaves, blossoms, and fruit can serve others. He did this
to shade people under the leaves of generosity, peace, and tolerance;
to make people intoxicated with the flowers of love, compassion,
and mercy; and to fill them up with the fruit of virtues.

Hodjaefendi did his historic duty once again by opening the
daily agenda of events that has been deadlocked due to some people's continuing mistakes; by opening the darkening skies and
bringing rain instead of storms and typhoons to the oppressive
atmosphere; by sheathing drawn swords and the binding artificial
wounds; and by turning an environment of conflict into a foundation for peace. Those who should benefit most from this historical
duty, which I have tried to summarize without going into specific
details, are the groups that appear most likely to be affected by the
coming crisis.[396]

---

[396] *Zaman.*

*At the National Reconciliation Evening 1997, Gülen presents a
gift to Turkey's Former President Demirel*

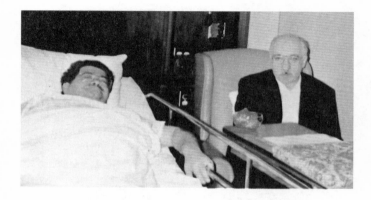

*Gülen visiting Turkey's Former President Turgut Özal after the
latter's operation  in Houston*

*Uzeyir Garih and Ishak Alaton, directors of the Alorko
Companies Group and leading members of Turkey's Jewish
community, visit Gülen*

*With Turkey's Prime Minister Bülent Ecevit*

*Gülen and Dale F. Eickelman, Professor of Anthropology and*
*Human Relations at America's Dartmouth College*

*Gülen sings the national anthem with Halide I. Begovic, Former Vice-Premier Tansu Çiller, Former*
*Deputy Vice-Premier Hikmet Çetin, and other spectators before the Benefit for Bosnia soccer match*
*sponsored by the Foundation of Journalists and Writers.*

*Gülen and international soccer star Maradona watching the match*

*Gülen with His Eminence, the late John Cardinal O'Connor of New York*

*Gülen and Pope John Paul II*

*Gülen with Bensiyon Pinto, leader of Turkey's Jewish
community, and leading Jewish figures*

*Gülen with Yusuf Sağ, Istanbul Representative of Syrian Catholic Community;
Monsignor Georges Marovitch, Istanbul Representative of the Vatican; and Yusuf Çetin, Istanbul
Representative of Syrian Community, and his deputy Samuel Akdemir*

*Gülen with Alpaslan Turkeş, Riza Akçalı, and Turkey's Chief Rabbi David Aseo
at Fatih Universityís opening ceremony*

*Gülen and His All Holiness Patriarch Bartholomeos I,
Archbishop of Constantinople, New Rome and Ecumenical Patriarch*

*Gülen together with Leon Levy, former president of America's
Anti-Defamation League.*

*Gülen with the Vatican Ambassador to Turkey, Pier Luigi Celata,
and Monsignor Georges Marovitc*